A
PERFECT
HELL

Also by John Nadler
Searching for Sofia: a Tale of Obsession, Murder, and War

A PERFECT HELL

THE TRUE STORY OF THE BLACK DEVILS,
THE FOREFATHERS OF THE SPECIAL FORCES

JOHN NADLER

PRESIDIO
PRESS

BALLANTINE BOOKS
NEW YORK

2006 Presidio Press Trade Paperback Edition

Copyright © 2005, 2006 by John Nadler

Published in the United States by Presidio Press, an imprint of
The Random House Publishing Group, a division of
Random House, Inc., New York.

PRESIDIO PRESS and colophon are trademarks of Random House, Inc.

Originally published in hardcover in slightly different form
in Canada by Doubleday Canada, a division of
Random House of Canada Limited, Toronto, in 2005.

Library of Congress Cataloging-in-Publication Data

Nadler, John
A perfect hell : the true story of the Black Devils, the forefathers of the Special Forces /
John Nadler—Trade pbk. ed.
p.   cm.
Originally published: Toronto : Doubleday, 2005.
ISBN 978-0-89141-867-2
1. First Special Service Force. 2. World War, 1939-1945—Commando operations—Italy.
3. World War, 1939-1945—Regimental histories—United States. 4. World War,
1939-1945—Regimental histories—Canada. 5. World War, 1939-1945—Campaigns—Italy.
I. Title.
D794.5.N33 2006
940.54'215—dc22   2005056574

www.presidiopress.com

For Dorothy

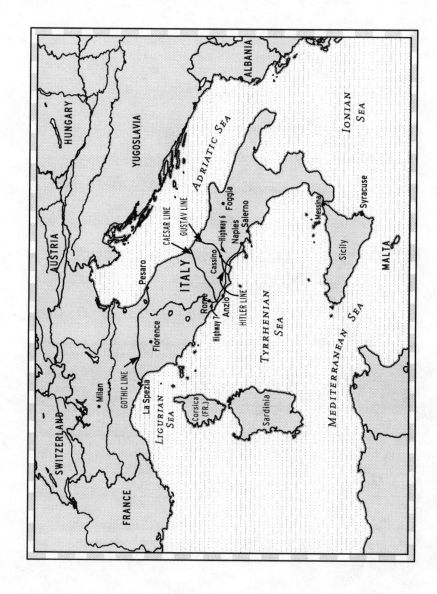

Italy and the Mediterranean Theater, 1944

CONTENTS

LIST OF MAPS

AUTHOR'S NOTE

The First Special Service Force was made up of three regiments with the numerical designations: 1st, 2nd, and 3rd Regiments. Each was made up of two battalions and six companies.

Since the companies in each regiment were numbered one through six, Force men identified them by "company number–regiment number." This book employs this system to identify the FSSF's various companies. Hence, the three companies discussed in detail, 1st Company–1st Regiment, 1st Company–2nd Regiment, and 3rd Company–3rd Regiment—are occasionally mentioned in the following pages as 1-1, 1-2, and 3-3.

Brave men are courageous from the first strike.

—Pierre Corneille, *Le Cid*

PROLOGUE

In June 2004, I traveled to Italy as a journalist to cover the sixtieth anniversary of the liberation of Rome from the point of view of a unique band of veterans who had been among the first Allied soldiers to skirmish their way into the Eternal City in 1944. They were the survivors of a commando unit known as the First Special Service Force (FSSF), or, as their enemies reverentially called them, the Black Devils.

On the surface, the assignment seemed little more than a pleasant excuse to visit southern Europe in early summer. The articles I would be writing would most certainly be ignored when the commemorations marking the Normandy landings began in France. Even sixty years later there was no bigger story than D-Day.

Still, I didn't really care if any of my articles were published. I was more interested in meeting the men of the FSSF, and I had been given an extraordinary opportunity to do so. William Story of Moneta, Virginia, the executive director of the FSSF association, had arranged for me to join the tour as the veterans and their families visited old battlefields and haunts. As it turned out, the Rome trip would be a turning point for me in my research of the Black Devils, which had begun almost a year before when I had read a brief, tantalizing reference to the outfit in a Tom Clancy book.

Just a cursory study made me intrigued by the unit's accomplishments. Despite being no bigger than a brigade, the FSSF had played a decisive role in key battles in the Italian war of 1943 and 1944. Moreover, as a cooperative effort between the United Kingdom and the U.S., the Black Devils had been a multinational force, and represented the only time to my knowledge that soldiers of a foreign military (Canadian) had been full-fledged members of the U.S. Army. The Force, as the men called their unit, had been created from the best available soldiers in North America, and during an astonishingly violent and intense campaign history, these special men performed feats that still seemed extraordinary when I first heard them mentioned in the 2003 TV documentary *Daring to Die*. In a single year of combat, for every Force man who fell in battle, the unit killed twenty-five of the enemy; for every Force man taken prisoner, the FSSF captured two hundred and thirty-five of the enemy.

FSSF engagements like the siege of Monte la Difensa, and the defense of the right flank of the Anzio beachhead were models of strategy, endurance, and field skills. But all these successes came at a cost. After their first battle alone, the Force suffered a 30 percent casualty rate; and after their first six weeks in combat, their casualty rate rose to 60 percent. According to FSSF historian Joseph Springer, by the time the unit was disbanded in late 1944, the Black Devils, which started the war with a fighting echelon of 1,800 men, had lost 2,777 personnel to deaths and wounds.*

But something else happened during the veterans' visit to Italy in 2004 that caught my interest, and ultimately compelled me to turn a fascination for the FSSF into a book. Among the former soldiers, family members, and assorted stragglers like myself on the tour, was a powerful-looking and youngish American who was introduced to me as Captain Lawrence Basha, a current member of the U.S. Special Forces.

At a quiet juncture, Larry and I sat down for a beer in the lobby of the hotel in which the veterans were staying (I had invited him, but for reasons I can't remember, he paid), and Larry admitted he was moved to be part of the FSSF tour. I understood why early on the morning of June 4 when the old soldiers solemnly and silently congregated to place a wreath at the gate of Rome where their unit had entered the city sixty years before. They would be honoring those comrades who had fallen in that day's battle, and all the battles that had led to, and culminated in, the liberation of this capital.

That the veterans considered this memorial an intimate and reverential act was underscored by their decision to do it alone. Thus far, the old soldiers had allowed friends, family, and journalists to accompany them everywhere on the tour: to battlefields, military cemeteries, official receptions, and excursions. But on that morning, the Force men would be paying tribute to their fallen friends by themselves. There was only one exception: Larry, who would participate in the memorial representing the Special Forces, which considered the FSSF one of its precursors. In fact, Larry had told me that the FSSF campaign record was officially considered part of the Special Forces' legacy. Moreover, as he stood among the veterans in a crisp dress

* Joseph A. Springer, *The Black Devil Brigade* (New York: ibooks, 2001), p. 283.

uniform, Larry's presence symbolized—to me anyway—a tangible link between these WWII commandos and the special operations units of today that had been playing such a prominent role in America's current conflicts.

Until this point, what I knew of the U.S. Special Forces was restricted to recent events. Dust had barely settled on the destroyed World Trade Center in 2001 when Special Forces operators began stealing across the border into Afghanistan. They helped organize and coordinate the disparate tribes and factions of the Northern Alliance into a relatively unified force, directed air strikes, and brought about a collapse of the Taliban and al Qaeda faster—I suspect—than anyone could have imagined. On November 9, 2001, Taliban forces retreated from the northern city of Mazar-i-Sharif. Four days later Kabul fell. In less than two months the U.S. Special Forces had accomplished what the Red Army had not been able to do in a decade: defeat its enemies in Afghanistan.

And so as the survivors of the Black Devils commemorated their march into Rome sixty years before, Larry's presence was a reminder of the most recent capital that had fallen to the unit. In this way, the FSSF and the Special Forces represented bookends on a crucial and special branch of military history.

More than ever, I was determined to learn what this history was, and as I read and questioned the veterans more details began to emerge that were echoes of the present. The FSSF, I learned, had been conceived in Britain at the beginning of the Anglo-American alliance that helped end WWII, a partnership that seemed to presage America's present-day partnership with Britain in Iraq. Indeed, the idea for launching the Force grew from meetings—and no less important, a budding friendship—between General George C. Marshall and Britain's reigning commando leader Vice-Admiral Louis Mountbatten, when the former had visited London in April 1942. Prime Minister

Churchill would lend his enthusiastic support for the plan Mountbatten had introduced, and Marshall brought back to Washington. Fittingly, the plan was bold and visionary. But just as importantly, it sprung from desperation. Today, WWII exists in our collective memory as an epic story with the happiest of endings: the defeat of Nazi Germany and Imperial Japan.

Not only has the euphoria of these victories clouded some of the worst aspects of the war (the suffering of civilians and soldiers alike, and the colossal waste of lives) it tends to present every year of the war as determined, decisive steps toward triumph. Today, it is difficult to consider the early bleak years of WWII in isolation from 1945. But for Marshall, there was no guarantee in 1942 that the war in Europe could be won. Even contemporary historians like John Lukacs speak of pivotal moments (the early collapse of the Soviet Union, for example) when a different course might have created an outcome where Hitler may "have been unbeatable."* For Lukacs, the crucial juncture was May 1940.

For Marshall, it is difficult to imagine a more desperate year than 1942. Weeks before its arrival, Pearl Harbor had thrust America into a global conflict it was not prepared to fight. Soon after, Japan invaded the U.S. protectorate of the Philippines, and Germany seemed on the verge of defeating the Soviet Union. Today, after September 11, 2001, it is difficult to imagine a more fearful time. But if any year in recent history was as unsettling as 2001, it was 1942 when the First Special Service Force, an innovation in warfare, was created to meet the challenges of a new and dangerous epoch.

But of course, despite the FSSF's compelling history, I still found the most fascinating aspects of this story to be the men

* John Lukacs, *Five Days in London: May 1940* (New Haven: Yale University Press, 1999), p. 188.

themselves. Earlier, I had asked the documentary filmmaker Wayne Abbot, one half of the directing team that had made *Daring to Die,* if the veterans of the FSSF shared a single quality. Yes, he said after a pause. "They're tough." In Rome, I understood what he meant. All the veterans exuded confidence, defiance, and a zest for life. Herb Peppard, a youthful octogenarian who had the health of a fifty-five-year-old, entertained his fellow veterans with old wartime songs still at the tip of his tongue. William "Sam" Magee, a Silver Star recipient, devoted his retirement to visiting schools and educating the young on the WWII experience. General Ed Thomas, the tour organizer and leader, still conducted himself with a dignified military bearing. Sam Finn from St. Louis, Missouri, told me a fascinating tale of how he marked the liberation of Rome by sitting in the chair of Fascist leader Benito Mussolini and placing a pair of dirty boots on the dictator's desk. Despite the grim business they had returned to commemorate, Lloyd Dunlop, Hector MacInnis, Charlie Mann, Jack Callowhill, Emil Brodofski, Edwin Edwards, Arthur Pottle, and the Texan Eugene Gutierrez were conspicuous for their laughter and energy.

Either the call to the FSSF had attracted men who were inordinately spirited, or the experience had steeled them for a lifetime. I suspected the former, because what was most impressive about their collective history was the way in which they had responded during that horrible year of 1942. The FSSF was a volunteer outfit, and many of the call-up notices that appeared in mess halls across North America made it clear that the duty posed inordinately high risks. The notices asked for single men only, and some bulletins plainly called the unit a "suicide outfit."

Still, thousands volunteered. These were indeed special men, and my interest was peaked. So the next time I was at my family home in the West, I gassed up the car, and headed in the direction of Montana: the place where the FSSF had been created, and the setting where this story began. When I reached the state capital of Helena roughly eight hours later, I immediately searched for two Force veterans: legendary scouts, legendary friends, and among the last survivors of some of the unit's most harrowing battles.

Of the two friends, I found Joe first. A robust eighty-four-year-old with thick salt-and-pepper hair, Joe kindly indulged me, and invited me to talk at length about the Force at a bar he and his wife, Dorothy, tended on weekends. Under dim tavern lights and the soft blare of country music, Joe Glass focused his memory and described a mountain in central Italy, and a small army that crept onto its slopes during a winter's night in his youth. All the while, Dorothy Glass busied herself by wiping counters and filling a coffee machine, and listened. I could tell by the look on Dorothy's face that she was part of this story. She knew the tale intimately, because it began here, in her lifelong home of Helena, during the best and worst times of her life.

PART I

THE MOUNTAIN

CHAPTER ONE

THE ASCENT

Helena, Montana
Winter 1943

Montana is famous for many things—deep coulees, high mountains, gold, a spirit of defiance—but in the early part of the twentieth century visitors to the state often remarked upon the intensity of its quiet—particularly at night. Towns such as Helena often bustled during the day, but night, outside the saloons along the rowdy stretch of the town's main street, Last Chance Gulch, was a different matter. With vehicles silenced, horses in their stalls, dogs in houses, and the townsfolk in bed, the stillness of the Montana wilderness enveloped the community with a silence so rich and deep that the world became hollow, like the cavity of a dead tree or an abandoned mine shaft on a nearby ridge.

For most of her eighteen years Dorothy Glass, born in East Helena, had considered this silence one of life's givens. It was as natural as the yellow hills and the broad canopy of Montana sky. But in the summer of 1942, a little more than a year earlier, the silence had been broken by the soldiers who filled her town with noise and weekend revelries.

They had come almost like an invading army. They came from across America and Canada, the best of them tough and earthy, and almost every one of them calloused by a life of labor. Throughout the week they lived in tents on the nearby army base, Fort William Henry Harrison. During the weekend they swarmed into Helena and neighboring East Helena, and fre-quented such saloons as the Casino Bar, where Dorothy had worked. Dorothy had tended bar since she was sixteen, and over those two years she had met a lot of men. But the men who came in July and August 1942 were different.

They were special not only in name—the First Special Service Force. Some strutted and boasted that they were members of a "suicide" outfit, most charmed the local fathers, courted the daughters, drank, brawled, and during the week trained relent-lessly as warriors—leaping from planes, floating to earth under chiffon-light parachutes, marching endlessly across the country-side, blowing up derelict bridges, scaling mountains, and living in boxcars on the Continental Divide. The élan of these 1,800 men quickly made them sentimental fixtures in Helena, adopted sons of the community. But months ago these special soldiers had left, and with them went one unique man, Joe Glass, the husband she barely knew. The silence returned and on snowy nights Dorothy, nursing Charles, the newborn son Joe had never seen, could not help but wonder: Where was he?

Monte la Difensa, Italy
December 2, 1943

As the day passed and a cold darkness settled, an army of six hundred commandos began to stir from its hiding place in a narrow copse of trees on an alpine crag in central Italy.

The men had been hiding the entire day after spending the previous night slogging through rain, thorny brush, frigid creek beds, and stretches of knee-deep mud to reach the cover of trees on the lower slope of the mountain. Unable to continue their march in daylight without being detected by the enemy, the commandos—from the 2nd Regiment of the First Special Service Force (FSSF)—had kept low, warmed themselves in the sunlight breaking through the clouds, and waited for nightfall to continue their climb to the mountain's summit, where the Germans were entrenched. Their mission was both simple and seemingly impossible: scale this mountain's face in the dead of the wintry night, steal up to the German positions, and then drive their foes off of the peak.

As the regiment waited for the day to pass, Private Joe Glass of Sarnia, Ontario, cleaned his M1 rifle and sharpened his dagger and bayonet. Other men ate cold rations and tried to rest. Everyone, including Joe, dwelled on whether or not the night, or the next day, would bring a successful mission.

Glass, a lean youngster of twenty-three years who had been a seaman on the Great Lakes in civilian life, was about to enter combat for the first time. Indeed, the entire unit, the "Force" as the commandos called it, were virgins in this regard. Sitting under the trees, there were other things Glass would have preferred to dwell on, but he fought to keep these thoughts from his mind. To obsess on the wife he hadn't seen in months and the son he had never laid eyes on would be the surest way to lose focus and guarantee that he would never see either of them again. So he cleared his mind and occasionally chatted with friends in his unit, 3rd Platoon.

He might have preferred to speak with his best friend, Lorin Waling of Grande Prairie, Alberta, but Lorin was elsewhere in the trees with his own unit, 1st Platoon. Where Lorin was and what he was thinking, Joe could only imagine. Joe and Lorin shared a history that was only as long as Glass's fifteen months in the outfit. But their friendship had been rollicking, marked by clandestine nights spent in the East Helena lock-up, where the local jailer offered them beds after evenings spent with their girl-friends, now their wives, and surreptitious returns to the base in the rear of a milk truck driven by another local conspirator who always got them back in time for reveille.

Glass was distracted from his reveries when he sensed a slight movement around him. When he looked up, he saw what the muted excitement was about: the Force's commander, Robert T. Frederick, had just arrived.

Glass was both surprised and pleased to have the "Old Man" visiting their position. It was a surprise because the regiment was "out in front," facing an enemy that was proving itself as lethal in defense as it had been in attack, when it had surprised the world again and again with its ruthless efficiency. And he was pleased because, like so many of the men, Glass deeply admired Frederick. To Glass he looked "awful young" for his thirty-six years and high rank. Slight and wiry, Frederick was not imposing physically, but he carried himself with a posture as straight and soldierly as a bayonet. And there was a quality to Frederick—an ease, a manly empathy, perhaps—that was set in the officer's pleasing face and evident in every decision. Frederick was a commander who was tough on officers and generous with soldiers, and his men loved him for it.

Frederick mingled, greeted his commandos, and wished them good luck in the attack. And then, standing among the slim trees, Frederick delivered an impromptu speech. It was the standard pep talk any commander might impart to his troops before a battle. "I expect every man to do his best," Frederick said. But what set this commander apart from others was that Frederick had deemed it important to see the commandos off personally.

The afternoon passed quickly after Frederick left. When dusk fell, the men hiding in this belt of slender trees and scrub brush began to stir. To men such as Joe, who had grown up beside lush, dense Ontario forest, this copse was almost anemic. But it had provided the only cover on the hillside to hide the soldiers from the heights above, where seasoned and heavily armed German units were entrenched. Now, with darkness on its way, the men prepared for the last stage of their mission: leave the trees under the cover of night and make their way up the mountain's precariously steep slope, to their final destination, the mountain's enemy-occupied summit.

At approximately 4:30 p.m. the order was given for the regiment to pack up and move out. Shouldering a rifle, a pack filled with supplies, and ammunition—while rooted to the earth with calf-high "jump boots" and warmed with a fur-lined, hooded parka—Glass headed out near the front of a thin column that wound from the trees.

For Glass and the men of FSSF's 2nd Regiment, the months of training on the other side of the ocean, the preparations and marching, and the day's inertia under the trees were finished. Before the night was up, they would either fail or succeed in their assignment—an assignment on which balanced the future of the Allied campaign in Italy.

In a huddle just before the mission, the big picture had been explained to Joe and the men. In November 1942, Operation Torch had brought the Allies to North Africa; in June 1943, Sicily; and finally, in September of that year, British, Canadian, and

American armies landed in southern Italy. For the first time since Dunkirk, Allied armies stood on European soil.

The Allies began fighting their way up the Italian peninsula, but by November their onslaught had ground to a halt in the mountains of central Italy, where they ran up against Hitler's Winter Line, which the Germans held with determination. The cold and rain of the worst winter in years quenched Allied morale and stalled their advance. To end the stalemate, the U.S. Fifth Army attacked a gap in the mountains near a village named Mignano that led to a valley that in turn carried on to Rome. Their losses had been enormous against the well-dug-in Wehrmacht.

A strategic height, Monte la Difensa—the mountain Joe and the others were now scaling—guarded the way into this gap. Their orders: take this mountain and the entire German line will collapse. Take this mountain and Allied armies will be in the Liri Valley in days, and in Rome in weeks.

Joe and the others knew this would not be easily achieved. The entire U.S. Fifth army had been pinned down at Mignano since early November, thwarted by the German defenders occupying the high ground. Repeated assaults by the Thirty-sixth Infantry Division, the Third Infantry Division, and the British Fifty-sixth "Black Cat" Division had been turned back. The Force, a handful of men by comparison, was attacking defenses that had repelled thousands.

Joe's regiment, now making this fourth attempt, comprised only six hundred soldiers. The audacity of this, their first mission, was lost on none of them. Success, they believed, could change the tide of the war. If they failed, they would accomplish no more than the transformation of dozens of young brides like Dorothy Glass into widows.

Few knew that their journey up this mountain had really begun two years before, at the start of one of the worst years anyone could remember.

CHAPTER 2

THE TERRIBLE YEAR

April 11, 1942. Twenty months before the 2nd Regiment of the First Special Service Force mounted the dark slopes of Monte la Difensa in central Italy, an official meeting took place at Chequers, the draughty Tudor-style mansion in Buckinghamshire, eighty kilometers north of London, that had been the rural sanctuary of British prime ministers since 1921. The meeting was part of a diplomatic initiative by the U.S. to influence Britain to change the direction and focus of the war. This never happened. But the meeting would lead to an unprecedented military partnership between Canada and the United States, and like many decisions made by diplomats and bureaucrats and staff officers, these talks would affect the destinies of scores of ordinary men and families across North America.

One of history's great alliances had been cementing over the previous months and in a sense this meeting was its culmination.

A series of conferences known as "Arcadia" had drawn to a close in Washington in January. Great Britain and the United States had agreed to defeat Germany before decisively settling their accounts with Japan. Their strategy was to soften up the Germans with bombing raids and material support for the USSR and Resistance fighters before attempting a European landing. The Arcadia meetings also brought into being the Combined Chiefs of Staff (CCS), senior British and American officers well-placed to advise Churchill and Roosevelt.

At the meetings were two of America's most influential officials: presidential envoy Harry Hopkins and the most prominent American on the CSS, General George Marshall. They had come to Britain on April 8, and gone on to Chequers on the weekend of April 10, to persuade their host, the rotund, puckish, and resilient Prime Minister Winston Churchill, to sign on to a plan—two plans really—that Marshall's office had conceived. The Americans were impatient to tackle Germany, if only to get it over with, the sooner to turn their full attention to the Pacific.

Soon after arriving in London, Hopkins—so frail and sickly even his friend and mentor President Roosevelt referred to him as "that half-man"—and the older, graver, and much more robust Marshall paid a visit to the prime minister at his residence at 10 Downing Street. Churchill, a resident of Number 10 for two years, greeted the men warmly, particularly Hopkins. "Your visits always have a tonic effect," Churchill told him. Churchill wasn't simply being polite. His enthusiasm for Hopkins—and for American emissaries in general—was as enduring as his war. Churchill had spent much time since becoming prime minister in May 1940 courting the U.S., trying desperately to seduce it into the conflict against Nazi Germany. "No lover ever studied every whim of his mistress as I did those of President Roosevelt," he admitted.

Hopkins had been to Britain on two previous occasions as a presidential agent, and Churchill had laid on the charm each time. There were whiskey-soaked weekends at Chequers, garden parties with Churchill's aristocratic crowd, and private late-night viewings of movies like *Night Train to Munich* at Churchill's alternate retreat at Ditchley in Oxfordshire. Hopkins was impressed. As the son of a poor Iowa harness maker, he was fascinated by moneyed aristocrats (even broke ones, like Churchill). And perhaps because of his ailing, fragile constitution, he was attracted to matters of the flesh, and appreciated beautiful women. But it was Churchill's resilience and goodwill that affected him most, and on his last visit Hopkins had reciprocated by ending a dinner with a quote from the Book of Ruth: "Whither thou goest I will go; and where thou lodgest, I will lodge; thy people shall be my people and thy God my God." And when he ended with his own declaration "even to the end," tears filled Churchill's eyes.

Ultimately, it was the Japanese who would persuade America to join the war, by bombing Pearl Harbor on December 7, 1941. America had entered the war reluctantly, but once in was determined to conclude it—quickly and decisively. Marshall's aide, Dwight Eisenhower, captured the American sentiment in a January 22, 1942, diary entry: "We've got to go to Europe and fight." Indeed, the first American troops, the Thirty-fourth Infantry Division, were already arriving in Northern Ireland in early spring.

The grim-faced Marshall concurred with Eisenhower. A famously reticent man, Marshall lacked Hopkins's easy way and was congenitally incapable of a similar intimacy with Churchill. But Marshall's grimness reflected the times: April 1942 represented a particularly bleak chapter in both his life and American history.

America had not only found itself at war, it had found itself losing a war—on every front. At that moment in 1942, Japan was conquering the U.S. dependency of the Philippines. Only two days earlier U.S. forces numbering 79,500 men had surrendered on the Bataan peninsula. In Europe, Germany had overrun the

Continent right up to the English Channel. The previous summer had seen Hitler's seemingly invincible armies sweep across the vastness of the USSR, encircling Soviet troops by the million. The Luftwaffe had utterly shattered the world's largest air force in a few days. January had seen a major Russian counteroffensive, which recaptured lost ground. But by March the offensive had stalled, and the Germans still seemed to have a stranglehold in the east. Many wagered the USSR would crumble under the German hammer-blow sure to fall that summer. And Churchill knew better than the Americans how bad the war could get. The Eighth Army was on its heels in North Africa, the Japanese had been bloodying Commonwealth troops and seizing British possessions in Asia, and German U-boats were strangling the U.K. Though the Blitz had ended, the rubble of Britain still smouldered.

Shared misfortune and common enemies had made Churchill and Roosevelt fast allies. Now Marshall and Hopkins, hunkering down to business, presented Churchill with a letter from Roosevelt that explained what they wanted from their new alliance.

> Dear Winston,
>
> What Harry & Geo Marshall will tell you has my heart and mind in it. Your people & mine demand the establishment of a front to draw off pressure on the Russians & these peoples are wise enough to see that the Russians are to-day killing more Germans & destroying more equipment than you & I put together. Even if full success is not attained the big objective will be.
>
> Go to it!

Establishment of a European front: this was the essence of the two military plans—Roundup and Sledgehammer—that the envoys had brought. Roundup, Marshall explained, was the code name for an attack on German-occupied France along the Atlantic

Wall, but it would be neither a rehearsal nor a raid. A full-scale invasion of forty-eight infantry divisions, the attack would be a direct cannon shot, landing between Le Havre and Boulogne at a narrow point of the Channel, a route that ran straight through Paris and on to Berlin. Roundup would establish a second front in western Europe, and it would do it soon: April 1, 1943, one year from the meeting at Chequers.

As Churchill digested Roundup, Marshall explained Sledgehammer, an emergency operation that called for putting a much smaller Allied force on the European continent as early as September 15, 1942, five months on. Sledgehammer was an expedient to be used in desperation only—a suicide operation to be carried out if the Russian front was in danger of collapsing. Because the U.S. could not bring troops to the British Isles before September, British soldiers would be the ones committing suicide if Sledgehammer went forward.

Moreover, Marshall was determined not to wait a year before unleashing Allied wrath on the Germans. He recommended incessant, small-scale attacks across the Channel. "The enemy in the West must be pinned down," he had written in a memo to Roosevelt, "and kept in uncertainty by ruses and raids."

When Marshall finished, Churchill tried to sound matter-of-fact. He and his staff too had plans for an invasion of France, he said. "[We] had them under consideration for many weeks, and were prepared to go ahead." But Churchill admitted he didn't take these plans as "seriously" as the Americans. He had misgivings. Weren't the Germans still too strong, and the Allies too weak, for any attempted breach of the Atlantic Wall to succeed within the next two years? Churchill's warnings raised the simple question that was at the heart of Roundup: At what point does a bold step, a full frontal attack against an awesome enemy, become a reckless one?

That question would torment Allied commanders until the

end of the war, British commanders in particular. The memory of the horrific carnage of the First World War haunted all who had experienced it. Generals were desperate to avoid repeating it. Taken to task by Churchill for his slow advance into Germany later in the war, General Montgomery defended himself by noting that it had been the prime minister who had warned him against risking the casualties of the Somme. And what about the citizen soldiers who would be doing the fighting and dying? Could the volunteers and conscripts of the U.S. and Commonwealth armies be called upon to make the fanatical sacrifices that marked the German and Russian approaches to warfare? Even the most courageous Allied troops, driven by a sense of honor rather than the desperation and fear of their German and Russian counterparts, had little enthusiasm for a bloodbath.

Churchill liked the idea of invading North Africa. In his last face-to-face meeting with Roosevelt over the New Year, they had decided that their first decisive counterattack as allies would be Gymnast—the invasion of Algeria, Morocco, and Tunisia. (The invasion of North Africa would later be called Super Gymnast, and ultimately Torch.) Churchill had pushed Gymnast hard, wanting to shore up Britain's beleaguered forces in both Africa and the Middle East, to control the Mediterranean, and perhaps to groom the Allied armies for a winner-take-all fight on the Continent by means of an introductory campaign on the war's periphery.

Still, Marshall and Hopkins wanted to fight the Germans, and Churchill couldn't argue with that. "I'm favorably disposed to it," Churchill declared finally of Roundup.

After they left the prime minister, Hopkins felt deflated. He was not encouraged by Churchill's reception of Roundup. He believed the prime minister was unduly haunted by the prospect of turning the English Channel into, as he put it, "a river of blood." But Marshall, imbued with a soldier's pragmatism, saw the day's skirmish as a victory for the simple reason that it hadn't been a defeat. According to Hopkins, he said, "Churchill went a long way. I expected far more resistance than we got."

———

That evening, Marshall and Hopkins returned to 10 Downing Street for dinner. This time Churchill wasn't alone. The dining room included General Alan Brooke, the brooding Irishman who was Churchill's Chief of the Imperial General Staff (CIGS) and Marshall's opposite number on the CCS; Clement Attlee, Churchill's deputy in the War Cabinet; and Britain's tall, Errol Flynn look-alike foreign minister, Anthony Eden.

Marshall had been pleased by Churchill's relative agreeableness in the afternoon, but would his tune change in the company of subordinates? The chorus of discontent Marshall braced for never came. Churchill, who loved domineering over a dinner, seized control of the conversation from the outset, and outflanked the issue of a second front. Imbibing more wine than it was ever Roosevelt's habit to consume over a meal, Churchill steered clear of the current war, delving instead into the American Civil War, a topic close to Marshall's heart, and the last war, the Great War, a conflict the ageless Churchill had helped lead as well, as First Lord of the Admiralty and then later, after a hiatus as commander of the Sixth Royal Fusiliers in the field, as minister of munitions.

Before the evening was up, General Brooke acted as the prime minister's conscience. He raised the issue of Roundup, and expressed his misgivings, the same ones Churchill had brought up earlier: an assault on "Fortress Europe" was unnecessarily risky when the North African campaign would succeed in opening a second front without descending into a disastrous bloodbath. (In his capacity as First Lord of the Admiralty in the First World War, Churchill had pushed for the disastrous landings at the tip of the Gallipoli peninsula in Turkey, where the sea had literally run red with blood; 300,000 of the 500,000 men who landed became casualties.) As a former soldier, as a prime minister, and as a strategist husbanding Britain's strength, Churchill would not countenance another Gallipoli.

———

The next day, Marshall rose early and ventured off alone to meet the British chiefs of staff at the trapezoid-shaped monolith that served as the British War Office in Whitehall. Passing through the Ionic columns at the front, Marshall was ushered to the second floor, where he found the bulk of the chiefs: Admiral Sir Dudley Pound, the First Sea Lord; Air Chief Marshal Charles Portal, Chief of the Air Staff; and Major-General Sir Hastings Ismay, Churchill's chief of staff. All these men were as reluctant as Churchill to attack Fortress Europe before the time was right. Except for one.

At forty-two, Lord Louis Mountbatten, chief of a fledgling branch called Combined Operations, was a generation younger than Marshall and the other chiefs, and his manner was markedly different. Great-grandson to Queen Victoria, he hailed from aristocratic stock. But Mountbatten, who had left a naval command to become adviser to and later head of Combined Operations, eschewed snobbery, at least when it came to influential American officers.

In Mountbatten, Marshall found a willing partner. Because Combined Operations specialized in unconventional warfare, such as amphibious landings, securing beachheads, and the execution of small surgical raids against the enemy, Mountbatten and Marshall were potential kindred spirits. Marshall was becoming increasingly convinced that this type of fighting was essential to the war effort.

Combined Operations (CO) had been dispatching lethally trained commandos against German positions in Europe for over a year. On March 4, 1941, a CO unit cryptically known as No. 4

Commando raided German positions on the Lofoten Islands, in Norway. They blew up armaments and fish-oil factories, seized secret German radio ciphers, and returned home with over two hundred German prisoners and three hundred Norwegian volunteers. The only casualty of the operation was an officer who inadvertently shot himself. An attack against Vaargso, Norway, on December 27, 1941, wasn't as charmed. Combined Operations lost seventeen commandos. But they captured almost one hundred Germans and four Norwegian collaborators, and successfully shot up the local German garrison. As recently as March, 1942, Operation Chariot had successfully raided the French coast at St.-Nazaire, destroying U-boat pens.

Seizing on Marshall's interest, Mountbatten invited him to visit his headquarters at Richmond Terrace. Marshall agreed, and later that day toured the Combined Operations offices and was introduced to a member of Mountbatten's staff. Marshall found himself standing before one of the strangest men he had encountered in forty years of soldiering. Geoffrey Pyke was a scientist working for Combined Operations. On the cusp of the nuclear age, Pyke was a forerunner of the physicists and game theorists who a decade later would strategize the Cold War. A 1940s Dr. Strangelove, Pyke looked almost as morbidly comical. When Marshall shook hands with Pyke, he looked up into a long thin face sharpened at the chin by a goatee beard and topped by a hopelessly disheveled mop of hair. Tall and lean, as jumbled and angular as a long math equation, Pyke towered over Marshall, who was six feet tall.

But Pyke had one pleasing attribute: a face that blazed and sometimes charmed. Mountbatten himself had been a victim of Pyke's appeal. Pyke had won his current job by appearing at Combined Operations headquarters and declaring: "Lord Mountbatten, you need me on your staff because I'm a man who thinks." He was indeed. Pyke had spent most of his life a slave to wide-ranging and galloping ideas that at least one biographer believes were fueled by undiagnosed epilepsy. In some cases he rode these ideas to success; in other instances the wild brutes trampled him to the ground.

Educated in public schools and at Cambridge, Pyke approached a London newspaper at the start of the First World War and offered to spirit himself into the German capital to write dispatches. He made it to Berlin, lounged around in cafés, and was promptly arrested for spying. Incarcerated in the Ruhleben prison camp, Pyke applied his unconventional intellect to the goal of escaping. As was his habit, he tackled the problem backward. Seeing that German guards had foiled every nightly breakout, Pyke marched out of the camp in broad daylight, and eventually crossed into the Netherlands on foot.

Two decades later, as Europe careened toward another war, Pyke's theories took on military applications. During the Spanish Civil War he fabricated motorcycles with sidecars to transport hot food to the front. In the run-up to 1939 he tried to dissuade Hitler from his ambitions by conducting a secret poll of the Reich's citizens (the pollsters posed as inquisitive Brits on golfing holidays). The survey proved that the majority of Germans wanted peace. The Führer invaded Poland anyway.

There was a method to Pyke's eccentricity. Unlike most academics, Pyke was without a discipline; he was a scientist without a science. His talent was an ability to question an assumption and approach it from the freshest of angles. Sometimes this was a formula for silliness. Tackling the problem of how to destroy Nazi oil fields in Romania, Pyke suggested releasing St. Bernards carrying casks of alcohol against sentries, the assumption being that the guards would get drunk and leave the oil wells vulnerable to commando attack. If booze didn't do the trick, Pyke suggested dispatching beautiful women to distract the lonely men.

Despite these clunkers, Pyke had come to Combined Operations with a theory that fascinated Mountbatten, a strategy the chief wanted General Marshall to hear. So, as the American listened, Pyke passionately expounded on a memo he had written entitled *Mastery of the Snows*. And within minutes Marshall found himself persuaded by this strange man's reexamination of the obvious: the military viability of snow. Pyke argued that in winter so much of Europe was covered in snow that the substance was not merely a factor of weather, it was a fourth element: "a sea which flows over most of Europe each year and which usually tends to act as a brake on military operations. We must obtain mastery of the snows," Pyke declared, "as we have of the sea." And just as great warships ruled the waves, Pyke argued, snow could be conquered and exploited if the Allies developed, as he wrote, "cross-country snow machines . . . [that] would enable us to move over snow at speeds greater than that of the enemy and to go where he cannot follow."

According to Pyke's thinking, snow machines, plus the element of surprise, could enable an impressively small number of specially trained commandos, schooled in winter warfare, demolitions, and so on, to do enormous damage. Moreover, their mobility and specialized training would allow them to subdue a much larger force of Germans. Pyke listed Romania's oil fields as a target. But of even greater strategic interest to Marshall and Mountbatten was Pyke's plan to neutralize Norway as an "economic asset" to the Germans by unleashing snow commandos and their armor against the fourteen Norwegian electric power stations that generated 49 percent of the country's power. This northern attack, Pyke said, could prepare "the way for an eventual reoccupation of Norway, thereby forming a link with Russia."

Pyke may have been reaching a bit, but he was saying things that Marshall wanted to hear. The plan was Sledgehammer on skis, and it could be launched within the year.

By the time Marshall and Hopkins arrived in Buckinghamshire for the weekend, Mountbatten had already decided to give Pyke's idea to the Americans. Britain lacked the resources to realize the plan, he believed. Only the United States had the money, men, and talent to make it work. Marshall agreed. The U.S. War Department would plan the raid, and U.S. defense scientists would design the state-of-the-art snowmobiles. Both men agreed that Pyke would go to Washington to help and that some British commandos might serve in the Norway operation.

The April 11 meeting at Chequers served as the final endorsement of the Pyke plan. Hopkins, who never met the quirky scientist, showed little interest; he was too preoccupied with Roundup. But Churchill paid attention during Mountbatten's briefing, and declared that if the scheme became reality "never in the history of human conflicts would so many have been immobilized by so few."

On April 15, Marshall and Hopkins left for home. Much had been accomplished. The British had agreed to a proposal, called "Bolero," for a massive build-up of American forces in Britain, to be equipped for bombing and air combat operations over Europe, and in anticipation of an invasion of the continent. Only a few months later, Major General Eisenhower would arrive to oversee the preparations.

Roundup and Sledgehammer, however, would never happen. The latter was shelved in the summer of 1942, amid preparations for a large-scale rehearsal of an amphibious assault on the French coast to be called Rutter, and later renamed Jubilee, which would demonstrate unequivocally the inadequacy of Allied tactics and planning. The debacle of this landing would help convince the CCS to postpone Roundup until 1944, by which time it would be called Overlord. The invasion of Europe would have to wait.

CHAPTER 3

THE STAFF OFFICER

When Marshall returned to his offices on Constitution Avenue in Washington, he still believed that the British were supporting U.S. strategy to establish a second front in Europe.

No one was more relieved by this unanimity than Dwight Eisenhower, Marshall's assistant at the War Department. As head of Operations Division, Eisenhower and his team had been the authors of Roundup and Sledgehammer. "We are definitely committed to one concept of fighting," Eisenhower confided to his diary. And that concept was to invade Fortress Europe head-on from across the English Channel and march directly on Berlin. All of Washington seemed to share Eisenhower's enthusiasm. Roosevelt dispatched a jubilant cable to Churchill: "I believe that the results of this decision will be very disheartening to Hitler." And the capital operated as if propelled by a new sense of purpose. America was no longer fighting a rearguard action. The nation was on the attack.

It was during this hopeful period that Marshall briefed Eisenhower and his staff on the eccentric plan to invade Europe with a force of winter commandos. Marshall whipped off a memo, going over the salient points of Pyke's plan: how a specialized "motorsled" that is "armored, carrying adequate guns" could "be used to considerable effect against critical points." Marshall wrote of the vision of Pyke and Mountbatten: "They have in mind establishing a base from the air in Norway. They have in mind the use of these vehicles in sudden raids so as to force German troop concentrations in a wasteful manner . . ."

Now officially dubbed Plough Project, the scheme took on momentum. In a span of days the wild musings of a British academic had found their way into Eisenhower's Operations Division as a potential mission. At first some officers were more intrigued by the proposal than impressed. Eisenhower himself considered the scheme a "curiosity." But on May 22, General Crawford, Deputy Assistant Chief of Staff, Operations Division, walked the proposal to one of his officers: Robert Tryon Frederick, a West Point graduate and former artilleryman. Already a lieutenant colonel at the tender age of thirty-five, Frederick was an up-and-comer. Affable and serious, possessing both a sharp intellect and a diplomat's ability to soothe egos, Frederick shared many of the same traits as his boss, Eisenhower.

Frederick had been one of the youngest in his class when he graduated from Command and General Staff School at Fort Leavenworth in 1938. He joined the War Department in 1941 from a posting at Fort Shafter, Hawaii, after a report he had filed caught the attention of General Marshall. By the spring of 1942, Frederick was serving in Eisenhower's Operations Division, where he spent twelve days poring over Plough. Weighing it as a military operation, Frederick was less concerned about the loftier aspects of the plan (how the state-of-the-art armored snowmobiles would be designed) than the practical questions. Was it logistically feasible for the raiders and machines to perform the tasks Combined Operations had set out?

At the end of twelve days Frederick submitted his report. Eisenhower read it after he returned from his own fact-finding trip to London on June 3. London had been a revelation for the American general. On the positive side, the Brits had generally impressed Eisenhower despite their interference in his four-pack-a-day smoking habit. Eisenhower found General Bernard Law Montgomery "energetic" and "able," even though Monty refused to let Eisenhower smoke in his office. Eisenhower struck up "an immediate and lifelong friendship" with Lord Mountbatten. But he was less impressed by the Britons' appetite for a fight. The realization was beginning to dawn on him that British officers had no stomach to invade Europe that year by way of Sledgehammer or in 1943 with Roundup. What is more, U.S. forces already on the ground there were in disarray, and a new leader for the European Theater of Operations (ETO) was needed.

With London a vivid memory, Eisenhower read Frederick's report, and was surprised. Frederick had declared Plough Project militarily unworkable. It was, he contended, a suicide mission. Once the commandos were in Norway, there was no conceivable way of getting them out. But that wasn't the only problem. As far as Frederick knew, there was no easy way of getting the raiders *in*. The obvious route, of course, was an airdrop, but there were no planes available to carry the parachutists. And even if the problems of getting the men in and out were solved, Frederick wasn't convinced that a small force could do sufficient damage to justify the risk and resources. "Plough was a beautiful paper concept but a strategic farce," he wrote.

Neither Eisenhower nor anyone else could argue with Frederick's reasoning. Militarily speaking, the young lieutenant colonel's analysis was flawless. But there was one problem: the Allied leadership supported the plan. It may have been flawed, but for political reasons it had to go forward. "General Eisenhower . . . was very much disturbed over the unfavorable report on the project," Frederick later wrote, "and said that in view of the fact that both General Marshall and he had assured both the Prime Minister and Lord Mountbatten that the United States was going ahead on the project there was nothing to do but proceed in an energetic manner."

Eisenhower may have had his own reasons for not wanting to see Plough die, particularly given the apparent demise of Roundup in London. Plough envisioned taking the fight to Europe—in Norway, in Romania, in Italy. And in the bleak spring of 1942, Eisenhower had hardened himself to the fact that the Allies had to start fighting in Europe and men would have to die. Already he was using a great balance sheet to rationalize the loss of lives. He admitted as much when he confessed in a memo that the trade-off for losing every man in the suicidal Sledgehammer operation, "would be to keep 8,000,000 Russians in the war."

Like it or not, Plough would be reality, and Frederick was asked to help get the project off the ground. Frederick went with Eisenhower to the Soviet embassy for a meeting that included Lord Mountbatten, who was in Washington on business. The Soviets expressed keen interest in the snowmobile the project envisioned. After all, during Russia's endless winter the Great Steppe was transformed into an immense, flat inland sea of snow. The Soviets had already developed their own snow craft to navigate this expanse. (Pyke had studied and was fascinated by the Archimedean screw-powered propulsion system of at least one Soviet snow machine.) The cruel efficiency of the eastern winter had destroyed Napoleon's Grand Army and taught subsequent generations of Russian generals that snow and cold were their best allies. Finnish soldiers, who had fought off an invading Soviet army in 1939 with technology no greater than skis, white camouflage, and honed winter combat skills, were the most recent reminder that in wars in the North the snows always choose the victor.

Days later, when it was announced that Plough would get a full-time officer to breathe life into it, Frederick asked his direct superior, General Crawford, if he could detach himself from the issue and get back to his other work. Crawford said no.

Then Plough began to speed out of control. On June 6, an American army officer was selected for Plough: Lieutenant Colonel H. R. Johnson. Two days later Johnson met with Plough's creator, the British scientist Pyke, then in Washington to assist in the project, and conflict erupted immediately. Pyke made Johnson's skin crawl. Mountbatten met with Johnson and seems to have been no more impressed by the American than was Pyke, particularly when Johnson told the vice admiral that he would take part in Plough only "if the project was really going to amount to something and be carried out . . . but if it is just another idea that might come to no real operation, he was not anxious to have anything to do with it." Johnson had also said the same thing to Eisenhower. It was strike three for him. By June 9, he was banished from Plough.

Late that same evening, a British officer from the Combined Chiefs of Staff called on Frederick and dropped a grenade: Frederick had been selected to lead Plough. Lord Mountbatten, he would learn, had lobbied hard for him. Clearly, Mountbatten had been watching Frederick closely and was impressed by the young officer.

Frederick was "stunned." He was delighted to have earned the trust of a man of Mountbatten's stature and he had been given a fascinating assignment. But he knew better than anyone that the command was a death sentence. "Every man will be sacrificed," he wrote in his diary. "I'm hard pressed to find anything welcome in [it]."

———

A weary Lieutenant Colonel Frederick strode into his house and was greeted in the living room by his wife of fourteen years, Ruth. For Frederick, it was no exaggeration to say that his marriage and the army shared equal weight in his life. For many soldiers, then and now, duty supersedes family. Frederick was no less responsive to duty, but it was not for nothing that his lives as soldier and husband began synchronously: Frederick had married Ruth Adelaide Harloe on his graduation day from West Point in 1928. He had met her during his second year at a West Point dance, and must have been desperate to marry her, unable as he was to wait a single day after his release from school.

This relationship influenced his career in many ways. Frederick immediately signed up for the coastal artillery to get himself back home to California, but most of all to obtain access to some of the best family housing in the army. That Frederick had found something—marriage—to equal the army in his life is telling, since the army was all he had ever wanted. Born and raised in San Francisco, a short distance from the Presidio, Frederick had gravitated toward a soldier's life at an early age. Fit and agile, he possessed a physique that would have excelled at baseball or track and field. But while Frederick was never known to take any interest in team sports, he did have a hunger for adventure. At fourteen years of age, perhaps inspired by the travels and writings of another wild son of San Francisco, Jack London, Frederick served as a deck boy on a steamship bound for the South Pacific. But the sea never hooked Frederick. He returned home and single-mindedly pursued his passion to be a soldier. Having already joined the Reserve Officers Training Corps at thirteen, he later lied about his age and joined the National Guard. After that he enlisted in the reserves, and was an officer by the time he was admitted to West Point.

After West Point, Frederick spent a dozen seemingly quiet years in the coastal artillery. While by most accounts he was not dissatisfied with his military career, he suffered frustration when his incisive intelligence collided with the will of less perceptive superiors. When posted at Fort Shafter, Hawaii, the vulnerability of U.S. forces was as clear to him as the Pacific moon, and he wrote a six-page report citing precautions that he considered elementary. He recommended emptying Pearl Harbor, the clear target of any attack, of its warships, and having them remain scattered offshore, where they could be supplied and fueled by barges. He also suggested flying barrage balloons to help the islands' "meager" antiaircraft system ward off a Japanese air attack. "Raiding forces will steam toward Oahu during the night," he predicted, "releasing planes about daylight."

Frederick hoped his insights would be passed up the line. Instead, they were returned to him with the response: "Maj. Frederick, we are not much impressed with your ideas." About six months later Frederick won an assignment to the War Department; four months after that, the Japanese attacked Pearl Harbor in much the way he had foreseen.

Now it was 1942, the world was at war, and Frederick seemingly had everything he had wanted. Or did he? A posting in the War Department was an accomplishment, but staff work did not ignite a fire of ambition in him as it did in others. Eisenhower, for example, had nominally been a colonel when he joined the War Department on December 15, 1941, and now, barely six months later, was a major general on his way to command the European Theater of Operations.

Nor did Frederick necessarily yearn for the field. As his daughter would say sixty-two years later, "He wasn't looking for anything unusual or unique." But he had been offered Plough, arguably the most "unusual" command in the U.S. Army. Frederick didn't tell his wife what the assignment was. He simply told her calmly that he had taken an assignment and, in an aside that made the enigmatic mission even more perplexing, added: "I've got to go to Canada."

If Bob Frederick had reservations about Plough, he didn't show them. The muted weariness he had displayed to his family contained more doubt than he ever revealed to the rest of the world. Once he had accepted Plough, he moved like a bulldozer. He left for Canada on June 11 with Mountbatten and Pyke to feel out Ottawa for possible participation in Plough. Mountbatten was now certain that Britain would not be able to assist Frederick with Plough in any substantial way; it just didn't have the resources. Plough needed partners, and Mountbatten decided that Canada could represent Britain and the Commonwealth in the unit.

In many ways Canada was the perfect choice as an ally. Mountbatten knew that its soldiers were acquainted with snow and cold, and most—presumably—could ski. And he also knew they were willing to fight. Canada had declared war on Nazi Germany on September 10, 1939—a week after Britain, France, Australia, and New Zealand had declared war, and five days after the U.S. had announced its neutrality. If Canada had entered the conflict after greater deliberation than some of its allies, it was because of the lessons of the First World War—a conflict that had claimed 65,000 Canadian lives, and extinguished all naïveté about the meaning and costs of warfare in the twentieth century. Canada's reputation in the First World War was proof to Mountbatten and other British leaders of its tenacity under arms. That 58,000 Canadian men and women (out of a total population of 11 million) volunteered to join the war before the end of September 1939 proved that the people were as determined as their leaders to fight this war as well.

On the technical side, the nation's wintry climes could be useful for testing the snow machine that was currently being developed by the U.S. Office of Scientific Research and Development and the War Production Board, all under the watchful eye of Brigadier General Raymond Moses, formerly with the Army's Fifth Engineer Regiment. Canadian scientists might also be able to expedite the research.

With Mountbatten smoothing the way, Plough's three leaders, Frederick, Mountbatten, and Pyke, lunched with Canada's governor general and met with the Canadian Army Chief of Staff, Lieutenant General Kenneth Stuart, as well as top officers who might have something to contribute. Frederick exchanged ideas with Tom Gilday, a young captain who was in charge of the Canadian army's winter warfare school. The meetings proved more constructive than anyone in Plough had hoped and the only tensions that arose surrounded Pyke, whose quirky, deeply unmilitary behavior was clearly grating on the nerves of some of the soldiers. During a meeting on June 12, Pyke was extrapolating on his vision for the project when a Canadian officer passed Frederick a note that read: "What the hell does he want?" Pyke also irritated Frederick. Back in Washington, he had regularly phoned at all hours of the night, and talked endlessly. In Canada, he fussed, insisting that their hotel-room doors be double-locked, and wanted to be part of every meeting that Frederick attended. But Frederick, perhaps by exerting simple soldierly discipline, treated Pyke with patience and courtesy.

On June 13, 1942, Frederick's discipline in this and other matters paid an important dividend: Canada and its northern warriors joined the mission to invade Norway. General Stuart and his staff had discussed Plough and its inherent problems, and decided they liked the project. Wrote Frederick later: "They assured me that Canada was willing to enter the project 100 percent in cooperation with the United States." They also agreed that Plough should have its headquarters in the U.S., and that the U.S. Army should carry out the planning and intelligence. A Canadian would be second-in-command; half the officers would be Canadian, as would one-third of the enlisted men. Scientists from the National Research Council of Canada would help in snowmobile research. Frederick returned to Washington on June 14 a satisfied man. The project had moved one full step closer to completion.

At home, Frederick needed a mandate, so Eisenhower asked him to write up his orders. The young lieutenant colonel sat down and wrote himself a blank check. To keep himself free of War Department politicking and office disputes, Frederick put Plough under the aegis of the deputy chief of staff. Frederick specified that he, and only he, was responsible for creating the unit. (He would not be sharing decisions with eccentric British professors or well-meaning officers in Combined Operations.) In paragraph four he gave himself the power to get what he wanted from where he wanted. ("The facilities of other agencies of the United States will be utilized as fully as is practicable . . .," he wrote.) Paragraph five allowed him to hire foreigners as advisers, trainers, and instructors. Paragraph six allowed him to place Canadian, British, or Norwegian officers in command of Americans. (He was determined to put the best men at the top, regardless of nationality.) Paragraph seven enabled him to liaise directly with foreign governments and armies.

Paragraph nine was the keystone. It ordered the "Commanding Generals, Army Ground Forces, Army Air Forces, and Services of Supply, and the Divisions of War Department General Staff" essentially to do Frederick's bidding "in the vigorous and thorough accomplishment of this project."

The orders bore General Marshall's name. Frederick and his future commandos were now on the way to their expected suicide, and they would not be hindered by red tape.

———

Even before Frederick climbed into Plough's driving seat, researchers had been driven hard by General Moses and pestered mercilessly by Geoffrey Pyke. Strangely, and probably to Moses's great surprise, under Frederick's control the research team made immediate progress. Experts at Combined Operations had already decided the snowmobile should be able to travel over all types of snow, and a certain distance over solid ground. It had to carry two tons of men and arms, travel at a top speed of thirty-two kilometers an hour, climb a 20-percent-grade hill, and cover as much as four hundred kilometers of territory. To achieve these goals, military researchers would have to push existing snow sled technology to its limits.

Snow craft did exist in 1942. Eighteen years before, Carl Eliason, a Wisconsin outdoorsman with a handicapped foot, had begun working on a mechanized sled, which he hoped would help him get around on the snow while hunting. He patented his invention, the Motor Toboggan, in 1927. With wooden runners and an open engine, the early Eliason toboggan, driven by a 2.5-horsepower motor, was a far cry from the long-distance, speedy winter war machines dreamed of by Pyke. Just before the war, 150 Motor Toboggans were sold to the U.S. Army. But even these improved models (by 1937, Eliason was powering his sleds with 25-horsepower engines) were not advanced enough for the Plough mission. (The first Ski-Doo, which was invented by Joseph-Armand Bombardier of Valcourt, Quebec, and possessed the basic structure of modern-day snowmobiles, did not become available commercially until 1960.)

To meet the October deadline, Moses would have to devise a new prototype. He gathered an eclectic team to help him. In addition to the consortium of scientists at his disposal, Pyke had hired a Norwegian air force officer named Sverre Petterssen, a meteorologist of almost psychic ability. He had also tapped an Austrian-born snow expert named Herman Mark. The Austrian might officially have been an "enemy alien" living in New York, but he knew snow. In the beginning, the team tried to save time by seeking to adapt the army's armada of Eliason Motor Toboggans, which were being used by the Eighty-seventh Mountain Infantry at Mount Rainier, Washington State. But in tests in the frigid highlands of California, the Eliason, little more than a motorcycle engine powering a slat-studded canvas tread, puttered along too weakly for anyone's liking.

Pyke's vision, derived from the notion of ruling Europe's snows as if they were waves, was of a snowmobile driven by two giant rotating screws. Pyke envisioned a hull that sat atop horizontal screws as large as logs that propelled the sled by gobbling up the snow and churning it out the back.

The Russians had similar machines, and they reportedly bored through the snow of the wintry steppe like high-powered drills. But the steppe's flatness was key to the success of screw-driven technology. When tested, the snow screws couldn't climb hills, and since Romania, Norway, and Italy had a lot of them, Pyke's dream collided with hard reality. The Plough scientists even tested a versatile new military vehicle called the jeep. So state-of-the-art that it was featured in the January 1942 edition of *Scientific American*, the jeep was touted as the American answer to the German Panzer. In tests as a snowmobile the jeep did have some success moving around, but it eventually got stuck in a snowdrift.

Finally, the scientists decided they would have to invent something. A design was fleshed out for a machine that would run sleek and low over the snow on mighty rubber-coated tractor treads. Moses and his team went over the plan, and they liked what they saw. (The only dissenter was Pyke, who still clung to his dream of a sled running on Archimedean snow screws.) The Weasel, the code name for the Plough snowmobile, had now been conceived. By July, four prototypes would roll off the assembly line.

Plough Project would get its machines. Now all it needed was men to drive them.

———

By mid-June, Frederick's team occupied offices on the third floor of the War Department's Munitions Building in Washington. The rooms must have felt cavernous. Plough, for all its promise and bravado, was the loneliest prairie outpost in the army. The unit at this point was made up of Frederick, Pyke, and a few secretaries.

Frederick immediately set to work building a staff, flexing the muscles his orders had given him. He hired a major by the name of Orval Baldwin, who had been an engineer with the National Resources Planning Board as a logistics officer, or G-4.* From military intelligence he signed on Captain Robert Burhans to be his G-2, or chief of intelligence. And from the coastal artillery just outside of Boston he tapped an old colleague from his years in Hawaii, Major Ken Wickham, to be his adjutant, or G-1. Frederick's commandos would need to be airborne-certified in an inordinately short time, so he looked to Fort Benning, one of the country's top jump schools, and hired away Major John Shinberger

* The G designation denoted staff in large army units. G-1 handled personnel; G-2, intelligence; G-3, operations; G-4, supply. In army units smaller than a division, the S designation is used. Because of the FSSF's compact size, some of the staff referred to themselves as S-1, S-2, etc.

to oversee operations and training, and two Fort Benning instructors to teach his men the art of combat parachuting.

Now equipped with a staff, Frederick looked for a venue in which to train and house his men. The base needed to be as unique and special as the Plough force itself, and it had to be big enough for landing strips and training-drop zones so that his men could learn to jump out of airplanes. It had to be near an extremely cold place, so his troops could be taught how to ski and survive the winter, and readily accessible to the mountains, so that the men could learn mountaineering and high-altitude warfare. And lastly, ever mindful of Plough's top-secret status, Frederick required privacy.

Focused on the western half of the U.S., where mountains, snow, and space were to be found, Frederick learned of an old fort in Montana named after America's ninth president. Erected in 1894 by order of Congress, Fort William Henry Harrison was available and—standing five kilometers from the frontier town of Helena—isolated. And like everything in Montana, the fort was immense, taking up about two thousand acres of empty land, which was in turn surrounded by open space and wilderness. As for Plough's unique training requirements, this stretch of Montana seemed to offer everything. Hard on the Continental Divide, the area had harsh winters, endless snowfalls, and a varied landscape—flatlands that had been cattle country since 1866, when the first herd of longhorn arrived there from Texas, and mountains that contained gold, which brought prospectors even before the cattlemen.

At a glance, Fort Harrison was suitable. After Shinberger returned from Montana with a glowing report, Frederick was convinced. Plough now had a base.

Finding the right men was an altogether more complicated matter. Frederick was keenly aware that he needed soldiers with a unique temperament. But the question was, what type? He consulted with a psychologist and was told that men already accustomed to the isolation and rigors of the wilderness were most likely to excel in Plough's missions. After a quick inventory Frederick learned that the army currently had 327 men who had been employed as outdoorsmen before the war. He would need more. So he sent Wickham and Shinberger to canvass at major bases in the U.S. He contacted the Canadians to comb their barracks as well. Finally, he put out a call that winged its way in notice form to bulletin boards and messes across the United States and Canada.

The notices varied. Some advertised for volunteers for a suicide outfit. Other notices asked for men interested in joining a new airborne unit. Most of the notices called for:

> Single men between ages 21 and 35 who have completed three years or more grammar school within the occupational range of Lumberjacks, Forest Rangers, Hunters, Northwoodsmen, Game Wardens, Prospectors, and Explorers.

=====

In July 1942, a nineteen-year-old prairie boy named Lorin Waling was languishing in the military stockade—the "jug" as he called it—at the Canadian army base in Petawawa, Ontario. Waling was despondent. The army, it seemed, was conspiring to keep him out of the war. When Waling signed up, he was seventeen years old. He had lied about his age to get into uniform, but he fooled no one. "They knew I was underage, and they treated me like I was underage," he said. By the summer of 1942, Canadians were on combat duty in the Pacific and awaiting action at bases in Britain. But Waling was in Petawawa, and doomed to stay there. Desperate to fight, he had gone AWOL, stolen across the border at Windsor, and attempted to join the

U.S. Army in Detroit. But American recruiters were wise to the fact that Waling was already a Canadian soldier, and he ended up in the brig.

After two weeks the gates of the stockade swung open and he spotted a notice posted at the base. The bulletin asked for volunteers for a special parachute unit, a new form of warfare almost unheard of until German paratroopers had startled the world by leaping into and seizing the Netherlands in 1940 and the Greek island of Crete in 1941. The notice was addressed to men with outdoor experience, and promised rigorous training and quick entry to combat. Waling immediately went to see his commanding officer.

———

In Hawaii, New Mexico–born Mark Radcliffe, a member of the 161st Infantry, had just been accepted to Officer Candidate School in Fort Benning, Georgia, when he spotted a notice asking for volunteers for a special unit. He signed up. By mid-July 1942 he had graduated from officers' training and been retained as an instructor. He was lecturing to a new batch of trainees when a runner appeared in the classroom and told him to report to camp headquarters on the double.

Minutes later, Radcliffe found himself standing in front of a pensive major named Wickham.

Wickham showed Radcliffe a document. "Is this your signature?" he asked.

Radcliffe looked it over and said yes.

"You have four hours to clear this base."

That afternoon Radcliffe was on an airplane headed west. Similar plays were being acted out in bases across North America as ambitious, bored, or disgruntled soldiers saw Frederick's call for volunteers as an invitation to something dangerous and enticing. In a short time men began making their way to Montana.

CHAPTER 4

MAVERICKS AND MOUNTAIN MEN

One of the first men to arrive was Frederick himself, who stepped from the fuselage of a commercial plane and set foot on the hot tarmac at the Helena, Montana, airport on Sunday, July 19, 1942.

Frederick took in his surroundings—a huge, heavy sky and mountains that encircled the area like the rim of a bowl—and even though it was late afternoon, he left immediately to inspect the new home of the Plough Project: Fort William Henry Harrison.

What he found when his car pulled through the gates that Sunday in July could not have pleased him. The base was dry prairie covered by derelict buildings. A throwback to an era when the Indian wars were remembered as America's great conflicts, Fort Harrison hadn't been used as a regular army base since 1912.

But the regional army unit IX Corps was now hard at work repairing, maintaining, and guarding the post. Frederick was satisfied with this. He wrote in his diary that he liked the "energy and initiative" being exhibited, and was "pleased with the progress that had been made." More than half of the tent frames to be used as temporary barracks for the troops were already standing. Mess halls, latrines, and administrative buildings were ready to go.

Since D-Day for the Norway invasion was set for December 15, Frederick knew that no time could be lost. So even as the base was being constructed, his staff was hard at work. His operations chief, Major Shinberger, and the force's jumpmaster, Captain Tug Wilson, were on their way and would arrive the next day. Frederick had a dynamo in Shinberger. Immaculate in his dress, Shinberger was so fastidious that he pushed himself to the brink of caricature. A quick study of men, Frederick saw Shinberger as a martinet. But he also saw that Shinberger was showing impressive enthusiasm. Things were getting done. A space would soon be earmarked as a runway to accommodate troop transports, essential for airborne training. The fort already boasted a serviceable rifle range, and as Frederick noted in his diary: "There are excellent sites for additional ranges for sub-machine gun, pistol, machine gun, and field firing."

Other staff would include Dermot "Pat" O'Neill, an Irish-born former cop with the Shanghai Municipal Police, who had been an instructor with the Office of Strategic Services (OSS) when Frederick tapped him to teach his men hand-to-hand combat. O'Neill had not arrived yet, but Ken Wickham, Frederick's bespectacled and bookish G-1, was on the ground and running. Acquaintances when they shared a post at Fort Shafter, Hawaii, Frederick and Wickham were fast becoming friends. With his talent for organization, Wickham, whom Frederick called "Kenneth," became a sounding board, confidant, and an essential member of his staff. Frederick's Executive Officer (XO), or second-in-command, was the ranking Canadian, Lieutenant

Colonel John McQueen. A fitting counterpart to Frederick, McQueen sported the same wiry, compact physique and finely trimmed moustache. An officer with the Calgary Highlanders, McQueen had come to Montana from Britain, where he had seen something neither Frederick nor his staff had. McQueen had stared across the English Channel at Fortress Europe, Plough Force's ultimate destination.

One of Wickham's first contributions was to draft a Table of Organization for the unit that cleverly served its mandate as a stealth outfit. With Frederick's approval, he broke the unit into eight-man sections, each under a sergeant. Each section would travel the snows of Norway in four state-of-the-art Weasels: two men per snowmobile. The entire outfit grew from this eight-soldier building block. Two sections made up a platoon under a lieutenant; three platoons formed a company under a captain. There would be three companies to every battalion under a lieutenant colonel; and two battalions would compose a regiment under the stewardship of a full-fledged colonel. The total regimental body count would be 32 officers and 385 enlisted men—a preposterously small number. A real army regiment, as Wickham later wrote in his memoirs, "was four times as large." The entire combat echelon of the Plough force would be made up only of three of these lean regiments. Counting medics, communications officers, and staff, Plough comprised 108 officers and 1168 enlisted men. The outfit would in fact grow to 11 men and later 16 men per section. Still, even at its largest, Frederick's army remained small. But grouping the small force into regiments served a purpose: it would mask its true strength from the enemy.

The night of his arrival, Frederick invited Wickham to join him for a dinner with Lieutenant Colonel Sawkins, the "blunt, go-getter" (as Frederick would call him) who commanded the IX Corps Area complement that was caring for the fort. Sawkins's wife made them a foursome, and they retreated that evening to the Montana Club, an old social club that occupied a wedge-shaped six-floor mansion on the corner of Sixth and Fuller Avenues in Helena. The members-only Montana Club was Frederick's introduction to the community, and it had impressed its openness and lack of pretension on him by offering to extend membership privileges to all the officers at Fort Harrison. Helena's most exclusive society was embracing him and his men. Frederick couldn't have felt more at home.

But he had other reasons to celebrate with Wickham and Sawkins. Frederick had been promoted to full colonel on the day the formal order had been published announcing the formation of the Force headquarters and naming Frederick commanding officer. Frederick's outfit was a unit of the U.S. Army, and had recently been given an official name. In a bid to replace the top-secret moniker "Plough Force," Frederick had mulled over a host of titles. He toyed with giving it a native Indian name. The army seemed to prefer dramatic titles designed to horrify the enemy and titillate headline writers. Darby's Rangers, an American unit being formed in Britain by Colonel William O. Darby, had informally named itself after the colonial paramilitary Roger's Rangers. But Frederick wanted something more restrained. He rejected the epithet "commandos," derived from the *Afrikaaner Kommando* of the Boer War, which Mountbatten's Combined Operations HQ called its raiders.

Frederick certainly knew that in 1941 David Stirling, a former British commando, had formed a band of raiders that blew up sixty-one grounded German aircraft in their maiden operation in North Africa. Stirling called his unit the Special Air Service, a name that was both vague and, in the context of the U.S. Army, highly ironic given that the entertainment division would be named Special Services and soldiered by the likes of Mickey Rooney. True to the British commando tradition of Stirling, Frederick named his unit the First Special Service Force.

The men enjoyed their dinners, as the work would only become more intense in the days to come. Wickham had gone personally to Forts Benning and Belvoir and harvested the graduation classes of the Officer Candidate School (OCS) and Engineer OCS respectively. These young second lieutenants would become the unit's future platoon leaders and company commanders. Collectively, these men, most in their early twenties, would represent the spine of Frederick's force, and they were already arriving.

———

Just before 8 a.m. on July 18, 1942, a taxi deposited Mark Radcliffe and another second lieutenant by the name of Brown at the entrance of Fort Harrison. Standing in the dust, these recent OCS graduates were reporting for duty. But as he stared through the fence at the base, Radcliffe wondered what he had done by volunteering for this mysterious unit.

Brown knew. The night before, soon after the two officers had stepped off a plane at Helena, Brown had gone to the base to inspect it. The shock drove him into the nearest saloon. He returned drunk to the hotel room he had booked with Radcliffe. "Wait till you see what we're getting into," he shouted. "We'll be living in tents on skids."

Admittedly, Fort Harrison's prairie-like sparseness and decaying buildings that lay in the yellow grass like carcasses were not what Radcliffe had imagined. Still, he was no stranger to sun, dust, or isolation. Raised in New Mexico in and around a Navajo reservation where his engineer father was employed, Radcliffe thrived by learning the unique skills of the badlands. He profited by catching and milking the fangs of rattlers and selling the venom to serum makers. Outside of school he picked up enough Navajo to be able to appreciate that vast culture. Given where he had sprung from, he saw nothing austere about Fort Harrison.

It was primitive and dusty, to be sure, but it was surrounded by gorgeous land. In fact, Radcliffe was already feeling at home in Montana. The moment he had stepped down from the plane the day before, he looked around him at the ridges in the distance and the yellow hills and told himself, "This place is for me."

Radcliffe reported to the guard post and passed through the gate. He was not alone. Out of a batch of ninety newly commissioned second lieutenants whom Wickham had tapped at Benning and Belvoir, eighteen men showed up with Radcliffe that morning. They first presented their orders to Major Wickham and then reported to Major Shinberger, who made an impression. Shinberger's eccentricities were visible to all the new arrivals. In a book written by Force veteran Adna Underhill, a native of Albany, New York, Shinberger greeted new charges from a bench in the shade of his tent while he gripped a riding crop and barked "yard training instructions to two, half grown, black Labrador puppies."

Many officers would get similar tastes of Shinberger's eccentricities—the crop, the jump boots, the general balls-to-the-wall intensity—before being sent off to Supply for uniforms and assigned quarters, which for lucky ones like Radcliffe consisted of a tent. For others it was open ground.

———

The next morning, Frederick and the Force's brass strolled out to meet the first wave of officers, who fell out for inspection. The young men sized up their commanders. Most recognized Major Wickham, who had recruited them. Shinberger's refrigerator-shaped physique and affectations stood out in contrast to the man who stepped forward and identified himself as Force commander Colonel Frederick. With the morning sun burning on the horizon, Frederick briskly but sincerely welcomed the men.

Radcliffe eyed his new commander and wasn't sure what to think, other than the observation everyone made—that he looked young for his rank. The reception was brief, and perfunctory given what it represented. From that moment on, the First Special Service Force ceased to be a paper concept. It now consisted of the blood and bones of some of the best young officers in the U.S. Army.

Fittingly, their first training operation was a night assault. The recruits were divided into two groups. Radcliffe was given command of one; Dan Gallagher, an earnest city boy from Chicago, was assigned the other. Armed with canteens of water, belts, and blankets, the two teams were pointed toward a hill behind the fort called Pine Mountain. Two gullies ran up the hill's face like vertical riverbeds on the north and south sides. With Radcliffe ordered to attack from the south and Gallagher the north, the mission was a competition to see which young officer could get his men on top first.

That evening the men slipped into the dark and raced across the plain toward the oversized knoll. They didn't need to run the whole way, but they did. Mercifully, the night had cooled, making the trek easier, and the officers couldn't rein in their ambition. By dawn Radcliffe, Gallagher, and the others stood at the top gulping warm mouthfuls of morning air. From Fort Harrison, Shinberger would have seen them as khaki-tinted ants swarming over a dry mound of dung. Pine Mountain was the Force's first mission, and in some ways it never ended. "Sixty-two years later we're still arguing who was first," recalled one of the men. "I still say we beat them."

The Pine Mountain assault was a gentle entry into a rigorous, and astonishingly accelerated, training program. The men had no way of knowing it, but the pace was based on this premise: there is no time. Airborne training was the first important hurdle, and it was the best example of how the program was sped up. The Fort Benning jump school took up to six weeks to prepare candidates for their first leap, a fastidious program that included instruction on how to pack your own chute. At Fort Harrison, Mark Radcliffe and the others had their chutes packed for them to save them the time of learning. To prepare them physically for their first jump, the instructors whipped the men into shape by calisthenics, double-time marches, five-kilometer runs up and down another knoll behind Fort Harrison (the soldiers dubbed it Muscle Mountain), and repeated trips through an elaborate obstacle course that Frederick had designed. After a few days of toughening up, jump instructor, Captain Wilson, held an orientation meeting. "You men will be making your first jump in less than a week," he said.

They hurried through the finer points of jumping. Step from the door; you don't dive, since diving will cause a man to get fouled up in his shroud lines. Don't wait at the door, since even a second's delay going out of the plane creates a huge distance between the jumpers on the ground. When you land, keep your feet apart—an instruction that would later be changed to "keep your feet together" after an epidemic of broken legs and a frame-by-frame viewing of film footage of injurious jumps that showed men with their feet apart touching down on one leg a fraction of a second before the other.

Next, Radcliffe and the others leaped from a mock-up of a C-47 fuselage suspended about a meter and a half off the ground, and learned the proper method of hooking up their equipment and leaving the door of the airplane. And then, to educate and orientate them on how to land, the men were placed in harnesses and hoisted as high as 4.6 meters in the air before being dropped. (A 4.6-meter free fall offered roughly the same impact as hitting the earth with a parachute.)

Only hours later, they found themselves in the belly of a transport ascending for their first real-world jump. This early in the training program, the men wore little in the way of specialized equipment (their jump boots hadn't arrived yet), apart from their chutes: a main, and a spare. They tried to remember to shove their soft caps into their jackets so they wouldn't be lost in Montana's big sky. Before going up, the men had discussed what they would shout on the way out the door. Would they scream "Geronimo"? It was the call of America's other jump schools, adopted, according to one rumor, by the Eighty-second Airborne after watching a cowboy-and-Indian movie at a local theater. Eventually, the Force men chose "Powder River," a stream in eastern Montana. The name was perfect: it provided a prolonged four-syllable curse; it originated from a local Indian dialect; it was theirs.

As wind and engine noise spilled into the cabin through the open door, the jumpmaster shouted: "Stand up, hook up!" Radcliffe and the others stood and attached the static line of their chutes to the cable that ran like a clothesline down the fuselage. On the order, Radcliffe checked the line of the man behind him, in this case his new friend, Tommy Pearce, who in turn checked his. The last order, "Stand to door," sounded out, and then Radcliffe, standing at the front of the line, which was called the "stick," waited for a pat on the shoulder from the jumpmaster. The shove came, and as Radcliffe moved out the door he was hit by an unexpected blast of back-stream air whipped up by the monstrous props that chewed the sky off to the side, and by the force of the plane, which the pilot was trying to keep under 160 kilometers an hour. Stepping into 1,200 meters of oblivion,* Radcliffe let out a guttural cry, slipped down five meters in the first second of his fall, and plunged to the end of his static line,

---

* Radcliffe remembers the altitude of that first jump being as low as 460 meters (1,500 feet). But records and testimony seem to suggest that most first jumps were between 900 and 1200 meters, high enough for soldiers to deploy their backup chute if necessary. Many Force men did leap at 460 meters on subsequent jumps; combat jumps were as low as 180 meters, or 600 feet.

which yanked his chute from its bag. Radcliffe was airborne, and an instant after he disappeared from the door Pearce reflected on his shout and thought: "That wasn't Powder River."

Radcliffe's chute deployed above him like a giant sail. Below him, the Montana plain spread like a yellow blanket covered with patches and holes. Thankful that his chute had opened, Radcliffe enjoyed the ride. Quickly the ground rose up, and by manipulating the risers Radcliffe was able to steer clear of a fence that seemed intent on catching him. Finally, the upward-rushing earth slammed into the soles of his feet and sent him tumbling into nothing more harmful than grass.

Around him, men floated to earth. Tommy Pearce landed moments after Radcliffe, and within minutes the drop zone was littered with relieved men holding silk in their arms like laundry, each wearing an expression of exhilaration and relief. The hatch of the C-47 had been a threshold that almost everyone had wondered whether he could cross. In jump school, men did freeze at doors, and often it was the unlikely ones, brawny and tough-mouthed kids, who iced over. When they froze, they did so literally, and often had to be pulled out of the way by the jump-master and deposited at the back of the cabin. Sometimes they tumbled onto the floor mannequin-like, locked in the posture in which they had been standing. If anyone had frozen on this jump, Radcliffe and Pearce, numbers one and two in the stick, would never know. These men would remain in the C-47, land, and then disappear. At some point their comrades would notice an empty bunk and realize the missing man had fallen short and been sent packing.

The first moment he had a chance, Tommy Pearce asked Radcliffe the question that had followed him to the ground. "What the hell did you yell when you jumped?"

Recalling the fearsome blast of wind, Radcliffe answered: "Judas Priest."

Every day, volunteers with orders, often recorded in a top-secret code Major Wickham couldn't decipher, appeared in the dust of the front gate and swung in. The full complement of ninety second lieutenants eventually arrived. Enlisted men, EMs, came from across the U.S., each lured to Fort Harrison for different reasons. As Frederick had hoped, frontiersmen—miners, rangers, trappers, and farm boys—were answering the call. Others also stepped forward: high-strung city kids, and a few malcontents who didn't fit in anywhere else in the army. Base commanders took advantage of Frederick's invitation by emptying their stockades of troublemakers and dispatching them to Helena, sometimes under armed guard.

But the most notable arrivals were the foreigners.

———

On August 6, a train from Canada filled with thirty-five officers and 450 enlisted men, most but not all of Ottawa's total complement, hissed to a stop along the fort's rail siding. The train had originated from a "concentration center" in Ottawa where final selections had been made for the Canadian contingent, officially known as the Second Canadian Parachute Battalion. The journey had been a long one for the soldiers and officers on board, and they knew what they were crossing into when the train reached the Alberta–Montana border. They were joining the U.S. Army, which meant they were not only leaving Canada behind, they were giving up the familiar values, trappings, and traditions of their Canadian regiments, no small thing, particularly for the professional soldiers. Shortly before arriving, the officers had eaten a valedictory dinner and toasted the monarch for the last time with port donated by the Canadian Pacific Railway, singing "God Save the King."

Word spread on base when the train carrying the Canadians was pulling up, and Radcliffe and a few others sauntered out to the siding to take a look. For some of the men, the show was like the circus coming to town. The new arrivals hailed from strange-sounding outfits: the Eighth Princess Louise's Hussars, the Algonquin Regiment, the Black Watch of Canada, the British Columbia Dragoons, Lord Strathcona's Horse, Les Fusiliers Mont-Royal, and Le Régiment Maisonneuve. And the men themselves were dressed just as strangely. Some were clad in summer-issue short pants and sleeves, others were in leggings or puttees that looked to the Americans like WWI issue. On their heads they wore broad overseas caps that rode so precariously close to the ear they seemed to defy gravity. The strangest of the lot were the Ladies from Hell, the First World War sobriquet for the fighting Scots, some of whom wore "plaid trousers, better known as *trews*, only to be followed by others in kilts, complete with *sporrans* to the front and *dirks* in the knee-length woollen stockings," wrote force veteran Bill Story. "These drew extra stares and comments . . ."

Radcliffe watched as the new arrivals fell in and listened to Colonel Frederick's simple welcome. The Canadian second-in-command, Lieutenant Colonel McQueen, was also on hand, having arrived by plane the night before to greet his countrymen. Then one of the skirted men produced a strange bladder, and the wail of a bagpipe sounded as the soldiers marched to base. Radcliffe decided immediately that he liked the martial scream of the bagpipe. It was a sound that pierced the core of a soldier, and electrified him.

None of the Americans were sure what to make of the Canadian salute. The American salute, in which the bladed hand is raised crisply to the soldier's brow, seemed utterly lax beside the Canadian version, in which the hand, held palm out like a paddle, was raised in a lightning-swift arc from the hips to the side of the head. The salute ended with fingertips positioned only millimeters from the soldier's temple, at the apex of a hand

and upper arm that often vibrated like a tuning fork, and ended with the exclamation point of a loud stamp of the foot. This was not a salute that acknowledged respect and high rank; this was a salute a soldier would die for.

In fine British tradition, many of the Canadian soldiers wore immaculately groomed moustaches—some as thin as pencil lines, others heavy and magnificent. As the column passed by him, Radcliffe noted the long arm swings, the fast pace, and the crisp precision of the drill. Radcliffe and the others would later learn that the impressive Canadian parade drill had a very practical design. In order to instill in its infantry an unhesitating understanding of how to attack a position in combat (first by establishing a line of fire and then using this fire as cover to attack the enemy flank), the Canadian drill featured an elaborate series of quick turns and flanking movements that ceremoniously imitated such an assault. As the last of the Canadians marched by, Radcliffe concluded his first long glance at the exotically named, colorfully kitted, and disciplined foreigners who had just arrived in his outfit, and could not help being impressed.

But Colonel Frederick wasn't. The Canadians may have looked sharp, but they were still foreign, and Frederick needed utter unity of purpose, spirit, and action to make his outfit work. Years later he recalled the Canadians as they filed in from the train and admitted that he "watched with some apprehension . . ."

On August 11, the last 149 Canadians arrived at the rail siding, and among them was Lorin Waling, the young private who had dreamed of combat from the interior of a stockade. After reporting in, he was assigned a spot in 1st Company–2nd Regiment (1-2), commanded by Captain Bill Rothlin, a soft-spoken Californian. Waling would eventually find himself in 3rd Platoon, but in those early days the soldiers of 1-2 mixed and trained together. Waling's barracks was a tent that he shared with three others, and the parade field was the plain around the fort that now included an airstrip and a drop zone as well as firing ranges.

Waling began training the moment he arrived, and it was a challenge. After rising at 5:15 a.m., he had cleaned his quarters and breakfasted by the time real work started at half past six: marches of fifty-five kilometers and more, relentless circuits of obstacle courses, and those seventy push-ups that marked the end of every long day. Waling didn't mind; he was too busy. Training sessions were held all day, and the men marched double time from one to another. Like everyone, before Waling knew it, he found himself in the windy cabin of a C-47 with a parachute strapped to his back. Unlike Radcliffe's first jump, Waling wore a football helmet on his head and impressive leather jump boots on his feet. When it was his turn at the door, Waling leaped without hesitation. And he landed comparatively softly. (The same wasn't true for Waling's Canadian CO, Lieutenant Colonel McQueen, who broke his leg on his jump, thus ending his career as Frederick's second-in-command. McQueen was replaced by Lieutenant Colonel Paul Adams, a West Point classmate; Lieutenant Colonel Don Williamson, 2nd Regiment's commander, became the highest-ranking Canadian in the Force.)

Although Waling soldiered like an adult, everyone still recognized that he was underage, with his gangly teenager's physique and youthful complexion. There were other overgrown boys in his platoon as well, like Don MacKinnon, who was seventeen years old. However, 1st Company–2nd Regiment also had men on the other side of the generation gap. Howard Van Ausdale was born on May 16, 1905, to a father of Dutch ancestry and a mother who was a member of either the Apache or Yavapai Indian nation. After growing up in and around Mayer, Arizona, Van Ausdale lived as a prospector and sometime trapper in Oregon and Washington, and then for reasons no one knows he enlisted in the army at the outbreak of war, and became at thirty-seven years one of the oldest members of the FSSF.

Slight, wiry, and fit, Van Ausdale had the dark skin and high cheekbones of a native Indian and the slender face of a European. Despite his solitary past in the wilderness, Van, as he was called, mixed easily with his fellow soldiers, and early on he took an interest in Waling, whom he called Kid. During training he mentored him about the things he knew best. Van Ausdale's finely honed skills as a tracker easily transferred to man-hunting war games, where one group in the company was given the mission of overtaking another's position. On Sundays, Van Ausdale would lead Waling into the hills and hunt snakes for Major Shinberger, who had offered a reward for every bagged rattler. Van Ausdale made soldiering fun. But Waling, after his first weekend on leave, realized there was better fun to be had.

Force men got leave on weekend nights, and Sundays off. Waling noticed that some of the soldiers in 1-2 stayed in the barracks during off-hours. But most of the men spent Saturday nights in Helena, which offered innumerable places to drink, dance, and meet people. The epicenter of a weekend night was Last Chance Gulch, Helena's main street, named after the camp of down-on-their-luck gold miners who bivouacked in the area in 1864 and eventually found the pay dirt that gave birth to the town. Seventy-eight years later Last Chance Gulch still retained the hard, boom-and-bust temperament of the miners in saloons like the Gold Bar. Helena boasted other taverns—the Cabin, and the Cheerio Bar in the Placer Hotel—but the Gold Bar became the favorite watering hole of the Force men, where they mixed, and sometimes clashed, with local cowboys, mill workers, and miners. Fights erupted. Energetic and high-strung, many of the Force men were natural-born brawlers, and their training made them more inclined to respond to any insult, real or imagined.

In the early days, before the standard uniform was issued, Force lore has it that some of the burly locals once taunted Canadians wearing the shorts and kilts of their home regiments. It is not difficult to imagine: bearish Ontario loggers and tough, wiry B.C. miners are nursing beers in the Gold Bar when local cowboys take umbrage at the exposed hairy knees of the Canadians. The cowboys hurl insults and invective, trying to provoke a fight, and the Canucks long to oblige them. But the Canadians have been warned by their officers that as representatives of their country, they will be held to the highest standards of conduct, and that any troublemakers will be sent home. So they stare into their drinks, clench their fists, and bite their tongues. But their American comrades know what is holding the Canucks back. Finally, the American Force men can take no more. Sure, the damn fool Canadians are dressed like old women, but only *we* can call them old women. Then one of the American boys falls on a yokel, and as fast as it takes for a beer glass to break over someone's skull the Canadians join in and a fine old-fashioned brawl breaks out.

Some Force men claim this barroom dust-up was the first time Canadians and Americans fought together, and that as a result it did much to erase the distinction between the two nationalities within the unit. That may be true. But there were numerous weekend fights in the Gold Bar, and they could be easily counted by the number of times the establishment's long plate-glass windows were smashed by an airborne chair or body. News of the broken windows reached Wickham. The first time, he braced himself for an angry demand for compensation. It never came. Nor did it come the next time. The third time a window was shattered, Wickham contacted the bar's manager and offered to pay up if his men were responsible. "Forget it," said Bob Kelly, the proprietor. "I sell whiskey, and that sort of thing is a natural result."

Montana wasn't necessarily a supporter of the federal government, the army, or the war. Like elsewhere in the American West,
Montana tended toward isolationism, and some resented the
incursions of Washington into their lives more than they resented
Tokyo or Berlin. A day after Pearl Harbor, when the U.S. Congress
declared war on Japan, Jeannette Rankin of Montana was the only
representative to vote against the decision. (Rankin was no flip-
flopper; she had also voted against America's entry into the First
World War twenty-four years earlier.) But the West was also a
place of grand hospitality, and Helena, as a frontier town, had
a soft spot for brave young men. The townsfolk took a special
interest in the soldiers since their own sons with the 163rd
Infantry were already overseas. People opened their doors to the
Force men, and adopted them. "Everyone had a family there," said
Bill Story of 2nd Regiment. Story found his in the local Methodist
church on Sunday. After one service the preacher, Reverend
George Morrell, invited him home, and Sarah Morrell, the minister's wife of thirty-four years, fed young Bill a plate of delicious
apple pie with ice cream. Before long Story was spending nights
in the room of their son Douglas, who was away at war.

There were other places for soldiers to spend the night, including Ida's Rooms, the more popular of Helena's two brothels.
Ida, the establishment's owner, did not have the girth, feathered
robes, or a long cigarette holder of a great-breasted Hollywood
madam. She would be remembered as rather ordinary-looking.
This canny woman offered Force men comfort at a price. But
even for her and her girls, the exchange wasn't all about money.
At least one marriage resulted from the men's visits, and Ida
would later write to some of the boys after they had gone to war.

If a madam's heart could be warmed by the boys, so could a
banker's. Alfred T. Hibbard, the president of the Union Bank
and Trust Company, floated loans to cash-strapped young Force
men, particularly the American boys, who were paid only once a

month and had a tendency to blow their salaries long before the next payday. John Morrison, an engineer, skiing enthusiast, and rancher, responded immediately to Frederick's request for space to train his men to ski and climb mountains. Morrison offered up any parcel of land he owned that could be of use. When jump training raged, Helenans would drive as close as they could to the drop zone, congregate on the road, and watch the sky explode with silk as soldiers glided to the earth.

Not everyone liked the Force, however. Absent Helena men with the 163rd liked it the least. They had journeyed as far as Australia during the war only to learn that their home was being set upon—as one veteran later put it—by "this bunch of ivory-peckered bastards." The taunts the strangely uniformed Canadians sometimes received in barrooms were more than compensated for by Helena's daughters, who found the Canadians' foreign dress and ways exotic, and infinitely attractive. To be a presentable-looking Canadian Force man in Helena that summer was tantamount to having a member made of gold, not ivory. "A Yank's only hope for a date," one American boy pointed out, "was if there should be more girls than Canadians."

Within the ranks of 1-2, Lorin drilled, perspired, and caroused with a lot of good men. H. G. "Herby" Forester was a hot-tempered rooster of a man from Edmonton who battled to make the grade despite his tree-stump-sized physique. On double-time marches Herby had to pound his stubby legs at twice the speed of everyone else just to keep up. James W. "Jimmy" Flack, from Renton, Washington, was barely any taller, but he elevated himself by being one of the few soldiers who had been in the army before the war. He wore those years like a badge. "I been in more pay lines than you been in chow lines," he said constantly. Walter Lewis was a native son of Montana, from Butte. At thirty years, he was one of the oldest in the platoon, apart from Van Ausdale, and the men called him Pop. "Frenchie" Daigle from Montreal spoke English with an accent and sometimes segued into French. Percy Crichlow was the oddity in the platoon. A volunteer from Canada who hailed originally from Barbados, Crichlow was a soft-spoken intellectual, thoughtful, reserved, and sophisticated. Among the men rumor had it that he was a Rhodes Scholar. As far as Lorin Waling was concerned, Crichlow even dressed differently from the others on the rare occasions he was seen in civilian clothes. There were a lot of good kids: Walter Wolf from New Jersey, Sam Eros from Saskatchewan, Dennis George from the Kootenays in B.C., and Don Fisher from Marysville, Washington.

Lorin generally liked the sergeants. Staff Sergeant Kotenko was another prairie boy from Winnipeg who tried to act tough but was actually soft-hearted when it came down to it. A logger from Oregon, Sergeant McGinty was tough as raw timber, and didn't need to act it. Edwards from Colorado was another sergeant. He was quiet, and more deadly at cards than any of the weapons he was learning to fire. While most of the men lost their pay at the poker table, Edwards was often the one who pocketed it.

First Company–2nd Regiment was also filled with characters. Tommy Fenton was another prospector and tracker, and a kindred spirit of the half-Apache Van Ausdale. Although a generation younger than Van Ausdale, Fenton had spent years before the war combing the mountains and streams of British Columbia for nuggets. Everyone called Chester Kroll a gangster for no other reason than that he was from Chicago. Joe Dauphinais, a prairie boy from Starbuck, Manitoba, always seemed to be smiling, even at reveille or the aching end of a fifty-five-kilometer march. Johnny Walter, a son of Montana, was a bona fide cowboy from Ekala.

But in the early days, as Lorin got to know his fellow Force men and explored Helena's nightspots on leave, he met one soldier who would change his life. The meeting took place on a weekend night in the Casino Bar in East Helena, a little smelter town thirteen kilometers away, where Waling had enacted a soldierly tradition: falling for a local girl. He had just arrived at the Casino when he noticed a cute young woman sitting to the side. She was accompanied by a curly-haired girlfriend who was with a slender, dark-haired Force man he recognized from his company but didn't really know. Waling sent his date away with his sergeant, and sat down beside the girl. Her name was Steffie Broderick. She was eighteen years old. The other girl was her best friend, Dorothy Strainer. And the corporal with them, Joe, was a recent addition to their lives. Dorothy had met Joe there in the Casino Bar days before.

This was Lorin Waling's first meeting with Joe Glass. Immediately, they became fast friends. Whether it was simple chemistry or the bond of their new girlfriends Dorothy and Steffie, who in turn were best friends, the two soldiers became inseparable. Since they were both in 3rd Platoon, they were able to arrange it so that they shared the same tent. The men were true opposites. Where Lorin had grown from the wild grass of the Alberta prairie, Joe had grown up by and on the waters of Lake Ontario. Born in Sarnia, Ontario, Glass hailed from a long line of Great Lakes shipmasters. His forefathers originally sailed schooners on the lakes; one of Glass's earliest memories was of standing on the deck of his grandfather's steamship. When Glass was sixteen years old he left home, went to Toronto, and signed up to crew on the ore freighter *Gleneagles*. True to his heritage, Glass thrived as a mariner. Before long he became a junior officer. Serving as a watchman, Joe began by running the crews that painted and cleaned the great ship. But before long he learned the entire craft's operations. "I really felt this would be my life's work," he later wrote in a brief memoir.

After color-blindness foiled his attempts to join the Royal

Canadian Navy in 1939, Joe Glass jumped ship from the USS *Noronic* to join the army a year later. He was attached to the Kent Regiment and, like Waling, ached to see combat. But two years later he found himself instructing bayonet drills at Lansdowne Park in Ottawa. He feared he might spend the war there, until he spotted the fateful notice on the base.

Waling and Glass were different in many ways, but they seemed to complement each other. Waling was a forehead taller and perhaps a half-inch thinner than Glass. Joe's facial features were sharper and squarer. The one thing they shared was a love of training. They were at an indefatigable age, and they enjoyed the competition of a long march or grueling run.

They particularly liked weapons training. Joe preferred the M1 rifle, the gun George S. Patton called the "greatest battle implement ever devised." It was heavier than the Lee-Enfield Glass had shouldered in the Kents, but the M1 was powerful, capable of punching a target accurately at four hundred meters. And the M1 was semiautomatic (the Lee-Enfield was bolt action). When Glass—the former bayonet instructor—mounted a dagger on its barrel, he was in heaven.

The men also trained with .45 handguns and grenades. Live grenade training provided some exciting moments. It was not an easy thing to pull the pin, arm the grenade, and toss it. It was harder yet to hold it a moment before tossing so that it would explode roughly as it landed.

Demolition training created even bigger explosions. With an eye to blowing up electrical power plants in Norway, Frederick had acquired Ryan's Special (RS), a state-of-the-art explosive with twice the power of TNT, and brought two experts from Fort Belvoir's Corps of Engineers to instruct on its use. To make the training more meaningful, Wickham and Frederick found targets in the community that needed to be demolished. The result was a level of destruction that trivialized any damage done at the

Gold Bar. A mining company allowed the Force men to blow up an abandoned shaft since its aged equipment in the vicinity could only be sold for scrap metal. But the men stuffed so much explosive into the hole that the equipment was pulverized beyond the definition of "scrap." Ken Wickham, the officer responsible for this damage, would later lament: "They also blew up buildings at the mines and started a rather bad forest fire."

It got worse. "On one occasion they blew up the wrong mine, [and] another man's summer home." And when they targeted an "abandoned bridge" for demolition, they used so much explosive that the blast managed to slant chimneys in a nearby town. As Colonel Frederick would say years later with profound under-statement: "In several instances [the men's] enthusiasm carried them away."

The Force men would have other lethal toys to play with. Frederick had resolved to arm his unit with the very latest in weaponry, and the flame-thrower and a cumbersome two-man rocket launcher nicknamed the "bazooka" joined the arsenal. Frederick also armed his men with mortars, the Thompson M1 machine gun, or "Tommy gun," and the Browning automatic rifle, or BAR. Everyone was pleased when the Force's supply chief gave the Marine Corps a cache of its precious RS explosives in exchange for Johnson light machine guns (LMGs) or "Johnny guns." Each platoon would have two BARS, two Johnson LMGs, a bazooka, and a 60 mm mortar.

Frederick's staff even considered arming the men with blow darts until it was determined that such a weapon might consti-tute a war crime. Carrying a knife wasn't against any international law, however, and Frederick himself drew a blue-print for the unit's dagger, officially designated Commando Knife No. V-42. Pat O'Neill, the former Shanghai cop and hand-to-hand-combat instructor, also made sure that Force men could kill without any weapons at all. O'Neill was an expert in a martial art called Defendu, which had been developed within the Shanghai Municipal Police to combat everything from mafia thugs to Communists. (The long list of criminals O'Neill hunted down in his police career included a firebrand named Mao Zedong.)

When men like Waling and Glass arrived at O'Neill's first class, they faced a banal-looking, heavyset man with an Irish accent. O'Neill really only got their attention after asking the biggest and huskiest in the group to attack him with a bayonet. The soldier did so, with a natural reluctance to skewer an instructor. O'Neill responded with a hair-raising scream: "I said, 'Attack me, hard!'" Eventually the burly commando-in-training lunged at the Irishman, and was promptly sent sprawling—"the guy flying one way, the knife the other," as one witness put it.

Lorin Waling called O'Neill a "miraculous" man. But in fact, there were no miracles in O'Neill's repertoire. He taught simple moves from a variety of disciplines, choosing moves that could be learned rapidly and employed without thinking. He focused on the essential point of combat. "I'm not here to teach you to hurt, I'm here to teach you to kill," he would say. He taught them to focus an attack on the eyes, throat, groin, and knees. He taught them to kill with a knife and with their bare hands. He taught them how to quick-draw a .45. He had the men attack each other with sheathed bayonets, and later with real blades. Blood was spilled, and for O'Neill that was the best lesson of all.

Major Shinberger provided lessons as well, many as eccentric as he was. Eventually, Mark Radcliffe was promoted to Force headquarters to work directly beneath Shinberger in operations and training. The job was difficult due to Shinberger's odd nature. He always had some strange obsession: taking the men to an abattoir to accustom them to scenes of bloodletting and slaughter, or dragging Radcliffe out on the prairie to shoot tin cans from a fence post with his .45. Once, Shinberger got it into his head that Force men should be able to wander naked onto the plain and survive indefinitely. For Shinberger this meant eating rattlesnakes, and for days and weeks he pestered Radcliffe to go rattler hunting with him. One day some base engineers told Radcliffe about a huge den of snakes in a dump under Pine Mountain. He went there with his snake pole, found the den, roped a bagful, and presented the cache to Shinberger, thinking this would quiet him. Shinberger was crestfallen: "I wanted to be there when you got them."

Radcliffe kept Shinberger's snakes in a box near the latrine, which nearly caused an involuntary evacuation when one officer poked his head in to see what was inside. Ultimately, as was his plan all along, Shinberger took his rattlers to the mess and presented them to the kitchen. One cook was ethnic Japanese and knew how to prepare exotic meat. Later a few officers came in for chow, dished up, and dug in. Shinberger looked on until the meal was half consumed, stood up, and launched into his lecture. "A soldier must be able to live off the land," he said, "survive on whatever is at hand. Like rattlesnake, which—gentlemen—is what you are eating."

So it went. Within weeks, Waling, Glass, Radcliffe, and their fellow Force men were being transformed into some of the most extraordinary soldiers in the U.S. Army. They had acquired a range of specialized skills that was virtually unprecedented. For the men who survived the cut, their accomplishments were rewarded on August 29 when Frederick called a parade. Wearing crisp shorts and standing under an oppressive Montana sun, Frederick pinned jump wings on 1,125 qualified parachutists. Despite the heat, the colonel made sure he personally decorated the chest of every man.

Lorin Waling and Joe Glass were among the successful Force men who had become airborne certified. Off base, while some of the men were carousing like true paratroopers, Lorin's relationship with Steffie was growing more serious, which only fueled his friendship with Joe and bonded the couples as a foursome. They were inseparable. Joe and Lorin saw the girls every weekend and, in time, most nights. Captain Rothlin, 1st Company's commander, had already identified the close friendship between Glass and Waling as a problem and had moved them out of the same tent. Smelling trouble, he would often stick his head in Glass's tent after lights out and say: "You still here, Glass?"

"Yes, sir."

"Good night, Glass."

Moments later, Joe would be out. He would rendezvous with Lorin and head out behind the base near the airstrip, where the two girls waited in Steffie's sister's car. They got there by leaving the road and driving through the grass with the lights out.

The plan worked because the base guards were more concerned about the front gates than the endless range behind the fort. But one night the sentries did spot the car and ventured out to take a look. When Dorothy and Steffie saw them coming, they lay down on the floorboards and drew a blanket over themselves. The guards shone a flashlight, kicked a tire, and left, probably thinking the car belonged to a local rancher.

Once free of the base, the four of them would head for East Helena, which had no MPs to keep an eye on the soldiers, and on to the Casino Bar or Tivoli Tavern. They usually danced, to whatever was playing. Sometimes it was Hank Williams. More often than not it was Glenn Miller or Tommy Dorsey, who had recently performed in Helena. Joe and Dorothy had a song they already considered *their* song. It was "For Me and My Gal."

When they drank, the boys had a Coke Highball (whiskey and Coke) or a Whiskey Ditch (whiskey and water). But they danced more than they drank. The girls insisted on it, not because they hated drinking; they just loved to dance. This went on—the dancing, the highballs, and the singing—until about

1 a.m., when small-town decorum demanded that the girls go home. Dorothy and Steffie worked, after all. And the boys needed to get back before reveille. Usually Joe and Lorin spent an hour or so sleeping in cells in the East Helena lock-up, where the night constable always had room for them. Because they knew where the keys were, they could let themselves in if the jailer was out.

The boys usually slept until about 4 a.m. and then took a taxi to the dairy. The local milkman drove a shipment to Fort Harrison every morning, and Joe and Lorin would help load the truck and then ride in back with the rattling bottles. On the way, they always cracked open a bottle and consumed as much milk as they could to ease their stomachs. The milk truck was invariably waved through at the gate.

But one morning a guard told the milkman to open up the truck. Joe and Lorin sat there thinking: "It's over. They're going to catch us." But the milkman turned mean, and shouted at the guard: "If you open the doors of this truck, I'll turn around and take this milk back to town."

The guard waved the truck through, and Joe and Lorin, as always, helped unload before making their way to their tents.

———

One Friday morning Mark Radcliffe reported to his desk in Force headquarters and his boss, Major Shinberger, threw him a quizzical look. Radcliffe seriously wondered if his days on Shinberger's staff, and in the Force, were numbered.

Radcliffe had tired of Shinberger's antics, and resented being dragged off to shoot tin cans or catch snakes. He had better things to do. Like so many other Force men, Radcliffe had met a local girl. He had been at a dance at the local armory. Tommy Pearce, the same man who had been behind him on his first jump, was with him. Pearce gestured at the single girls sitting off to the side and said: "Go ask one of those gals to dance." Pearce, already married, didn't want to meet new girls.

Radcliffe wasn't so sure. "They don't want to dance with me, a poor second lieutenant." He was at that innocent soldierly chapter of his life when he measured everything by army values. Why would a young woman be interested in dancing with him when she could have a first lieutenant or a captain?

"Go ahead, what's it gonna hurt?"

Radcliffe plunged, and for a young man the act of walking across a dance floor to speak to a woman is often as terrifying as a 1,200-meter jump. The whole way he imagines that every eye in the house is on him, and that the girl will turn him down.

But Edith said yes. And Radcliffe started seeing her. Every Saturday, when Shinberger wanted to catch a snake, Radcliffe thought of Edith in Helena and how she was waiting.

So on that Friday morning Radcliffe felt a sense of dread when Shinberger gave him that all-too-familiar look.

"You're being kind of secretive, aren't you?" Shinberger said.

Radcliffe asked what he meant.

"I hear you got married last night."

Shinberger had heard right. Tommy Pearce had stood up for him as best man. A Force man named Chet Ross lent the newly-weds his car. The problem was, there was a regulation that forbade Force men to marry.

Radcliffe expected to be fired. But Shinberger only said: "Why the hell didn't you let me know? I could have gotten you some time off."

For a few days Force men waited on tenterhooks to see if Radcliffe would be expelled. When he wasn't, one after another married local girls. To some this change in policy was strange, given Frederick's determination that all his orders be followed to the letter. But with December 15 approaching, Frederick may have asked himself: Why deny his men a few last months of happiness?

———

Before the soldiers at Fort Harrison bonded with the community, Colonel Frederick had worried that the outfit's two armies might never unify and truly work as one. He had been apprehensive about the Canadian army's alien drill and culture. In the beginning, seemingly innocuous traits like the long arm swing of the Canadian drill represented a fundamental difference between the two armies. There were a host of others. It took the Americans some time to figure out what the Canadians meant when they referred to an officer as "lef-tenant." The marching orders Canadian officers gave their soldiers differed from American commands. Bill Story, a young sergeant from Winnipeg, later wrote: "Canadians were accustomed to hearing: 'Company will move to the right in column of threes by platoon. Right turn! By the left, quick march!' Americans would mutter: 'What-in-hell does he mean "by the left"?' In drill, Canadians did 'About-turns'; Americans did 'About-faces.'" According to Story, "Most Americans couldn't master the about-turn. Many Canadians didn't master the about-face. So everyone did what came naturally." Neither Canadians nor Americans could make sense of a former U.S. cavalry officer who tried to stop a drill by calling out, "Hoo."

In the beginning, the two nations couldn't even agree on how to kill the enemy, either. The Canadians were partial to the Bren light machine gun, and universally hated the U.S. army issue BAR, which they believed fired slowly, and was hampered by its long, awkward barrel. The Americans thought the Canadians' constant harping on the virtues of the Bren to be almost irrational.

The inconsistencies between the Canadians and Americans were precisely what Frederick had dreaded when he learned that his force would be the amalgam of two armies.

At first he tried to diminish these differences by thoroughly mixing the two groups throughout the three regiments of the Force. He even tried to unify them with a song. Frederick wrote Irving Berlin and asked the composer to pen a special piece for the FSSF emphasizing "the reckless, fearless spirit of the men." An exasperated Berlin, who had received many similar requests, demurred: "I have done so many of these special songs in the past that it's just impossible to do any more." Hugh McVeigh of 5-2 wrote and sang a Force song, but it probably wasn't quite what Frederick had in mind:

> Oh we are the jumpin' paratroopers
> You've heard so much about
> The mothers all hide their daughters
> Whenever we walk out
>
> So all steer clear of the paratroopers
> They're always in a jam
> For half the regiment is CB*
> And the rest don't give a damn
>
> Our parachutes are trailing
> The right chute for us has ne'er been made
> Swinging and swaying,
> The jumpin' paratroopers are on parade

Frederick got the Force a single uniform, but he was stymied when the Canadians began wearing their old regimental

* CB: Confined to Barracks.

halyards over their shoulders. Every regimental halyard was a different color, and the Americans didn't have them. To eliminate
this inconsistency, Frederick had a Force halyard made. It was
woven red, white, and blue, the colors of both the Stars and
Stripes and the Union Jack, and he forbade his men leave until
they bought one. To his delight, the girls in Helena loved the
accoutrement and the halyards sold out. And the Force's most
spectacular pieces of kit, the snow-traveling Weasels, were due
to arrive in the autumn.

In the end, the uniforms, halyards, snowmobiles, and
marches didn't seem to matter. The competing arm swings
found a happy medium, which was longer than the American
and shorter than the Canadian. The Canadian bagpipes were
largely replaced by a unit marching band, which sounded reveille
every morning and performed for parades and special ceremonies. The men bonded through training and unity of
command: two factors dictated by Frederick. As if to prove
Frederick's concerns unjustified, an esprit de corps grew that
was stronger than he could have hoped. The tough men being
selected for the Force were congenitally prone to loyalty to each
other and the outfit. As hard as they played, they trained harder,
and in a sense set their own high standards. Wickham marveled
at this himself when he noted how the men identified a weakling
in the ranks and "rejected him spiritually." Wickham later wrote:
"There were very few of these cases, but we simply had to trans-
fer those few men out. . . . . The Force was bonded together
strongly." They still had months of training ahead of them, but
they were now an army.

On the evening of August 31, Frederick appeared on radio station KPFA Helena and tried to explain to listeners what the Force
was. "Because the history of both the United States and Canada
is so rich in Indian lore," he said, "we believe that a term derived
from the Indians would be fitting in describing this Force of both

nations. The popular name by which the First Special Service Force is becoming known is the 'Braves.'"

Braves never really stuck as a name. But Frederick knew he had created a close-knit tribe of warriors capable of fulfilling its mission. Their shoulder patch was a red arrowhead with "USA" stitched across the tip, and "CANADA" along its length. The summer was drawing to a close and preparations for Plough Project were entering the endgame. On September 16, Frederick took off in a flying boat from Botwood, Newfoundland, which in 1942 was still a Dominion of Great Britain and not yet part of Canada. His destination: London, where he would make final arrangements for getting his men onto British soil, and then into the skies over Norway.

CHAPTER 5

WARRIORS WITHOUT A WAR

Shortly after 3 a.m. on September 17, 1942, a stewardess awoke Colonel Frederick as he slumbered in a berth in the great belly of the seaplane as it roared over the Atlantic. By day's end he would be in the British capital, and ready to begin a series of meetings that would finalize the Norway mission.

Frederick flew in a Sikorsky S-42-A. With a fuselage shaped like a whale and kept aloft by four great propellers, these aircraft, which took off and landed in the sea, regularly made the journey between Newfoundland, and Foynes, Ireland. Before the war, civilian travelers had taken advantage of this fast and exotic mode of transport, made the journey from coast to coast in hours instead of days. But after war was declared, Pan American's flying clippers primarily ferried officers, officials, and politicians across the Atlantic and back, including First Lady Eleanor Roosevelt, who made the trip in 1942.

Within an hour of being awakened, Frederick could see the Irish coast illuminated in weak pre-dawn light, and it struck him that the scene looked like a "toy land" from the air. In wartime, seeing the world from on high seemed to make philosophers of even the toughest pragmatists. By 4:30 a.m. the great underbelly of the flying boat was touching down, and by late evening Frederick was settled in an austere room at his London hotel. The next morning he sat before his old boss, General Dwight Eisenhower.

As commander of ETO Allied Force Headquarters, Eisenhower had come a long way since June, when Frederick had been given command of Plough Project. Ike looked the same, still possessing a wide grin and an easy manner that—as any former subordinate could attest—belied the man's fastidiousness and demanding temperament. But London had changed Eisenhower. Before, he had been an anonymous War Department bureaucrat. Now he was the foremost American in Britain, an idol of the newsreels, and the man who would ultimately oversee Allied troops into their first clashes with Germany.

Frederick briefed Eisenhower on the Force's progress and why he had come to London: he needed a temporary base in Britain and, most important, RAF transports to fly his men over Norway for the drop. The arrangements, Frederick believed, were almost a formality. While in Washington, the day before flying out, he had checked in with General Joseph McNarney, U.S. Army Deputy Chief of Staff. In McNarney's contention Plough Project was almost ready to be presented to the British War Office. The U.S. Army had completed its end of the bargain by forming, training, and equipping the Force. Once Frederick and the FSSF set foot in the British Isles, the responsibility fell to Whitehall to get the men into battle.

Eisenhower listened to Frederick's briefing with interest. Plough was an audacious strike at the Continent, and Eisenhower had been an advocate of Roundup and Sledgehammer. The decision not to fight first in Europe had depressed Eisenhower, who said with astonishing exaggeration that the day this was declared was "possibly the blackest [day] . . . in history." Here was someone who could be counted upon to support Plough.

However, at that moment Eisenhower was in the midst of planning Operation Torch, the landing of 100,000 troops on the North African coast. Frederick's arrival with an army and a plan to raid the Continent was fascinating, even heartening, but the focus of the European war had shifted, and Plough did not fit within Eisenhower's new marching orders. "Although [Eisenhower] was interested," Frederick wrote in a diary, "he did not express himself as believing the project was within his province."

The discussion with Eisenhower had not gone as expected. But Frederick anticipated a different reception at his next meeting, at 14 Richmond Terrace, Whitehall, the home of Combined Operations HQ and its chief, Lord Mountbatten. Plough had originated with Mountbatten, the Combined Ops chief who had not only given Plough its momentum, but had recommended Frederick for the job of leading it. Over the next hours Frederick looked forward to getting down to the brass tacks of "progress and planning."

But he immediately ran into a brick wall with the gentlemanly commando leader. The point of contention was aircraft. Frederick had wasted no time. He told Mountbatten that Plough Force was a reality and that the operation as originally conceived was on schedule. But to execute, he needed six hundred aircraft large enought to airdrop his men and their armory of snowmobiles. Could Mountbatten help arrange this? To Frederick's amazement, Mountbatten said no.

Any shock Frederick felt hinged on his understanding of the Plough deal: America would create the Force, the British would transport it. But Mountbatten saw things differently. "When the project was proposed to General Marshall," Mountbatten argued, "it was agreed that the project would be American entirely." Furthermore, Mountbatten said, "Marshall had given the impression that there would be ample U.S. aircraft in the British Isles for the project."

Mountbatten had a reputation for charming Americans. But he showed no inclination to compromise on his stance that it was up to the U.S. to provide the aircraft for attacking Norway.

In truth, Mountbatten was no longer the same brash military chief who had first proposed Plough in April. His fellow chiefs of staff had always viewed him as an upstart. "Mountbatten's inclusion in the COS was a snag," chief of staff General Alan Brooke confided to his diary. "There was no justification for this move." By late September, "Dickie," as Brooke called Mountbatten, was reeling from the aftermath of his latest ambitious operation, code-named Jubilee.

On 19 August, an Allied force of 5000 troops from the 2nd Canadian Division, who had been languishing in Britain and begged to see action, along with 1000 British commandos and 50 U.S. Rangers, landed at Dieppe in the newly-designed amphibious craft stockpiled for the eventual full-scale invasion of Europe. It was the first European landing since the butchery of Gallipoli. The Canadians were supported by eight destroyers and seventy-four air squadrons (including eight from the RCAF). The assault depended on surprise and the cover of darkness, and also the flanking support of Nos. 3 and 4 British Commandos, which were to take out the Germans guns.

These advantages were lost when No. 3 Commando bumped into a German convoy as it headed for the beach. The landing craft were scattered, and the exchange of fire alerted the German defenders. When the Royal Regiment of Canada hit the beach at Puys behind schedule, in the light of morning, they walked into a lethal firestorm; few of them, or of the Black Watch sent to reinforce them, returned to the boats. In the western sector No. 4

Commando was successful, and the South Saskatchewan Regiment and Queen's Own Cameron Highlanders of Canada met only light resistance. They made their way inland to their main objective, an airfield, but suffered severe casualties as they withdrew. In the main assault on the beach of Dieppe, the Essex Scottish Regiment made some progress against heavy machine-gun fire, and Les Fusiliers Mont Royal were sent to reinforce them; both forces became trapped. The Royal Hamilton Light Infantry also made it ashore and engaged in street fighting, but the tanks of the Calgary Regiment were delayed, leaving the infantry grievously exposed. Those tanks that made it ashore were quickly knocked out.

When the sun set, Mountbatten had an amphibious fiasco on his hands. Of the 5000 men who had gone ashore, 3,367 were casualties. German casualties were 600. Moreover, the RAF had lost 106 planes, including 13 of the RCAF; the Luftwaffe suffered less than half that number. For those chiefs of staff who had argued long and hard against an invasion of France, Jubilee, as one historian would later put it, once and for all was "to demonstrate how difficult was a landing on a fortified coast." For Canadians, Dieppe would become a potent symbol of the tenacity and bravery of Canada's fighting men, as well as a reminder of the tragedies that arose when Canadians went into battle under the direction of foreign commanders. Although Canadian commanders like Major General John Hamilton Roberts (who famously called Jubilee "a piece of cake" on the eve of the attack) endorsed the raid, many Canadians would eventually blame the bloodbath on Mountbatten, the operation's ranking planner.

These Canadians were not alone. Jubilee had clearly weakened Mountbatten's position in Whitehall. And there was something else that affected Plough. In recent days Churchill had been pushing his generals to sign on to Jupiter, the invasion of Norway. That very day Churchill's Norway scheme had been thrashed out within the COS, and rejected. General Brooke opposed the idea. Invading Norway "is quite impossible at the same time as the North African expedition," he wrote in his diary on September 15. On September 17, the day Frederick appeared in Mountbatten's office, Brooke practically bragged to his journal how today's "COS meeting [was] mainly devoted to defeating Winston in his latest venture."

Nevertheless, Mountbatten decided to raise Frederick's plan with the COS anyway, and so he quickly drafted a paper on Plough and went over it with Frederick, whom he invited along to make his case in person. The cause was not hopeless: the COS might go for a Norway invasion that—supplied, funded, and manned by the U.S. and Canada—cost them nothing. Perhaps they would see Plough as a rough compromise on Jupiter.

At noon, Frederick sat down with the British chiefs, and they were an intimidating lot. There was Sir Charles Portal, the Chief of Air Staff. Portal had displayed exemplary pluck in the First World War as a pilot for the Royal Air Corps. At the start of the present war Portal was serving as commander in chief of Bomber Command, and had impressed Churchill greatly with his relentless attacks against German cities. His ferocity had prompted Churchill to promote Portal to Chief of Air Staff in October 1940. Portal was more than a bulldog. He was keenly intelligent, and purposeful. Eisenhower would compare him to Churchill in his abilities. But he was not nearly as communicative as the prime minister, in either speech or body language. Portal's face, which seemed always to be falling forward under the weight of a heavy nose, gave little away.

From the moment the meeting opened, Portal took the offensive. Chief of Navy Staff Sir Dudley Pound and Vice Chief of the Imperial General Staff Lieutenant General Sir Archibald Nye were present, but Portal did most of the talking, and it was clear from the beginning where he stood. As air marshal, Portal was not dispatching monstrous bombing sorties against Germany every night merely out of duty. His subordinates at Bomber Command were certain their raids would win the war. They even believed an invasion of Europe might not be necessary.

Frederick was quizzed on the potential of the U.S. Air Force to speed up production to churn out enough C-54 transports to fly Frederick's men to their target. Frederick was not in a position to answer, and the questions made it clear the British chiefs wanted the U.S. to come up with its own transportation. But in the end what Portal really wanted from Frederick was justification. Could Plough polish off Germany any faster than his bombers?

The meeting ended. Portal promised to give Frederick and his plan every consideration, and Frederick returned to his room to pack. The next morning, upon arriving at the Irish coast, Frederick learned that his transatlantic flight had been canceled due to bad weather.

He retreated to a hotel room, waited for the Atlantic to calm, and pondered what had happened in London. He was discouraged and perhaps even a little confused. Four days before, he had arrived in London triumphant, the commander of a British scheme to penetrate the Continent. There were many ways in which Eisenhower and the Brits might have greeted him, but cold indifference was the last reception he could have imagined.

The more he thought, the more Frederick realized he had to know. Impulsively, he boarded a plane, returned to London, and appeared at Richmond Terrace. He met a surprised Mountbatten, who decided to dispense with diplomatic niceties. He told Frederick straight out that he didn't think his Force would get British air transport and there was nothing Mountbatten could do about it. Furthermore, and perhaps not surprisingly, Norwegian officials in exile had recently criticized the plan for the destruction it would wreak on their homeland. Without Norwegian support, Portal and the Chiefs of Staff Committee would never endorse Plough.

It was over, Frederick concluded. Mountbatten could only concur. Plough Project, the raid on Norway to seize mastery of Europe's snows, was dead. On September 26, Frederick sent a coded cable to his intelligence chief Burhans that tersely said it all: "Suspend effort on present line."

———

Nine days later, Frederick was in Washington. After concluding that Plough was unfeasible, he had bucked up and decided that the war was still big enough to accommodate his men. Even his September 26 cable to Burhans contained optimism (perhaps more than reality justified), suggesting there could be other missions. "New plan may be radically different and not concerned with hydroelectric or other industrial installations," Frederick had written. ". . . Inform [Executive Officer Paul] Adams at Helena to . . . stress general tactical training to include attack of fortifications, pill boxes, barracks, and troop concentrations."

He had promised Burhans he would return as soon as the weather permitted. But the hope that his force could still see action prompted him to stay on, meet with Eisenhower and Mountbatten again, and inspect Combined Ops' raiders in No. 12 Commando, to compare notes and get ideas. Marshall's fortuitous meeting with Mountbatten in April had not only given birth to Frederick's force, it had also spawned the U.S. Rangers. Marshall was so taken with Mountbatten's strategy to launch amphibious raids against the Continent that he had assigned nine U.S. officers to work in Combined Ops. The ranking American was Brigadier General Lucian Truscott, a former cavalry officer whose days moving soldiers on horseback convinced him of the importance of speed when mobilizing infantry. Mountbatten's commandos were not just fast, they were bolts of lightning.

In May, Truscott proposed creating an American version. Marshall agreed, and the First U.S. Army Ranger Battalion was formed. The Rangers not only had the same grandparents (Marshall and Mountbatten) as the FSSF, the two elite units were linked through Frederick's snake-hunting subordinate Shinberger, who had roomed at school with the Rangers' leader, Colonel William O. Darby. Predictably, Darby and Frederick were similar in many ways. Both were West Pointers. Both were young (although Darby was four years younger). Both had climbed the ranks rapidly, revealed promise, and been staff officers before being tapped for their current commands.

Their destinies were tangentially linked to Britain and its Commando Training Center in Achnacarry, Scotland, but their fates diverged the moment Frederick came to London. Where Darby's Rangers would play a role in the North African campaign, Frederick's Force men were without a mission. And any hope Frederick had that his force would live on took a blow three days after his arrival in Washington.

Ottawa had just announced it wanted its soldiers back. Learning that the invasion of Norway had been scrapped, the Canadian Army General Staff decided it could deploy these soldiers elsewhere. The Canadian army was under pressure to make use of every warm body it had since mobilizing more soldiers would eventually require conscripting them, something Prime Minister Mackenzie King had vowed not to do.

At stake was Canadian unity, he wrote in his diary on April 27, 1942, and he resolved "to do all in our power" to avoid conscripting Canadians to battle. The prime minister believed that imposing conscription, which Quebecers passionately and almost universally opposed, would not only scuttle his government (no small consideration for a political survivor like King) but might drive

Quebec from Confederation. However, volunteer enlistment had trailed off after its initial surge at the outbreak of war, and many in the country believed that conscription would eventually be necessary to drum up sufficient reserve troops. Furthermore, the Tories and most of English Canada supported conscription, which placed King squarely in the middle of a historic confrontation. For the present, King had time to find a solution and—in the words of King's biographer, Brian Nolan—"delay, postpone, divert and avoid the question." With the exception of Hong Kong and Dieppe (though both grievous losses), Canadian forces had not yet entered sustained battle and were not incurring a steady rate of casualties that required reinforcements. But even in 1942, King knew that he could not dodge this issue forever; his government was eager to utilize every man in uniform.

Before King could get his hands on the Canadians in the Force, however, an unlikely savior intervened: General Marshall. Frederick may not have known it, but Marshall was an ally in Frederick's determination to strike Europe in 1942. A fierce advocate of Roundup, Marshall was so disgusted when the British shelved the plan in favor of attacking Africa that he recommended Roosevelt tell Churchill that if the British insisted on waging war on Europe's periphery, "the US [will] turn to the Pacific for decisive action against the Japanese." Roosevelt had overruled Marshall, and Marshall, like Eisenhower, lacked the political heft to save Plough. But Marshall could save the Plough force. He asked Ottawa to reconsider; pulling the Canadians would destroy the FSSF, and Marshall had plans to use it to raid the Caucasus.

The King government acquiesced. Ottawa may have been annoyed that the FSSF's mandate had been changed and was now uncertain, and the Canadian army may have needed the men, but the Canadian War Committee decided to give America's highest-ranking soldier and the FSSF the benefit of the doubt, with the stern proviso that it must "review any operational project that might be contemplated." For the time being, Bob Frederick still had an army.

———

Snow fell in Helena for the first time on September 8, an early date for winter's arrival even in Montana, although the snow would come and go in the following months. Winter huts replaced tents at Fort Harrison, and wood stoves were fired up to warm soldiers as they slept. Around the fort, the landscape transformed. The snow made the Montana range appear flatter and emptier. For some of the Southern boys, the arrival of snow was strange and wonderful. For prairie boys like Lorin Waling, the cold was all too familiar.

Lorin, Joe, and the other men in 1-2 had no idea of the Force's change of mission. They had never known about Norway. But they noticed the shift in training. Earlier, the arrival of the Johnny guns had been a message that someone had plans for them. Now they noticed they were blowing up the Montana countryside less and performing combat exercises more.

By autumn, the imperious Shinberger had disappeared from the Force. So involved were they in training that the soldiers barely noticed. Later, Radcliffe guessed that Shinberger's eccentricity had shaken the confidence of Colonel Frederick. He was right. Years later Frederick would call Shinberger "irrational," and admitted he had been troubled by the officer's enthusiasm for snakes.

By December, the snow had arrived for good, and with a vengeance. It was the deepest snowfall some Helenans could remember, and the Force launched into winter training. The Weasels, the Force's snowmobiles, had already arrived off the assembly line. Compact (for airdrops), box-shaped, and propelled forward on bulldozer-like treads, the Weasels looked like mini-tanks (minus the cannon) or smallish armored personnel carriers. But the state-of-the-art snow machines did everything promised. They cruised across the snow like wolves, and proved handy in training. The men drove them, raced them, and learned how to fix them. The two-man Weasels sometimes pulled entire platoons on skis. To Joe Glass these rides were great fun for everyone except the man on the very back, who was snapped around like the end of a bullwhip.

Ski training was given high priority. The men were taken in groups to Blossburg, a desolate rail terminus near the Continental Divide, and put through their paces by a team of Norwegian experts. At night they slept in boxcars, each heated by a single wood stove. Before dawn they would pile out, bundled in fur-lined parkas custom-made for the Force, and follow the Norwegians. Each man carried a lunch in his parka, and it always froze. They always skied in single file, and always uphill on either side of the Blossburg pass and into the mountains, which reached into the clouds. The Canadians and the American men from the Northwest were usually accomplished skiers. Most of the Southern men, who called skis "torture boards," weren't.

As 1942 drew to a close, Joe, Lorin, and the rest of their battalion were on the Divide. On New Year's Eve day, Joe and Lorin had just returned to the boxcars from training when Joe came up with an idea. Why not ski to the Blossburg station, jump on a passing train to Helena, and spend New Year's with Dorothy and Steffie? The next morning they could catch a train back and no one would be the wiser. Yes, they would be going AWOL. But a man couldn't spend New Year's in a cold boxcar filled with snoring soldiers; and there were worse things you could do in the Force than go AWOL.

In no time their skis were sticking from a snowdrift outside the station and the boys were riding a caboose bound for Helena. Before leaving Blossburg, Lorin had called Steffie's sister, Ann, to warn the girls. Ann found Steffie and Dorothy having an early drink in the Tivoli Tavern and told them the boys were on their way. They could only shake their heads. Leave it to Joe and Lorin to find their way to a party during the worst winter in years. Joe and Lorin made it to East Helena at the cusp of evening, and rang out that miserable year 1942 in grand style at a big party in Union Hall. They danced, drank, laughed, and caught not one moment of sleep before heading back to the station to ride the next train back to Blossburg.

On the train, the two met up with a guy on his way to Seattle who shared a bottle of whiskey with them, which helped Joe and Lorin fight off their hangovers by staying drunk. True to the plan, the boys got off the train at Blossburg, strapped on their skis, and plowed back to the boxcars. They were late getting back and knew that their platoon would already be out. When they arrived, they noticed skis sticking from the snow and found a few men inside the boxcar tucked in their sleeping sacks, sick from the cold. Lorin and Joe were about to hit the sack themselves when their platoon commander, Lieutenant Larry Piette, a pious and serious soldier from Wisconsin, appeared at the door. He had come to find out what had happened to the men who hadn't left on that day's exercise, and he questioned each one.

"What's wrong with you?"

"I'm sick, sir."

"And you?"

"Me too, Lieutenant."

Finally, Piette got to Joe. Of all the sick men in the rail car, Joe may have looked the sickest. A great alibi was plastered on his pale, hungover face.

"What's wrong with you, Glass?"

"I was in town last night, sir."

Piette turned to Waling and repeated the question, perhaps not quite believing what he had heard.

"I was with Glass, sir."

Piette snapped like an icicle, "You two are under arrest."

Being under arrest didn't mean much in the Montana wilderness at fifty below, and that's how the incident was left until the men returned to Fort Harrison. Days later, Glass was called in to see 1st Battalion's 27-year-old commander, Major Tom MacWilliam. In civilian life MacWilliam had been a history teacher at Sackville, New Brunswick's Mount Allison Academy. He was a studied man, tall and lean, and well spoken. Because of his sharp intellect he did not suffer fools gladly, and could be sardonic when faced with idiocy. Still, MacWilliam had an affable, small-town look about him that to some was reminiscent of the actor Jimmy Stewart. According to fellow officers, he led through affability as well. In an army like the Force, which was manned by confident, high-strung achievers, simply pulling rank was rarely effective in winning respect. MacWilliam led by knowing his charges, and by speaking to them as men as well as soldiers.

MacWilliam did the same with Joe Glass when the errant soldier reported to him as commanded, but only after MacWilliam had given Joe hell for going AWOL during critical ski training. "You're too intelligent to do these things," MacWilliam said. "What's the matter with you?"

Joe didn't know how to answer this, so he said nothing.

Then MacWilliam spoke candidly, expressing what was really on his mind. "We don't want to lose you," he said.

The reprimand came with no real punishment. Lorin was moved to the 1st Platoon so that he would be away from Joe in 3rd. Joe was busted down to private from corporal. As a private, Lorin couldn't be busted down to anything. But the demotion didn't mean much except in pay. By virtue of the awesome array of weapons and techniques at their disposal, privates in the FSSF were superior to most sergeants in the regular army. Still, facing the prospect of expulsion from the unit, Joe resolved to behave himself.

Joe not only wanted to stay with his friends in the Force, he wanted to stay in Helena. He borrowed ten dollars from Lieutenant Piette (who clearly had not been too upset about the Blossburg AWOL incident), bought a ring, and proposed to Dorothy. She said yes. She had just turned eighteen years old and she was ready, but didn't know how to break the news to Ma and Pa. She was sure they liked Joe. Both were from the old country of Austria, though, and they weren't prone to chatter or verbal soul-searching, and it was not easy to know their minds. They worked hard, plodded through life, and said little about things other than practicalities. So Dorothy decided to say nothing until the wedding was over.

On the afternoon of Saturday, March 6, Dorothy put on her best dress and did herself up. As she headed for the door, her mother smelled trouble. "You aren't going to do something silly like getting married are you?" she asked.

Dorothy met Joe at the office of the Justice of the Peace in Helena. Lorin stood up for Joe; Steffie stood beside Dorothy. A certain Judge White pronounced them man and wife. Afterward the four celebrated together as they always did. But later that evening, Joe said to Dorothy, "We've got to tell your mom and dad."

To ease the shock, Joe bought a bottle of whiskey, and when the newlyweds set foot in Dorothy's old East Helena home, Joe sauntered over to Pa in his chair and silently slipped that bottle onto his lap. Pa accepted the bottle with barely a word, and Joe could see that he warmed to the idea of the marriage with every dram he downed. Life had just presented Antone Strainer with a grown-up, married daughter and a new son-in-law—and how could he not be happy about that?

The men who survived the cut and were still in the Force in early 1943 loved training to the point that sometimes, at the end of a day's march, Lorin Waling would suggest a final run up Muscle Mountain just for the joy of it. The weekends in Helena—the girlfriends, wives, friendships, families, saloons, fun, and fights—were part of the package, and the Helenans might have been forgiven for wishing the boys could stay on at Fort Harrison indefinitely.

But that wasn't to be. The men didn't know it, but Colonel Frederick had been lobbying for an assignment. Marshall's plans to deploy the unit in the Caucasus didn't come to pass. But the general had other plans, and this was made clear when orders came down in April for the outfit to move to Norfolk, Virginia, for amphibious training. Frederick ordered a fitting good-bye.

On April 6, 1943, Army Day, Frederick stood atop a reviewing stand in downtown Helena with local dignitaries like Helena's mayor, Jack Haytin, and the governor of Montana, Sam C. Ford. They watched the men as they marched by in a grand parade. Led by the Force's band, men marched bayonet-straight, looking ahead with eyes shadowed by the brims of their combat helmets. All of Helena crowded into Last Chance Gulch to see the boys, who were barely recognizable as the same men who had arrived in the summer of the previous year. Back then they were green officers, bored privates, lonely prospectors, frustrated warriors, rebels, and ruffians from two nations who shared an ambition to get into combat as quickly as possible. Now they were an extraordinary military unit.

Dorothy Glass and Steffie didn't go to town to watch the parade. They stood in the yard of Steffie's sister, Ann, who lived on the outskirts of Helena where the parade began. They watched as the boys passed, and felt moved. The parade was impressive—poignant and sad. There was no doubt that these men had become formidable soldiers, but they were marching literally to war. On April 11, the railcars containing the Force men pulled away from Helena. For some reason, the train chugged slowly for a while, and Dorothy and Steffie, driving Ann's car, followed the train for as long as they could as Lorin and Joe and dozens of other boys hung out the windows and waved.

The Force stayed at Norfolk for six weeks. They learned how to board landing craft and storm beaches. When practicing getting in the landing craft, they moved up and down the webbed hull of the ship like insects. They learned their lessons so well that the Force broke a record previously held by the Marines for scrambling down the nets from the troopship into the bobbing boats. The Force was then sent to Fort Ethan Allen, Vermont. There they learned how to attack bunkers and fortifications. The base had a roller skating rink, and some of the men from Joe's platoon went. Jimmy Flack skated. (Joe decided that Jimmy was a lousy skier but hell on roller skates.) Dorothy came to be with Joe, and other Helena wives came too. Then Colonel Frederick was ordered to report to Sixth Army headquarters at the Presidio in San Francisco.

Once there, any fear Frederick had that his men would never be permitted to prove themselves vanished. Frederick was presented with a mission: Operation Cottage. The FSSF was slated to be part of the largest amphibious operation in history, the invasion of a Japanese-occupied island just off the coast of Alaska. And Frederick's army, true to the red arrowhead patch each man wore on his shoulder, would spearhead the attack.

Before dawn on August 15, 1943, rafts emerged from a cold fog, and the men aboard them fought the currents, paddling their way to the rocky coast of Kiska Island to surprise the legion of Japanese defenders entrenched there. In one of the rafts moving toward Broad Beach on the northern end of Kiska sat Mark Radcliffe, his face smeared with camouflage paint. Radcliffe, now a first lieutenant, was leading a platoon from 3rd Regiment toward the Japanese. Radcliffe and his fellow officers expected the fight, only minutes away, to be tough as hell. Kiska sat on the eastern end of an island chain called the Aleutians that stretched to the Alaska Peninsula, and American territory. Occupied by the Japanese in June 1942, Kiska was Tokyo's closest outpost to North America, and the U.S. Army was determined to take the rock back.

The Americans knew that the Japanese defenders would be equally determined. The Japanese attack on the U.S. naval base at Pearl Harbor on December 7, 1941, had inspired many American soldiers to hate this enemy, but few could honestly question the tenacity, ferocity, and ambition of the Japanese imperial forces. Japan had followed up its strike against Hawaii by making its first landing in the Philippines, America's prized Pacific holding, three days later. In early 1942, Japanese forces landed in Dutch Indonesia, New Guinea, and Sumatra as part of a bid to control the breadth of the Pacific, a goal that looked more than plausible when U.S. forces surrendered at Bataan on April 8. The fall of British forces (which included 1,975 Canadians from the Royal Rifles of Canada and the Winnipeg Grenadiers) at Hong Kong before the end of 1941 educated both London and Ottawa on the threat the Japanese posed, and some even feared the Japanese might strike the coast of British Columbia. Though these spectacular early defeats may have caused the Allies to overestimate Japanese strength, the men of the FSSF believed Japanese defenders would fight as doggedly for the barren rock of Kiska as they had for Guadalcanal.

True to tradition for amphibious landings, Radcliffe and his men had wanted to feast on steak before departing for the invasion, but the navy cooks served nothing better than sauerkraut, and only the battle that awaited him made him forget his anger. Everyone expected a vicious fight this day for the simple reason that the Japanese had fought zealously to defend Attu, the nearest island in the chain. Attu had been considered an easier target than Kiska. Still, the invasion force had needed three weeks to take that rock from fewer than 3,000 defenders, and suffered a staggering body count for its trouble: 3,800 casualties, one-quarter of the invasion force.

By contrast, according to intelligence, Kiska was defended by almost 12,000 Japanese. Third Regiment was ordered to meet them at the northern end of the island. First Regiment had already landed to the south the day before, and they had completed their mission—securing and marking landing areas, seizing the nearby ridgelines, and paving the way for the first wave of the main invasion force, which in total numbered 30,000 Americans and Canadians. But neither the Force men nor the invading infantry found any Japanese. These were anxious hours as 1st Regiment waited for a trap to spring in the south and 3rd Regiment paddled into a potential ambush in the north.

Radcliffe, like so many of the others, found merely getting to shore amid the chop and strong current a fight. And the landing zone was no beach. What looked like pebbles from a distance were huge chunks of rock—a "boulder spit," he would later say—and landing his men was more difficult than he had expected. The consolation was that they were fighting the sea and the rock, not the Japanese. Not a shot had been fired at them yet. The enemy was obviously inland. According to plan, Radcliffe and his men marched a short distance to Kiska Lake, deployed their rafts again, and for the second time that night began paddling. And for the second time the elements conspired against them. The fog had lifted, and in the moonlight you could see the rubber fleet on the water as if it were daylight. Radcliffe waited for the bullets. But they never came, and the men kept going. They landed, left the boats, and headed up into the ridgeline. Still no Japanese, only a wind so potent it threatened to blow his men clear off the trail.

Radcliffe eventually reached a vantage point where he could see the Japanese camp below. Their orders were to ease up from behind it for the attack. As they came down the ridge and started to move into position, Alaskan Scouts were sent forward to locate the enemy. Radcliffe was uneasy about the eerie stillness of the place when gunfire erupted ahead. Out front, the Scouts had spotted movement and opened up on a dugout in the tundra. Lieutenant Radcliffe's war had finally started.

Or had it? When the men noticed they were the only ones shooting, they ceased fire and spotted the enemy: a big hungry dog that immediately romped up to them looking for handouts. Radcliffe would soon learn the dog was all that remained of the Japanese detachment which had surreptitiously retreated from the island just before the invasion. Later, Al Lennox of Winnipeg, who at that moment was paddling across Kiska Lake with 4th Company (4-3), put it best: "There was nobody home."

———

Had there been war on Kiska, Joe Glass and Lorin Waling, along with the rest of 2nd Regiment, would have jumped from the sky to join it. On August 15, Joe, parachute strapped to his back, Mae West life preserver on his chest, had fidgeted on the tarmac with the rest of his platoon, and chain-smoked as he and they awaited orders to climb on the transport and wing off. They climbed aboard and disembarked several times. But the plane remained grounded, and finally word came by way of code: "Baby's got a new pair of shoes." Colonel Frederick had sent this message, and it meant "stand down." Joe's regiment would not be jumping that day.

Frederick himself had landed on Kiska by raft, although he only narrowly escaped being swept out to sea. He and his aides made it to shore by paddling like maniacs. A separate raft carrying staff officers and radio equipment had been carried away by the current and was later picked up by the navy. Frederick had personally climbed to the high ground near Quisling Cove and stared out at Kiska's inexplicably silent horizon. He had to wonder whether his braves would ever see action.

———

On August 18, Frederick received a message from Admiral Nimitz, commander of the Pacific Fleet, ordering his force to San Francisco. On that very day, Operation Husky, the invasion of Sicily, had been fully realized. Messina had fallen to the Allies, and the first round of the campaign, which had squared off against 167,000 Axis troops, had been won. Now the boot of the Italian peninsula lay open to invasion, and Frederick's force had been earmarked for this campaign.

On August 31, the Force arrived by ship in San Francisco, beginning a long journey that would take them to Burlington, Vermont; and then Hampton Roads, Virginia; and then by way of the *Empress of Scotland* to Casablanca. After that they would ride the rails to Oran, Algeria, board U.S. Navy transports, sail to Naples, and finally travel by truck to the tiny village of Santa Maria Capua Vetere. From this southern Italian base, Frederick would be compensated for the disappointments of Norway and Kiska; in fact, he would see enough warring in the next two years to last him a lifetime.

As would Privates Glass and Waling. But the privates had had other things on their minds during that long journey. After landing in San Francisco, Lorin and Joe were rushing to their next posting in Burlington, Vermont, when they stopped in East Helena, and Lorin married Steffie Broderick in the town's tiny Catholic church. Joe stood up for Lorin, and Dorothy watched on with a swollen belly. Lorin Waling was a new husband; Joe Glass was to be a new father.

After the brief ceremony, the two couples rented a one-room cabin for Lorin and Steffie's honeymoon. The boys hung a wool blanket from the ceiling, and after they drank, talked, laughed, joked, and planned their lives, the couples retreated to either side of the heavy fabric and settled in for the night.

Besides Mark Radcliffe, Glass, and Waling, as many as two hundred Force men married into the community. There were Herb Goodwin, John Marshall, and Stoney Wines, to name a few. In March, hand-to-hand-combat expert Pat O'Neill had married Mary Hardin, a delicate-looking blond schoolmarm.

The Waling–Glass honeymoon typified most: it was brief, charged by the drama of the times and the knowledge that the men were now leaving for war. But when Glass, Waling, and the others left, no one could anticipate the future: that the war would go on for another two years, bringing with it an avalanche of death and sadness. The first rumblings of that slide would begin four months later on a mountainside in central Italy.

CHAPTER 6

TWO PEAKS

The Force's new home was a shell-damaged barracks a couple of kilometers west of Santa Maria Capua Vetere. Not long before, it had been home to the Hermann Göring Panzer and Parachute Division, one of the enemy's crack outfits. Before that it had housed Italian artillery cadets. From their barracks, the men could even see Monte la Difensa and Monte la Remetanea looming in the distance.

On November 20, 1943, as they settled into their base, neither Joe Glass nor Lorin Waling of 1-2 realized the significance of those mountains. No one could know that these would be their first battlefields, but there was every indication they had reached the war; all around them was the damage left behind by Allied explosives. Indeed, much of southern Italy had become rubble after almost three months of warfare. The Allies had invaded Italy on September 1 at the coastal town of Salerno, setting foot on Axis-occupied Europe for the first time since the British had been driven from the Continent at Dunkirk, France. Ironically, the Allies had invaded the homeland of an enemy that no longer wanted to fight. Weeks before, reeling from the invasion of Sicily, Italy ousted Fascist leader Benito Mussolini, and attempted to seal a unilateral peace deal with the Allies—a gesture that triggered a full German invasion.

From the moment they landed on the Italian shore, the Americans of the Fifth Army and Brits of the Eighth Army, which included the Canadian First Infantry and the Canadian Fifth Armored Divisions, encountered tough resistance.

The invaders were stymied by several factors: difficult terrain (mountains creased with chasms and gorges), problems with transportation (bad roads or none at all), and unfavorable weather (rain and fog). But the biggest obstacle was the enemy itself, led by Field Marshal Albert Kesselring, a resilient one-time balloon observer and former air force chief of staff who was nicknamed "Smiling Albert" by colleagues for his constant optimism. By fortifying natural barricades like the Sangro and Garigliano rivers and the Apennine Mountains with razor wire, bunkers, and outposts, Kesselring was able to create three defensive belts that stretched across the peninsula. These belts, known collectively as the Winter Line, proved nearly impregnable. Before the landing, conventional wisdom among Allied leaders had it that the Germans would not contest southern Italy, but instead make a stand farther north. Instead, Kesselring's strategy was to make the Allies claw for every inch of ground, and ultimately grind the invasion down into a stalemate. For an Allied army blooded in North Africa, where the campaign was fought in free-ranging mechanized confrontations on open battlefields such as the desert of central Tunisia, the creeping Italian campaign, confined to mountains, valleys, and rivers of mud, was a cruel surprise. Tanks were nearly useless, and air cover was often fogged in; it was the infantry that would have to seize each bloody yard, a mode of warfare that favored the entrenched defender. Before its conclusion, certain chapters of the battle for Italy would better resemble the bloody inertia of the First World War than the blitzkrieg of the Second.

The U.S. Fifth Army, commanded by an ambitious former aide to Eisenhower by the name of Lieutenant General Mark Clark, had ground through the first line of defense, the Barbara Line, only to butt up against the more resilient Bernhardt Line on November 1. Midway across Italy, at the mouth of the Liri Valley and the mountains that protected it on either side, the two remaining lines of defense (Bernhardt and Gustav) merged into one thick system. This point would soon become the focus of the Italian war.

The Liri was the only valley that broke through the mountains of central Italy and provided a route to Rome wide enough to accommodate a large mechanized army. A modern motorway, Highway 6, ran down the valley, but the approach to the Liri and the Bernhardt and Gustav Lines was guarded by mountains on which the enemy had entrenched themselves with firepower capable of mauling any force that tried to pass Highway 6 and enter the valley. The first set of mountains, acting as sentry to this approach, was the Camino Complex. In the shadow of the Camino massif was the village of Mignano, a quaint and ancient community that now found itself at the epicenter of the Italian war. In late November, Colonel Frederick was given the assignment of seizing two peaks in this complex: 950-meter-high Monte la Difensa and the adjoining Monte la Remetanea.

Frederick's force had been assigned to fight under the U.S. II Corps, and specifically had been attached to the Thirty-sixth Infantry Division. As Frederick was briefed about his assignment at General Clark's Fifth Army headquarters in the nearby city of Caserta, he learned that the Force's assignment on Difensa and Remetanea was part of a greater offensive, dubbed Operation Raincoat, against this natural fortification, which also included Monte Camino, located directly south of the FSSF's targets, and Monte Maggiore to the northwest. Camino, noted for the stone monastery on its summit, was to be attacked by the British X Corps in two stages—a diversionary attack by the British Forty-sixth Division against the southernmost outcrop of Camino on December 1 that would, General Clark hoped, distract the enemy while the Force and the rest of II Corps prepared for the real show that would begin the next day to the north all along the massif. While the Force moved against Difensa, with the intention of rolling all the way across the ridgeline to the adjoining peak of Remetanea before the day was over, the British Fifty-sixth Division would attack Camino's main summit. Taking nearby Camino would deny the enemy a position from which to cover Difensa with mortar fire when the Force attacked. Clark's armies would strike along a six-mile alpine front, but Difensa and Remetanea were the key objectives and the sole responsibility of the Force's 1,800 fighting men.

Given previous attempts to seize the massif, assigning such a small unit to sieze Difensa and Remetanea seemed almost absurd. A succession of large-scale attacks had been unleashed on the mountains, and all had failed terribly. On November 5, the U.S. Third Infantry stormed the slopes of Difensa. Nicknamed the "Rock of the Marne" for its stubborn refusal to give ground to the Germans in 1918, the Third Division charged up the treacherous approach, but the line of fire enjoyed by the German defenders above them proved too direct and overwhelming. The Germans rained down fire with killing precision. Those infantrymen who endured and survived the relentless barrage had to contend with the snow and cold, and the gullies, rocks, and craggy terrain of the mountain itself. The dogfaces of the Third died on the mountainside in staggering numbers. Those determined GIs who managed to make gains in this high-altitude brawl found themselves in precarious positions that couldn't be supplied.

Despite the setbacks, General Clark needed to control Difensa and the Camino Complex in order to enter Mignano and control the approach to Cassino. So he ordered the men of the Third Division on, and for ten grueling, bloody days the futile attack continued, until its inordinately high casualty rate and lack of success forced Clark to call off the attack. The British Fifty-sixth Division had also laid siege to the mountains, focusing their attack on Camino. But theirs was a foray into the same sausage grinder that had savaged the men of the Third Infantry. The Germans were proving themselves grim masters of the counterattack. As one historian wrote: "Whenever [the British] reached a peak, they would be counter-attacked off it, and ended up clinging to near vertical slopes." The Brits, surrounded on Camino at one critical point, were forced to break out in order to withdraw, a development that infuriated Clark.

On November 15, the bleeding and battle-weary Third Division limped off the line and were relieved by the Texas-based U.S. Thirty-sixth Infantry. Clark may have thought that bringing in the tough Lone Star Division might break the deadlock. But despite having spearheaded the Salerno landings that had brought the Fifth Army onto Italian soil, the Texans encountered the same impenetrable, dogged resistance when they threw themselves against the mountains.

When the FSSF arrived in late November, this was the recent history of Monte la Difensa and its sister peaks Remetanea and Camino. Entire divisions of thousands of infantrymen had tried, and failed, to uproot the Germans from the massifs' summits. The FSSF, which was now taking its turn, was no bigger than the size of a brigade.

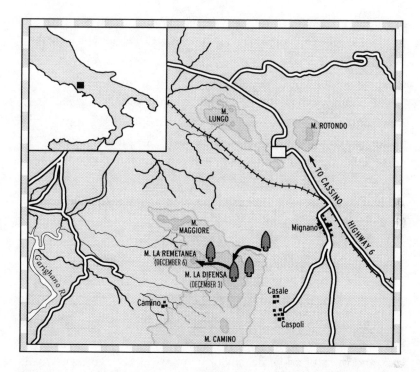

Second Regiment's assault on Mts. la Difensa and la Remetanea

Colonel Frederick took a look for himself, first scouting the lower reaches of the mountain and then, with his planning officer, Lieutenant Colonel Emil Eschenburg, doing reconnaissance from the cramped fuselage of a bouncing Piper L-4 Cub. Eschenburg stared out the window of the screaming spotter plane and didn't like what he saw. "I had my doubts about Monte la Difensa," he recalled. And he told Frederick so. "But [Frederick] was determined."

Eschenburg's doubts were understandable. There was a reason the roughly 400 Germans atop Difensa, members of the veteran 104th, and about half of the 129th Regiments of the 15th Panzergrenadier Division, had successfully beaten off so many previous attacks. Monte la Difensa was a natural fortress. According to some locals the mountain was a dead volcano, and its summit a former lava dome that had cooled into a concave bowl. This saucer-shaped plateau was a convenient high-altitude bivouac area for the defenders, and the only route to it was up the mountain's southern slope, which rose steeply, and fell perfectly in the line of mortar and machine-gun fire of the defenders. The other side of the summit—the northern slope—was an impenetrable line of 70-degree cliffs as high as sixty meters.

This was the conundrum, and Frederick gave the job of assaulting the summit to his 2nd Regiment, commanded by Colonel Donald Williamson, the highest-ranking Canadian in the Force. Williamson, who also inspected the mountain, assigned his 1st Battalion, commanded by Tom MacWilliam, now a lieutenant colonel, to spearhead the attack. As 1-2 was part of MacWilliam's battalion, Joe Glass and Lorin Waling, though they didn't know it yet, would finally have their wishes realized: they and their buddies in 1st Company would be seeing combat.

The sequence of events that led to Glass and Waling being two of the first to attack Monte la Difensa began when MacWilliam asked his Executive Officer, a conscientious young soldier from North Carolina named Major Ed Thomas, to reconnoiter the mountain. Thomas had joined the outfit late— September 1942—and he hadn't joined MacWilliam's staff until after the Kiska operation. But the two men quickly became friends, and MacWilliam's faith in Thomas was underscored by the assignment he had given him: find an attack route up Difensa that would not decimate the battalion.

In late November, when Thomas first ventured out into the brambles and uneven terrain at the foot of Difensa to reconnoiter, he brought 1st Company commander, Bill Rothlin, with him, and two scouts. Thomas found Rothlin quiet and "very dedicated," but 1-2 interested Thomas because of its resident scouts, Tommy

Fenton and Howard Van Ausdale. Specifically, Thomas knew that Van Ausdale had an uncanny talent for evaluating terrain.

On that first reconnaissance patrol, the four men marched sixteen kilometers to Difensa, and took in the approach and the overall landscape. For the most part, thick brush grew from the ground running up to the foot of the looming mountain, and a copse of trees sprouted from its lower slope. Thomas and his reconnaissance team spent the night in a barn at the mountain's base. The next day they braved mortar fire, scrambling onto Difensa's slopes to reconnoiter the spur itself. The mountain was just as the maps and reports depicted it. The southern approach seemed to be the only clear way to the top.

However, Van Ausdale focused on the sixty-meter cliffs at the north end of the summit, and in particular on a route that crept up the mountainside and stopped at the base of those cliffs. Like many problem solvers, Thomas and Van Ausdale attacked the riddle backward. Because the northern cliffs were seemingly impenetrable, they were the only place on the mountain where the enemy wouldn't be watching for an attack, and arguably the best possible route.

MacWilliam accepted the challenge. His men had alpine training. Colonel Williamson concurred. Ultimately, Frederick signed off on the plan as well. According to Eschenburg, after his flight in the spotter plane, Frederick believed the cliffs to be the only route to the top. Thomas's proposal was risky, but most agreed there was no other way. The 2nd Regiment would spirit themselves up the northern trail of Monte la Difensa under cover of night, and then mount the cliffs to the rear of the German positions. When 1st Battalion was on top, MacWilliam's men would attack and overwhelm Difensa's German defenders from behind. Once the summit was secure, the Force men would charge across the ridgeline and drive the Germans off the adjoining peak of Monte la Remetanea.

The plan looked promising on paper. But the risks were obvious. For this strategy to work, six hundred men would have to
scale a rock face in the dark of a wintry night, and creep to the
rear of the enemy lines without being detected. If anything went
wrong—if the Germans heard a sneeze, or spotted a shadow, and
got wind of the attack before the commandos were in place—the
men would be caught in the open and cut to pieces.

———

In the late afternoon of December 1, not all of this was known to
Joe Glass, Lorin Waling, and 2nd Regiment as they climbed
aboard six-by-six transport trucks and began a journey that would
end on the top of Difensa. But the men knew that a key mountain battle awaited them. Before their departure, II Corps
commander, General Geoffrey Keyes, had given the men a pep
talk, telling them of the battle's importance to the Italian war. If
they could win this mountain, Keyes said, "we'll be in Rome in
two or three weeks."

At roughly sundown, the trucks carrying 2nd Regiment, after
speeding and careening along the battered Italian roads, arrived at
the drop-off point: a sheltered area not far from the village of
Presenzano. Joe and the others from 1-2 got off, and as rain pelted
them from above, they left the road and began a long march
through thick brush and mud and along creek beds, with Difensa
looming over them like a gravestone. The going was difficult. Joe
and Lorin's 3rd Platoon had taken up the rear of the loose column,
and fell farther and farther behind the company. They would catch
up with the others just as they were finishing rest stops, and the
weary men of 3rd Platoon would have to carry on without a break.
The exhaustion this was causing the men angered Herby Forester,
who pounded forward on his short legs and at one point threatened to tear off his sergeant's stripes if his men didn't get a break.

Early the next morning Forester, Glass, and the others arrived at forward positions of the Thirty-sixth Infantry, manned by the jaded survivors of the past thwarted attacks on Difensa. Some men of the Thirty-sixth wanted to know who the hell this horde of six hundred "glamor boys" thought they were to attempt a mountain that had killed so many of their comrades. The crag was so lethal that neither they nor the Third Division had been able to retrieve their dead and wounded from the upper slopes. Difensa was a trap their hapless comrades had been sucked into without a trace. These forward guards of the Thirty-sixth knew what fate awaited the Force men. "Nice knowing ya, boys," one of the Texans shouted out to Glass.

The men marched all night, and by dawn reached the belt of trees on the base of the mountain. Restricting their movements, lighting no fires, doing their best to rest, the men of 2nd Regiment hid in these woods throughout the day. Mercifully, the rain stopped, the sky cleared, and a warm winter sun appeared. Under the trees, Joe Glass bided his time by cleaning his weapons, trying his best not to think of how his life had moved on since he left home. While in Italy, Joe had received word that Dorothy had given birth to their son on October 17, and had named him Charles.

During the day, while the men waited, Colonel Frederick arrived and wished them well. For Joe and many others, Frederick's presence "out front" on the dangerous slopes of this mountain proved an inspiration. Regimental commander Williamson also spoke, and urged the men to "follow" him.

In the late afternoon, as the daylight began to fade, Lieutenant Colonel MacWilliam gave the order to his battalion to move out. Joe Glass, Forester, Don MacKinnon, and the rest of 3rd Platoon stirred and got into place. They would now begin the last leg of the journey, which would end with the assault itself. From the trees, they would climb the slope that wound its way to the cliffs on the north face of the summit where the Germans were entrenched. Once there, the men would silently scale this sixty-meter-high cliff face and—assuming, indeed praying, that the Germans were all dug in on the opposite end of the plateau—sneak behind the enemy position and launch a surprise attack.

As the men exited the treeline, a deafening roar greeted them as II Corps guns far below Difensa initiated a devastating artillery barrage that was directed at the mountaintop and meant to cover the men's approach. The firepower was breathtaking, and Joe and the others could only stare up in awe as the mountain complex, including nearby Mount Maggiore, where the U.S. 142nd was going into action, came under fire from 820 artillery pieces, which would deliver 20,000 rounds over a single hour of firing, the heaviest Allied barrage since El Alamein. For Private Don MacKinnon, the shelling was "unbelievable." He later wrote: "Shells roared overhead in both directions like fast freight trains one after another." Some of the men immediately dubbed the target "million-dollar mountain," so spectacular was the violence and so high the cost in shells. One wag claimed it would be cheaper simply to pay the Germans to leave.

At that moment the Germans were huddling in recesses and crevices on the summit that were fortified with timber, and fashioned into makeshift bunkers. According to II Corps estimations cited by Force intelligence chief Robert Burhans, there weren't many Germans on the top. One battalion of the 104th Panzergrenadier Regiment, consisting of about 250 soldiers, represented the main force, bolstered by half of a battalion from the 129th Panzergrenadiers. The other half of the 129th Third Battalion stood vigil on the ridgeline, putting the total on Difensa's summit at anywhere between 350 and 400 defenders. The 115th Reconnaissance Battalion stood in reserve. The

Panzergrenadiers on Difensa were a well-trained and battle hardened contingent of artillery spotters and recon scouts who used the heights of the massif to repel any Allied movement along Highway 6 and the approach to Mignano and the Liri Valley, by calling in fire from well over 100 German artillery pieces positioned in and around Sant' Ambrogio, San Vittore, and Cassino.

Cold, isolated, and perched upon a dreary granite outcrop, the Panzergrenadiers lived in miserable conditions. The only consolation was that the remoteness of their posting had made it defensible. The Wehrmacht had already begun to show how tenacious it could be in defense, and the German soldier's ability to show initiative would slow the Allied advance until the bitter end of the war. Indeed, a handful of well-trained Germans could often stall a much larger Allied force by taking advantage of terrain. Most such skirmishes would be settled by over-whelming Allied artillery superiority, but the German doctrine of active defense and robust counterattack meant that Allied infantrymen often had to fight for the same ground more than once. The defenders on Difensa had every advantage terrain could offer, and they had already proved their mettle to American GIs in the fierce battles they had waged in the crags of Sicily, particularly their dogged and ultimately failed bid to drive elements of the U.S. 1st Infantry Division from Monte Basilio near the village of Troina. Sicily had tested and scarred these men. They would not give ground easily.

The slender column of soldiers in single file was led by MacWilliam's party, which included his young bodyguard, Private Stuart Hunt, and 1st Company commander, Bill Rothlin. Nearby were the scouts Fenton and Van Ausdale, who used every ounce of tracking knowledge his Native upbringing had instilled in him to pick his way along the dark, treacherous slope. As luck would have it, Joe's 3rd Platoon was first in line, and a short time after they set out, Glass and the others came upon the corpses of Allied soldiers, lying stiff and gnarled. The stench of death made the men gag, and the corpses delivered a troubling message: *Beware, boys. A month ago we were you.*

Even though the hailstorm of artillery above them was deafening, the men took no chances and moved as stealthily as possible. At about 10 p.m. the column stopped, according to one account, because shells were falling short of the summit and detonating on the slope. A short time later the artillery stopped, and the column picked itself up and set off again. The silence meant that the head of the column was now very close to the cliffs and the final ascent to the summit was almost at hand. At this stage Herby Forester struggled along with everyone else to remain silent. "Every little noise seemed amplified at least fifty times," he noted.

Eventually, the route that Van Ausdale and Fenton had been following wound into the face of the mountain. The head of the column had arrived at the base of the cliffs. After two nights of covert marching, the fight was now very close and the two lead scouts had one last job, something the Germans had deemed impossible. Gripping crevices with fingertips and boot toes, the two men mounted the precipitous face in a bid to find a route to the top. As they broke a trail up the face, Privates Joe Dauphinais and Johnny Walter followed them carrying coils of rope, which they strung down the mountainside, forming two rope-lines.

Fortunately, Van Ausdale and Fenton found that the face was not vertical all the way to the top. Although sheer in places, the cliff now and then relaxed into a steep grade, allowing the scouts to take a breath, pound life into numbed appendages, and consider the route ahead. The task before them was not only to find a way up, but to blaze a route that could accommodate the others, who were lugging guns, ammunition, and over a hundred pounds of gear each. But as Van Ausdale clawed at the rock face, his instincts served him well: he happened upon a natural chimney that offered a steep but accessible channel for climbing.

Finally, after an ascent that seemed interminable, Van Ausdale and Fenton sat on the edge of Difensa's summit. They had found a route to the top that they were confident the others could manage with the help of ropes. It was now time to get back down. But before doing so, they probed forward to reconnoiter and locate the enemy. Moving ahead, they found they still had to scramble up a rocky incline to reach the cusp of the plateau. And when they got there, Van Ausdale raised his head above a rock only to stare through damp, wintry air into the shadowy back of a German sentry, who had been standing in that spot seconds before and was now moving away.

Van Ausdale and Fenton eased back to the cliffs and then made their way back down. The news they had for Lieutenant Colonel MacWilliam and Captain Rothlin was good. They had found a route to the top of the cliffs and had been able to secure two rope lines the length of the escarpment. After the cliffs, the plateau was only about 105 meters on, and their side of the summit appeared to be clear of Germans except for possibly a sentry or two. Van Ausdale and Tommy Fenton then collected their gear and weapons and mounted the face for the second time, once again leading the way. Third Platoon followed them up the ropes a man at a time, and perhaps a half-hour later Joe Glass arrived at the top of the cliffs, exerting the final pull that brought him onto the summit.

The night was quiet, wet, dark, and cold. The men were taking off their packs and piling them to the side so that they could fight unencumbered. Glass did the same, and then eased forward in the dark to get into position. From the ropes, men were going off to either the right or the left, around the edge of the plateau. Joe headed right. As he stepped gingerly over stones, the only noise he heard was a whisper from his platoon commander, Lieutenant Piette: "Fix bayonets." Glass obeyed, and as he crept toward the German line, his bayonet probed the darkness like a white cane. Edging forward, Glass lost contact with everyone else, moving utterly alone, prepared to continue advancing until he found the enemy. The rest of the one hundred men who made up 1-2 were at that moment rapidly filing up the cliffs behind him.

Those already on the summit were creeping somewhere to Joe's left. Lorin Waling had moved left, keeping close to Sergeant Boodleman, a tough Oregonian whom Waling had grown close to. Like Waling, most of the men were edging forward in a rough skirmish line toward the German position. But Glass had no idea where the rest of his platoon was. Nor did he know how close he was to the enemy.

But others did. On the left side of the plateau some of the 3rd Platoon men in the advancing line, like Dauphinais, Van Ausdale, and Fenton, were so close to the enemy position they could hear German sentries joking and smell food being cooked. The simmering breakfast underscored one desperate fact lost on none of the commandos: morning was approaching, and when dawn arrived, the battle would certainly begin. Right now all of the commandos were covered only by darkness, and when the night disappeared, there would be nothing separating them from the enemy. The challenge was to ensure enough men were on top to engage the Germans before first light.

Just before dawn, the last men of 2nd Company were making their way up the cliffs. Captain Rothlin, advancing with a line of men on the right, had lost contact with Van Ausdale and Fenton. According to one account, Rothlin sent Joe Dauphinais and Johnny Walter to find Van Ausdale and get information. "In no time at all," Dauphinais later wrote, "we found our scouts. And the enemy. Aroused."

At this moment events unraveled so rapidly that none of the men were certain of the order. On the cliffs a young soldier by the name of Jack Callowhill was pulling himself up the rope line when the man above him slipped, and kicked Callowhill in the head with a heavy jump boot. He managed to hold on to the rope, but his helmet went spiraling off of his head and clanking loudly down the mountainside. An instant before or later, Sergeant Howard Van Ausdale came face-to-face with a German sentry. The German issued a challenge, which the scout answered with a bullet. What is certain is that at roughly 5:30 a.m., just as dawn seeped into the sky, a heavy firefight erupted on the summit. General Frederick, near his command post located beside a newly erected aid station farther down the mountain, heard it, and knew immediately that the battle for Monte la Difensa was underway.

———

Before the firing broke out, 3-3's new commander, Lieutenant Mark Radcliffe, waited for morning with his men in a gully at the base of the mountain. Because 3rd Regiment had been ordered to support 2nd Regiment in its assault, when the fighting broke out Radcliffe's men would be responsible for hauling ammunition and supplies to the top of the hill. From his position not far from II Corps's artillery placements, Radcliffe was forced to listen to the guns' deafening thunder as they lobbed shells at German positions. The artillery was so monstrous and the barrage so violent, according to Lieutenant Chet Ross, the ground trembled "like jelly" with every volley, and Ross's first reaction was an involuntary evacuation of his bladder.

For Radcliffe's men, the night was noisy but clear. Suddenly a mortar went off, followed by others that moved toward his position like footfalls. Radcliffe shouted, "Hit the dirt," and then ducked just as a shell exploded on the other side of the boulder that covered him. The rock deflected the power of the blast upward, and when the dust cleared, Radcliffe found himself sitting in about the same spot but with a twisted piece of shrapnel the size of a fat, long finger protruding from his forehead.

———

On Difensa, the firefight became mayhem, intermittently illuminated by the artificial dawn of magnesium flares launched by the enemy. The first man to fall, the German sentry shot by Van Ausdale, was also the first man Lorin Waling ever heard die. Somehow, the mortally wounded enemy stumbled past Van Ausdale and fell down an embankment that Waling was approaching. Waling heard him give out three raspy groans before fading. A moment later the man's gasps would be drowned in the clatter of BARS and Johnny guns, the rattle of the section leaders' Thompson submachine guns, and the roar of M1s.

The Force was aided at first by the confusion of its enemies. For the first few minutes the Germans, believing they were being assaulted from the front, opened up their guns in the wrong direction, firing on fixed lines down the empty southern slope. And even when they realized their attackers were behind them, turning their machine guns to the rear proved difficult. Some of the German gunners died trying. Others grabbed smaller weapons, such as Schmeisser machine pistols, and sought cover.

In the waning darkness Lieutenant Piette and most of the men of 3rd Platoon could just make out the German position up ahead. It was a bunker, and beside it was an apex forming the highest point of the mountain plateau. At three different spots along the German line, flames from machine gun barrels licked the darkness. Piette wanted the guns flanked, and ordered his

men to lay down fire so that Sergeant McGinty, an imposing logger, and roughly half of 3rd Platoon could scramble around to the
right. McGinty moved right while Lorin Waling and 1st Platoon,
who had somehow circled in, were hitting the positions from the
left. Waling pointed his M1 rifle at one of many Germans who
now stood visible and vulnerable in the dawn light. Waling shot
him and then ran back to Sergeant Boodleman. "I got one, Sarge,
I got one."

When the fighting erupted, 1st battalion commander
Lieutenant Colonel MacWilliam was already on the summit with
his runner and bodyguard, Stu Hunt, at his side. Positioned near
the lip of the saucer where he could take stock of the rapidly esca-
lating firefight, he directed the battle and at times even joined the
fight as a rifleman.

Joe Dauphinais of Starbuck, Manitoba, in his quest to find
Van Ausdale, had advanced ahead of the 1st Company's skirmish line. Still covered by a waning darkness, Dauphinais kept
low and kept moving. Suddenly he found himself crouched
behind a little bush, the only cover available on the plateau.
Knowing there were Germans nearby he didn't want to go
around it. So he went through it. The deafening clamor of the
firefight would mask any noise he made, even to an enemy positioned only a few feet away, he reasoned. But just as he dove
into the bush, an unexpected pause in the fighting brought an
eerie silence. "As will happen only in a war, suddenly—and just
for a fleeting moment—all war-like noises ceased," Dauphinais
wrote. The prairie-bred private likened the din he made to "a
rogue elephant, crashing along my path." Sure enough, the
noise alerted the Germans hiding among the rocks on either
side of him, who turned their guns in his direction. "I saw
more muzzle flashes in the next few moments than I was to
see for a long time afterward," he said. But Dauphinais survived the hail of bullets by keeping low. Still, rock chips sprayed

his face and a bullet hit him above the left elbow. All he could do was lie flat and bleed.

Somewhere out in front, Sergeant Percy Crichlow, the Barbados-born Rhodes Scholar, heard firing break out and dashed forward. Dawn was just breaking and visibility was still poor. At one point the plateau's bowl deepened considerably, and Crichlow descended into it with two men: Sergeant Deyette and Private Daigle (a different Daigle from Frenchie in 3rd Platoon). Daigle seemed to have disappeared, but Crichlow heard Deyette's voice call from nearby, "They're below here." Crichlow moved in the direction of the voice and found Deyette on the ground with a hole in his forehead, breathing hoarsely. Deyette died, and the next time Crichlow saw Daigle, he was dead as well.

The Force men had entered battle for the first time, and the utter panic and confusion transformed them quickly from green soldiers into killers. Morning arrived, and daylight, no matter how rainy and dim, transformed the battle into a frantic brawl, and made it clear what a mean, small place the plateau was.

Joe Glass received no orders from his officers, nor did he work in unison with another Force man. He never regained contact with his section. He fought for his life, ducking from and firing at the Germans, who seemed to appear everywhere he turned. The enemy was at times terrifyingly close. "I came face-to-face with [them]," recalled Glass, who was forced to fight his first battle at close range. At one point Joe turned to find a German pointing a rifle at him. The German was standing point-blank, so close that Joe could smell him. There was no time to move. Joe peered into the muzzle and realized what was going to happen. The German shot at him. And missed. In the frenzied second that followed, Joe ducked away—and found himself facing another enemy.

At crucial moments, the limited space of the plateau worked in the Force's favor. Many of the Germans had been bunched in their fortifications of rock and timber, and in some cases, according to reports, the men simply aimed at concentrations of enemy and opened fire. But Force men were falling as well. The left side of the plateau, where so many 1-2 men had moved, offered little cover, and the Force men who were there when the firefight erupted found themselves exposed. At the beginning of the battle, Joe Glass, fighting on the right side, was just as vulnerable. Only providence had saved him. Standing in front of a crowd of Germans ready to kill him, he watched them crumple and die from wild, careening bullets shot from weapons other than his. But eventually Joe and other Force men on the right, like Don MacKinnon, found a low ridge of rock they could crouch behind and fire from.

Their desperate firing paid off. An hour into the firefight, the FSSF had begun to push the Panzergrenadiers back. The Germans had been surprised, but they were masters of the counterattack, and could always be expected to retaliate. Some Germans were still making a stand on the southern half while others had retreated onto the ridgeline, where half of the contingent of the 129th had been positioned. Still others sought out positions behind particularly jagged boulders, and used these as vantage points from which to snipe at the Force men. But gradually, and then suddenly, the battle turned into a German rout. White flags began to rise from behind rocks all around the edge of the plateau. Many Germans were surrendering, but not all.

From his low vantage point behind a boulder, Joe could see rags waving like flags. But among them, he spotted a single German who was refusing to give up. Joe could see him clearly. He seemed crazed, and shot with a machine pistol at anything that moved. He was only about six meters away from Glass, who realized that if he edged around the rock he was lying behind, he could zero in on the sniper perfectly.

Joe gripped his rifle and—careful to keep the barrel below the rock, where it couldn't be spotted—pivoted to the right. As Glass rolled onto his stomach, he leveled his M1 through the slit between two boulders, and almost shot Jimmy Flack, who was crawling like a lizard out in front of him, perhaps himself trying to find a charmed spot from which to surprise the holdout sniper. Glass shouted at him to "get the hell out of the way." He raised his eyes to take a shot, and saw that the German had already taken aim at him.

It was the last thing Glass saw clearly for a long while. The spurt of bullets ricocheted from rocks on either side of him, spraying granite into his eyes and face. Another bullet clipped, but didn't quite sever, his thumb as it passed by the fist of his firing hand. The force of the shot drove Joe back around the rock, where he lay as low as he could, helplessly blind.

A moment later, Joe's left eye started to clear, and he swung around to try again. But every time Glass shifted to take a shot, the German spotted him and opened fire, forcing Joe back down. The German seemed to have drawn a relentless bead on his position, and Glass wasn't his only target; somehow Joe knew that Don MacKinnon was to his right. And just then Captain Rothlin crawled up from the rear, with Syd Gath close behind.

MacKinnon, for his part, registered the arrival of Gath, a close friend, and the four men huddled behind the cover. Rothlin turned to Glass, who was bleeding from the face and hand, and asked, "How ya doin', Joe?" So Joe told him: "There's white flags goin' up all over the place, but there's this one German who's not giving up." He told Rothlin the German was just on the other side of the rock, warning him for God's sake not to look, because the German had his sights on them.

Surrendering to the irresistible, Rothlin and Gath looked. Both soldiers raised their heads above the rock to catch a glimpse of the enemy, and almost in the same instant bullets tore into both their foreheads. They didn't so much die, they simply ceased, according to Glass, "folding" gently to the ground. Had it not been for the blood and brains that emptied all over Joe and his rifle, he might have thought they were slumbering. They died so quietly that MacKinnon, facing slightly to the left, felt the weight of Gath's body and shouted, "For God's sake, Syd, you're leaning on me," before turning to him and pushing him away. And as he pushed, Syd's head shifted position and MacKinnon could see the aperture in his skull.

Joe roused himself, grabbed his rifle, and removed some grenades from Rothlin's body with the intention of lobbing them at the sniper. He crawled up to MacKinnon, who had just discovered Gath.

"I'm scared, Joe," MacKinnon said.

Then Joe did the only thing he could think to do. He lit cigarettes for both of them. Glass never got to use his grenades against the sniper. Suddenly the German was gone—perhaps killed by Jimmy Flack, though he never thought to ask him. Ironically, Rothlin's death corresponded with the end of the major combat. In barely two hours the Force men had taken the summit that had repelled divisions for weeks.

———

Shortly after the summit was secured, Lieutenant Colonel Tom MacWilliam ordered his battalion to line up and prepare to rush out onto the ridgeline so as to continue the advance to the neighboring peak, Remetanea. Major Ed Thomas was at the rear of the column, MacWilliam and about six members of his HQ at the head. Although the last of the enemy had been driven onto the ridgeline, sniper and mortar fire still menaced the Force men. MacWilliam and his battalion now owned the top of Difensa, but they weren't any safer. Their position was vulnerable and dangerously fluid, and would remain this way until both the ridge-line and Remetanea were cleared of the enemy.

For this reason, MacWilliam was determined to press on with the attack despite his casualties, and diminishing ammunition supplies. The entire battle was now in MacWilliam's hands. Shortly before, he had sent Private Hunt to the rear to get orders from 2nd Regiment's commander, Colonel Williamson. Hunt found the colonel near the cliffs. But the commander was badly shaken by the violence and morbidly concerned with sniper fire. According to Hunt, Williamson was "out of commission," and when he returned and reported Williamson's condition to MacWilliam, his CO simply nodded. MacWilliam had already deter-mined with 2nd Battalion commander, Lieutenant Colonel Bob Moore, that when Williamson was not on the hill, MacWilliam, as the senior of the two battalion commanders, was in charge. Now he was about to lead the charge against Remetanea. Shouting "Let's go," MacWilliam began racing toward the edge of the plateau. The column was moving forward, and MacWilliam wanted to be at the cusp of the ridgeline to direct the attack. The six men had just started out when there was an explosion that stopped the attackers in their tracks.

Farther down the line, Major Thomas sensed trouble the moment the advance had stalled and did not start up again. After a few minutes of waiting, Thomas jogged to the front of the line to see what had happened. What he found was almost unbeliev-able: his close friend Tom MacWilliam was dead. A mortar shell had exploded beside MacWilliam and the others as they raced forward, killing the lieutenant colonel, his operations sergeant, Carl Siebels, and Sergeant G. S. Dewey. The others in his entourage, including his young runner and bodyguard, Private Stu Hunt, were seriously wounded. He had been barely four feet from MacWilliam when he died. Somehow the explosion that killed MacWilliam had spared him. As Thomas worked to put order back into the battalion in order to continue its advance, Colonel Frederick appeared.

Frederick accepted the news of the deaths of MacWilliam and Rothlin quietly, and after conferring with Major Thomas about ammunition stores, he ordered that the Remetanea attack be postponed. By evening they would be resupplied with bullets, and Thomas could resume the attack the next day.

In the meantime, the Force's tenure on the peak remained precarious. The Germans continued to rain fire onto them from the ridgeline, which they controlled. To make matters worse, the sky continued to drizzle, and the alpine air remained bitingly cold.

Amid the fire, Joe Glass, barely able to see from his good eye and nursing a swollen, bleeding hand, wandered the summit, checking on friends. He found Sergeant McGinty and Joe Dauphinais, who had miraculously survived when he stumbled across German lines, and narrowly escaped being shot by Herby Forester as he clawed his way back. Both soldiers had wounds in their arms that were serious but not life-threatening. Pop Lewis, the thirty-something oldster from Butte, was in worse shape. He had a thick bullet wound across his back that had severed muscle and almost opened a kidney. Don Fisher had been completely blinded from a spray of rock similar to that which had partially blinded Joe.

Sergeant Kotenko died, but not quickly. The section leader lingered, unconscious and mortally wounded, as an aid man worked to revive him. Don MacKinnon stood off to the side and watched wistfully as his former sergeant faded away. For a boy soldier like MacKinnon, the death of one of the platoon's leaders was difficult to fathom and accept. The medic must have felt the same way, because it took him a long time to give up on Kotenko.

As Joe stumbled around, he found Private Suotaila, one of the quiet kids in the outfit, who in Helena always preferred staying on base to going into town on the weekends. Suotaila too was dead, and in his last moments had spit out his false teeth, which were lying beside his face. Edwards, the best gambler in Joe's platoon, had also been caught out in the open, and was dead. Edwards's long string of luck ended that morning, and Joe could only think how he had just borrowed fifty cents from Edwards to buy a pack of cigarettes and now could never pay him back.

Van Ausdale and Fenton, two men who should have been dead, emerged from the carnage alive. Van Ausdale didn't have a scratch even though he had led a bayonet attack into a "cave" bunker at the summit's apex. Lieutenant Piette also survived, and marched the battlefield triumphantly. "So these are the German supermen," Piette said, strolling among German prisoners, "who are supposed to be so tough."

Once 2nd Regiment had secured Difensa's summit, 3rd Regiment's war was just starting. Assuming a support position, the men of 3rd immediately began ferrying supplies of ammunition, water, and medicine up the slope of Difensa, so steep and treacherous in places that pack mules couldn't negotiate it. The Service Battalion also transported supplies and empty stretchers that would bring back wounded. The men of 3rd acted as their own beasts of burden, lugging five-gallon jerry cans of water in their fists, and straining under pack boards weighed down with bullets, mortars, and grenades.

The climb was exhausting and seemingly endless, taking the men, who climbed in groups of about five men, eight hours to scramble from the base to the summit. Lieutenant Chet Ross, a 25-year-old platoon commander in 2-3, had not scrambled far through sleet and rain when he realized his leather jump boots were utterly soaked, and rubbing his feet raw. Others in 3rd Regiment braved sniper fire and shrapnel from mortars that the enemy, which still controlled the ridgeline and Monte la

Remetanea, were able to lob down. But most of the regiment's casualties were from sheer exhaustion. At 5 p.m. Corporal Sam Magee of 6-3 was among the first of the 3rd Regiment to reach the summit. When he and the four others in his group mounted the rope lines on the cliffs, Magee was astonished by what his 2nd Regiment comrades had managed to do in the dead of night, but knew "we [in 3rd Regiment] would have done the same" if called upon. When Chet Ross arrived at the cliffs he was limping but otherwise unhurt. During his eight-hour march to the peak one of his wet jump boots had dug a silver-dollar-sized hole into his sole. When he emerged on the summit, the scene that greeted him was infinitely more painful than trench foot. Ross's nostrils filled with the smell of cordite, and his ears with the moaning of wounded and dying men.

Each man who pulled himself up the ropeline and witnessed Difensa after the battle experienced his own unique dread. When Tom O'Brien, a 28-year-old salesman for Kraft Foods from Toronto, arrived, combat had ended, and dead men lay on the rocks. O'Brien looked them over, recognized faces, and remembered drinking with a few of them only days before. Right then he made a decision: "It's time for us to do some killing of our own." When Lieutenant Roy Cuff arrived at the summit, he stepped into a curiously peaceful place. The mist that covered sections of the plateau opened at one spot and revealed a few of the boys who were quietly sleeping after the fight. Only later did Cuff realize these snoozing soldiers were corpses. Most of the dead were Germans: about 75 in total. By comparison, the first hours of the battle for Difensa had killed about 20 Force men and wounded another 160.

Force men were still dying on Difensa from fire from Remetanea and its ridgeline. But they were also vulnerable from the south. Along with the materiel ferried to the top by 3rd Regiment came a message from Colonel Paul Adams, Frederick's second-in-command who was overseeing the battle from the Force HQ below the mountain. The British assault on Camino, the peak looming to the south, had not been as successful as the Difensa operation, Adams reported. Camino's peak was no longer in British hands. The British Fifty-sixth Division had attacked during the night, and by morning had occupied the monastery. But only briefly. A German counterattack had driven the Brits off the top, and back onto the treacherously steep southern slope. The enemy across the mountain complex, as one Force man said, "fought just like they didn't have any intention of losing the war."

The Panzergrenadiers' dogged defense of the mountain had earned the grudging respect of the entire Fifth Army. But some of the prisoners on Difensa earned gratitude as well, for unexpected gestures of soldierly goodwill. One young Panzergrenadier medic offered to stay on the summit and attend to wounded Force men. Sergeant Bill Story watched him save a Force man's life by covering a sucking chest wound with a patch torn from a poncho. Eight German prisoners helped carry litters of badly wounded soldiers down the cliffs and mountainside. When Colonel Frederick met them at the aid station, he shook the hands of each of the enemy and thanked them for saving his men.

Private Lorin Waling survived the day's battle. He had helped retrieve Kotenko's dying body from the south side of the plateau while mortar fire was raining in, and later went looking for Sergeant Boodleman. He found him sitting on a rock beside the regimental commander, Colonel Williamson, who stared at a line of dead Force men and wept: "Oh my boys. Oh my boys."

That night the men bedded down with the wounded and the dead on Difensa's newly conquered plateau and tried to sleep. The Germans fired at them with mortars and the dreaded *Nebelwerfer* rockets, whose sound had earned them the nickname

"Screaming Meemies." The next day, Major Ed Thomas left the battle after receiving a bayonet wound to the leg. Because the British had been unable to seize Camino, the Force once again postponed their action against Remetanea, although the Force men did bring the battle to the ridgeline.

Remetanea did not fall until December 6, when 1st Regiment was dispatched to the summit to bolster 2nd Regiment in the attacks. On December 7, FSSF patrols rendezvoused on the ridgeline with British soldiers who had finally been able to secure Camino. On December 8, relieved by the 142nd Infantry, 2nd Regiment began their long march back down the hillside.

———

Joe arrived at the field dressing station realizing that the Force's first battle had been brutal for everyone, not just 1-2. So when a doctor offered Joe a blood plasma can half full of whiskey, he drank it, and then resumed his march down the hill "drunk as a skunk."

By the time the Force left the mountain, casualties from all three regiments would add up to 73 dead, 429 wounded, and 9 missing. So grueling were the conditions, many men who escaped bullets nevertheless found themselves casualties. Out of a unit of commandos in peak physical condition, more than a hundred were hospitalized for exhaustion; others were taken from the line to be treated for trench foot. In total, the casualties were almost the size of a regiment.

Joe Glass recuperated quickly. After collapsing in a hospital, he woke up the next morning clean, wearing fresh clothes, and feeling renewed.

Mark Radcliffe, struck in the forehead with shrapnel seconds into the battle on December 3, had survived as well. The long sliver had pierced the bone but had not cut into his brain; his wound was harmless, though it looked ghastly.

When he entered an aid station with the metal protruding from his head, a doctor, unnerved by the strange sight, began treating him but couldn't stop trembling. Finally, Radcliffe shouted: "What are you shaking for? I'm the patient."

"But you're my first one."

CHAPTER 7

TELEGRAMS

The firefight on Monte la Difensa resonated across North America.

In Moncton, New Brunswick, a single mortar detonating on the crag's summit reverberated in a knock on a front door. Harriet MacWilliam, a "camp follower," as one officer described her, who had journeyed to Helena, Norfolk, and Burlington to be with her husband, had returned to the Moncton home of her parents after Lieutenant Colonel Tom MacWilliam, commander of 2nd Regiment's 1st Battalion, and formerly of the New Brunswick Rangers, was shipped overseas. Just shy of her thirtieth birthday, Harriet had already established a career as a teacher. But in the early winter of 1943 she was facing an indefinite absence from work; she was pregnant. Though her husband was far away and in danger, she had few immediate worries. She had her family, and of course, Tom's parents and four older sisters lived in the nearby hamlet of Cails Mills. But Harriet MacWilliam had no idea how dramatically her life would change until that day in late December 1943 when a caller appeared at the door of her parents' home with a telegram.

———

While rain and metal descended on Monte la Difensa, snow fell on Helena, Montana, during a winter that was memorably deep and frigid.

A thick crust of white covered everything; men and women, heavily bundled, waddled when they moved down icy walks; and cars, leaving dirty clouds of exhaust behind them, rolled gingerly along Helena's frozen streets. But despite appearances, the community did not feel quite the same after the Force had left Fort Harrison. The saloons of Helena were again the sole domain of cowboys and miners. Weekend nights at the Montana Club, which had become the Force's unofficial officers' mess, were no longer uniform-studded affairs crowded with young men and women and resonating with their laughter. The absence of the Force men was felt in the most unlikely of places, such as the Union Bank and Trust Company, managed by the 53-year-old town father, Alfred Hibbard.

The whole town knew how Hibbard had befriended many of the officers and soldiers who had walked into his bank as potential customers, causing Hibbard to defy any moneylender's best instincts by making it Union Bank policy to give the Force men loans ahead of pay almost any time they asked. According to some, it was Hibbard who had smoothed the way for Force officers to have access to the Montana Club. And perhaps out of simple hospitality, Hibbard displayed an interest in the Canadians. He had grown to like boys like Jimmy Ariott, a first lieutenant from London, Ontario. He seemed to revel in the unions taking place between the men and the local daughters. When Lieutenant W. R. Bennett, a Toronto man attached to 5th Company–2nd Regiment, married a local girl in November, Hibbard and his wife hosted the reception in their home. Gray, and always nattily attired, Hibbard may have looked like Lionel Barrymore, but in the wonderful life that was 1940s Helena, his demeanor was more like that of Jimmy Stewart's George Bailey. For Hibbard, a bank's purpose was to build the community, and bolster people's lives. He would even say: "The banker is the closest person to the residents of any community, except members of the family." He was a man who could only have missed the excitement that had left the town, and his parlor, when the Force shipped out.

The cavernous space inside the Cathedral of Sacred Hearts of Jesus and Mary that loomed over Helena on Catholic Hill echoed with the names of Force men at least once a day. Georgina Morgan visited to pray for her new husband Roland "R. O." Morgan, an enlisted man in 1st Regiment. She went to Mass daily, got down on her knees, and prayed for God to "let R. O. keep his arms and legs."

The absence of the soldiers was apparent even in the smallest crannies of East Helena. Eddy's Bakery had once employed three Force men's wives. Local girl Dorothy Strainer, now Dorothy Glass, had left her job at Eddy's in order to have her baby son.

In the beginning, motherhood gave Dorothy a reprieve from wage labor she had never before experienced. Like many others of her generation, Dorothy's girlhood had been short. She knew little else but work. Her immigrant father had found a job in East Helena's smelter only to break his neck doing some after-hours ranch work. Pa wore a cast for a year. When it came off, he was never right again. Barely in her teens, Dorothy quit school to earn money for her family. At first she picked potatoes in the valley, working her way up mile-long rows, filling a seemingly bottomless sack. Later she landed a job as a nanny for a well-to-do family who lived on Eleventh Avenue in Helena. She stayed in Helena during the week but spent every Thursday, her day off, at home after signing over her paycheck to Ma and Pa. After the nanny job, Dorothy worked behind the bar at the Casino club. She was sixteen years old. After that, it was Woolworth's. Then she found work at Eddy's Bakery. And then the soldiers arrived at Fort Harrison, and with them Joe Glass, and now her life revolved around their newborn son, Charles.

Dorothy would soon be leaving East Helena completely. She planned to move to Sarnia, Ontario, and live with her husband's parents. She wouldn't be the only Force man's wife to move away in the soldiers' wake. Steffie had already left town for a lucrative factory job elsewhere. And all the other Force wives who had worked in Eddy's Bakery had moved on as well. Bea Pederson, wife of Oli Pederson, returned home. Dora, Art Arsennek's wife, whom Dorothy and everyone else called Bucky, returned to St. Catharines, Ontario.

Dora wasn't called Bucky until she met Art Arsennek, who categorically refused to utter the name Dora, dwelling instead on her surname, Buckley, or Bucky for short. She was Bucky to him, and in Helena she became Bucky to the other soldiers and soldiers' wives. The sense of humor that inspired Art to give her this nickname had been the reason for their short courtship and rapid marriage. Art had worked at McKinnon's car factory in St. Catharines. Dora had met him through friends and was instantly drawn to him. His character seemed always focused on eking as much joy out of life as possible. He loved to sing, country and western being his genre of choice; he constantly joked; and he had intriguing talents: he could sketch well; was able to turn a witty phrase, and composed poetry. He was thin, as lean as the Depression itself, but wholesomely good-looking.

They married in 1942. Art enlisted in the army. Approaching his twenty-first birthday, Art had known he would probably be called up, and reasoned that by enlisting he could at least choose where he would serve. So Art joined the army, was posted to Camp Borden, near Barrie, Ontario, and volunteered for the parachute battalion that would eventually become the First Special Service Force.

Art was in Helena just days in August 1942 when Bucky realized how excited he was about this unit. "I got my wings," he told her over the phone. "I jumped three times in three days."

Dora was content to live out the war in St. Catharines, awaiting her husband's return. The thought of traveling to distant Helena seemed impossible even after Art had sent for her, telling her that other wives had come. Finally, another Force man's spouse wrote her a letter, certainly at Art's urging, explaining how lonely Art was, and convinced her. Dora Arsennek climbed aboard a train and, with thirty dollars in her pocket, the most she could bring along for a month-long stay, headed toward Helena. Eventually she found a job at Eddy's Bakery, and a two-room apartment where she and her husband could be alone. Whether approved by his superiors or not, Art spent most nights of the week with her in Helena. On weekends they rollicked with other couples, including Joe Glass and Dorothy Strainer and Bea and Oli Pederson, whom they knew through Eddy's. But they also spent time with Art's friends in the 1st Company–1st Regiment, like D. C. Byrom—or Dee for short—from Fort Worth, Texas. Large and lumbering, Byrom was a real Texan, as spirited and colorful as Art. And because Dee's wife, Joanne, or Jo, had come to Helena, Art and Dora (or Poison and Bucky, as their nicknames went) could socialize with them as a couple.

As a group, they cruised saloons such as the Casino and Tavern, or they bowled, or they congregated in someone's apartment.

Every time Dora's mother sent a letter, she included a ten-dollar bill, which easily funded a weekend of entertainment.

But the revelry did not last much longer than Dora's thirty-day visa. She had arrived in the spring of 1943, and soon afterward Art, Dee, and the other men left for Norfolk for amphibious training. Dora returned home to St. Catharines. After the Kiska operation, she saw Art in Burlington, Vermont, and there he entrusted her with a prized possession: his solid-silver jump wings. "I don't want to take these overseas," he said. "They might get lost or stolen."

Dora returned to her factory job in St. Catharines, and waited for word. Art was good about writing, and when he settled in, he would send a letter. In the meantime, Dora kept in contact with the other wives. She wrote to Jo Byrom in Texas, and to Bea Pederson in Hamilton, and to Dorothy Glass in Helena. She waited.

Autumn had disappeared and winter had fully arrived and Dora was at work when she heard the news quite by accident. A woman in the factory knew George Bradley, a Force man from nearby Ridgeville, Ontario, and Dora overheard her say that Bradley's family had just received a telegram: he'd been wounded in Italy. The men were in combat. Distraught, Dora phoned her mother from the factory. Because Dora was so upset, her mom wanted her to come home. But Dora said no, she'd finish her shift. At home she'd spend the day worrying; at the factory she'd be able to occupy herself. Soon after, she decided to inform the other wives, just in case they hadn't heard. She composed a Christmas card for Jo Byrom in Texas. "Merry Christmas Jo," she wrote. "This season we have to pray for our men because I've just heard that they—Art, Dee, Oli, and the rest—are in action in Italy. You'll let me know if you hear anything, and of course I'll do the same."

A little later, Dora received a letter from Fort Worth, Texas.

Art, Dee, and Oli were all in 1st Regiment, and on the morning of December 3 the regiment was mobilized, in reserve under the Thirty-sixth Infantry. The morning was still dark when the regiment started on its way up the mountain. The men were being dispatched because radio transmissions received at Thirty-sixth Infantry HQ seemed to suggest that both the Difensa and Remetanea peaks had been conquered that morning, and that 2nd Regiment, which had done the conquering, would need reinforcements. None of the senior officers—not 1st Regiment commander, Colonel Cookman "Cooky" Marshall, or 2nd Battalion's Lieutenant Colonel, J. F. R. "Jack" Akehurst, or 4th Company's G. W. "Gerry" McFadden—knew that this was a mistake, that Remetanea—Hill 907—had not been taken, and that they and the regiment were being ordered up a mountainside fully controlled by the enemy.*

But they knew something was up. The officers ordered absolute quiet as the men marched single file up the trail in utter darkness. The column was so blind that each man held the bayonet sheath of the soldier in front of him. This is how Art Arsennek, Dee Byrom, and Herb Peppard of Truro, Nova Scotia, crept up the mountain, clinging to the daggers of the men a step ahead of them.

A handsome, square-jawed kid, one of nine children, Peppard had come to the Force late. He had been part of a group of ninety-seven volunteers from the elite First Canadian

---

* Thirty-sixth Infantry's confusion over what hills had been taken that morning persisted for at least twenty years after the war. The army's 1969 history of the Dec. 3, 1942 battle states: "During the day, the leading regiment continued beyond Hill 960 toward a high and broken ridge, Monte la Remetanea, which overlooks part of Monte Maggiore . . . [T]he large area held by the 1st Special Service Force prompted General Wilbur . . . to use the reserve regiment." Martin Blumenson, *Salerno to Cassino* (Washington: US Army Office of Military History, 1969), p. 266. In fact, the FSSF did not occupy Remetanea until three days later.

Parachute Battalion, which was completing jump training at Fort Benning. Peppard and the others arrived at Fort Harrison on December 10, 1942, and immediately settled in. As an unmarried Force man, Peppard would have little opportunity to get to know Force wives such as Dora Arsennek, Jo Byrom, and Bea Pederson; he was too busy getting into trouble. Once, he and sixteen other men had decided to celebrate a windfall in back pay (an astonishing $123) by going AWOL and returning home for an unscheduled visit. (One of the ringleaders was Spud Wright, who grew up with Lorin Waling in Grande Prairie.) The seventeen planned their break well, and had somehow even forged passes. They boarded a bus, and made a stop at Shelby, Montana, just short of the Canadian border, for what seemed to be a customs inspection. Customs was actually the local sheriff's office, which had been instructed to watch for the errant soldiers and hold them—until military police could be dispatched.

Instead of enjoying an AWOL holiday, Herb found himself in a jail cell, sitting on the cold floor, playing cards. The sheriff and the town fathers were so pleased to have soldiers in their midst that they offered the boys a deal. They could go to the movies, have dinner in any restaurant, swill drinks in any bar, and all for free, courtesy of the town. The only condition, said the sheriff: you have to promise us you won't try to get away. Peppard and the others gave their word, and kept it. They went out on the town in Shelby, returned to Fort Harrison the next morning and took their lumps. Now, on December 3, [1943], they were marching in a column, blind as a child bride, up a mountainside in central Italy.

On that morning Peppard's only connection to Bucky Arsennek, Bea Pederson, and Jo Byrom was a fearful voice he heard behind him as he marched. "I was born to be a lover not a soldier," the voice said. "I was born to be a lover not a soldier."

The voice belonged to Sergeant Dee Byrom, Jo's Dee, the hulking and hard-hitting Texan in the company, and he repeated these words like a mantra.

"I was born to be a lover not a soldier."

Peppard didn't like what he was hearing. Byrom's words were, as he would later write, "unnatural."

Dee only stopped muttering when the shelling began, and mortar after mortar fell squarely onto the column, butchering the regiment. From a position of total blindness Peppard suddenly found the world illuminated in intense flashes that revealed men's bodies coming apart. The sounds that this violence occasioned were just as dumbfounding. Even if Dee had still been mumbling, he wouldn't be heard anymore over the screams, like those of one boy, gutted from shrapnel, certainly dying, who cried out: "Mama, mama, mama." Peppard would later note that this boy's words were not so much a cry of pain as a plea for help to "the person dearest to him in the world." Amid the screams, Peppard heard the order to dig in and, soon after, another to withdraw down the mountain.

The next day, Peppard volunteered to join a group of men who climbed back up the same trail wearing Red Cross bands on their sleeves and carrying litters. Unarmed, Peppard and the others retrieved the wounded, gambling that the enemy, high above them, would see their arm bands and understand their benign purpose. They brought back the injured men, some delirious from pain, others delirious from gratitude. Afterward they brought back what dead they could find, most of them in pieces.

On December 4, Joe Glass ran into his friend Lieutenant Herb Goodwin of Elmira, Ontario. He and Joe had met before either had heard of the FSSF, when Goodwin has been in the Scots Fusiliers of Canada. Now the young officer was pale with grief. "Joe, I can't believe it," he said. "I damn near lost all my men."

———

The letter Dora Arsennek received from Fort Worth bore an unfamiliar return address. After opening it, she immediately realized the correspondent was Jo Byrom's mother.

"I am writing on behalf of my daughter Joanne," the letter began, "to tell you that Jo's husband Dee is dead." The letter said Jo had received a cable on Christmas Eve notifying her that Dee had been killed in action on December 3. The cable did not explain that the maiden battle in which Dee had died had sapped the 1st Regiment of 40 percent of its strength. The cable would not have contained his last words, either, which only a few comrades like Herb Peppard heard before the mortars began to fall. Peppard did not see Byrom on the trail, but he would learn about his fate. One of the shells, Peppard was told, had killed the big Texan instantly.

———

A. T. Hibbard received no telegrams. But Helena was a small town, and word got to him quickly of the deaths of other boys, like Sergeant A. O. Gunderson, who had married a Helena girl and was one of two soldiers from 2-2 who had been cut down in the initial predawn attack on Monte la Difensa. Also dead was Jimmy Ariott of 6th Company–2nd Regiment, who died on the second day of the Difensa operation. These bleak announcements would not be the last.

With death very much on his mind, Frederick wrote Hibbard only days after Gunderson and Ariott and all the others had been killed in the Force's first operation. His words put Hibbard on notice. The Force's sojourn in Helena, a winsome summer in all of their lives, was over. "The Force has already been in action," Frederick wrote, "and, as must happen, has left some of its members fallen in battle. Future operations will certainly result in others of our ranks dying in combat." And then Frederick raised the issue of a fund of money that his men had collected when the cruiser USS *Helena* was sunk near Guadalcanal in 1942. The Force men had donated the cash for the construction of a new cruiser, but the navy returned their check and suggested the money be invested in war bonds. Frederick now proposed the fund "be used for the erection of a memorial to those members of the Force who die in combat operations."

Frederick's words, and the news that Ariott and Gunderson had died, cut Hibbard deeply. "Your letter of December 13 has brought a great surge of emotion to us," Hibbard wrote Frederick. "As a matter of fact, the whole community has been on edge, eagerly awaiting news after we knew the Force was in action . . ."

———

Harriet MacWilliam in Moncton may have been on edge over practical matters when news reached her of her husband's death through the telegram delivered to her home. After the initial horror and grief, she would be consumed by one question: Had Tom received her letter informing him that she was pregnant before he died?

Ultimately, Harriet would write Major Ed Thomas, Tom's good friend and Executive Officer, and pose this question to him. Thomas knew the answer. There had indeed been a mail delivery on the brink of the Difensa operation. But it had been a delivery for the American Force men only. The Canadians had not received letters, and as far as Thomas knew, Lieutenant Colonel MacWilliam had gone to his death never knowing his wife was expecting. Thomas would describe the letter he wrote in response to Harriet's as one of "the most difficult" of his life.

For the Force men, there would be more difficult times to come. It was December 1943, and a long year of fighting lay before them.

CHAPTER 8

MAJO

At 10 a.m. on December 12, the First Special Service Force gathered for a reflective pause. A memorial service was held on the Force's base near Santa Maria Capua Vetere, and the survivors of the Force's first battle stood solemnly in ranks in front of their barracks.

The base was still ramshackle, but it was more livable than before. While the combat echelon had been on Difensa, service battalion carpenters had patched up the building as best they could. And recently tents had been erected offering hot showers for the soldiers who—weary, wounded, and now freshly laundered—turned out for this parade to honor the seventy-three men who had died on the mountain that stood in the distance. The service battalion band sounded dirges and marches as living men thanked God they were not dead, and others simply asked themselves why. Even among the highly trained men of the FSSF, survival was often no more than luck.

Colonel Frederick stood at the head of the formation alongside the tall, lanky figure of Fifth Army commander, Lieutenant General Mark W. Clark, and inspected the survivors. The parade included both the able-bodied and the wounded. Only those men languishing in hospital beds and graves were absent. As in past days, the weather threatened to turn the Italian campaign into a muddy reprise of the Somme. The rain fell on Frederick's three regiments, each of which clearly bore the scars of the last battle. When Frederick took in 2nd Regiment, he could see just how depleted it had become, particularly 1-2, which had spearheaded the Difensa assault. Third Regiment, where Mark Radcliffe now stood, had also lost men, but the lion's share of its casualties were attributable to exhaustion and trench foot. The latter condition proved critical for Chet Ross, who developed such a serious case while delivering supplies up Difensa that his foot became gangrenous and was almost amputated. The depleted ranks of 1st Regiment, which had been mauled because of a blunder by another divisional commander, had to be particularly troubling for Frederick. In the last days of the battle, ten more from 1st Regiment had fallen while reinforcing 2nd Regiment in the effort to secure Difensa and take the saddle ridge and the adjoining Remetanea peak.

Prayers were offered, and thanks given by General Clark, and Frederick himself addressed the men. Perhaps with the dead of 1st Regiment in mind, Frederick vowed that they would fight on as a single unit, and intimated they would never be wasted by an outside officer again. Despite the losses they had sustained from this onerous mission, they were not "marked men," Frederick said, assuring them that their high casualty rate had not set them apart as a bad-luck outfit or suicide squad.

Herb Peppard, who had listened to Dee Byrom's last lament, absorbed Frederick's words and experienced a moment of elation when General Clark lauded the Force for fulfilling this task. "Most of us thought that his next words would be: 'I'm going to give you all a four-week leave in Naples!'" Peppard wrote in his memoirs. But instead, Clark promised the boys "bigger and better hills to climb."

Bigger and better hills. Monte la Difensa would not be the only misty mountaintop in their campaign.

———

General Clark's promise of more mountains in the Force's future was a tacit admission that the initial objective of the battle on Monte la Difensa had been naïve. General Keyes had told the Force men that if they conquered that crag, the Fifth Army would barrel into the Liri Valley and on to Rome in a matter of weeks. This never happened, mainly because II Corps, for all its might, just couldn't break through. The mouth of the Liri Valley began beyond the village of Mignano. Difensa, which towered to the southwest, was the southern frame of a doorway that was known as the Mignano Gap. And over this threshold ran Highway 6, which connected Mignano to Cassino, best known for the ancient monastery perched on the heights overlooking it, just after crossing a swift moat known as the Rapido River.

On the far, or northern, side of the Gap from Difensa stood another set of crags owned by the Germans. Just how formidable these enemy positions were did not become clear until late on December 7, when the Thirty-sixth Infantry Division advanced on San Pietro, the next village up from Mignano, just off the highway. The fighting Texans were a relatively seasoned lot, but the Germans, who owned mountaintops like Lungo, Sammucro, and Hill 720, which was Sammucro's western ridge, soundly repulsed them at San Pietro. Clearly, the Allies could not make headway toward Cassino and the Liri Valley so long as the Germans controlled the high ground above the route. Uprooting the Germans from Sammucro and Hill 720 became a priority.

By December 22, the Allies had made some progress. Monte Lungo and the village of San Pietro had been won, and the Germans had finally given up Monte Sammucro after a prolonged fight. But the way to Cassino was still far from clear. The Germans remained atop Sammucro's strategically important ridge, Hill 720, and this essential high ground was designated the next objective of the FSSF. By this time, Force men like Radcliffe had been rested and the Force itself temporarily revitalized. First Regiment was earmarked for the assault, with 2nd Battalion under Jack Akehurst chosen to lead the way up. The regiment's 1st Battalion, commanded by another high-ranking Canadian, Lieutenant Colonel R. W. Becket, would back up Akehurst in reserve. At that stage of the war, Akehurst held the distinction of being the highest-ranking Canadian in the outfit. Frederick had sent 2nd Regiment commander, Williamson, formerly the most senior Canadian, back home, having been disappointed by his performance on Difensa.* Some spare men from 2nd Regiment, now commanded by Lieutenant Colonel Bob Moore and still licking its wounds after

---

* By nearly all accounts, Williamson was transferred because Frederick had judged his leadership in the Difensa operation lacking. But Frederick was tight-lipped about Williamson. In the 1963 interview with Robert Adleman, Frederick said of the Williamson matter: "I think that is better forgotten." (Courtesy Adleman Collection, Hoover Institution.) This is a sentiment shared to this day. In 2004, FSSF association executive director, Bill Story, stated: "It is hard for us to talk about Williamson. It's not easy to explain just how disappointed we were in him." A historical appraisal of Williamson comes from Tom MacWilliam, son of the 1st Battalion officer killed on Difensa: "Williamson was an officer who was probably better suited as an organizer and administrator than a combat commander."

the difficult Difensa assault, would act as pack mules in support of the attack.

The attack was set to commence on the holiest day of the year for Germany's Lutheran soldiers: Christmas Eve. However, at the last minute, the attack was postponed until Christmas Day while final details of the operation were being ironed out. The early hours of December 25 might have found the Germans either keenly vigilant or soulfully distracted; Akehurst would never know which. Responding to the Allied artillery barrage from the Sixth Armored Artillery Group and two other artillery battalions that broke out about an hour before the operation was to get under way, the Germans unleashed shelling that began to fall on the slope of Sammucro (above the German positions on Hill 720) where Akehurst and his men, including Herb Peppard, were shivering from the "cold, cold rain" and waiting for the attack to begin. The shelling severed the battalion's lines of communication with the outside world and boxed the attackers in. As intelligence officer Robert Burhans later observed: "Mortar and artillery falling along the line of troops on the black mountainside . . . disorganized the assault battalion to such an extent that no forward movement was possible." Commanders like Captain George McCall and Lieutenant Omar Smith labored in vain to organize their troops amid the chaos. The situation deteriorated further when Akehurst's command post took a direct hit, which killed his adjutant and a reconnaissance officer, and peppered Akehurst's upper body with shrapnel.

With Akehurst severely wounded, the utter collapse of the operation was averted only when regimental leader Colonel "Cooky" Marshall rushed to the area and assumed leadership of the battalion and the assault, which got under way just as dawn was about to break.

In the weak light of their first Christmas in combat, the

freezing, weary men of 2nd Battalion stormed down Sammucro's slope in the direction of the Hill 720 ridge. Although morning had arrived, the men could still see the muzzle flashes of German machine guns in the distance, and they heard their own shells whistling over their heads on their way to the German positions. Fifth and Sixth, the two assault companies, attacked the Germans virtually leaderless. Omar Smith, who had spent the night rallying his men, was hit by a sniper bullet. George McCall took a shrapnel fragment to the neck. But the attack ground on, with 6th Company swinging around from the right and 5th Company squeezing the enemy from the left. According to Burhans, the men of 6th killed Germans in their makeshift bunkers with "well-pitched grenades and covering fire." The men of 5th silenced two machine-gun nests on the top of the ridge as the men of the 504th Parachute Infantry successfully beat the enemy off of the adjoining Hill 687, which was close enough to fire on the attackers. By 7 a.m., the battle was over. Lieutenant Smith lay dead; Captain McCall, despite his serious wounds, was still standing and giving orders.

Christmas had been eventful. The Force had won two hills and generated gifts for home: telegrams alerting the families of sixty-five Force men that their men had either died or been wounded on December 25, 1943.

Grief was also felt in the mountains among the survivors. The dead of Hill 720 included George "Smitty" Smith, Herb Peppard's best friend, who died in a mortar attack. "His death was a terrible blow to me," Peppard would later write. But the mountainous advance to Cassino had moved forward by one more peak.

Now General Clark believed the Fifth Army was able to enter the endgame in the campaign to break the Winter Line. His plan: beginning January 5, the Fifth Army would overwhelm the Germans on the east side of the Rapido River, which barred the

approach to Cassino, and push the enemy defenders into the Liri
Valley itself. This meant yet more summits to be climbed and
attacked. The Force was ordered to continue advancing from
mountaintop to mountaintop, and to eliminate the Germans
from the peaks of Monte la Chiaia and Vischiataro, which stood
over Highway 6 and the right flank of II Corps. Vischiataro, the
westernmost peak, was the focal point of the German line in the
mountains. And looming over it to the northeast: the 12,000-
meter-high spur Monte Majo.

Frederick gave the task of advancing on Vischiataro to Edwin
Walker and 3rd Regiment, which would move on these peaks by
hooking around from the far right of the line. Mark Radcliffe,
whose combat experience thus far had consisted of a single blade
of shrapnel received between the eyes before the battle of
Difensa, was finally embarking on his war. Joe Glass's undermanned 1st Company–2nd Regiment would support 3rd
Regiment by ferrying supplies and carrying their wounded. As
3rd Regiment and Joe's company hooked to the right, 1st Regiment
was assigned to clear the Moscosa Gap, a narrow, gorge-like
mountain pass.

The remainder of 2nd Regiment set its sights on an obscure
crag called Hill 724, which was important only because it overlooked the ancient alpine village of Radicosa, which Frederick
hoped to use as a forward command post for endgame operations on Majo and Vischiataro. A three-man scouting patrol that
had been fired upon as it crept toward Radicosa confirmed that
the Germans still held this tiny community of six stone houses
and a church.

As Adna Underhill later wrote, the plan was elementary:
"Bypass Radicosa on the north and east; take Hill 724 from the
north; consolidate that high ground, then move down into
Radicosa. Cold or no cold," he observed, "this was the kind of
action the Force understood and enjoyed, if there's enjoyment in

any military combat." And it *was* cold. On the night of January 3, when Moore's 2nd Regiment went into action, the Force men mounted the dark slopes of Hill 724 and climbed into weather as formidable as the enemy. The frigid weather that Herb Peppard had complained of days earlier seemed to worsen as a January winter descended on the mountains. "Strong winds whipped up the flat valleys and snow covered the lowlands," wrote intelligence chief, Burhans, in his history of the Force. Up high it was markedly worse. According to Burhans, the men had to plod through ankle-deep snow at the 500-meter altitude and snow-drifts at 600 meters.

Nevertheless, 2nd Regiment managed the climb and—as was becoming the Force's habit—attacked after dark. The advantage of these nighttime approaches became clear as the Force men surprised the Germans of Hill 724, who had been shivering at their posts when they were overwhelmed after what Burhans called a "light firefight." As Underhill observed: "As is rarely the case, everything went as planned." But as on Difensa, the Force men were punished after the battle was over when the enemy began pounding their positions with mortar fire, a barrage that again took the lives of leaders, such as the Canadian second lieutenant Fern Cox, who died instantly when a grenade detonated in his hastily dug foxhole, and first lieutenant D. J. Ekberg, who lived long enough after his wounding to die on a stretcher as it was being manhandled down the hillside.

The Force kept hold of Hill 724, and the next evening a nine-man patrol from Marshall's 1st Regiment crept up and eliminated a series of machine-gun nests on another summit within firing range of Radicosa: Hill 675. Again, cunning won the day. One German machine-gun crew was captured without the firing of a single shot. Marshall's men had virtually crawled into the gun pit with the Germans before giving the order to surrender. A German gunner later recounted: "We were standing alertly at our machine guns when a voice said, 'Hands up!'"

The strategy worked. On January 5, Force scouts again crept up to Radicosa, but this time they were met by silence. With Hills 724 and 675 lost, the Germans in Radicosa, outflanked on both sides, had withdrawn. As planned, Colonel Frederick, dressed in green fatigues and a battle helmet, and looking as nondescript as a private, marched into the tiny ghost town. His presence officially transformed this collection of booby-trapped stone dwellings into the Force HQ. Wide-ranging patrols then pushed and evened out the Allied line to the edge of the enemy.

While 1st and 2nd Regiments were clearing the way for the occupation of Radicosa, Walker's men had been busy as well. They began their advance on January 1 from the slopes of Monte Corno Vetese, and patrolled and bided their time until Radicosa fell. Then, on January 5, they began moving against outposts as well. The weather had not improved. Braving the biting cold, they seized and cleared Hills 968 and 1025. Farther to the south, they wiped out German positions on Hill 850. Placed in the hills to harass and warn rather than make a determined stand, the enemy manning the three positions had put up only modest fights. Underhill wrote: "These German soldiers . . . were cold, tired, disorganized, and confused; they did not act like the disciplined fighting men the Jerries had fielded on La Difensa. The Third [Regiment] patrols overran these outposts, inflicting heavy casualties, and bringing in more than 50 prisoners." One soldier in Underhill's *The Force* notes: "These Krauts who are manning at least part of this line aren't their first line troops . . . Somebody told me that the guys in front of us are Austrians who only like to fight when they're winning."

Third Regiment patrols then crept northwest to the village of Colle Stefano. They expected to find Germans there. Instead they found it empty, but scouts encroaching on the foot of Monte Majo to the north received mortar fire as a greeting. The Germans had pulled back to Majo and ultimately Vischiataro: the Force's target from the beginning of the onslaught. Seizing Vischiataro would complete the mountain campaign. But the key to this position was the mountain that towered over and beside it. This was clear even to young Lieutenant Underhill of 2nd Regiment. "It was evident to Colonel Frederick that in order to take Vischiataro (Hill 1109), his main objective, Mt. Majo must be under Allied control."

For Radcliffe and his men in 3-3, the skirmishes on their advance to Majo and Vischiataro had been agonizing. Estimations that the German outposts they attacked were not being passionately defended did not make the job easier. The men assaulted rocky slopes atop frozen feet, fueled by cold rations, and shivering at night under whatever inadequate bedding was at hand. On January 4, as he led his company through Hills 910 and 950, Mark Radcliffe wrote in his battle report: "[E]stablished a rest camp at the base of the hill out of the bitter wind that was blowing. Platoon drew off 2 men at a time sending them down to get bed rolls, water and rations and to get warm. Bed rolls were dropped too far back, ski mitts were needed, and foot wear was not warm enough."

The worst was yet to come for Radcliffe, now an acting captain, and his company. In the Force's final slog to oust the Germans from Vischiataro, 3-3 was assigned a role in seizing the adjoining heights—an anonymous spur known as Hill 1270, and Majo. So, at 6:15 p.m. on January 6, just as dark was settling on the mountains, Radcliffe found himself leading a column of men up a crag barren of everything except enemies.

Radcliffe's 3-3 ascended on the left of the mountain's attack area, climbing the trail single file; on the right was 2nd

Company–3rd Regiment, led by Captain Weldon B. Perry. Perry's men were actually leading the assault, with Radcliffe's men positioned to hit the enemy on its flank. They were facing a battalion from Germany's 132nd Infantry, an element of the 44th Infantry Division that in turn fell under the divisional umbrella of the expert alpine fighters of the LI Mountain Corps. Advancing in the dead of night in the dead of winter, Radcliffe's company could not depend on the element of surprise. The Germans of the 132nd, if not ready for them, were ready for *something*.

The proximity of the enemy was clear when 3rd Company approached the official Line of Departure (LD) for the operation and an enemy soldier appeared from the shadows. He had either blundered upon Radcliffe's position or—overwhelmed by cold and fear—had come to give himself up. A Force man couldn't be spared to escort the German back to battalion HQ, so the POW joined the column, forced to march in the one direction he most certainly did not want to go.

As the column edged up the mountain, Radcliffe knew that many of the prisoner's comrades-in-arms on Majo's lower slope had already been eliminated in a silent flurry of killing. Majo should have been virtually impenetrable. German machine-gun placements guarded both the summit and the slope, and these guns had been positioned with typical defensive acumen. Guns on the summit covered the flanks of the gun nests located halfway down the slope, which in turn covered a German gun outpost on the mountain's base. Together, these three tiers of gun place-ments made the storming of Majo a costly proposition, one in which men would pay with their lives for every foot of ground. As well, the gun nests lower down on the crag served as an alarm to the troops on the summit. If Radcliffe's 3-3 and the other compa-nies in 1st Battalion were to employ any element of surprise in their attack, these guns had to be taken out, and taken out quietly.

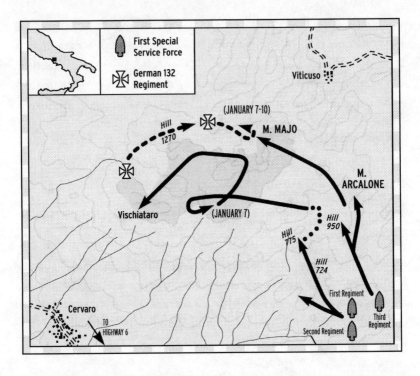

The FSSF's battle for Monte Majo

First Battalion operations and its commander, the 33-year-old Canadian winter war specialist, Tom Gilday, had chewed on this problem and come up with a solution: a secret weapon in the form of a brooding, barrel-chested scout by the name of Sergeant Tommy Prince, an Ojibway Native of the Saulteaux tribe who had spent most of his twenty-eight years on the Brokenhead Reserve at Scanterbury, Manitoba. Prince had reported to Radcliffe's HQ the night before the attack. In his reserved manner, he discussed the mission with Radcliffe, but there was not much to discuss beyond passwords and the exact composition of the squad. Prince's mission was clear: he was to lead a night patrol up Majo's dark slope and eliminate those outposts without the Germans on the summit knowing they had been eliminated.

Radcliffe hadn't known Prince before this mission, and despite his long exposure to the Navajo nation, the officer could not quite read the taciturn soldier. But Gilday had identified Prince as a talent in scouting and close-quarter combat. Like other Force men with Native blood, Prince had brought an impressive repertoire of skills in hunting, tracking, and wilderness survival to the army. However, Tommy Prince's greatest asset was difficult to quantify, and it was probably wrong to label it a technique or skill. He was able to immerse himself in any surroundings, and stalk the enemy with precision.

Radcliffe watched Sergeant Prince, at the head of a patrol, disappear up the slopes of Majo. "He moved just like a shadow," Radcliffe later said. When the patrol came upon the first bunker, Prince—who often silently communicated with other scouts by squeezing the hand of the man behind him (who in turn passed the unspoken message down the line)— signaled for the others to stop and stay still. He then slid into the German bunker and dispatched the gunners single-handedly.

When Prince and his patrol returned to Radcliffe's post before dawn, he reported his mission accomplished: gun pits at the base and in the middle of Majo's slope had been neutralized. There had been some shooting when the patrol first set out. A nervous German sniper had probably spotted some movement or a shadow, and had probed the night with bullets. But Prince's patrol hadn't responded, and instead circumvented the fire and continued undetected with the mission. Radcliffe never knew exactly how Prince neutralized the outposts and the men within them. But as Radcliffe's column made its way past these dark, silent bunkers, he knew that Prince had been successful. The company was marching on Majo's summit without firing a bullet. Prince, he had to admit, had done "a beautiful job."

The column, moving gingerly upward with eight meters between each man, advanced as quietly as it could given that every step of the march produced the footfalls of seventy-two enlisted men and four officers. The cold bit deeper the higher the men climbed. It was unlikely there was a single man in 3rd Company who hadn't been fighting in the past days to stay dry, reasonably warm, and effectively mobile. This meant constant vigilance of the condition of boots and socks. So cruel were the wintry conditions in the mountains just before the column set out that four men from 3-3 had to report to the aid station with frozen feet.

As the column got within a thousand meters of the top, two patrols—from 1st and 3rd Platoons respectively—probed ahead, one moving to the right and the other to the left. As the company neared its objectives on the summit, the patrols needed to be well out in front to—as Radcliffe wrote in his battle report—"prevent ambush, take enemy snipers under fire, and to assist the platoons in taking their objective."

While Radcliffe and his two assault platoons edged up the mountainside behind the patrols (Radcliffe's 2nd Platoon was poised in reserve), the battalion's other two companies were positioning themselves for the final attack, which was scheduled to begin at 11:30 p.m. The entire battalion's assignment was to seize the summit and overwhelm its defenders, which, in addition to Germans, reportedly included a detachment of "Austrians and Poles with the 132nd Regiment." In contrast to the sometimes lackadaisical resistance of their countrymen earlier in the mountain campaign, the Austrians and Poles were expected to fight fiercely according to their "strict orders to hang onto the eminence at all cost."

Like many crags in the Apennine range, Majo's crest did not consist of a single domed summit. Instead, a study of the spur with field glasses from an adjoining peak had revealed that

Majo's main summit was connected to two adjoining peaks by a ridgeline. Most certainly, there was enemy on all three eminences, and battalion commander Gilday ultimately ordered his three companies to seize the entire summit region in a pincer movement. Second Company had been ordered to climb the precipitous northeast slope and attack on the right, while Radcliffe's 3rd Company attacked on the left flank and concentrated its efforts on the two adjacent peaks or "knobs," as some of the officers called them, situated roughly eighty meters to the west of the main peak.

Not long after Radcliffe's two patrols had disappeared up the slope, gunfire from a single weapon sounded. Radcliffe knew that a German sniper had fired on them but was likely shooting at shadows. He decided to lead the column on and worry about the sniper later. Incredibly, with the objective just ahead, this lonesome sniper had been the only opposition the company had faced during their long advance up the mountainside. But 3rd Company's luck didn't hold. A mere twenty-two meters from the top, a cacophony broke Majo's silence. Radcliffe scrambled forward and saw by the light of the glowing moon that the inevitable had happened. He could see that 3rd Platoon's patrol had finally been spotted by a pair of machine-gun nests, and were pinned down, unable to advance or even retreat. The same moon that silhouetted the patrol now illuminated the entire company on Majo's hillside. The enemy gunners knew beyond any doubt that an assault was upon them, and they had to have called for reinforcements. Radcliffe was tempted to send a runner down the hill for more men, but he knew that by the time support troops clawed their way up the mountain, it would be too late.

Suddenly there was movement. Radcliffe realized that two members of a forward patrol, Sergeants Ralph Swisher and John Rich, had sprung into action. Swisher, another tough character

from a small town in Oregon, sprinted toward the gun placement from the left, firing a pistol as he ran. The German
gunners spotted him, and Radcliffe could see the flames spitting
from the enemy barrel as it turned toward Swisher and zeroed
in. Swisher fell, but then immediately pulled out a grenade and
tossed it into the nest. An explosion erupted, and the gun fell
silent.

While Swisher was getting shot, John Rich crawled up to the
side of the second machine-gun nest, lay as flat as a lizard, and
opened up on the Germans with his Thompson. His burst of fire
might have ended the battle right there had his weapon not
immediately jammed. There was Rich, positioned in point-blank
range in front of an enemy bunker, with a submachine gun as
useless as a broom handle. Rich's faulty weapon might have
been providential for the Germans had the man run, panicked,
or hesitated. Instead, Rich pulled out his pistol, opened fire, and
leaped into the machine-gun nest, a fortification the Commonwealth troops called a *sangar*—a barricade fashioned from
stacked stones. Swisher, on legs torn up by German bullets but
still somehow functioning, hobbled up to the gun placement
after Rich and pointed his gun into the nest. A moment later
Rich emerged from it, and both men, together with Radcliffe,
then turned their attention on a German sniper with a machine
pistol, positioned a little farther up the slope. They charged the
position head-on, and the sniper promptly surrendered.

Radcliffe would later nominate both "outstanding NCOs" for
decorations. But at that moment there was a real danger that
none of them would live to tell these tales. In the translucent
night, Radcliffe could see his men scrambling to the top. First
Platoon laid claim to their stretch of ridge to the left of the company's objective after a short, vicious firefight against two more
German gun nests that initially had them pinned down. Half of
2nd Platoon left its reserve position when it saw the trouble,

crept up to the machine guns from the flank, and put them out of action.

Farther down the ridge and the slope, 3rd Platoon, led by Minneapolis native Sergeant Sam Thomas, had less luck with the enemy. Unwilling to give up their position easily, the men of the 3rd badly depleted their ammunition supply in a firefight with the Germans that went on for an hour. Making matters worse, Radcliffe's men were limited in the weaponry they could employ. Because Perry's 2nd Company had not yet taken its objective on Majo's main peak, the men of 3-3 didn't dare use mortars for fear the Germans there would see the muzzle flashes and return fire.

The high-altitude skirmish, which had Thomas and his men clinging to the ridge only forty meters away from the Germans and their objective, tipped in 3rd Platoon's favor when the other half of 2nd Platoon climbed up to support them. Then, as Radcliffe noted in his report: "3rd platoon drove the Germans off and consolidated their objective." While this was happening, Perry's 2nd Company, attacking up the northeast slope, and 1st Company, led by Captain Dan Gallagher (who still quarreled with Radcliffe over who had conquered the top of Pine Mountain during the first exercise at Fort Harrison, way back in July 1942), fought to extinguish the last of the resistance on top by taking on German gun nests firing from the high ground on the northern-most end of the summit. Gallagher's men tried to use the last moments of darkness as cover to storm the enemy gun positions, but the moon—which Burhans described as "full . . . and reflecting starkly off the snow"—revealed them. As a result, 1st Company's fight was particularly costly.

Meanwhile, on the main peak and the ridgeline, the men of 2-3 and 3-3 "scissored back and forth along [its] length cutting out machine gun placements," and driving off the Germans, Poles, and Austrians dug in there, according to Burhans. As expected, none of these troops, the non-Germans included, were eager to withdraw or willing to surrender; Majo and Vischiataro was the end of the line for them. But the swiftness and surprise of the overall attack seemed to catch the enemy off guard.

The Germans who survived the initial onslaught fell back from Majo's peak to a lower ridgeline, which suddenly came under attack from Walker's 2nd Battalion, commanded by Montrealer Lieutenant Colonel John G. Bourne. It was tough going for Bourne's men. Devastating machine-gun fire from a southwest spur cut off and isolated his 6th Company from the main attack force until the rest of the battalion (mainly, Bourne's 4th Company) relieved them by overwhelming these gun posts. When resistance from this fallback line was silenced, it appeared for a moment that the battle had been won. The assault had been a lonely, cold, and deadly drama played out on an otherworldly setting of rock, ice, and snow. After skirmishes that burned fiercely and then died down like a meteor, 3-3 had taken its objective on Monte Majo.

But there would be no time to celebrate. From the top, the men could see silhouettes of enemy reinforcements charging up the slope toward them. They had barely taken Monte Majo and the Germans were already launching their signature counterattack.

———

Depleted and exhausted by its assault on Difensa, 1st Company–2nd Regiment had been placed in reserve, and this was all right with Joe Glass. Private Glass could now see out of his bad eye, but his thumb was proving slow to heal. Joe had not shown the wound, then festering, to a physician in the military hospital for fear that he would be pulled from the line to have it treated. "I saw our boys with so many bad wounds up there, I just couldn't show the doc my thumb," Glass would later explain. He could live with a swollen hand, and he was on the mend. After December 22, when the Force began its long mountain slog in the peaks northeast of Highway 6, Joe was placed on temporary duty to guard Colonel Walker's 3rd Regiment headquarters.

Walker's command post was a stone hut equipped with a radio and a table and maps, and Glass stood guard outside, doing his best to keep warm. When Joe first reported to the HQ for duty, he saw a soldier reclining against the building near the door and assumed he was a guard. It was only after Joe got closer that he realized the guard was actually a dead man whom they were waiting to ferry down the mountain for burial. The sight didn't surprise Joe. "There were dead men all over the place up there," Glass said.

As far as officers went, Joe respected Walker. He was not alone. In time no one would admire Walker more than Colonel Frederick, who must have seen more than a bit of himself in the Texas-born career soldier's obsessive, hands-on leadership style. Like Frederick, Walker, a West Point graduate of 1931, was a chronic worrier who was constantly wandering into 3rd Regiment's areas of operations to be sure all was going according to plan. Walker would get so engaged in an operation that he would refuse to eat, and even Frederick noticed how the man lost weight and "literally wore himself out." Indeed, as the mountain war dragged on, Walker's tall frame seemed to stoop slightly from worry, and his unshaven face took on the lined and world-weary look of a hobo in certain poses. But Frederick saw Walker's propensity to make himself sick for his men as a sign of excellence, and recognized Walker for what he was: "an outstanding soldier." Soldiers like Joe Glass warmed to Walker because of his no-nonsense demeanor. While Glass guarded Walker's command post, artillery started to fall in on top of them and Joe could tell from the sound of the eruptions that the shells were friendly. He ran into the outpost without so much as a knock.

"Colonel, those are our shells," he said.

"Can't be," Walker replied.

"Just listen," Joe said. Walker stepped out the door, cocked an ear to a detonation, and then raced back inside. A moment later he was on the radio to headquarters. And a moment after that, the shelling stopped.

After Radcliffe and 3-3, and Captain Perry and 2-3, had overrun the summit of Monte Majo, Glass and his company were supplying Walker's men with ammunition, medical supplies, food, and water as 3rd Regiment fought to hold this strategically essential crag. Glass and Jimmy Flack had just led a pack mule onto the summit, and were unloading the beast's cargo, when a German counterattack broke out. Germans were storming the slope, mortars were falling, and machine guns screamed.

Amid the crisis, Walker strode up, and Joe—ready to grab a rifle and defend the peak—said, "Can we help?"

"Get off of this mountain," Walker shouted.

Glass and Flack raced back down the rocky slope, narrowly keeping ahead of a persistent German mortar crew, which lobbed rounds that followed the two soldiers like hammer blows all the way down.

For Mark Radcliffe, the elation of seizing his objective was short-lived. The Germans stormed the length of Monte Majo's summit and ridgeline, and threatened to dislodge the Force men, who were nearly out of ammunition. To beat them back quick-thinking Force men turned the barrels of German *Maschinengewehr* 42s (MG42) down the slope and opened fire. The other defenders from 2nd and 3rd Companies lined up along the long edge of the slope, and joined the fray with what bullets they had left. Their fire managed to drive the enemy back down the mountainside. But the Germans, Austrians, and Poles who had just been on

Majo were determined to win back the summit, and perplexed at what was happening. Hearing the distinctive roar of their MG42s, some of them shouted: *"Schiessen Sie nicht! Wir sind es!"* Stop shooting at us, they called, thinking elements of their own army were mistakenly firing on them. Still, the counterattacks kept coming, and when daylight came Radcliffe understood why the Force's grip on the peak was so tenuous. The news came from a sergeant, who told him: "You better take a look at this." Radcliffe was led to a newly erected observation post (OP) on a high knob that directly overlooked a spur on their flank. Germans crawled all over the neighboring ridge. Radcliffe was aghast. The Majo operation had called for elements of 1st Regiment, which included his best friend and best man, Major Tom Pearce, to seize that ridge during the night so that 3rd Regiment's flank would be safe. But 1st Regiment was nowhere in sight, and the Germans were using the ground it was supposed to be occupying to launch mortar rounds and counterattacks.

The situation was worse than Radcliffe had thought. His men had a tenuous hold on the summit, and, with their flank exposed, were in real danger of being overrun. Radcliffe got Pearce on the radio.

"What the hell is going on down there?" Radcliffe demanded. "You're supposed to be up on our flank."

Pearce, a no-nonsense Westerner from Seattle, did not hide his frustration. During the night, 1st Regiment had followed orders, secured the mountain on Majo's flank, and were now dug in. "I am on your flank," Pearce said.

"No, you're not," said Radcliffe, who had already divined what was going on. Majo's flanking hill was not really a hill but an obscure ridge, which may not even have appeared on some of the maps that Force headquarters admitted were "fuzzy and inaccurate." Pearce, Radcliffe determined, now stood on a height that was one ridge too far away.

Pearce was a gung-ho soldier and a stickler for detail, who could only have been horrified by Radcliffe's suggestion he was in the wrong place. So Pearce agreed to come to Radcliffe's position and take a look for himself.

Later in the morning, Pearce arrived, tired from a trip that was little more than a rifle volley as the bullet flies but a grueling trudge around enemy positions on foot. Together the men scrambled up to and climbed inside the OP, which was a tent on a high outcrop offering a bird's-eye view of the peaks in the distance.

"See," Radcliffe said, pointing down to the ridge below them where a frantic unit of Germans worked busily. "You're supposed to be there."

"I got to get down there and straighten this out," Pearce said, and turned to leave. Radcliffe, about to step out ahead of him, hesitated, and turned to pick up his carbine which leaned against the wall. Pearce marched from the tent's entrance. As Radcliffe stooped, a blast blew into the tent, numbing his eardrums.

An instant later, Radcliffe, having blinked himself back to the moment, realized he was unhurt and ran from the tent to find Pearce sprawled on the ground, utterly transformed. His right leg had been sheared off by the mortar round; the left leg was horribly chewed but still somehow attached; and Pearce himself was conscious, pumped with awe, gazing down on what had become of him in the duration of a single moment.

There followed an indefinite period of commotion that filled the span of only minutes, if not seconds. Men raced and shouted, and suddenly there was Sergeant Latoz kneeling over Pearce, trying to stop the man's life from bleeding away through the end of his stump as mortars continued to fall. At some point Pearce recognized himself in the scene of mutilation that was the lower half of his body, and started issuing orders to Latoz or anyone who would listen.

"Just leave me," Pearce said. "I don't want to live."

Radcliffe couldn't agree, but he understood what Pearce was getting at. If ever there was a man whose spirit was attached to the physical, it was Tommy Pearce. His passions were sports and testing his body in the out-of-doors with a hunting rifle or fishing pole in hand. Moreover, his commanding demeanor seemed part and parcel of his impressive form, which now was cut almost in half.

When Latoz had patched Pearce up well enough to be transported, he was hoisted onto a litter and carried away in the direction of the nearest aid station. And all the way, as Radcliffe would later hear, Pearce kept on telling the litter carriers: "I don't want to live. I'm too beat up."

Pearce's maiming was distressing to Radcliffe for both personal and soldierly reasons. Pearce was his best friend, yes. But Pearce was also the one person who could have sorted out the chaos raging on his flank. To add to the confusion of the battle, Pearce wasn't the first officer to fall. At dawn, shortly after 2nd Company's objective on Majo's peak had been seized, Captain Perry received a bullet or shell fragment directly to the head as he was kneeling down awaiting the charging army. He remained kneeling, gripping his rifle, after life had left him, as if determined to hold his ground even in death.

There was no time for Radcliffe to mourn either loss. The Germans kept counterattacking, and those elements of 3rd Regiment on Majo's peak were in a bad way. As for 3rd Company, Radcliffe had done his best to shore up what strength he had. Earlier that morning he had reorganized his stretch of the line into a "defense in depth." He set up four warning outposts, and behind them he established a line of riflemen, and behind them he set up some Johnny gun placements and made his rocket launcher specialists the last line of defense, along with men armed with mortars, Thompson light machine guns, and rifle grenades. Radcliffe also set up dummy outposts so that attacking Germans would waste bullets and mortars on vacant placements.

The strange, uneven terrain, which limited the field of vision, didn't help. Radcliffe's men couldn't see the right flank that 2nd Company was defending, and 2nd couldn't see the left flank. Enemy attacking from the left would appear on top of Radcliffe's line without warning even though 2nd, on the right flank, could see them coming. Very quickly, the two companies developed a system whereby they would yell down the line, across the two companies, when the Germans began to storm the hill. "They're coming from the left!" someone would scream, and the word would be passed right down the line to 2nd Company, which would blindly wait for the onslaught.

No one waited long. The Germans came and came, determined and furious to win back the plateau. And 3rd Regiment hurled as much metal as they could to keep them back. The day, like the night, was crisp, clear, and cold. Radcliffe began to dread the winter as much as the Germans. Contrary to conventional wisdom, he had already decided that soldiers even within the range of shellfire should, whenever possible, leave their foxholes and help build shelters for one another. Working above ground was dangerous when a mortar round could whistle in at any moment, but on the march to Majo, Radcliffe had lost more men to frozen feet than shellfire. On Majo, the men of 3rd Regiment were too busy fighting for their lives to worry about the cold. Some of the Force men, like Captain Perry, were dying where they stood and kneeled. Lightly wounded soldiers had their gashes doused in sulphur and patched with dressing, and were then given back their rifles and urged to fight on. The seriously wounded suffered where they lay. As long as the counterattacks raged, there was no way to get them down the mountain to an aid station. And the dead, the majority of whom were Germans who fell either defending or attempting to retake the summit, simply "lay in piles on the hill," as intelligence chief, Burhans, observed.

They had only cold rations to eat, and were running short on medical supplies and water—none of which was making it to the top while the ongoing battle prevented support units like 1-2 from climbing the slope with supplies. But the only shortage they really noticed during the endless fighting was ammunition. Shooting the attacking Germans with their own well-stocked machine guns temporarily solved the problem. Third Company, for its part, did its best to target Germans with twenty rounds of their own mortars. Radcliffe also sent patrols out front into the gullies and chasms to prevent the enemy from stealing up a draw and pouncing on the defenders from the flank. The defenders also called in three separate artillery barrages to beat the attackers back.

The Germans assaulted Majo twenty-seven times on January 7 and the morning of January 8, and by 1 p.m. of the second day, when I Company of the 3rd Battalion, 133rd Infantry, came to relieve the exhausted defenders, Radcliffe's company had tallied an impressive body count: in two nights and a day and a half of relentless combat, they had killed fifty-three and captured twenty-four of the enemy. More crucially, they had hung on to Majo—but at a price. The fighting had wounded nineteen of Radcliffe's men and killed three. In addition, one of his men went missing, and countless others had to be sent down the hill because of frozen feet. "I never lost that many any other time," he said.*

---

* Radcliffe calculated his casualty rate for the period of December 25–January 9 as 135 percent in an interview with the author, October 8, 2004. His original battle report listed two men killed in action, one man died of wounds, and one missing in action. In an interview sixty years later, Radcliffe recounted losing as many as six men on Majo. The casualties in Radcliffe's company for the December 25–January 9 battles give a sense of the attrition during a series of these small-scale engagements.

By the time of their relief, 3rd Company consisted of two officers and thirty-one men. On the way down the mountain, Radcliffe's company limped past the infantrymen who were happily mounting the hill in close-order file. Radcliffe didn't like what he was seeing. His own men had climbed and were now descending the hill with a gap of several meters between each. "For Christ's sake, spread out," he shouted, "The Germans have observations posts and they can bring in fire."

This nonchalance proved to be an omen. Once at the rest area, the men of 3rd Company hadn't even had time to get a hot meal when Radcliffe was summoned to headquarters, where a grim-faced Frederick gave Radcliffe and his fellow officers of the battalion the bad news.

"We've got to go take Majo back," Frederick said.

It was maddening for Radcliffe. The 133rd had immediately lost the mountain to a counterattack. Walker's anemic 3rd Regiment was being dispatched back up Majo.

Walker realized he was dangerously under strength. First Battalion in particular was seriously short of men. So he combined the remnants of his regiment into two fighting companies, and for the assault placed Radcliffe in command of one and another seasoned combat leader named Hubert Neely at the head of the other.*

Such was the attrition during the winter war in Italy's Apennine Mountains. After little more than a month of action, battle casualties and frostbite had whittled 3rd Regiment down

---

* "And we were way down in strength, and finally when we were down in the bivouac area I was told to report to Force headquarters. So our battalion, the three commanders, all our key people, met with Frederick, and Frederick says, 'We got to go take Majo back.' So we took 1st Battalion, and 2nd Battalion (and the regiment), which formed two companies out of it. I got command of the first one, and a guy by the name of Neely got command of the second battalion." Transcript from Mark Radcliffe interview with the author, September 5 & 8, 2004.

to the strength of two companies of fighting men. When they left the line, Radcliffe's 3rd Company had been diminished to the firepower of a platoon. Now, as Radcliffe and his weary men put away any hope of rest, relaxation, and hot chow, and trudged back in the direction of Majo, their only consolation was that the enemy was as depleted and exhausted as they were. As before, 3rd Regiment set out after dark, and over-whelmed the defenders on top in an angry, concerted push. As tired as they were, the Force men now had special motiva-tion for hating the Germans. They were now battling against an enemy who had denied them showers and hot meals. By 9:30 p.m., Radcliffe and his men were kneeling behind the same rocks on the same desolate spur where they had been that morning.

At 1 a.m. on January 9, the dislodged enemy struck back with all their might. But the line held. At 6:30 a.m., two freezing, dis-couraged Germans appeared at a forward outpost with arms in the air and, after surrendering, told the boys to expect a devastat-ing mortar attack. Their warning was accurate. As Radcliffe's battle report crisply stated: "These guns hit our left flank the rest of the day and that night." But still the line held.

On January 10, Mark Radcliffe and 3rd Regiment were relieved from Majo for the last time. This time the 100th Infantry Battalion, an astonishingly fierce Hawaiian outfit made up of second-generation Japanese immigrants known as the Purple Heart Battalion (or, as they called themselves, the "One Puka Puka"), replaced them. The men of the 100th held the peak, and on January 24—the northern mountains having been cleared after the Majo "hump" had been overcome—these same men would ford the muddy, flooding Rapido River and spearhead an attack on Cassino, the last obstacle into the Liri Valley. The attack would fail, but by this time the First Special Service Force would be gone from the Mignano Gap.

They departed to fight elsewhere, but left many in their ranks behind. On December 1, 1943, the eve of the Difensa battle, the Force was made up of 1,800 men. In mid-January, only 400 Force men left the mountains unscathed. All the rest were dead or wounded. Radcliffe's friend and best man, Major Tommy Pearce, remained, having died in an aid station in the shadow of Monte Majo not long after his crippling wounding had him begging to be left to die.

In 1st Regiment Art "Poison" Arsennek and Herb Peppard came out of the mountains, each carrying his own memories of men like Dee Byrom, who been killed barely minutes into his first engagement in the war.

In 2nd Regiment, young Don MacKinnon, the underage soldier from 1-2 who had crouched with Joe Glass and witnessed the horrifying quick deaths of Syd Gath and Bill Rothlin, fell too. While working to supply 3rd Regiment in the early hours of the Majo battle, MacKinnon was engulfed by an explosion with an eerie yellow hue. When he regained consciousness, MacKinnon stared down at the lower half of his body and recognized his left foot hanging by mere sinews. A moment before, MacKinnon thought that he had died, but in the ensuing moments he decided to live. Colonel Walker helped administer first aid. Joe Glass, Tommy Fenton, and Herby Forester carried him down the mountain in a litter and deposited him at an aid station, where 2nd Regiment's chief medical officer, George Evashwick, kept MacKinnon alive by pumping plasma into his body. Eighteen-year-old Don MacKinnon would live on, but without a left leg.

As for Joe Glass, he survived the mountains of central Italy with life and limb intact. Glass's last enduring memory of this time was of a ridge near Venafro. Glass had taken a prisoner, "a tall, good-looking Austrian kid" who spoke perfect English and said he had relatives in western Canada. The Austrian helped Joe carry supplies and wounded, and then, during a gap in the work, the two enemies sat and chatted. Just like normal men. Eventually the prisoner was taken down the mountain, and Joe reflected on their conversation. Given that his new father-in-law was Austrian-born, here was an enemy he had much in common with. Here was a kid who was almost like himself in every way except his uniform.

Just off of the ridge Joe could see Cassino: the object of six weeks of miserable combat. It looked so close and vulnerable, he wondered why he and the others weren't allowed to run down the ridge and take the damn place. But much time would pass, and countless lives would be lost, before the Allies would set foot in the ruins of that monastery.

The American government awarded the FSSF battle honors for Difensa, Remetanea, Hill 720, Radicosa, Majo, and Vischiataro; the Canadian government awarded battle honors for Difensa-Remetanea, Camino, and Majo. The push to the Liri Valley was marked by Allied frustration and German tenacity. Supply and weather problems, and the Wehrmacht's resilience in defense and counterattack, yielded the Allies little better than a series of stalemates and Pyrrhic victories. In this theater of war the FSSF took every objective set out for them and cleared the heights on both sides of the Mignano Gap, where so many others had failed. The immensity of these accomplishments, and the brutality of the fighting and the conditions, were extraordinary.

But Cassino and the Liri Valley were no longer the Force's concern. They left the high mountains, where they had been baptized by fire. Their next destination would be a beach by the sea.

PART II

THE BEACH

CHAPTER 9

SHINGLE

Early on February 1, 1944, a convoy of landing craft and support ships ploughed north through the Tyrrhenian Sea along the Italian coast, and by the time the light of dawn streaked the sky they were anchored just offshore from the seaside villages of Anzio and Nettuno, which only ten days before had been the target of a massive invasion by the U.S. Fifth Army's VI Corps. The convoy carried the men and arms of the FSSF and the 456th Parachute Field Artillery to their next battlefield, this vulnerable beachhead.

Moving from the high Apennines to the Italian lowlands was not an easy journey for recently promoted Brigadier General Robert Frederick. When Frederick descended from the mountains of the Mignano Gap, he left much behind. In addition to 77 percent of his combat echelon, dead and wounded, and 50 percent of his service battalion, he had left behind a part of himself. He had seen too much to emerge from the mountains intact.

Due to Frederick's unique command style, which saw him lingering endlessly on the front lines, he was on hand to watch many of his men die. For the men, his entrances were always inconspicuous and his mood stoic, which seemed to add to the mythic quality of his sightings. Herb Peppard once spotted a soldier plodding up an adjoining ridge of Sammucro with the help of a warped cane, and thought nothing of it until he glanced at the man's forty-year-old face and remarked: "I didn't think we had any old men in this outfit!" Peppard was told that the old man was the "Old Man." Frederick sometimes had an entourage: Captain George McCall, a tough Montanan; the Norwegian Finn Roll; or the martial arts expert Pat O'Neill, for whom Frederick had arranged a captain's commission and a place in the Force as his occasional bodyguard.

Carrying the aura of an officer burdened by the loneliness of command, Frederick had few companions other than the cigarette that perpetually smouldered between his fingers. A few days after Sergeant Peppard spotted Frederick near Sammucro, another 1st Regiment sergeant spied a man lighting a match after a devastating bombardment had cut his company off and filled its foxholes with corpses. The light invited more mortar rounds and screaming meemies, and the sergeant cursed the man until he realized it was Frederick himself, crouching over a badly wounded soldier, placing a cigarette in his mouth. "I'm sorry about lighting that match," Frederick told the sergeant, "but this boy wants a smoke."

Not only was Frederick on hand after battles, he had an eccentric habit of crossing into territory about to be overrun in order to observe the operation firsthand, a style of leadership that earned him a reputation as a maverick, and epithets like "crazy SOB" and "probably the most shot-at, and hit, general in

history." The latter characterization was as accurate as the former was unfair. With the exception of rare fighting generals like
Theodore Roosevelt Jr. (who would win a Congressional Medal
of Honor later that year on the beaches of Normandy but die
soon after of a heart attack), Frederick was a unique commander. The scars that etched his body were a grim record of
his campaign history. First sliced by shrapnel on Monte la
Difensa, Frederick would be wounded four more times in the
mountains of central Italy, once on each of the crucial peaks
seized by the Force—Remetanea, Sammucro, and Majo—and in
the town of Radicosa. According to his daughter, Frederick took
these risks "to compensate while leading others to possible
death by being where his troops were and perhaps going even
further into danger himself."

As steep as the costs of Frederick's war were, the payback was
just as great. Professionally, Frederick had proved the Force's
worth as a fighting unit, and in the process advanced the argu-
ment that manpower alone need not dictate a unit's strength.
Careful selection and rigorous training could make an army infinitely stronger than its numbers.

Proving this point had made Frederick a bona fide military
star, at least in the Italian war. The Force had so impressed Mark
Clark that Frederick was promoted to brigadier general.
Moreover, even Frederick's former colleagues in the Munitions
Building in faraway Washington had noted the FSSF's accomplishments. On January 23, 1944, General Thomas Handy,
Frederick's former boss, sent him a cable: "Hearty congratulations and wishes for continued success are offered you by your
old friends in the Operations Division and myself." In a later letter that began "Dear Fred," Handy added, with surprising
sentimentality: "We have heard a great deal of the operation of
your Force and all of us are very proud of you."

In the past, even the War Department secretaries had shown

a touching affection for Frederick and his ambitions. Early in the Force's history, way back in 1942, eight of the female clerical staff had baked cookies and cupcakes, and dispatched these goodies to the FSSF's top officers along with a four-stanza poem that began:

> Last night we labored long and hard
> With Rationed sugar, pecans and lard,
> To send to you this package small
> In hopes that you will like it all.
>
> There was candy stuck on windows,
> And candy on the door,
> While "First Special Service Force Girls"
> Sat sifting flour on the floor.

These verses represented the misconceptions Frederick and the Force left buried in a grave under the shade of crag on the frustrated approach to Cassino. The surviving Force men carried no romanticisms or false hopes of glory when they stood on the decks of their ships and contemplated their next theater of war: a drained marsh that would be universally known as Anzio.

In the 1940s, Anzio was a collection of white-and-rose villas on the Italian shinbone with a classical pedigree. In the Roman epoch, the coastal village had been alternately a bustling port, a resort town, and the birthplace of a pair of royal tyrants: the Emperors Caligula and Nero. By 1944, Anzio had enjoyed almost two millennia of tranquil obscurity, when it suddenly became an object of fascination for Allied leaders who saw it as a key to ending the wintry stalemate that had settled along the Gustav Line. The FSSF had helped put the Fifth Army within reach of Cassino, but the slowness of the advance, and its inordinate cost in lives and munitions, had given Winston Churchill, for one, an idea.

Over two world wars Churchill had a history of conceptualizing strategy in bold flourishes as colorful as a brush stroke on the portraits he painted in his spare time. Gallipoli, the attempt in the First World War to collapse the German trenches of western Europe by amphibiously invading Turkey, was one such design that proved to be catastrophically fanciful. Almost three decades later, Churchill's schemes to enervate Nazi Germany by attacking Norway through Projects Plough and, later, Jupiter were equally daring. As the advance on Rome bogged down, Churchill contemplated the map of Italy, stared at the stars, and conjured up a "dazzling vision," as one historian put it, that would reverse Allied fortunes and inertia. Churchill's vision centered on a single question: If the Gustav Line could not be broken, why not go around it?

Churchill's scheme, which Allied generals on both sides of the Atlantic eventually bought into on January 8 under the code name Shingle, was to land an invasion force north of the mountains and then, in concert with the Fifth Army at Cassino, push for Rome, a city Churchill "passionately" wanted to occupy, and without which, as he wrote to General Clark, "the campaign in Italy will have 'petered out' ingloriously." The Allies selected the soft beaches near the villages of Anzio and Nettuno as the invasion point. This spot was a mere fifty kilometers from Rome, and the terrain was invitingly flat and accessible.

Churchill may have dreamed that the Anzio landing force would be an army capable of liberating Rome on its own. Both Clark and his British boss, Fifteenth Army Group Commander

General Sir Harold Alexander, saw Anzio as a diversion that would allow them to break the standoff along the Winter Line at Cassino, where the fighting had descended into a gory deadlock. Although the battle for Cassino was much smaller in scale and strategic importance, the German defenders who held the monastery compared the bitterness of the siege to the brutal fighting at Stalingrad, the city that had given the world a new name for privation and horror.

The Allies' failure to break through the Gustav Line at Cassino after a month of treacherous warfare both in the mountains and on the lowlands along Highway 6 convinced Alexander and Clark that if a breakthrough didn't occur soon, the Italian war would bog down indefinitely. This was Kesselring's strategy: a bloody stalling maneuver and battle of attrition. But with the invasion of coastal France planned for mid-1944, the overweeningly ambitious Clark did not have time for a protracted campaign. If the Italian war were not won before Eisenhower's invasion of France, it would be overshadowed by the march on Germany.

Anzio was conceived as the spark to reignite the Allied war effort in Italy. By attacking Cassino on the eve of the Anzio landings, Clark gambled that the Fifth Army would draw enough assets of the German Tenth Army to the Gustav Line to ensure that the invasion force could get ashore en masse. And then, after the Anzio landings, he believed General Heinrich von Vietinghoff would withdraw to the north in terror that his Tenth Army would be cut off and surrounded. Vietinghoff's departure would then allow Clark to burst into the Liri Valley from the south. In short, the Anzio landings would unleash a chain reaction, as one historian wrote: "the first attack on the Gustav Line would contribute to the success of the Anzio landings, which would in turn threaten German Tenth Army's line of communication and thus its hold on the Gustav Line."

Clark's prediction would prove wrong. For him, the Anzio invasion would become a wasted opportunity and a grave disappointment. But for Frederick and the FSSF, who at 10 a.m. were given permission to dock and unload, it would be the battlefield that would define them.

CHAPTER 10

THE LONG COLD NIGHT

When Privates Glass and Waling of 1-2 arrived at Anzio, they set foot in a strange world of mayhem and violence. Freighters filled the harbor of the city like flotsam, and landing craft like the ones the Force men sailed in on lay in the docks and against the piers like beasts with men and materials streaming out of their gaping mouths. Transports tore along the coastline, and some trucks, such as the eccentric amphibious vehicle known as the DUKW, motored through the harborfront as well. Military stevedores worked feverishly to unload the arms, supplies, and men necessary to the survival of the beachhead. The beachhead's harbor looked "like a big market," a German POW on hand told one historian, "like a big business without confusion, disorder, or muddle." These men worked fast, Force men like Glass soon realized, out of fear for their lives. Above, German bombers regularly tried to drop ordnance on the piers, while P38 fighters and antiaircraft batteries flailed away at them—and with some success. By the time Glass and the others set foot on the shore, ninety-seven German fighters and bombers had been shot down. What couldn't be shot down were shells, particularly those lobbed from a monstrous 280 mm railroad gun the men would eventually christen Anzio Annie.

Annie attacked the harbor almost exclusively, but still, Glass had only to scan the horizon to know that no one anywhere on the beachhead was safe from enemy artillery. The entire area was as flat as Saskatchewan, with the Alban Hills—where Annie was perched—rising in the distance. There was simply no place to hide in this implausibly small theater. Where the Force's

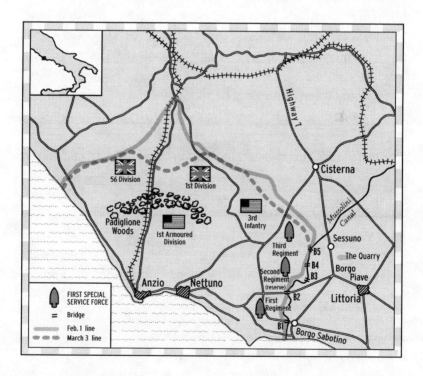

The Anzio beachhead

last battleground, the mountainous approaches to Cassino, had been an immense ocean of craggy white caps, the Anzio–Nettuno beachhead was a modest wedge of land shaped like a badly cut piece of pie that was only forty-eight kilometers wide and eleven kilometers deep. To date, 61,000 soldiers had piled onto this small swath of real estate. On the far left of the beachhead, along the Moletta River, stood the U.S. Forty-fifth Division, also known as the Thunderbirds, which had originated as the Arizona, Colorado, New Mexico, and Oklahoma National Guards. The U.S. Third Division, which commanded Darby's Rangers, was positioned directly opposite the village of Cisterna, strategically vital because it was located along Highway 7. In reserve behind the Third was a pair of regiments from the Forty-fifth. The U.S. First Armored Division, "Old Ironsides," headquartered behind the line in an inhospitable tangle of bush called the Padiglione Woods, were poised to plug any holes should the beachhead come under pressure. And on February 1, 1944, three regiments of the First Special Service Force, consisting of only 68 officers and 1,165 men, now joined this crowded army.

The first night they spent in a troop concentration area on the west side of Anzio. The next morning they moved inland into the bridgehead, which was nothing more or less than rustic farmland accented by peasant houses, simple rectangular two-story affairs that sprang up here and there along the roadsides. As he moved up with his men, Frederick noted that those same houses in enemy territory would offer excellent "opportunities for observation and for ambush." Frederick, at 2 p.m. on his first full day on the beachhead, had the advantage of knowing the Force's assignment. It was information that would take a while to trickle down to Joe and the others in 1-2, but by nightfall every officer and enlisted man in the Force would be informed that the outfit's overall mission was to protect one-quarter of the front line beginning on the far right of VI Corps's territory. The 1st Regiment, where Joe's friend Art Arsennek now served, would defend the line on the far right, from the coast running north about five kilometers. From there, the 3rd Regiment, where Mark Radcliffe served, would defend the remaining eight kilometers of the front, chiefly because Colonel Walker's regiment was now the strongest in the outfit; replacements had brought it up to close to full strength. First Regiment was still at half strength, as was Joe's 2nd Regiment, which was put in reserve.

The new faces of replacements were visible to Joe amid 2nd Regiment's thinning ranks. Most of these men were volunteers from the Canadian and U.S. armies who had been put through special training at Santa Maria Capua Vetere. Eventually, the Force would be bolstered by the remnants of Darby's Rangers, a unit that was like distant family of the FSSF, which had recently become a cautionary tale.

———

Ranger leader Lieutenant Colonel William O. Darby did indeed have much in common with Robert Frederick. He was equally dynamic and handsome, and, at thirty-four, even younger. Like Frederick, he had an innate ability to inspire men. According to historian Rick Atkinson: "No one who met him ever doubted that Bill Darby was born to command other men in the dark of night." But there were differences between these two leaders. Darby had a greater personal flair for the dramatic, making statements such as: "Onward we stagger, and if the tanks come, God help the tanks." And his career as a pioneering commando leader had been more charmed, at least in the beginning. Tapped to participate in the invasion of North Africa, the Rangers were able to prove their mettle in February 1943 with raids against the infamous Italian Tenth Bersaglieri Regiment at Station de

Sened, Tunisia, an operation that netted an enemy body count of fifty dead and a dozen prisoners. In March 1943, the Rangers spearheaded General George Patton's assault against the heights of El Guettar, Algeria, an operation that earned the unit a Presidential Citation, and Darby a Distinguished Service Cross. Later, three Ranger units led the Seventh Army onto the beaches of Sicily, and helped capture Messina; and after that, Darby's Rangers spearheaded the Fifth Army's landings on the ankle of the Italian peninsula at Salerno. Darby stepped onto Italy a battle captain with ten thousand men under his command, a force that included elements of the Eighty-second Airborne Division and the Thirty-sixth Division in addition to the Rangers. Eventually, Darby battled in the same terrain as Frederick, waging alpine warfare at the Sorrento Chiunzi Pass and near the villiages of Venafro and Ceppagna. Now a full colonel, Darby was not only selected to participate in the Shingle landings, he had been chosen to spearhead them.

After midnight on January 22, British Landing Craft Assault (LCAs) put ashore at Anzio two Ranger battalions, which seized gun batteries, and secured the village. To their right, three regiments of the Third Division, commanded by Major General Lucian Truscott, who had first recruited Darby, also hit the beaches.

By noon of that day, VI Corps, the army entrusted with the operation, was well on its way to consolidating a beachhead, which within two days reached eleven kilometers into the plain along twenty-six kilometers of shoreline. VI Corps commander, Major General John P. Lucas, received congratulations from fellow generals as transports carrying men, armor, and supplies poured ashore—where they remained. Determined to reinforce the beachhead (and influenced by General Clark, who cautioned "Don't stick your neck out, Johnny"), Lucas did not immediately press on. The Germans, however, did. On the day of the landings, an alarmed Field Marshal Kesselring mobilized the German Fourth Parachute and Hermann Göring divisions and began positioning them to prevent the Allied army from crossing the plains and seizing the high ground overlooking them, the Alban Hills. Kesselring need not have hurried. A small man who looked old at fifty-four and by his own admission felt "every year of it," Lucas waited five days before meeting with divisional commanders to discuss pushing on—a decision that would affect no unit in Lucas's invasion force as much as Darby's 6615 Ranger Regiment.

On the night of January 29, three Ranger battalions crept across German lines in and around the village of Cisterna. Two battalions were to take the village and the third was to clear the road. The raid would be a preliminary foray in what was to be Lucas's massive breakout. Darby's men would occupy Cisterna and await backup from the Third Division, which would be close on their heels once the offensive got underway. The Rangers brought along firepower for a lightning strike, and a short and intense skirmish. Leaving heavy machine guns behind, each of Darby's riflemen carried two "bandoliers" of ammo strung over their shoulders, all the grenades they could carry, and mortar crews armed with three rounds for each cannon. The sheer flatness of the ground made Darby wary of armor, so he had his battalions bring along "sticky grenades" and rocket launchers. The Rangers departed for the operation, charged with the same raw confidence that the Force men always exhibited before a fight. What Darby couldn't have known was that his commandos were stepping into the path of two locomotives on a collision course. Convinced that he was facing a conventional-thinking, if not timid, commander, Kesselring had already begun amassing troops in the Cisterna area for his own siege, which he hoped would drive VI Corps back into the sea. The Rangers unknowingly stepped in front of Kesselring's juggernaut, and this time neither their élan nor a charmed past could save them. The Germans heard the Rangers coming, and let the unsuspecting commandos advance into an ambush before unleashing a storm of machine gun and tank fire. Trapped and absurdly outnumbered, the battalion that fought to clear the road was badly mauled, but the two Ranger battalions bound for Cisterna were enveloped on open ground. Sergeant Sam Finn, a 21-year-old from St. Louis, was a member of Darby's Fourth Battalion. A tall kid with a sharp smile and an easy Missouri accent, Sergeant Finn realized he and his comrades were in trouble immediately. "There were Germans where there weren't supposed to be any," he wrote in a memoir. Finn and Fourth Battalion were nearing the village of Isola Bella when flares lit the sky and the German ambush began. Finn, who ran a mortar crew, was able to leap into a shallow irrigation ditch with his men when the Germans attacked. He tried to provide covering fire for his company as it advanced up the road. But German machine-gun fire pinned him down. When Finn and a fellow sergeant rose to pull a wounded Ranger to safety, the sergeant was shot by a sniper and died instantly.

The situation was even more desperate for the other battalions near Cisterna. In a sad foreboding of the unit's fate, Third Battalion's new commander, Major Alvah Miller, was killed by the first shell of the ambushing enemy. The Germans were so close that when Ranger Carl Lehmann sprinted to the left to escape the bullets, he stumbled into an enemy encampment where some Germans lay under blankets. Lehmann raced through the bivouac literally "shooting from the hip." The Rangers, despite being divided, and surrounded, put up a vicious fight, and the day might have ended differently had the Third Division been able to break through and provide reinforcement. But the German line held firm, and the Rangers remained trapped.

Finn ultimately survived by hiding in an irrigation ditch all the next day and then slipping back at night. But he was one of the lucky few. That night, Darby's Rangers simply ceased to exist. Only 6 of the roughly 800 men who attacked the village would return; 12 were killed, 36 wounded, and 767 captured.

For Darby, the calamity unfolded in his headquarters slowly as his squawking radio brought increasingly grim reports from the field. The silence that overwhelmed the frequencies when the battalions' radios went dead said even more. Darby was with Sergeant Carlo Contrera, his longtime jeep driver, when the realization struck him that his battalions had been obliterated. "[Darby] put his head down on his arm and cried," Contrera would later say.

Arguably, Darby's men helped to deflect and absorb the burgeoning power of Kesselring's attack. Still, Lucas's breakout had stalled, with British infantrymen on the right of the line advancing only two thousand meters in the face of the German defenses.

Churchill captured the disappointment and inertia. While he had expected the Anzio landings to be like "hurling a wildcat on the shore," he was forced to concede that "all we got was a stranded whale."

———

Eventually a Ranger gun company of howitzers mounted on half-tracks would become part of the FSSF, as would orphaned soldiers like Sam Finn. Most of these men arrived sullen, shaken, slightly embittered, proud, and utterly undefeated. They found a place in the Force, but Rangers and Force men took a while to accept each other. No one wanted to make new friends because, as one Force man said, "They had lost too many."

But the Rangers wouldn't come until later, and meanwhile, 2nd Regiment was still shorthanded. So, just before leaving the barracks at Santa Maria, Colonel Moore had reorganized the regiment into three solid companies. Joe's 1-2 merged with men from 6-2, with Lieutenant Tom Gordon, soon to be Captain Gordon, serving as the company commander. Lieutenants Piette and Langdon oversaw 1-2's platoons, and the company's staff sergeants were now Lebras, Boodleman, and Percy Crichlow. Joe would grow to respect Crichlow, with whom he later shared a foxhole. But the arrival at Anzio brought a greater, more welcome change: Joe's buddy, Lorin Waling, was promptly transferred back to 3rd Platoon, and the two friends were finally reunited.

Neither Gordon nor Piette brought these men together for sentimental reasons. Captain Gordon, a scion of Canada's Gordon's gin distillery, had decided to make both Joe and Lorin scouts. Their job would be to work together out front, doing reconnaissance, conducting raids, taking prisoners. Working "out front" meant behind German lines, and always in the dead of night. Their elevation was directly germane to 2nd Regiment's role as a reserve force. Of course, in reserve the 2nd Regiment would be called upon to reinforce any part of the long, thin FSSF line where the enemy was in danger of breaking through. But "reserve" also meant that the 2nd Regiment would conduct more than its share of patrols in enemy territory, and to accomplish this mission the regiment needed trained scouts.

Joe was pleased by the change in his fortunes, but Lorin was jubilant. "When they made us scouts, they made a team," Waling would later say. In a short time Glass and Waling would develop a reputation roughly equal with that of the heroes of the Difensa operation, Howard Van Ausdale and Tommy Fenton, still officially the company's chief scouts. Joe and Lorin's previous reputation as hard-fighting and fearless troublemakers qualified them for no other job. "I guess the best thing [our officers] thought they could do with Joe and me is hide us" behind German lines, Waling would say.

After dark on February 2, the Force moved to its new area of responsibility on the far right of the beachhead. Even in the night, the men of 1-2 could see the challenges they were up against. The far right of the beachhead was bordered by a waterway, about fifty meters across at its widest, named the Mussolini Canal, which was part of a network of ditches that had drained and transformed the entire lowlands, from a mosquito-infested marsh into workable farmland. A little more than a grenade throw away from the far side of the canal, at a distance of about one hundred meters, were the Germans. The enemy's close proximity combined with its vantage point in the Alban Hills across the plain gave the Germans a commanding view of the beachhead, parts of which the men came to call "the billiard table" because it was flat and open.

The only sanctuary was beneath the earth. So, after dark on February 2, 1-2 moved to a support position just behind the line near a dry creek bed with a high bank. Grabbing their shovels, Joe, Lorin, and Jimmy Flack started to dig a three-man cave. On each side of them other guys did the same. When Joe and Jimmy decided the cave was deep enough, they threw down their shovels and crawled inside. When Lorin crawled in, he realized they needed to dig a foot more to make room for him. But they'd had enough digging. So Lorin Waling spent his first night on the Anzio beachhead as he would every other night for the next ninety-nine days: with feet dangling from his foxhole.

———
———

When the sun rose on the Force's first day on the line, Frederick already had casualties. During the night's relief deployment, enemy outposts facing 3rd Regiment had divined the movement of men in the shadows and had opened fire with 88 mm guns, a German cannon originally designed as an anti aircraft weapon that was so effective it became ubiquitous on the battlefield. It was a weapon the Force men would become intimately acquainted with as time progressed. Two officers in 5-3 had died when the level, almost point-blank fire had driven them into foxholes that enemy infiltrators had mined. Lieutenants D. W. Cuddy and C. R. Scoggin were dead, and the company commander, Captain D. G. Fletcher, of Trois-Rivières, Quebec, was grievously wounded.

These were bitter casualties for the Force to take, but they were instructive. Frederick's orders had been to dig in his heels and defend the beachhead. But with the enemy so near, a passive defense was an invitation to be overrun. Frederick resolved to be aggressive. He ordered forceful night combat patrols with the goal of driving the German line back, in order, as he would later write, to forge "a kind of no man's land between the two [armies]" and give his men some breathing room. Frederick had no doubt what this warfare entailed. The fighting would be brutally intimate and done mainly at night. With knife, gun, and grenade, the Force men overwhelmed, killed, captured, and demoralized the Germans one outpost at a time. The entire Force, taking an aggressive lead from 3rd Regiment, set to work to do what General John P. Lucas, the beachhead's commander, could not seem to accomplish: permanently expand the beachhead. An army of a thousand men could only hope to win territory by meters, and this is what they did. Their own survival depended on driving "Jerry," as they called the enemy, back. Their blood was up, and they fought mercilessly. Though in general the fighting in the European theater was not marked by any special hatred of Germany (Nazi crimes were as yet largely unknown, and it had been Japanese, not German, aggression that had drawn the United States into the war), the proximity of the two armies soon led to bitter animosity. "In the Force,

Germans were regarded much as the frontiersman regarded Indians," wrote veteran Adna Underhill, "the only good German was a dead German."

The enemy may have felt the same about the Allies. The Germans facing the Force were members of the Hermann Göring Division, which began its life in 1933 as a simple police force (the Polizeiabteilung z.b.V. Wecke) under the control of Göring. Soon after, Göring's cops were absorbed by the Luftwaffe, which Göring commanded, and then in 1936 ascended into the pantheon of German special warfare when their best soldiers were selected to be among the first members of the *Fallschirmjaeger,* Germany's pioneering paratroopers. Göring's fighters never permanently became an airborne unit. When war broke out in 1939, the German air marshal employed the unit as an antiaircraft ground force with the 88 mm cannon as its weapon of choice. By as early as 1940, Göring's fighters were engaged in ground battles, and they found devastating success in aiming their 88s horizontally against enemies rooted to the earth.

But by January 1944 the division, like the entire German military, was no longer what it had been. German defeats in North Africa and Sicily, and most notably the Battle of Stalingrad, which had ended exactly a year earlier with the decimation of the German Sixth Army and the loss of 300,000 troops, had depleted its armed forces. The German war machine stretched across the 2000-kilometer front in the east, a staggering drain on manpower and logistics. At the same moment, with the Allies in control of the skies in the west, and aircraft production stifled by bombing, Luftwaffe air- and ground-crews sat idle in their barracks. In a move that marked German desperation, these men were eventually pressed into service as infantry. By the time of the Anzio landings, some of the enemy units were "Alarm Companies," brand-new recruits from the air force with a minimum of training.

These warriors were disciplined, but they clearly lacked the skills of the steely Wehrmacht veterans. And they paled in comparison with the Force men. As Adna Underhill wrote: "For 7 days, 2 to 9 February, the Force was busy moving the Germans back from the Mussolini Canal . . . Every night, the widening 'no man's land' was alive with black-faced Forcemen in baggy britches knocking out posts, blowing up enemy-occupied houses, and pushing the German forward positions back."

Having shocked the Allies with their stubbornness in their defense of Italy, it was the Germans' turn to be astonished by the ruthlessness of the FSSF's tenacity and aggression on their perimeter. Frederick was one of the first to recognize this. "It is certain that the enemy acquired a distinct distaste for the aggressiveness of our numerous patrols," he later wrote, "which knifed into his positions each night."

Within one week, the Force men pushed the line back 1,400 meters. The outfit was already on its way to Rome, clawing every step of the way.

———

In 2nd Regiment, 3rd Platoon's new scouts Glass and Waling would experience their share of patrols, but one of their first forays into the night was on a reconnaissance mission led by Sergeant Crichlow. The mission was memorable because Crichlow also selected little Herby Forester and Rusty Kroll for the patrol, creating a five-man scouting team that would work together for the duration of their time on the beachhead. This "recce" patrol was also noteworthy because it almost segued into combat, and would have become a raid had Glass been in charge. For Glass, the patrol was a lesson in the art of blending into the night, which was more than a matter of blackening faces and the shiny surfaces of weaponry with the soot of burned wine corks.

That night, Crichlow had come to them and said he had received an assignment to reconnoiter an 88 mm gun that was positioned somewhere along the road to their right, which intersected the canal. Some sort of action was being planned for that road, and headquarters needed to know the location of the gun and any outposts in its area. So the men set off after camouflaging themselves and collecting their weapons.

Forester, in defiance of his size, lugged a Johnny gun. Crichlow, as patrol leader, carried a Thompson submachine gun. But Glass always took his M1 rifle, and fixed a blade to the end of the barrel. Waling and Kroll shouldered rifles as well, although only Glass, the former bayonet instructor, had an enthusiasm for wielding a knife at the end of his M1. The men approached the line where 3rd Company–3rd Regiment manned an outpost. Mark Radcliffe was there, and briefed the patrol before they crossed the line.

"You men are going to have it all to yourself tonight," Radcliffe told them. That sounded great to Glass; there was no need to keep an eye out for your own people. The patrol of five men left Radcliffe's outpost, crossed the Mussolini Canal, and slipped into German territory. They moved single file and dead silently, with Crichlow in the lead. All the men had been out here before, and they knew the general lay of the land. If you moved east you'd eventually find the tiny village of Borgo Piave, a strategic point that Glass and the others would come to know well in the coming weeks. East of that was the small city of Littoria, where the enemy was firmly ensconced. And on a corner formed by two farm roads not far from where they had crossed the canal was an enemy machine-gun nest.

That gun would eventually have to be eliminated, but not tonight. Instead, Crichlow began to lead the patrol around the nest. Glass and Waling could just make out the outline of a bunker in the dark, and they knew they had to move quietly.

Glass, even though he was new to both scouting and the beach-head, had already found these machine-gun nests to be unpredictable: sometimes they exploded into violent fire and sometimes they didn't. Glass knew that it was a gun pit because he had previously seen it firing. But now it was still and quiet, and Glass couldn't figure it out. Was the pit empty at that moment? Or were its occupants terrified? This last point was possible. Ever since the Force had begun clearing outposts with knives and grenades, Glass had the distinct feeling the inexperienced Germans he was facing now spent their nights in terror. A little later, on combat patrols, Germans would surrender to Glass as soon as his blackened face came into view, as if the enemy had been waiting for him all along.

Crichlow's patrol was creeping around this gun bunker in expert silence when it became clear to Glass that its gunners were not asleep. From somewhere near the Force's line, firing erupted against the German position, probably—Glass decided in that instant—from a combat patrol that Radcliffe hadn't known about. For Crichlow, Glass, and the others, the firefight broke out at the worst moment. They were standing squarely in the crossfire, and could do nothing but fall to the ground, crawl, and hope that the bullets above their heads remained above their heads.

Crichlow led the men away from the gun pit, and soon all five were clear of the firefight. With no one hit, Crichlow led the patrol as it skulked toward the 88. They hadn't moved far when the German patrol appeared.

Like any good scout, Lorin Waling would hear the Germans long before he could see them. It wasn't that they talked, although they did. Their weapons and gear were clattering, and it was clear from the racket that they were coming straight toward him and the others. The Force men were on a trail with an irrigation ditch running beside it. When it became unmistakable the patrol was approaching, Waling and the others ducked into the trench and lay flat against its bank, with the tops of their heads roughly level with the path. Waling knew which path the Germans were treading, and also understood that if the Germans continued on this route, their path would steer them just clear of the Force men. But at the intersection of the two trails, the lead German turned and set foot on the path the Force men had stood on just moments before.

If the Germans got close enough to the ditch, they would spot Crichlow and the others. Even in the dark, the men were visible. Glass palmed a grenade and leaned toward Crichlow.

"Jesus, Crich," Glass whispered, "there must be a platoon coming. Are we gonna take them?"

"No," Crichlow answered.

Glass was incredulous. The Germans would be there in a moment, and what was the patrol supposed to do, wait for the Germans to shoot them first? Glass figured the job could be done without any shooting. All he'd have to do was raise his bayonet under the nose of the first German in the rank and the entire platoon would surrender.

"That's not our orders," Crichlow said. "Our orders are to get our information and get back."

Glass didn't agree. Their orders in this war were to take out Germans. But he obeyed Crichlow, clung to his grenades, buried his face in the bank, and listened as enemy boots bore down on them.

Lorin Waling, peering up like a gopher, would swear that he saw a German spit on his friend Joe as he walked by. This was the only ordnance discharged. A moment later the troop turned right and was gone. Crichlow summoned the men from the ditch and gave the order to move out.

A short time later, they found the 88. They noted its position, and the layout of the gun pit, and the bunker where the gun crew was garrisoned, and then—ready to move on—all five of them bolted in a flash across the main road that separated them from a series of farmhouses they needed to "clear." But another enemy patrol had been standing farther up the road, and they spotted the flicker of shadows. Hiding in the drainage ditch on the far side of the road, Glass, again clutching a pair of hand grenades as if they were rosary beads, begged Crichlow to let him take out the three Germans who were moving gingerly in their direction to investigate.

"No fighting," Crichlow hissed for the second time that night. "We can't risk it. We might get shot, and we have to get back with this information."

So Glass kept quiet and watched as the Germans sniffed around above their heads, walked past, and then broke out in frantic whispers. Glass was certain the Germans had seen them, but had done the prudent thing and pretended they hadn't. So the Crichlow patrol moved on.

They checked a few designated farmhouses to confirm whether or not they were being used as German command posts. The houses were empty, and Joe sat in one and smoked a cigarette, and finally suggested that they head back to their lines even though the patrol was not supposed to return before 3 a.m. Crichlow, anxious to report back, agreed, and a short time later they appeared at Captain Radcliffe's command post. They gave the password, accepted the countersign, and were soundly chewed out for coming in early.

They had taken no prisoners. They hadn't killed anyone, nor had anyone tried to kill them. Crichlow, whom Glass now saw as a first-class commander and smart as hell, had obeyed orders perfectly, returning with exactly the reconnaissance report demanded of him. There were lessons in all of this. Information could be as useful as a dead German or a prisoner. The night could envelop and protect a soldier if he immersed himself in it, and moved carefully and decisively. Strangely, being close to the enemy offered some rewards. Out front you were safe from artillery. Out front you were safe from snipers. If you had talent, good judgment, or, even better, luck, you lived and completed your mission. If you blundered or your luck ran out, you could die, get mutilated, or, worse yet, become a POW. But skill, judgment, and knowledge generated luck. All lucky men knew this. These were crucial lessons for Joe Glass and Lorin Waling.

CHAPTER 11

GODS

After a week on the line, the Force men became more accustomed to the new style of fighting the terrain of Anzio
demanded of them. The transformation was shocking. They had
come from the ceiling of central Italy to lowlands so flat and
desolate that only a few trees, randomly positioned farmhouses,
and a water tower and church steeples in the nearby village of
Littoria jutted from the horizon. For cover, the Force men dug
trenches into the banks of dry creek beds or wadis and the
mound that ran along the Mussolini Canal. (The high water
table of this former marsh made it impossible to dig trenches
on flat, open ground.) The German artillery spotters enjoyed a
clear view into the beachhead from Littoria's steeples and tower,
and from the Alban Hills and Lepini Mountains on the far end
of the plain. And they called in fire when they spotted gatherings
of men and vehicles, particularly in the rear where most of the

soldiers and materials were situated. On the front line, the ever-widening no man's land put enemy snipers out of range and sometimes made it possible for a single Force man to emerge from his trench, and enjoy a pleasure as dangerously banal as basking in the sun.

Mark Radcliffe would tell the story both on the beachhead and off. Sometime after combat patrols had beaten the Germans back so that a relatively secure no man's land separated the two fronts, a soldier sat on a blanket in broad daylight reading a book near a forward outpost. Radcliffe knew the soldier well. He was a 3-3 fixture from Indian Lake, New Jersey, by the name of Herb Morris. But Radcliffe couldn't imagine what Morris would be reading on the front line of the Anzio beachhead, so he grabbed a pair of binoculars and deciphered two words on the book's cover: *Charles Atlas.*

Radcliffe let loose a gale of laughter. Morris was reading a book on muscle building by Atlas, the famed, reformed "97-pound weakling." Radcliffe had what soldiers called a "command voice," calibrated by God to deliver orders. With that voice, he gave Morris the nickname "Muscles."

Morris, who turned twenty-one years old on the beachhead, would never confirm or deny that he read Charles Atlas at Anzio. "Maybe I did, but I don't remember," he once said when asked. But Morris answered to Muscles and understood why he was called it. "I was a little guy, 120 pounds," he would later say. "They called me Muscles because I didn't have any."

Morris looked like a kid who might have had sand kicked in his face in an Atlas brochure. His body was wiry and topped by a slender head, which—due to a pair of seashell ears and a prominent nose—seemed to taper to his chin. But his long narrow eyes did not blaze as much as they bore into people and things. Radcliffe and others would grow fond of Morris because of this determination. It was evident from the get-go. When Wickham came to the base where Morris was garrisoned to recruit for Plough, he stared into those eyes and asked Morris if he could "handle" the outfit. Morris met the stare. "Sir, I've been able to handle everything the army has handed out so far." Wickham, like Radcliffe later on, admired Morris's spunk and signed him up. For all of them, Muscles was the biggest smallest man they knew. But in a way, Morris's decisions to fight the war and to join the Force had come by default.

The choice may have been sparked in his youth in the very stove that young Herb lit every Sunday in the primary room of the nearby Denville Community Methodist Church, where his mother oversaw the church school's primary program. She was a strong and devout woman who believed in her duty to God and family, and never lost sight of her own blessings, such as her nine children and the chickens that the family raised for additional food. Not only did the Morris family say grace in thanks for these gifts before every meal, but Mrs. Morris, far from wealthy, also felt she was duty bound to volunteer to do God's work. Herb stoked the stove every Sunday simply because he felt someone had to ensure that his mother was comfortable while serving the church. Morris's father's contribution to the world was both simple and grandiose. He was a "hoisting engineer," a tall-boom crane operator in New York City, who eked out enough to keep the family clothed and fed, with the help of the chickens. His special crane lifted steel for skyscrapers, and over his career he helped fashion the New York City skyline.

Morris didn't join the army to topple Hitler or take vengeance on Japan. His father, who passionately disliked President Roosevelt, never pushed him to go. "Why can't we put Roosevelt, Stalin, and Hitler in a room and let them fight?" he once said. Young Herb signed up though, so that others, namely his brothers, wouldn't have to. When the war finally came to the USA in

1941, Herb was leading an uncomplicated life. He had his three brothers and five sisters. He had his mother and father. In the summer he loved to go to dances at Indian Lake, and he once met a "real doll" and danced the jitterbug with her. But the relationship never progressed further than the dance floor, and when the opportunity arose to join an outfit destined for combat, his unattached state was very much on his mind. His brother Bob was married. His brother Sam had a girlfriend. "All I had was the girl I jitterbugged with," he would later say. It wasn't that he had nothing to lose by dying; it was that the world, he believed, would lose little if it lost him.

Morris's modest sense of himself flew in the face of his ferocious personality. He was a complex young man who possessed resolve as fiery as any Methodist sermon. Defiant to begin with, the Force had made him tougher. That element of rebelliousness in Morris's character had found a perfect outlet in rigorous commando training, which he thrived on just as much as he thrived in the dangerous hinterland of the Anzio beachhead. Not technically a scout, Morris's place in the gung-ho 3-3 ensured nighttime action behind the lines. Like a scout, Morris felt his best when on patrol surrounded by enemies. "On patrol, you're running your own show," he said.

But being out in front brought a loneliness which seemed consistent with Herb's pensiveness and general search for purpose. This search would be interrupted on February 16 when Germany's 1st Parachute Corps, in step with the LXXVI Panzer Corps, fronted an assault against the beachhead with the intention of ploughing the Allied soldiers into the Tyrrhenian. Emerging from a thick fog that descended that morning, German soldiers and tanks, able to traverse the frozen ground of the marshy fields, lashed out with a massive counterattack that Kesselring had first intended to unleash against the beachhead two weeks before. He had been foiled when by sheer coincidence the Allies had attacked first. The German offensive began as a diversionary strike against the U.S. Third Division by two green companies of the Hermann Göring's Parachute Demonstration Battalion, whose gambit was weakened by an epidemic of dysentery that had swept through the ranks. The German Fourth Parachute Division also conducted a feigning attack against the center of the front, which succeeded in rupturing the line where the 56th Division stood vigil, and penetrated as far as two miles. The main enemy thrust took place along the Anzio-Albano Road and crashed through the Thunderbirds of the Forty-fifth Infantry. The entire front bucked and strained. Morris was manning a position on the line that was about to be overwhelmed by a panzer that was "running back and forth" in front of him like an angry, pacing dog.

In a short time Morris would find himself under the earth, his trench transformed into a grave. And the terror of that day would not be absent in Denville, New Jersey. Despite Herb's selfless enlistment, all of his brothers signed up anyway. With all of their boys in the services, Morris's mother and father whispered prayers before going to sleep each night. On one night, Mrs. Morris was shaken awake by a horrible dream. She immediately roused her husband. "Something has happened to Herbert," she said.

———

Frederick's aggressive posture on the beachhead was accruing a body count. By the end of February, the FSSF had taken 145 prisoners and, according to Frederick, killed and wounded "a considerably larger number." The Force may have been losing fewer soldiers, but it was hemorrhaging steadily. "We lost people every night during these raids," an officer in 2nd Regiment admitted years later. "We were getting diminished."

Nevertheless, it soon became clear that Frederick's strategy was working. The enemy had identified the right-flank defenders as the FSSF. (Axis Sally, the Italian war's version of Tokyo Rose, began to refer to them by name: "that murdering First Special Service Force.") The Germans appeared convinced the Force was much larger than it actually was, and—more important—they were afraid. The proof came in writing a day after the Force's first audacious raid on the beachhead.

Frederick had ordered 5th Company–2nd Regiment, commanded by Captain Adna Underhill, to seize the village of Sessuno. Frederick's scheme was ambitious and set the tone for the campaign: Underhill's men would not just attack the Germans, they would seize the village and occupy it for the night. Six days before their own counterattack, the Germans were to be forced to believe that a major Allied breakout was in the works. Under cover of artillery, Underhill's company crossed the Mussolini Canal at Bridge 5 and marched east on each side of the main road.

The Force men edged toward their objective expecting a vicious fight. They knew a bulked-up platoon from the Hermann Göring Division, roughly the same size of an FSSF company, was garrisoned in the town. They also knew that the Germans had reserve troops in Littoria, only five kilometers away. The Force men boasted no advantage in manpower or firepower, given that the enemy had armor at its disposal. But Underhill's raiders did enjoy the element of surprise. Worried that they would be spotted in the moonlight, most of the patrol advanced along the edge of the Allied shelling zone, a strategy that courted death from friendly fire but ensured the raiders would emerge from an area where the Germans wouldn't be expecting them. After the Force men got underway, they found that visibility under the bright moon only extended about 200 meters, and even at that distance, if spotted by enemy sentries, they could easily be mistaken for Germans.

Sessuno was located at a crossroads. Underhill put a platoon on each flank and then assaulted the town with a third platoon of black-faced marauders the moment the Allied artillery fell silent. (Underhill had coordinated his advance with the barrage so that his men were barely thirty meters away from the German positions in Sessuno when the shelling stopped.) While two platoons on the flank, armed with Johnny guns, took on enemy machine gun nests, 2nd Platoon, commanded by Lieutenant William Ivey, from Seattle, Washington, charged up the Bridge 5–Sessuno Road. Though three mortar crews covered this advance, Ivey's men met stiff resistance from the German gunners and mortar men who already had the road targeted. But the opposition did not last long. When the firefight erupted Underhill's flanking platoons were so close to the German gun pits the Force men silenced them with a few grenades. Ivey's platoon stormed into the town with such force that the Germans spilled into the crossroads and tried to flee.

The enemy who tried to escape south in the direction of the nearest German-controlled town, Borgo Piave, were mowed down with automatic-weapon fire from Force men waiting in ambush at the intersection. The frontal assault on the farmhouses killed or captured the rest. In the early hours of February 11, the village of Sessuno belonged to Adna Underhill and 5-2. Sometime around 2 a.m. the raiders started to pull out. A platoon covering the withdrawal ambushed four or five trucks of German soldiers speeding to Sessuno to deliver a counterattack. The raiders cut down as many as thirty of the enemy, who, according to Adna Underhill, "were falling like leaves in a windstorm."

When 5-2 reached the canal, their dead included two first-rate sergeants, and a young private. But they had killed up to fifty of the enemy, and taken seven prisoners. That this attack and others were scarring the psyche of the Hermann Göring Division became clear some days later when a story spread across the right flank of the beachhead like mail call. A German platoon commander had been killed and a diary had been found on his body. On February 11, the day after Adna's attack, the officer, a lieutenant in Alarm Company Pauke, had written: "Reports from Sessuno of *Schwartzer Teufel* [Black Devil] raid last night." Two days later, the doomed man wrote that there had been "sharp attacks on [Alarm Company] Vesuv," and he finished with the lament: "We never hear these devils when they come."

The Force men had to be pleased. They had toyed with sobriquets such as the Braves and Freddy's Freighters for two years, but finally a fitting name had been found. The Force men were Black Devils. Whether, as some historians now speculate, this hellish moniker had actually been invented by Frederick and his intelligence chief, Burhans, as another barrage of psychological warfare was irrelevant. The name stuck, found its way into the press, and was even reportedly mumbled by a dying German on the beachhead. "I could actually hear the Kraut trying to say *Schwartzer Teufel* as they were slicing his throat," Sergeant Victor Kaisner of 5-2 later told an historian. "That really surprised us that he knew who was killing him."

———

On any given night, a hulking man with a broad face, a wide nose, and crow-black hair as thick as prairie grass would leave 1st Battalion, 3rd Regiment headquarters, pass a Force outpost, commit a password to memory, and disappear alone into the Anzio night.

With skin so mahogany in hue it almost needed no camouflage, the lone soldier was Sergeant Tommy Prince, and his patrols were overseen by no god Mrs. Morris had ever worshipped, or perhaps heard of. A pantheon of deities lived at Anzio, even among the unruly Force men. There were Catholics, Jews, Protestants of every denomination, atheists, and hardened sinners in this group. But the Force also had older faiths that fixed soldiers to the contours of the earth and were rooted in nature. These were the beliefs of the Force's Native soldiers. Their spirituality was an amalgam of legends, values, customs, and practices that dictated how they lived, how they hunted, and, for some in the Allied armies in Italy and the Pacific, how they waged war. On another Italian battlefield a Saskatchewan Indian named George Munroe routed a group of Germans and saved a patrol of comrades by simply going "around the gully, just like hunting moose."

Tommy Prince, the Saulteaux Ojibway from Scanterbury, Manitoba, became the most famous, the most controversial, and arguably the most tragic Native to apply his ageless soldiering to the Second World War. In the Force, Prince was respected, feared, suspected, envied, dismissed, and genuinely puzzled over. Somehow, in an era when the U.S. Army was largely segregated, and Canadian Natives possessed no citizenship rights, Prince overcame official limitations and etched out an unprecedented record of bravery. He would win two decorations for valor and numerous campaign medals. At the war's end he would be touted the highest-decorated Native Canadian to emerge from the conflict. The accomplishment was spectacular given that the FSSF was an outfit that issued citations sparingly. According to Joe Dauphinais of 1-2, Canada's ranking officer Colonel Akehurst believed "to serve in the Force was reward enough."

The officer who recognized something special in Tommy Prince was 3rd Regiment's 1st Battalion commander, Tom Gilday. Admired himself for his skills in winter warfare, Gilday—according to a fellow officer at 1st Battalion HQ—was "the guy who could break a trail in new snow during ski training in Montana and leave the rest of us behind." Gilday was tough: "a strict disciplinarian and a good soldier." He was also a good judge of men. He spotted Prince's potential as a scout in the mountains near Cassino and took the big Indian under his wing at battalion HQ.

As time passed, Gilday would keep Prince close. He would keep him busy. He would give him medals and praise. Indulging his desire to work alone whenever possible, Gilday seemed to admire Prince for his uniquely Indian way of bringing bedlam and sudden death to the enemy. "He'd slip away at night and get behind the German lines by himself," Gilday would say years later. "He moved with absolute quiet because of a pair of moccasins he'd wear . . . Sometimes, instead of killing the Germans, he'd steal something from them . . . Other times, he'd slit their throats and not make a sound."

Prince came by his talents honestly; his Native pedigree was illustrious. Not only was he a direct descendant of the Saulteaux patriarch Chief Peguis, he was also related to Chief William Prince, a member of the Nile Voyageurs, Indian and Métis rivermen mainly from Manitoba who in 1884 joined a British expedition to help rescue Major General Charles Gordon, under siege at Khartoum. In spite of his noble Native bloodline, however, Prince may have become a soldier to escape Indian life, with its poverty and humiliation. At five years of age Prince was enrolled in a residential school, the infamous state institutions that proved to be dens of abuse with, according to one Indian Affairs report, a 24 percent death rate.

Outside of the classroom, life on the reserve was just as tough. At Brokenhead there was sharing between families and a sense of community, but there was also despair and relentless work. Prince found relief in the army cadets. Of course, he liked boy soldiering because he was good at it. Hunting with his father had taught him marksmanship and—according to his biographers—how to plant "five bullets through a target the size of a playing card at one hundred meters." In a world where he was relegated to inferior status (according to the *Indian Act* in force at the time, Native peoples were not defined as "persons" but as wards of the state), the military elevated him. "As soon as I put on my uniform, I felt a better man," Prince once said.

Prince was twenty-four years old when he left his job as a farm laborer to join up after war broke out. Enlisted in First Corps Field Park Company, he set sail for Britain in 1940. Once there, he served as a sapper, grew bored, and eventually volunteered for parachute training at the jump school at Ringway, Manchester. He excelled at it. In addition to fine shooting, his Saulteaux education had taught him how to read the land and its subtle contours. In the early summer of 1942, Prince returned to North America and found his way into in the Force.

At Fort Henry Harrison, Prince kept quiet, stuck close to the other Natives, and drank only in the Helena bars they drank in. When in the presence of non-Natives, Prince sometimes felt the need to clown. In barracks in Britain he called a letter from his father "a smoke signal from the chief." According to a Force man named P. L. Cottingham, after Prince momentarily froze at the door of the transport during his first jump at Fort Harrison, he told his friends he'd been a "chicken Indian."

He would never accuse himself of that again. In the mountains of Italy he began to find his way. Prince may have joined the army to be a better man—the equal of a white—but he discovered that he performed best in the white army when he drew upon the skills usually associated with the traditions of his people, and it was then that he came to Gilday's attention. The moccasins that Lieutenant Colonel Gilday claimed Prince wore on patrol symbolized his new determination to fight the Germans as an Ojibway warrior. Many of Prince's actions were audacious and linked to his Native sensibilities. Some marveled at the terror Prince inflicted on the enemy: the stories of how he slipped into foxholes and augmented his reputation by stealing shoes from the sleeping enemies' feet. Mark Radcliffe recounts how near Cassino Prince would slice the throat of just one snoozing enemy so that the cold body would be discovered by his comrades the next morning.

Prince didn't invent the Force's use of psychological warfare, nor was he the only one to employ it. General Frederick had psychological ploys of his own. Aware of the usefulness of "Psy-ops," Frederick had small, card-sized brochures printed. They bore the Force's red spearhead emblem, replete with the national identities "U.S.A.–Canada," and a very personal message to every German soldier along the beachhead: "Das Dicke Ende Kommt Noch." *It Will Only Get Worse.* These flyers proliferated at Anzio. The soldiers carried them in their cargo pockets, and deposited them on the foreheads of German corpses or on the bunker thresholds of the living enemy they wanted to unnerve.

Prince unnerved his share of Germans, but he killed many as well. According to Bill Story, Prince was an accomplished sniper who would make his way out into no man's land, choose a vantage point as secret as a duck blind, and shoot any German who fell into his sights. If Prince began to discover his potential near Cassino, he began to realize it at Anzio. Any fears he wrestled with at the beginning, such as his hesitation at Fort Harrison's jump school, were put aside to be replaced by a cold, single-minded aggression that would inspire acts of bravery and, later, recklessness. Years later, Prince explained what had driven him: "All my life I had wanted to do something to help my people recover their good name."

———

Around February 5, whatever was driving Prince compelled him to venture out alone deep into no man's land, and to creep within two hundred meters of the enemy.

Prince was late returning from that mission, and by the end of the first day Gilday began to worry that he had been either killed or captured. Finally, just after dark, Prince's sturdy form emerged from the shadows at an outpost, and when he reported to Gilday, he explained that he had found an abandoned farm-house near the German position. After slipping inside, he had climbed into the attic, hoping to get a clear view of the enemy's assets. Soon after, a German patrol, probably on a routine search, barged through the door. Prince managed to elude them, and remained in the attic the entire day. He watched and listened, and when he returned, he told Gilday that he had found a perfect observation post.

Gilday agreed, and the next day, before dawn, Prince set out again. This time he carried a reel of 1,400 meters of telephone wire, which he uncoiled all the way up to the farmhouse. For three days he observed and reported back by phone. He called in shelling, directed the fire, and by February 8 had orchestrated the destruction of four German tanks.

When Prince returned, he regaled Gilday with the details of his mission. At one point, Prince explained, the phone had gone dead. He knew what had happened: a shell fragment had clipped the telephone wire. Faced with a scuttled mission, Prince knew it would be suicide for him to leave the farmhouse in broad daylight and try to repair the line. But the line had to be repaired. Prince reasoned it would be impossible for an Allied soldier to mend the wire, but it would be an easy matter for an Italian, would it not? There were Italian civilians on the plain. Some peasants had refused to leave their homes in the combat zone, and were still occasionally spotted puttering in their farmyards as if a world war wasn't raging around them. Unfortunately, there was no resident Italian near Prince's out-post—until the Saulteaux put on some clothing that had been abandoned by the previous occupant, grabbed a hoe, and ven-

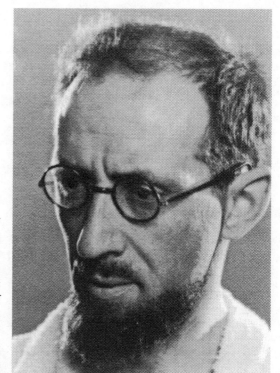

Portrait of a troubled mind: Geoffrey Pyke devoted himself to topics ranging from warships made of ice to a unified theory of economics. His suggestion to Mountbatten that the Allies master the snows of Europe the way the British had mastered the seas led eventually to the creation of the FSSF. (Rob Silcocks photo)

Winter training on the Continental Divide. This Force man learns how to wage war in arctic conditions near Blossburg, Montana, where the soldiers slept in box cars, and spent most of their days on skis. (U.S. Signal Corps, Library and Archives Canada, PA-183758)

Bayonet training on the Montana plains near Fort Harrison. Bayonets were only one of the many weapons with which the Force men were trained to kill. (JFK Museum/Lew Merrim collection)

A former Shanghai policeman and martial arts expert taught the Force men a particularly lethal form of hand-to-hand combat derived from Defendu. "I'm not here to teach you to hurt, I'm here to teach you to kill." (JFK Museum/Lew Merrim collection)

Force men clown during a light moment at Fort Harrison in 1942. Art Arsennek, hatless and shoeless, sent this photo as a card to his wife, Dora. (Courtesy of Dora Stephens)

Because attacks against electric power facilities in the mountains of Norway was an early mission of the Force, the commandos received alpine training at Fort Harrison. These skills served them well in their maiden battle on Monte la Difensa. (JFK Museum/Lew Merrim collection)

"Powder River": Force men board a C-47 aircraft during parachute training at Ft. Harrison. Due to the compressed training schedule of Plough Project, the FSSF's jump training was rapidly accelerated with Force men making their first jump within days or even hours of arrival. Underscoring their unit's uniqueness, the men rejected "Geronimo" and chose their own parachute cry. (U.S. Signal Corps, Library and Archives Canada, PA-183759)

The endless Montana plains became a parade ground for the Force in marches of 35 miles or more. (National Archives)

Second Regiment's Don MacKinnon as a novice FSSF paratrooper at Fort Harrison in 1942. Note head protection is a football helmet. (Courtesy of Heather MacKinnon)

Designed to transport the Force men across the snows of northern Europe, the state-of-the-art M29 Weasel snowmobile became redundant for the Force when the Norway invasion was scrapped. The Weasel was used in training, saw action in both Europe and the Pacific, and was part of the U.S. (and French) arsenals in the Vietnam war, where it plowed through swamp and mud as effectively as snow. (Courtesy of the John Dallimore/FSSF Living History association)

Legendary scouts and friends. Force men Joe Glass and Lorin Waling in southern Italy in 1944. (Courtesy of Joe Glass)

A prince at Buckingham Palace: Lt. Col. Jack Akehurst (left), the Force's highest ranking Canadian officer, inspects the Military Medal granted to Native soldier Sgt. Tommy Prince by Britain's King George VI in February 1945. (R. Woods, Library and Archives Canada, PA-142288)

Lt. Col. Tom MacWilliam, the commander of 2nd Battalion–2nd Regiment who led the assault on Monte la Difensa, and his wife, Harriet, in Saint John, New Brunswick. According to MacWilliam's son Tom, this was the last photograph taken of his parents. (Courtesy of Tom MacWilliam, Ottawa)

Lt. J. Kostelec of Calgary in a pose that highlights the Force's unique shoulder flash. Kostelec disappeared during an operation on the Anzio beachhead in early March 1944 shortly after being commissioned as an officer. He was Presumed Dead. (F. G. Whitcombe, Library and Archives of Canada, PA-183879)

Herb Peppard and his younger brother before leaving for war from a home "where I knew every nook and cranny . . . as if it were a part of myself." (Herb Peppard photo)

Art and Dora Arsennek in Helena, Montana in 1942. Dora came to Helena and found temporary work while Art trained at Fort Harrison. Dora was one of many "camp followers" who moved to base towns to be near their husbands. (Courtesy of Dora Stephens)

Force men smile at Anzio even though this photo is taken in late April, after three months on the beachhead line. Back row center is Larry Piette of Wisconsin, one of the first officers to scale the cliffs of Monte la Difensa during the Force's first operation. (C. E. Nye, Library and Archives of Canada, PA-183884)

March on Rome.
Brig. Gen. Frederick (far right) confirms his bearings with Lt. Gen. Mark Clark, Brig. Gen. Donald Brann, and Maj. Gen. Geoffrey Keyes on June 4, 1944, on the outskirts of Rome. "Frederick got so bold in his pursuit of the city, 1st Regiment's commander, Jack Akehurst, was forced to politely ask the general to not get ahead of advance units." (National Archives, 111-SC-191385)

Three Force men move along a mountain trail near Venafro, Italy through a cluster of peasant homes. (F. G. Whitcombe, Library and Archives Canada, PA-128979)

Force men and Fifth Army soldiers gather in front of the FSSF clearing station near La Noc Italy in January 1944. Note the German POW, in a posture of bored relief, in the center of the shot. For him the war is over. For the Force, the war would move from the mountains of central Italy to the Anzio beachhead. (National Archives of Canada, PA 128982)

General Frederick and Bob Moore of 2nd Regiment stand before a torched U.S. tank after the raid of Cerreto Alto on April 15, 1944. "From the cover of a drainage ditch, Joe watched the 88s rake the vehicles, and he couldn't help but think: 'Those poor bastards in the tanks.'" (National Archives, III-SC-437-685)

On April 14, 1944, an FSSF patrol invades Anzio's no-man's-land by way of an irrigation ditch to clear an enemy outpost from a nearby farmhouse. (National Archives, III-SC-312789)

May 24, 1944, a day after the breakout from the Anzio beachhead, a Fifth Army tank powers toward a German position 500 yards away. (National Archives, 111-SC-421412)

A Force man scrounges eggs on the Anzio beachhead. "Soldiers fought the Germans for henhouses in no-man's-land. Literally." (National Archives)

Lt. W. H. Langdon of Timmins, Ontario loaded down with full kit prepares to move out north of Venefro. (F. G. Whitcombe, Library and Archives Canada, PA-128981)

An FSSF unit prepares to venture out for a night patrol on the Anzio beachhead on April 20, 1944. Their blackened faces became a symbol of terror for the Germans, who reportedly christened the Force men *Schwartzer Teufel,* Black Devils. Lt. H. Rayner of Toronto kneels in the foreground. (C. E. Nye, Library and Archives Canada, PA-128986)

Mail became one of the Force's few pleasures during the long, arduous Anzio campaign. Third from left is Tom O'Brien of Toronto who, in 2004, was President of the FSSF Association. (C. E. Nye, Library and Archives of Canada, PA-183868)

Force men Capt. S. L. Dymond (helmet under his arm) and Lt. J. D. Mitchell plan their next move at Anzio. (C. E. Nye, Library and Archives Canada, PA-183735)

Art Arsennek illustrated this envelope with a scene, entitled "A Lonely Night in Italy," a depiction of his life on the Anzio beachhead. The machine gun is pointed at a mouse in the corner, and the cartoon depicts the boredom and banality that accompanied the terror of that long campaign. (Courtesy of Dora Stephens)

Force men left this calling card on enemy corpses. It means "It will only get worse." This form of psychological warfare helped generate terror among the enemy, and reinforced the Force's mythic reputation as Black Devils. (Courtesy of John Dallimore)

USA CANADA

DAS DICKE ENDE KOMMT NOCH!

Pvt. Dan Lemaire of Rouyn, Quebec, PFC Richard Stealy of Chicago, Sgt. Charles Shepard of East Franham, Quebec, Lt. H. Rayner of Toronto, and PFC James A. Jones of Quincy, Massachusetts prepare for a patrol on the Anzio beachhead. Force patrols took the war to the enemy lines in the dark of night. (C. E. Nye, Library and Archives of Canada, PA-183862)

Survivors: Steffie and Lorin Waling in the late 1970s. (Joe Glass photo.)

LEFT: Herb Morris, the son of Denville, New Jersey who found life's purpose on the killing fields of Anzio. (H. Morris photo) ABOVE: Rev. Herb Morris at his home outside of Portland, Oregon in 2004. (Author photo)

RIGHT: Wedding photo of Lorin Waling and Steffie Broderick (bottom row). Joe Glass stood up for Waling, and Steffie's sister, Ann, was maid of honor. (Courtesy Joe Glass) BELOW: Joe and Dorothy Glass in their Helena home in 2004. (Author photo)

LEFT: Capt. Mark Radcliffe in southern France in late 1944. When Herb Morris set eyes on Radcliffe in training in 1942, he told himself: "Now there is a soldier." (Courtesy of Mark Radcliffe) ABOVE: Mark Radcliffe in Helena in 2004. Fit and trim, Radcliffe says his voice never recovered after being struck in the throat while being interrogated at Anzio in 1944. (Author photo)

LEFT: Friends in arms. Force men Herb Goodwin (far left) and Floyd Schmidt (center) grew up next door to each other in Elmira, Ontario. But only one would return after the war. (H. Goodwin photo) RIGHT: Herb Goodwin in 2004 in his home in Helena, Montana. (Author photo)

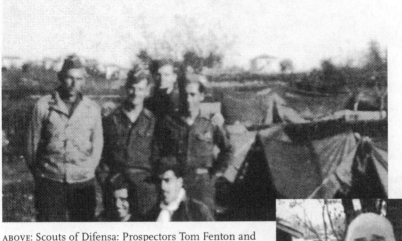

ABOVE: Scouts of Difensa: Prospectors Tom Fenton and Howard van Ausdale (middle row, 2nd and 3rd from left) in southern France in 1944. Fenton and van Ausdale scouted the route up Monte la Difensa, the Force's first and perhaps most legendary victory. (Courtesy of Joe Glass) RIGHT: Last known photo of legendary FSSF scout Howard van Ausdale outside his home in Baker City, Oregon, not long before his death in 1983. Although the photo is attributed to Tom Fenton, it may have been taken by Fenton's longtime friend Cliff Turner, who paid Van Ausdale a visit in the early 1980s. (Courtesy of Joe Glass)

Heroes' row: FSSF veterans gather on May 31, 2004, just before ceremonies marking U.S. Memorial Day at Nettuno, Italy. L-R Ken Jones, Maine; Herb Peppard, Truro, Nova Scotia; Jack Callowhill, Stony Creek, Ontario; Lloyd Dunlop, Yarmouth, Nova Scotia; Hector MacInnis, Dartmouth, Nova Scotia; Charlie Mann, Kincardine, Ontario; Sam Finn, St. Louis, Missouri.

tured outside. Pretending to be tilling the earth, which must have looked strange in February, Prince hoed a row along the telephone wire until he reached the break. Then, ostensibly stooping to tie a shoelace, he mended the communications wire, shook a fist at the German line for dramatic effect, and returned to the farmhouse, where he resumed telephone contact with the artillery.

Gilday must have loved the story. But based on what he knew for sure—Prince's penetration behind German lines and his three-day stint as an artillery observer—Gilday had already decided to recommend Prince for the Military Medal, a bravery citation tailored for men ranked as noncommissioned officers and below. This decoration would launch his career and his reputation. Within an outfit where acts of valor were commonplace and went largely unrecognized, Gilday's decision would also stir resentment. It could be perceived in whispers in Gilday's HQ and in the mumble of an anonymous comrade heard by Force man Bill Johnson, another Manitoban from The Pas, as Prince strode to the line one night: "There goes Prince trying to win another medal to prove he is brave."

———

Herb Morris's home in Denville, New Jersey, was just the way he remembered it: a welcoming, expansive house that was big enough to absorb a family with nine children. There was the living room, and the pillars you walked through on the way in, and the heavy coal furnace, and the adjoining parlor that connected to the dining room. With every room somehow linked and the house literally enveloping him, Herb edged toward the great fireplace and the tambour clock that sat on the mantel. Young Herb didn't notice the time. He was obsessed with a single thought. "Is this real?" he asked himself.

Slowly, deliberately, Morris dug his fingers into his flesh, and—as he feared would happen in his dream—he awoke in his slit trench to the reality of the Anzio beachhead. On February 16, he awoke to a nightmare: a German offensive that threatened to smash the VI Corps line, and push the defenders into the tide. Morris's first hint of what was coming had been the pacing tank flanked by German infantrymen, which bore down his position. Morris wasn't sure how many men he was facing, but there were a lot, and in this stretch of the front he was one of only three or four. The machine-gun nest up ahead had at least one gunner for certain, and another Force man shared the trench with Morris. But what they lacked in men, they made up for in firepower. The previous night, a Force man had been hit near him. Morris had cleaned and loaded the rifle the fallen man left behind, and it now leaned against the wall of the adjoining dugout. In addition to the extra rifle, Morris had a bazooka, which he and his fellow Force man already had aimed at the German tank.

With the armor tight in his sights, Morris fired. A flame spit out the back of the stovepipe barrel and a shell burst from the front. Morris, despite the roar and kick of the weapon, watched the rocket streak toward the tank—and bounce off. At that moment 50 mm fire bored in on them, followed by a jarring explosion. His last memory was of a wave of earth washing over, burying him and the other Force man in the trench. If Morris lost consciousness, it was only for an instant, or perhaps what he thought was unconsciousness was simply his head trying to blink its way back to full awareness after being numbed by the blast.

When Morris came to, he pulled himself out of the partly refilled ditch and realized he was alone. His partner had retreated without him, probably assuming he was dead. With the tank and men still approaching, Morris grabbed his extra rifle from the communications trench and sprinted forward to the conspicuously quiet machine-gun nest to make a stand. When he got there, he found the gun pressed into the skull of the gunner. The weapon was inoperable, and the Germans were advancing toward him.

Morris had one last idea. Racing back toward the slit trench he had just occupied, he focused on mortar tubes and grenades set up near the position. As was the practice elsewhere along the thin line, Morris and his partner had aimed their mortars at fixed spots along the approach. In the event of an attack, they could fire without aiming. Now that the thin line was in danger of being overrun, Morris frantically began pulling pins and dropping ordinance into the tubes. Within seconds Morris knew that the rounds pumping out of multiple mortar barrels were having an effect. German infantrymen were going to ground, and the advance was wavering. He fed the tubes so obsessively that he didn't notice exactly when support began to appear around him, and he wasn't even sure what had happened to the panzer. Among the Force men who had rushed up to meet and counter the German attack was Harold Pence, the 3rd Regiment medic, who stared at Morris and said: "Herb, you been hit."

Morris put a hand to the back of his head, waved a blood-covered fist in front of his eyes, and had to agree. He was wounded and disoriented, so he obeyed when the medic said he had to come with him to the aid station, situated about a couple of kilometers back of the line. With reinforcements still fighting to protect that narrow swath of front, Morris headed back with Pence, who asked him and a third man to carry a stretcher cradling a soldier. Morris, at one end of the litter, staggered along. Soon he was in the dressing station, and not long after that he found himself in the crowded tent hospital near the shore of the beachhead.

Suffering from a concussion, arguably more serious than the

shrapnel wound to his neck, Morris collapsed onto a hospital cot as German warplanes screamed overhead and anti-aircraft guns ack-acked nearby. Along the line that Morris had just come from, defenders fought all night for their lives in the face of a grinding and determined enemy. The attack had begun with an unexpected push by two inexperienced German battalions that overran the British Fifty-sixth Division, ploughed three kilometers into the narrow beachhead, and—in the words of one historian—brought "profound anxiety to the Allied command." The Brits, the American infantrymen of the U.S. Forty-fifth Division, and the FSSF rallied and made up lost ground, and by the end of the first day the German penetration extended no more than two and a half kilometers into the beachhead. But the beachhead's commander, General Lucas, had drawn a final no-retreat line that the Allies were forbidden to withdraw behind, and at times the enemy penetration drew frighteningly close to this boundary.

German Fourteenth Army commander, General Eberhard von Mackensen, continued the pressure throughout the night. Mackensen was so confident of a decisive breakthrough that he kept two critical divisions out of the fight to be used to deliver the coup de grâce when the moment was at hand. That moment never came. The Allied position became dire at the spearhead of the German attack, the vulnerable point between the U.S. 179th and 157th infantry regiments. But, as the historian Martin Blumenson noted, the Allies "refused to break. Supported by a reckless expenditure of artillery, tank, tank destroyer, and mortar fire, the infantry held." The outlook of the 179th Infantry improved when the inspired decision was made to put former Ranger commander William O. Darby in command of the defense, with orders to hold the line at all costs. As a leader who had already lost so much, Darby was a soldier unwilling to withdraw a step more.

Ultimately, the enemy offensive petered out under the weight of tremendous losses (German battalions had been reduced to the size of mere companies of no more than 150 men), and by the night of February 17 even "Kesselring thought it was probably already too late to win the battle." The offensive ground on a while longer, mainly to assuage Hitler, who would not readily accept failure. But the beachhead survived.

While the battle continued to rage, Morris slept like a dead man. Meanwhile, a continent away, his mother at that moment stirred from a nightmare that featured her son and woke up her husband. Soon she would receive a telegram that confirmed to her the dream had been true.

CHAPTER 12

DEVILS

For Lorin Waling and Joe Glass, the war, now restricted to the nightscape on the enemy lines, became myopic, furtive, and literally dark. Anzio offered few amenities and rare relief. Because they were undermanned, the Force men were constantly on the line, and tired. Different from the mountains, the cold of Anzio was achingly damp. It penetrated clothes, flesh, and bone. Sometimes Joe and Lorin warmed themselves by lighting a small fire, boiling water in their canteens, and seasoning it with shavings from the high-calorie chocolate bars they had been rationed. The only time they ventured to the rear was in search of booze—usually locally made wine, since whiskey and beer were hard to come by. When at the harbor, Joe and Lorin sometimes visited Joe's friend Bill Lindsey, an affable young sailor with the sturdy and squat build of a fire hydrant who served on the HMCS *Prince Henry*, a former merchant steamship converted into a cruiser. Joe had sailed with Billy on the Great Lakes before the war, and was amazed when he bumped into him on the beachhead.

But those visits were rare. Joe and Lorin found themselves ahead of the front line more than they did behind it. Like most of the 2nd Regiment, and the FSSF for that matter, their engagements were limited to night patrols, and their experiences were becoming increasingly nightmarish.

Combat patrols were still being aggressively pursued by the 1st and 3rd Regiments in a bid to "kill as many Krauts as possible, [and] put the fear of God, or rather of us, in them," as Adna Underhill would later write. These patrols were variations on the now familiar maneuver: move in behind enemy outposts and then strike ruthlessly, eliminating soldiers and their weapons, which Joe liked to bash into junk with rocks. Other Force men brought German weapons back as souvenirs, or to trade. And the men always, when possible, brought their own dead back, which ratcheted up the terror among the enemy, who would find German dead in the detritus of a raid but rarely Force men. They had to wonder: Could these men be killed?

They could, and Glass and Waling experienced that early on, after being assigned to act as litter carriers for a massive battalion-sized raid that was being led by 2nd Regiment's bear-sized commander, Bob Moore. In the spirit of Frederick and Walker, Bob Moore was a commander who liked to take control of the big operations with his frying pan–sized hands, and lead the way. The mission in the early hours of February 20 was to probe a derelict quarry near the village of Sessuno, sniff out the German guns and armor deployed there, and destroy as much hardware as possible. First Company–2nd Regiment men were conscripted to carry wounded after an incident two nights before when another 2nd Regiment operation in the same area had led to the deaths of at least two unarmed service battalion stretcher-bearers. After those losses, HQ had declared that only combat personnel would carry wounded back across the canal, and on that night the litter carriers would include Glass and Waling, armed with pistols, knives, and an army stretcher.

Glass had groaned when he received the order. He looked at a potato-fed private from Boise, Idaho, by the name of Jimmy Nielson, and said, "Don't you get hit, you big sonofabitch, I don't want to carry you back." Nielson had to laugh. Who the hell had any intention of getting hit?

The Quarry wasn't far away from the canal, lying due east from Bridge 5 at the far right end of the 3rd Regiment line. In addition to the Quarry, several spots across the plain's broad patchwork of wet fields and crisscrossing ditches were becoming infamous for the Force men: innocuous landmarks like Hell's Corners (east of Bridge 2 on the edge of the Pontine Marshes), House 13 (virtually on the coast), and, on the left side of the line, the Factory, the Bowling Alley, and Dead End Road.

The Quarry on that night would become surreal and bleak for Glass and Waling, as the Force incurred losses amid the burning German armor they ambushed and the irate Panzers that prowled the roads as the men hid in the dikes.

The night began spectacularly. Early in the raid a bazooka shell breached a half-track that must have been transporting ammunition. When the vehicle blew, the flames literally lit the area like morning, and any jubilation the Force men felt watching enemy equipment blaze vanished when they realized they were now visible. But for Joe the burning half-track was a wonderful sight, and he almost hooted when one of the men (he would later swear it was Colonel Moore himself) leveled a bazooka at a German *Flakwagen* and let a shell fly that passed right between the vehicle's wheels.

It was that same vehicle, spewing 20 mm shells, that somehow found the soft belly of Jimmy Nielson. Joe could see Nielson lying in the field trying desperately to find cover in a plow furrow that would certainly have hidden a skinny kid like Glass, but not Nielson, whose body protruded above the level field like the mound of a fresh grave. Whether a bullet dug underneath Jimmy or clipped the young man as he was diving for the ground, Joe would never know. What he did know was that Nielson had been gut-shot. Glass found that out by rolling him over, probing his wound with his hand, and feeling the sticky warmth. The numbness of the injury quickly disappeared, and Nielson was gripped by the inevitable agony of a stomach wound. One Force man from 6-2 would remember the screams: "My guts are spillin' out."

What Joe and Lorin would remember more than Nielson's screams were his pleas. They had loaded him onto their stretcher and had just begun to transport him back across the fields toward the canal when Nielson begged the men to make the pain stop.

"Joe, shoot me, shoot me," Nielson said. "It hurts so bad. Kill me, please kill me."

"Jimmy, we're going to get you back," Glass said. "Don't worry."

Nielson was beyond worrying. And Glass and Waling had more to contend with than his pleading. Glass, at the front of the stretcher, wavered under the man's weight, and because Lorin at the back was taller, the litter sloped toward Glass and drove him to his knees whenever he stumbled on the uneven ground; and every time he fell, poor Jimmy Nielson screamed.

Joe prayed Jimmy would be quiet when they passed by the last German outposts on the approach to the canal. But now there was another problem: Lester Granville, a private from 6-2. Lester was a good kid, but he had cracked—a dishearteningly common occurrence at Anzio. Somewhere at the Quarry, fear, horror, and relentless stress had reached an unbearable crescendo inside of him. Lester had imploded in the midst of the raid, succumbing to "combat fatigue," a complaint that affected nearly one in ten

American troops. Transfixed by the chaos, explosions, and hail of 20 mm fire, he suddenly became unable to move, focus, or speak coherently, and the nearest officer—immediately sensing shell shock—told Joe and Lorin to take Lester back. So helpless that Waling had to shoulder his rifle, Lester staggered alongside the two as they struggled to keep Nielson aloft.

As the four approached those forward German outposts, Nielson ensured his silence by dying. Both Glass and Waling knew the moment they were carrying a dead man, and all they wanted now was to get back. After slipping by the German gun pits, the men approached the 3rd Regiment's line and crept up to an outpost, which was situated on the other side of a patch of brush and manned by wary Force men. With a noisy raid raging to the east, and the sounds of explosions and gunfire echoing, Joe knew that the sudden appearance of a group of soldiers might alarm them, so he wanted to approach the line carefully. He grabbed Lester and whispered to him to walk around the brush slowly and deliberately, and give the password and get help.

Lester, dazed and passive, seemed to understand. He turned and headed to the outpost. Glass's eyes were so accustomed to the dark, he could see Lester clearly as he wandered around the brush, passed the outpost without a word, and came full circle to where Joe and Lorin were waiting.

"You didn't give the password," Joe said.

"Nobody asked me," Lester replied.

"They ain't gonna ask you. You're lucky they didn't shoot you." Reaching his own limits of fatigue, Joe pulled out his pistol. "Now you go back and give the password, and don't come back without help."

Lester did as he was told, and a short time later Lorin and Joe were sitting near 2nd Regiment HQ with Jimmy Nielson stretched out beside them. Captain S. L. Dymond from 3rd Regiment strode up and approached a group of men congregated nearby. They were a patrol that had gone out with Moore's raiders, got separated somehow, and had stumbled in just after Glass and Waling.

"Get your butts back out there," Dymond said. "Moore is going to need you."

Hearing this, Joe got up and told Dymond to forget it. "Captain, these guys can't go back out there. They'll never find 'em. You gonna send 'em back to get lost and die?"

Dymond chewed on the scout's words and then turned to the patrol. "Okay, you better stay and wait."

Joe knew that no one would be able to help Moore and his men other than themselves; behind the line and surrounded, they would have to fight their way out. After the firefight sub-sided, Moore's men took refuge in the center of a farmer's field while angry German armor patrolled the roads around it, and German officers shouted for Moore and his men to give up, though they had no idea exactly where and how many they were. Moore had no intention of surrendering. As the fire of the burn-ing German half-track subsided, the Force men melted back into the night, and then, with 3rd Platoon covering the rear, darted across a road between the rumbling tanks, and crawled along an irrigation ditch to another road 200 yards away, which they fol-lowed back to the safety of the Mussolini Canal. While this was going on, Joe Glass resumed his place beside Jimmy and Lorin. Jimmy, of course, represented a friendship lost for good that night. Joe's relationship with Lorin, on the other hand, had been solidified in a way that only the act of ferrying a dying man and a traumatized boy across a foreign killing field can do. There was nothing for the two living Force men to do now but wait. They both knew they were in for the night.

On the morning of February 17, the day after the German counteroffensive began, Captain Mark Radcliffe came off the line. The beachhead had held, but at a price. By the offensive's end, Allied casualties tallied five thousand. As many as one thousand men from the Forty-fifth Division had vanished, and were either POWs or MIAs. But the fight had been a turning point for all of them, particularly the enemy, who—as the Force's intelligence officer, Robert Burhans, wrote—"was slowly realizing that the beachhead had become a rock that could not be wiped out with one or two isolated attacks." A stalemate was settling along the Anzio front, the Germans realizing they could not break into the beachhead any easier than the Allies could break out of it. Farther south, the cruel impasse continued at Cassino as Generals Clark and Alexander renewed the offensive to break into the Liri Valley and draw German troops away from Anzio. But despite taking the extreme step of destroying the fifth-century Benedictine monastery on Monte Cassino overlooking the town, the offensive failed.

During a brief breathing space that he used to check on wounded men, Radcliffe went to Anzio's tent-city hospital and paid a visit to Herb Morris. Radcliffe was pleased to find Morris alive and conscious, but he was surprised by what he was asking.

"I want to go back to the line," Morris said.

"Muscles, you can't even straighten out your head," Radcliffe said.

But Morris was insistent. "They need us up there."

"Well, it's true we need everybody up there," Radcliffe said, "but why not stay here a while?"

"Last night the ack-ack came right through the tent," Morris said. "You can get killed that way."

Radcliffe pulled strings, and later that day Morris found himself back on the line, feeling relieved. Like many other Force men, Morris considered the rear echelon of the beachhead, near the pier, ships, and big guns under attack from air and artillery, more dangerous than the front, where the Germans rarely bombed for fear of hitting their own.

Before long Morris had his dream again, identical to the first time. He stood before the hearth in his parents' home in New Jersey and stared at the tambour clock on the mantel. And again in that dream Morris, somehow disengaged from the dreamscape around him, decided that he had to be sure he was really home and resolved to pinch himself. But just as he was about to do it, he thought: if I do wake up this time, and arrive back home a third time—I won't pinch myself again. When Morris squeezed his arm and awoke in the trench, it was settled. The next time he was home, he would not test it. He would stay put.

He had to wonder whether he would ever fit in at home. Morris realized he was changing.

Like all the men of the FSSF, Morris had been hardened by training and combat into an instrument of violence scarcely recognizable as the recruit who had been tutored by his family and his church to respect his fellow man and turn the other cheek. The Forcemen had adopted a code of no surrender. The men of 3-3 had honed this tenet to a rhetorical question that did away with the niceties of civil society: "Why give a guy an even break?" This was no mere matter of military expediency; it was a new moral compass, which permitted previously unthinkable violence against not only the Germans, but against anyone at all, including MPs and other GIs. The world of violence had so marked these fighters that any impediment, any disagreement, any unwelcome form of authority could be a provocation to massive retaliation. If an SOB gives you hell, give him more back. If he insults you, hit him. If he hits you, throw him down the stairs. The world was full of trouble, so why invite more by giving a guy an even break?

Violence had become instinctive and ubiquitous. Morris found himself focusing on the details of the war raging around him.

When he looked hard enough, he sometimes recognized a strange harmony. One night Morris was on the line, sitting in a hole in the earth, and there was a Johnny gun off to the side. The gunners were firing in short, rhythmic bursts, answering the blasts of a German gun and probing the night for infiltrators. The Johnson, firing four hundred rounds per minute, went *tat-tat-tat tat-tat, tat-tat-tat tat-tat*; and then a German gun sounded with its own *tit-tit-tit* of a different pitch. Above him, Morris heard the drone of a single plane that seemed to lay down a chord of melancholy buzzing, interrupted only when the plane's engine coughed as it changed course. The bomber brought on the *ack-ack* of antiaircraft fire, and suddenly the sounds merged: . . . *zzzz zzzz tat-tat-tat ack-ack tit-tit-tit tat-tat-tat zzzzz*. Languishing in that dark hole on the line's edge, Morris marveled at how these noises somehow came together into what he would call "music of this total war." The sensation inspired him to write a poem:

> As we lay prone and still,
> The hollow sounds in sequence come,
> Leave holes no-one will fill

Morris found symmetry in the most common objects, and one of the most common on the right flank of the beachhead was the Force's dagger, the sleek V-42. During the first frantic days on the line, the Force had set upon the Germans every night, obliterating outposts in a bid to push their line back. The killing and destruction were mainly done in sudden eruptions of fire: grenades were tossed into surrounded gun pits that were then raked with gunfire meant to extinguish every living thing in the enemy bunker. But on many occasions silent killing was necessary, and then the V-42 became the primary weapon. Morris grew familiar with the dagger, and so did almost every other Force man who operated for any length of time behind enemy lines.

Contemplating the tool, Morris recognized a balanced beauty in its 7 5/16-inch blade of blue steel that tapered to absolute perfection. In fact, the point was too perfect for some of the men, who blunted the end so that the dagger would not become stuck in German bones. Perfectly balanced, the ricasso was devised so that the knife would naturally fall into the best grip to thrust between the ribs of an enemy. A pommel at the base served as an excellent skull crusher when the dagger was wielded like a club. And the stiletto's horsehide sheath, which rode low from the hip like a six-gun, placed the weapon at a Force man's fingertips.

Frederick had devised the V-42 long before he had ever heard or conceived of the Anzio beachhead. But the weapon was eerily tailor-made for the warfare the Force needed to bring to the Germans, and extremely effective. The knife, designed specifically for man-killing, always cut easily and profoundly, severing arteries and trachea, and sometimes seemed capable of decapitation. Victims of the V-42 died quietly and immediately. Drowning, their death was little more than a gasp and some gurgles.

Ironically, while on patrol at Anzio, Captain Pat O'Neill, who helped design the V-42, rarely used the dagger. He would creep up to a sentry and ask in German for a cigarette. Then, when the man turned, O'Neill would simply shoot him in the face with a single bullet from a submachine gun, which let off a soft, indiscernible report when only one shot was discharged. But you couldn't take a gun pit with a single shot from a Thompson, and so knives necessarily left their sheaths.

The V-42 proved edifying for the men who brandished it. It eliminated the distance between killing and dying. In the field there was a gap between the act of squeezing a trigger and the violence unleashed on a body violated by bullets. The distance between a mortar man and his dying target was a chasm. But when you killed with the V-42, you embraced your enemy. The weapon reduced combat to its primal form—raw, direct killing—and it forced a soldier to share in his enemy's death. The experience affected soldiers in different ways. All, at some profound level, were greatly troubled. Some responded to the horror by vowing to kill only when necessary. Others lost all restraint, and killed easily and prolifically.

Either way, these were not men who had volunteered out of ideological fervor, nor had they been rounded up by the press-gangs of a desperate government. Most had enlisted because they had deemed it the decent thing to do. Somehow that decency had been turned on its head; somehow, doing the right thing required deeds of grisly violence that would have shocked them only a year earlier. Whereas many Allied infantrymen never had to do anything more morally troubling than laying down covering fire against an unseen enemy, the Force men were called up to stain their hands with another man's blood, to tug their knives from the bones of their victims, to violate much that they must once have deemed inviolable.

None of this was lost on Morris, who after long contemplation wrote the poem "Silent Death":

> Blades of steel
> Though blackened for protection
> Turn the moon's rays
> Into a slight reflection;
> Reflection of life, before death
>
> Keen hewn points
> Wake the enemy section.
> They quake and shout,
> Each voice changing inflection;
> Inflection of life, before death

There may well be a discordant harmony in the white noise of war, and equilibrium in a dagger kill, but for Morris his purpose in the war became clear the day he was called upon to do reconnaissance from an abandoned farmhouse in enemy territory not far from the canal. By that time Morris was working in battalion headquarters as a radio man. Setting out just before dawn, Morris crept to the house, unreeling phone wire as he went. Once inside, he set up the phone and found a perfect vantage point in the attic, where a small hole opened onto German lines. It was an ideal keyhole to stare through with field glasses, and he was prepared to sit in that spot until dark. Then the phone rang. "We want to shell in that direction and we don't want you in the way," HQ said. "Come on in for a while. You can have a hot lunch, and by the time you're finished it will be time to go back."

So Morris crawled back to his line like a snake, had lunch, and, when the shelling was finished, wriggled back to the farmhouse. When he climbed to the attic, he saw something that almost made him tumble back down the stairs. The part of the room where he had been sitting was gone, blown away by a German shell that the enemy had started lobbing in when the Allied barrage began. If he had not been called back, he would now be dead. He decided this wasn't a coincidence. None of it was: the fact that he had been lunching when he might have been dying; the fact that he was in Europe fighting when he could have been somewhere else. How could he not think that God wasn't watching over him?

Morris would have one more dream where he stood in front of the fireplace and stared into the face of the mantelpiece clock. True to his promise, he refused to wake himself. But when morning came, he wasn't surprised to find himself in the same slit trench near the Mussolini Canal. "God," he would later say, "this is where I'm supposed to be now." Herb Morris knew what his purpose there was.

He was a devil doing God's work.

CHAPTER 13

ESCAPES

One night on the line Joe Glass was given an assignment to take out a gun pit with knives, and to take along a new scout—a former Ranger by the name of Dick Houseman, one of two brothers who had joined 1-2 after Darby's Rangers were wiped out. Dick was a skinny kid. He was supposed to be the twin of his brother Roy, also in the company, but Roy was heavier, and Joe had no idea what the third Houseman brother, captured by the Germans at Cisterna and now presumably a POW, looked like. The brothers were hearty youths from Kansas City, Missouri.

Tonight would be Dick's first time scouting, and the first time he would be using a knife. Joe knew the mission was connected to a bigger operation. A night or two before, the regular 3rd Platoon patrol men, Crichlow, Kroll, Lorin, Joe, and Herby Forester, had been out front, trawling for prisoners. They nabbed

a placid group of Germans, and at least one Pole. Being a
Chicago Pole himself, Rusty Kroll spoke to the man, and learned
that there were other Poles in his unit who were fighting under
duress and desperately wanted to give themselves up. Kroll
would be going out that night to get them. But there was one forward German gun pit that was in the way, and this was the
outpost that Joe and the Ranger were ordered to take out. They
were using knives because they couldn't use grenades and guns,
which would open the front lines to fire, and endanger Kroll and
the throng of prisoners he would be leading in.

Joe went over the procedure with Dick Houseman. They
would creep up behind the German bunker and identify the gunners. With a hand signal Joe would tell Dick which man was his,
and then the two would leap into the pit and dispatch the
Germans with their knives. Joe showed the best way to wield a
dagger, exactly the way Captain O'Neill had taught him: seize the
man by the helmet, pull back, and then slash.

Standing off to the side was the other Houseman brother,
Roy, who was a mortar man. He scowled, and when it was time
for the two to get going, Roy approached Joe.

"You Silver Star–hunting sonofabitch, don't you go getting
my brother killed trying to be a hero," he said.

Roy Houseman had lost one brother at Anzio, and he didn't
want to lose another. But Joe took offense. He told Roy that he
was not out to win medals, and then he told him where to get off.
Joe went on a bit, and later regretted giving Roy hell. But he was
angry at being accused.

Dick didn't say much about the confrontation, and the
scouts set out. The gun pit wasn't far, and Joe knew the area as
if it were his front yard, which in a way no man's land had
become. Dick crept along behind him, about to cross the line.
This might have been what Roy Houseman feared as much as
losing his last brother. Killing a man by slitting his throat

means crossing a line and occupying another place in the world.

When Joe and Dick reached the vicinity of the outpost, Joe led Dick around behind it. They edged up close enough to see inside—and found it empty. So they crept back, and reported to the command post that the gun pit was empty. Rusty ventured out with a patrol, found the contingent of Poles bent on surrender, and brought them back before dawn.

It had been a night of escapes: for the Poles who gave themselves up, for Kroll who pulled off the operation, for the Germans who should have been in the pit, and for Joe and Dick who were spared having to kill them. But Joe's biggest escape had nothing to do with the activities on the front. In March, he was given leave. Tommy Fenton, it turned out, would get a pass at the same time, and the two men would be able to travel to Naples and southern Italy. Glass and Fenton were happy men.

———

Joe and Tommy braved the shelling in Anzio harbor, boarded a landing craft and rode it south as it heaved through the Tyrrhenian Sea toward the open mouth of the Bay of Naples. For the first time since arriving in early February, they were leaving the Anzio line and the beachhead itself. For both men, leaving the front was a strange sensation. They should have felt they were getting out of harm's way; in fact, they felt more fearful.

While the German warplanes intermittently attacked southern Italy, the most dramatic strike in March 1944 came not from the Luftwaffe but from nature. The men could see the violence from the deck of their landing craft: smoke and ash billowing into the sky in great clouds as Mount Vesuvius erupted for the first time since 1872. For some Allied servicemen, the mountain represented a surprise attack from a seemingly quiet flank. Hot ash rained on the nearby 340th Bombardment Group, bettering the German air force in destruction. Eighty-eight B-25 bombers were smothered in the burning snow, which ate away at the skin of the planes, scarred the glass, and weighted the birds down so much they tipped over.

Joe and Tommy were fascinated with the volcano and resolved to visit it. The crag must have been particularly intriguing to Fenton, with his affinity for mountains and the treasures and mysteries that lay within them. Here was a mountain that lived, and fought back. After the landing craft deposited the two soldiers onshore, Glass and Fenton decided to make some other stops first and then move on to Vesuvius.

They went to Naples, which had seen scores of other armies over three millennia and had no trouble adjusting immediately to Joe, Tommy, and their fellow soldiers. Not long after the Allies seized Naples from the Germans, street vendors had appeared on the avenue Rettifilo in the ancient Spaccanapoli district, selling trinkets passed off as Roman relics, fabrics, cameos, and sexually explicit postcards based on the ribald wall paintings in the ruins of nearby Pompeii. When soldiers such as Joe and Tommy appeared, street salesmen would employ the hard sell, following them down the street, pulling on their sleeves, unwilling to let them go with their wallets intact.

There wasn't much in the way of food for the local Italians. At desperate moments, prostitutes sold themselves for government-issue tins of beef. Still, a few restaurants opened for the liberators, serving wine, which was always plentiful, and fresh catches from the sea, grilled on coals.

Naples before the war had been a dusty collection of crumbling buildings as sun-baked as old bones. The war, however, had turned it into a modern wreck. Hulks of sunken ships protruded from the harbor like whale carcasses. The city lacked basic utilities, and buildings had been reduced to rubble through which sharp-eyed MPs, starving locals, black-marketers and leave-taking soldiers swarmed. This in March 1944 was the city's riotous new temperament, a carnival of sex, food, fraud, racketeering, escape, and survival.

Joe and Tom didn't spend much time in Naples. They were more interested in visiting a few wounded friends at the 32nd Station Hospital in Caserta, another old city about twenty-four kilometers to the north, where Mark Clark's Fifth Army had set up a headquarters in the former palace of the Bourbon king of Naples, Charles III. A place like Caserta was a strange venue for the two Canadian boys. In Joe's hometown of Sarnia, a man would have been hard pressed to find a building more than one hundred years old. In Caserta the Bourbon palace, completed in 1772, was a relatively recent construction in light of the Roman amphitheater that stood in nearby Santa Maria.

The war and the Fifth Army had turned this grand, ancient city into a base town like Helena, and so it should have been no surprise when a racing jeep suddenly stopped while the two Force men were walking down the street and a voice shouted, "Joe!" Joe turned and was greeted by the smiling face of a Native girl from Helena named Cora. Back in Montana, Cora was known for her loop earrings, appetite for partying, and devotion to a saloon called the Night Owl. Back in Helena she had gone around with Jimmy Flack for a while and then joined the army, and now here she was: on a street in Caserta, and in her WAC uniform look-ing as a cute as a USO girl.* Joe and Tommy watched her climb from a jeep overloaded with WACS, and they couldn't help but feel gladdened. With the exception of a friendly face from home,

---

* The Women's Army Corps (WAC) was a noncombat unit of the American Army. More than 15,000 women served in it during the Second World War. The United Service Organizations (USO) is a nonprofit civilian body brought into being to provide comfort and recreation to American soldiers.

what more could two soldiers on leave possibly want than a jeep full of wacs?

Cora and the girls invited Joe and Tommy to a party, and the two had a grand time in Caserta. Eventually they found their way back to the coast, and their curiosity wouldn't let them miss Pompeii. They found the ruin in better shape than many European cities at that moment in history. Ironically, the dead city was covered by a layer of ash from the same mountain that had destroyed it almost two thousand years before.

After peering into doorways, they left the ruins and searched for a place to have a drink and a bite to eat. They stumbled on some Italian students who spoke English, and they invited Joe and Tommy to a restaurant installed on the top floor of a house. Darkness fell, red wine flowed, food was served, and the two soldiers settled in. As the horror of their war began to fade for a moment, a howling erupted in the distance. From their restaurant perch, the revelers watched in fascination as German warplanes attacked Naples and ack-ack tracers streaked the sky. The air raid was little more than a spectacle—until the warplanes shrieked over the Pompeii area and began firing. Suddenly, Joe and Tommy found themselves all alone. The students, feeling their position vulnerable, had fled the restaurant. Joe and Tommy decided to stay and keep drinking. If they hadn't been killed on the beachhead, they weren't going to die in an Italian restaurant.

———

Mark Radcliffe's journey off the beachhead began after dark on March 13 as he slipped across the Mussolini Canal at the head of a combat patrol.

February had been a brutal month for 3rd Regiment and 3-3 in particular. Force and German raids had resulted in the deaths of twenty-six men from the regiment, six of them from Radcliffe's company. Gone were Sergeants Lanzi and Barnhill, and Private Ogle. Another, Private Charles McMeekin Jr., had vanished in the night on February 9 and was officially declared MIA, Presumed Dead. Many more had been wounded, but the patrols ground on each day with the certainty of sunset. There was little good that could be said about the campaign now, particularly after the death of his friend Tom Pearce on Monte Majo.

Like all combat officers, Radcliffe had long ago resigned himself to the inevitability of casualties. But at Anzio, despite all the friends who had been lost, and the interminable ugliness of the fight, Radcliffe at least enjoyed the company of his comrades. He liked Muscles Morris, whose pluckiness and humor made him a popular member of 3-3. Both Radcliffe and Morris grew fond of a son of Cheyenne, Wyoming, named Major Ed Clay, who was with headquarters. A new officer joined the Force at Anzio, a boisterous, spirited Cajun from Louisiana named Ray Hufft. In no time Hufft was calling Radcliffe and Clay his "Boudreaux," vernacular for "buddy." Soon all three were calling each other Boudreaux, forming their own little club.

There were inspiring leaders in 3rd Regiment. Major Jack Secter, the regimental XO from Winnipeg, would boost morale by taking daylight hikes along the line armed with nothing but a swagger stick, and by exchanging small talk and jokes with the soldiers he encountered. The beachhead line never seemed quite so dangerous after Jack Secter sauntered down it. Secter even took his stick with him on operations across the line, using it to point out the targets he wanted the men to shoot at.

Radcliffe grew to especially admire regimental commander Walker, whom he found astonishingly open in planning meetings, despite his propensity to worry. Walker didn't bully or overrule subordinates who disagreed. When you announced a plan of attack, he simply asked questions: What would happen if you went to the right instead of the left? What happens if the Germans counterattack on your left flank? And so on. And if you disagreed with him, Walker always listened to your reasons.

His obsessive habit of wandering into combat zones only increased with time. On one occasion Radcliffe almost cured him of it. On or around March 1, Radcliffe had led a patrol across the line and was about a kilometer into enemy territory when a German flare exposed their position. The men scattered and Radcliffe leaped into a nearby foxhole, where he realized he was not alone. Certain that no one from the patrol had leaped with him, Radcliffe had to assume that the shadowy figure nearby was German. Grabbing the man, Radcliffe pulled his knife from his sheath and was about to use it when a voice said, "Radcliffe, is that you?" in a familiar Texas drawl.

About two weeks after almost knifing the colonel, Radcliffe was back across the line. It was around 8 p.m. and, of course, dark, a time when the nocturnal warriors began their work. That night he had been ordered to check on some farmhouses only 450 meters away from the beachhead line and determine if the enemy occupied them. Radcliffe was on the left of the patrol, near one of the houses in question, when he spotted something. There was a flash of movement at the corner of the house that appeared to be a man heading for cover. Sure that he had a prisoner, Radcliffe quietly followed. This fateful decision to leave the patrol didn't reveal itself as a mistake until he found himself surrounded by five German soldiers, who immediately overpowered him.

That was the last Radcliffe would see of his patrol, and the last his patrol saw of him. Radcliffe's mouth was gagged and his hands were tied. He was led to a road and loaded into an armored vehicle. When finally able to see, he noticed that the men who had captured him wore a strange insignia on their uniforms, a lightning flash intersected with an arrow that was pinned to their chests on the right-hand side. They wore caps bearing the emblem of an eagle outlined in silver. Radcliffe would learn later that they were search commandos, a special unit an FSSF report would later describe as an outfit of released convicts fighting for redemption and as "fanatical suicide troops."

Radcliffe was driven to Littoria and brought to a battered building on the edge of town that served as the HQ for the Seventh Luftwaffe Jaeger Battalion. Before being led into the cellar, where two other prisoners were being held in a makeshift jail that looked more like a cage, Radcliffe noticed that he was being paraded around and shown off. Due to their ferocity and their unorthodox methods of engaging the Germans, few Force men had fallen into enemy hands, which made an FSSF company commander a rare find. Unbeknownst to Radcliffe, German soldiers on the line had been offered a lengthy leave as a reward for capturing a Force man, and now they had an officer.

Once in the cellar, Radcliffe looked over his fellow prisoners in the cage. By their uniforms he surmised the two were American GIs with the Eighty-eighth Division. They were in a miserable position: alive, but trapped and hopelessly lost.*

Just like Radcliffe.

---

* An unsigned Army report on Radcliffe's captivity states there were seven prisoners in the cellar: a British national named Tony Powell; a French national in civilian clothes, René Reunault; a German soldier incarcerated for drunkenness; and two FSSF personnel: Charles McMeekin Jr., from Radcliffe's 3-3, who had disappeared on February 9 and been listed MIA, Presumed Dead; and another unidentified Force man described as badly wounded either from combat or beatings while a POW. Radcliffe, however, denies seeing any Force men in the jail area. He remembers only the two prisoners (described as Powell and Reunault), but states both appeared to be wearing U.S. uniforms.

The Germans wasted no time in interrogating Mark Radcliffe. His reprieve lasted only as long as he waited for his interrogator to arrive. This gave him a chance to notice his surroundings: German maps of the Littoria Plain pinned to the wall, assorted debris on the floor, including a heavy length of window frame that had shaken loose from the building's structure during a shelling.

Finally, a certain Captain Erlich arrived by car and greeted Radcliffe with his best impersonation of American can-do bravado. After shaking Radcliffe's hand and asking if he had been treated well since his capture, Erlich regaled him in fluent English with his accomplishments. He had lived in Philadelphia for seven years, where he had succeeded as a stockbroker, earning as much as $30,000 a year. If Erlich hoped to impress Radcliffe, he failed. The Force man found the young captain's good-cop routine "obnoxious," and the reason he gave for Radcliffe to co-operate smacked of sycophancy. "Don't you know you can't win?" Erlich said. "All your troops are not like your outfit."

Then Erlich came to the point. The Germans had reason to believe that a British unit had replaced the FSSF on the line, or were scheduled to do so in the near future. Was this true? he asked Radcliffe.*

Radcliffe responded to Erlich's inquiry with his name, rank, and serial number.

Erlich must have realized he was dealing with an obstinate character, and either lost his temper or made a calculated decision

---

* A plan was afoot, code-named Operation Wildcat, to fool the Germans into believing, that "the Fifty-sixth [division] had moved into the FSSF sector for an attack." In fact, the Fifty-sixth was being pulled from the line, dispatched to Naples, and replaced at Anzio by the British Fifth Division.

to turn violent. In any case, he palmed a rubber truncheon hanging from his belt and swung it hard against Radcliffe's throat. The blow knocked Radcliffe back and left him gasping for breath. As the other prisoners watched and Erlich waited for Radcliffe to compose himself, the building suddenly lurched, the air filled with dust, and an explosion rattled their eardrums. An Allied shell had just struck beside the HQ. An artillery barrage was beginning.

Captain Erlich and the other Germans made a hasty retreat from the cellar, leaving a guard behind to watch the prisoners. And there it was: a fortuitous shelling had interrupted whatever tortures Erlich had planned, and Radcliffe was left to sit and wait until the barrage ended and his interrogator, fresh from the safety of a bomb shelter, returned. The situation seemed hopeless, until Radcliffe saw his opportunity. His guard now stood at the cellar window, peering out, with his back to him. Glancing at the floor, Radcliffe contemplated a plan. He rose to his feet, picked up that heavy length of wood from the floor, and edged toward the guard. When he got within striking distance, Radcliffe swung the club with all his might against the man's skull. The soldier collapsed, and didn't move.

Searching the fallen sentry, Radcliffe pulled a compass from his pocket, and then he removed a map from the wall. After freeing his comrades from their jail, Radcliffe and the two other prisoners raced up the stairs and out the door.

Although out in the open, the three were not yet free. It was a long way to their lines, with enemy soldiers, mines, and razor wire in between. Radcliffe expected the Germans to discover their escape sooner or later, and if they deployed dogs, the three would be in trouble. The question now was: Which was the best direction to go? Standing on the western edge of Littoria as dawn began to break, the three debated the best route out.

Minutes later, shouts and the barking of dogs filled the dark area where the escaped POWs had just been standing. The Germans had detected their escape almost immediately and were in pursuit. Knowing the three could only be a short distance ahead of them, the pursuers might have been confident. Many of them knew these trails, fields, and roads well, while the prisoners would be disoriented. But they found nothing. Even the keen ears and noses of the dogs failed to track down the fugitives.

The Germans were frustrated, and Radcliffe and the two GIs knew it. As dawn approached, the three watched from their high perches in the trees on the outskirts of the village as the Germans raced around on the ground below. That morning and all the next day, soldiers of the Seventh Luftwaffe Jaeger Battalion combed the front looking for the three escaped prisoners, never imagining the men hadn't left the outskirts of Littoria. All the Germans needed to do was look up.

The next night, the three escapees gingerly descended cramped, exhausted and weak with hunger. It was time to make a run for it, and even though the Germans were still looking for them, the pace of the search had diminished. Radcliffe knew he wasn't far from his patrolling grounds. Borgo Piave was just a little north and to the west, and after that it was only a short distance to the canal. This route was the shortest and surest way in, and Radcliffe suggested they take it.

The two others were from the left flank of the beachhead, and wanted to return by this route. "We want to go to our lines," said one of them. "We know where the minefields are."

"I know where *our* minefields are," Radcliffe responded. "Let's go to my line. It's closer."

The two men seemed to agree, but within a hundred meters of setting out, one of the men disappeared, and Radcliffe could only assume he had changed his mind and was going out on his own. A short time later, the other GI, who spoke partially in

French, announced he too was going his own way. So Radcliffe plodded west alone, evading enemy patrols and cautiously crossing roads along which German armor coursed. But the going was arduous. His throat ached, and exhaustion coupled with not having eaten in two days rendered him so weak that Radcliffe wondered whether he had the strength to make it back. Complicating the journey was the care he needed to take to avoid minefields. Radcliffe knew his swath of the line, but he didn't know the fields directly west of Littoria, and had to rely on instinct and take great care. He found himself changing direction and avoiding fields for no other reason than the warning from his gut. When he could, he climbed into dikes and moved beneath the earth through the cruel brambles. Radcliffe never felt the need to use the compass he had taken from his guard. His childhood in New Mexico had instilled a keen sense of direction, and at no time did he doubt where the Force lines were; it was just a matter of getting there. Finally, as morning neared, Radcliffe came upon a small shack that appeared to be a grain crib. Dead exhausted and in need of cover, he removed a plank or two, crawled into the little granary, and slept for the first time in two days.

Resting throughout the day fortified Radcliffe enough to continue on once darkness fell. Although his goal was only a short distance away as the crow flies, Radcliffe continued his careful, zigzag route, working his way deliberately and by dead reckoning to his area along the Mussolini Canal.

After a night of wandering, Radcliffe found himself less than a hundred meters from the beachhead line as dawn light began filtering into the sky. Moving forward, Radcliffe had to admit that morning would beat him to the canal, and that if he crossed the last fifty meters, he'd be doing it in daylight. So close now, he decided to take the risk—and that was when the German patrol spotted him. They were positioned just to the east, probably a group that had been searching for Radcliffe all night. Radcliffe had no idea who they were until the mortars came, spewing shrapnel into his legs and a single shard into his face. Now on the ground and "bleeding like a pig," Radcliffe's flight had been stopped dead only forty-five meters from safety.

At that moment he looked up and saw the Force patrol.

A group from 2nd Company–3rd Regiment, led by a sergeant named Grant Erickson, had spent the last two nights behind the lines looking for Radcliffe. So determined were they to find their company commander, Erickson's patrol had stayed on past dawn in no man's land, and thought Radcliffe was a German soldier when they first spotted him in the distance. It was when the mortars came in that they realized they had found their man and rushed to the scene.

Radcliffe focused his gaze and recognized Erickson's face above him. "Get me the hell outta here," he said.

Erickson bent down, grabbed Radcliffe by both ears, and joyously hammered his head into the earth once or twice. "You little sonofabitch, where the hell you been?"

CHAPTER 14

GUSVILLE

By March, General Frederick could see that his strategy on the beachhead was having an effect. The outfit, despite its small relative size, was holding the line, and more. Not only was the German line being progressively pushed back, the Force was consistently turning back enemy raids, as the Germans tried unsuccessfully to infiltrate the beachhead. Raiders did get in, but they never got back out. On February 29, the Germans launched a company-sized attack against the far right of the pocket, where 1st Regiment held the line. But the 1st had divined what the Germans were up to, and let them penetrate the front before encircling and trapping the entire raiding force. In that one operation the 1st Regiment took 111 German prisoners.

═══

On March 14, Frederick received a roughly but carefully sketched greeting that was headed: "Anzio Beachhead, Italy." From the officers and men of his command, the message read: "Happy Birthday to Brigadier General Frederick," and it was signed using the Native code names of the Force's different units: Sioux, Shawnee, Seminole, and Seneca (as well as Sabotage). The hardships of the beachhead had not diminished the men's loyalty to him. Indeed, the only officer to suffer gravely from the stalemate was the last officer to be passed the buck: commanding general, Lucas. Harold Alexander pressured Clark to fire Lucas after the German counterattack in mid-February. Lucas had considered halting the counterattack "something of a victory," but he was alone in thinking this. Although he wasn't prepared to blame Lucas for Anzio's near failure, Mark Clark agreed he should be relieved, saying that Lucas was too "worn out" to continue the fight. Lucas was tired, to be sure. His trademark corncob pipe stuck between his clenched teeth, the diminutive Lucas had taken on more and more the appearance of a beleaguered prairie farmer facing ruination from blight. Lucas rarely strayed from the expansive wine cellar that served as his bunker HQ, which gave the appearance that he was hiding underground.

In truth, when made commander of the Anzio invasion Lucas had been given an impossible task. To protect his beachhead he needed to seize and retain the high ground of the Alban Hills, which he lacked the men and firepower to do. Given his limitations, probably his main—and irreparable—mistake was not seizing the key towns of Cisterna and Campoleone when they were ripe for the taking, a move that would have won Highway 7 for the Allies, cut German transport lines, and possibly locked up the plain.

Major General Lucian Truscott replaced Lucas, and Truscott, Colonel Darby's mentor when the Rangers were created, was a man after Frederick's own heart. Behind that grim face was a flexible intelligence that matched Frederick's; and, like

Frederick, Truscott had turned his outfit (the Third Division) into a model of well-greased efficiency. Truscott must have admired Frederick as well. After Truscott's promotion, a couple of Frederick's high-strung men overpowered Truscott's guards and broke into his HQ, looking for booze. The men reportedly thought the MPs were guarding a valuable stash of alcohol; they had no idea the wine cellar was actually the VI Corps command post. Under any other commander, a court martial might have resulted, but Truscott lodged a mild complaint and, according to Ken Wickham, "forgot about the whole thing."

Truscott knew as well as Frederick that they couldn't spare a single man. In late February, Frederick had been officially ordered to absorb the remnants of Darby's Rangers into his unit. But even this infusion wasn't enough, and Frederick was forced to deploy elements of the service battalion as combat troops. In all, he managed to make two fighting companies out of the cooks, carpenters, and litter carriers willing to bear arms. Frederick ordered them to man machine-gun nests and defend a line about 450 meters behind the main front, which may have been a safer assignment, given the shelling and strafing they endured in the rear.

In late March, the famous war correspondent Ernie Pyle, whose columns were the voice of the average GI, visited the beachhead and marveled at its vulnerability. "On this beachhead every inch of our territory is under German artillery fire," Pyle wrote. "There is no rear area that is immune, as in most battle zones. They can reach us with their 88's, and they use everything from that on up." Pyle did find temporary sanctuary on the front lines, where he met a handful of Force men just back from patrol. One was Joe Glass. Somehow, in the course of their conversation, Joe told Pyle that he was color-blind, an ailment that had kept him out of the Royal Canadian Navy. Pyle was incredulous: "How the hell did you get in the army being color-blind?" Joe: "Nobody asked."

In March, the Hermann Göring Division left the line. They were in the final stages of redeploying when Mark Radcliffe was captured, and he had noted that the Germans looked suspiciously cheerful. The 735th Grenadier Regiment of the 715th Infantry Division replaced the Göring Division, backed up by a pro-Axis battalion of Italy's elite San Marco Marines, one of Italy's most illustrious units (other units of the San Marco Marines joined the Allies). Joe Glass and Lorin Waling had been scouting near Hell's Corner on a moonlit night when they flushed two enemies out of a hiding place. One was a San Marco Marine, and the two scouts gazed in amazement at the near seven-footer as if he were a circus freak. The incident proved that the giants of the Axis armies were willing to surrender even if their generals weren't.

This fresh blood didn't alter the stalemate. In early March, Field Marshal Kesselring had dispatched his chief of staff to meet personally with Hitler and inform him that further offensive action against the beachhead was futile; Allied artillery and air power at Anzio were overwhelming. Better to conserve their strength and unleash it on the invaders when they attempted a breakout. Kesselring was applying to Anzio his overall strategy of containment, which had successfully ground the Allied advance to a stop at the Gustav Line in the mountains at Cassino. Hitler agreed. The battle over the beachhead was entering the endgame.

———

The 1st Regiment manned the far right end of the Force's line, a stretch as contentious as any other on the beachhead. First Regiment men such as Art Arsennek, Herb Peppard, George "Spud" Wright, and Herb Goodwin understood the dire situation they were in. Undermanned, their grip on the front they held was decidedly tenuous. When 2nd Battalion commander Major Gerry MacFadden, a native of Brockville, Ontario, arrived at Anzio, he had only sixty-nine men left with which to defend a line a kilometer long. "If you can't do this," he was told, "get out of the way and I'll get somebody who can."

MacFadden's boss was 1st Regiment's commander, Colonel "Cooky" Marshall. A Pennsylvania native and West Pointer who graduated three years after Frederick, Marshall epitomized Frederick's vision of regimental leadership. Like Walker (and Frederick himself), Marshall was an obsessive commander who stayed on or near the front lines of 1st Regiment operations just to keep tabs on progress. Frederick's right-hand man, Ken Wickham, considered Marshall "witty, polished, and a good professional soldier." Robust and self-assured, Marshall didn't share Walker's inclination to worry away pounds. But worry he did, endlessly. His regimental radio man, Private Norm Smith of Boissevain, Manitoba, considered him "one of the best officers I ever seen in my life."

The military career of "Gus" Heilman was a perfect illustration of Marshall's flexibility. Before the war, while still at college in Charlottesville, Virginia, Heilman opened a bar and grill. After being drafted into the army in 1941, he applied for Officer Candidate School only because a posting in Fort Benning, Georgia, would allow him to be close to his profitable establishment. A rebel and troublemaker, Heilman was on the verge of washing out of OCS when he read the notice asking for volunteers for what would become the FSSF. Knowing that if he failed OCS he'd be shipped to an overseas-destined infantry outfit as a dogface GI, Heilman signed up.

A number of misfits and hardened criminals had volunteered (or been volunteered) for the Force during that period. "Post officers [across the U.S.] seized the opportunity to get rid of undesirable men," Wickham said. "They literally emptied their stockade." Most of the misfits were incorrigible, but in some cases raw soldierly talent, such as Lorin Waling of the Petawawa jug, emerged from these jails. And Heilman was a member of this exclusive group. "Big, tough, mean, and resentful," in the words of two historians, Heilman would become the prince of the Force's foul-ups.

When 1st Regiment took their positions on the far right of the Anzio line, Lieutenant Heilman led a patrol of thirty-two men across the canal, via Bridge 1, and entered the eerily vacant village of Borgo Sabotino, which sat less than a kilometer from their line. On that night Heilman's men pressed as far south as the beach, and another five kilometers due east, creeping as far as a lock house for the waterway that the Germans used as an outpost. Lieutenant Heilman and his men flushed the Germans from the building. As they passed again through Borgo Sabotino, they decided to stake a claim. The men quickly christened the town "Gusville," voted Heilman its mayor, and took up residence of sorts.

News of Gusville's founding spread down the line and boosted morale. Such esprit de corps had to be permitted. Colonel Marshall saw the stunt as an opportunity. He crossed the canal and set up positions on the east bank of the waterway, where 1st Regiment stayed. Gusville became the regiment's capital city, and a fiefdom for the enterprising Heilman, who immediately set up a bar, which he kept juiced with alcohol (mainly wine) obtained during raids and sold to Force men at a bargain. Heilman appointed city bureaucrats and named streets, the two most famous being Prostitute and Tank. At that intersection Heilman's raiders launched a newspaper, *The Gusville Herald Tribune*, mimeographed on 8½ × 14 inch sheets of paper and distributed to soldiers passing through. In one edition, the front page was headed up by an editor's note: "Have to run down to the Medics and get a good shot of paragoric befo' takin' this issue to press." (Paregoric was an opium-based cure-all drug, related to laudanum, that was eventually outlawed.) The main news of the day concerned Gusville's Guest House, and the *Tribune* listed the "rules for visitors to abide by." Rule number three: "Make out your will before retiring.—Who Knows? ? ?" Number five: "Insect powder will be a standard issue to all guests." Lastly, the editor promised: "from time to time we will publish the names of the prominent people that are killed while spending the nite in it." And prominent people did spend the night. Gusville fascinated the beachhead, and a few war correspondents visited it just for the exotic dateline.

Art "Poison" Arsennek was not a member of Gus Heilman's 2nd Company–1st Regiment, but the boys in Art's 1st Company (1-1) reveled in the audacity of Gusville. In the beginning, triumphs like Gusville offered a rare reprieve for Art and his comrades. The fighting was tough in Art's sector, and oddly freewheeling. Some in the regiment stood vigil in trenches, foxholes, and gun pits along the Mussolini Canal. Others went on the attack, creeping after dark to farmhouses, establishing outposts, and then retreating before dawn. They competed with 3rd Regiment for these houses, and also with the Germans, who took to blowing the peasant dwellings up in an attempt to deny the Force men nightly command posts. According to the Force's intelligence officer: "Each morning would show fewer houses dotting the landscape to the front." Arguably, this German tactic hurt the Germans more than their enemies simply because they relied on the protection. As the houses disappeared, the German line continued to creep back, ultimately more than a kilometer. Distance brought some stability to the 1st Regiment front, save for air attacks by Luftwaffe pilots mistaking Gusville for the city of Anzio.

Anzio remained an extremely dangerous place, but a frontline soldier such as Arsennek no longer had to worry about being downed by a sniper's bullet or mortar every time he left a trench. Simple pleasures infiltrated the line. Men scavenged for livestock and fought the Germans over henhouses on farms abandoned by peasants who quite understandably fled in the night in the path of the Allied invasion force. The plundered beasts included—as *Yank* magazine reported—"a herd of cattle, [and] three pigs" corralled at Gusville. But some locals remained, out of defiance or age or poverty. Once, while on a patrol to check a farmhouse for Germans, Joe Glass and Lorin Waling found a young Italian woman who had remained in her home because of her advanced pregnancy. Whether the desperate woman stayed because she could not walk or because she judged that fleeing through the mine- and enemy-infested war zone would be just as dangerous as staying was not clear to Joe. She allowed the men to carry her to the beachhead, where Allied physicians delivered her baby. Such emergency deliveries happened more than once, and according to Force lore, after 2nd Regiment's doctor, George Evashwick, helped bring a young Italian into the world, the grateful mother named her newborn in his honor.

Hens, eggs, and babies were not the only treasures the men found in no man's land. They requisitioned ponies from abandoned farmyards, and held bronco-busting competitions and horse races. All this made life more bearable, but for many of the men writing letters home offered the best escape. Art Arsennek for one enjoyed writing letters; this was clear from the care he put into each one he composed for his wife, Buck, whom he still refused to call Dora. Many of his letters bore elaborate, funny sketches on the envelope. On one envelope Art sketched the interior of a front-line Anzio farmhouse, a bare room lit only by a single candle. Inside is a frazzled Force man with a machine gun trained on a mouse in the corner. "I got him men," the soldier calls out. "Call in the artillery." Back home in St. Catharines, Dora Arsennek's mailman chuckled when he delivered them. Standing at the window, Dora could always tell if the postman was gripping a letter from Art just from his grin.

May 9 was comparatively quiet on the beachhead. Not a single Force man died that day. But for Art Arsennek the morning dawned memorably, because it was his second wedding anniversary. Art and Dora's nuptials had been as fast and simple as their courtship in an era when people never hesitated to launch into and get on with life. Art had been thinking of this day for a while. On one of his last leaves he had gone to a market and purchased some delicate cameos that he hoped Buck would have made into a bracelet to mark their anniversary. Now, on the day, he picked up a pen, imagined his wedding day, perhaps a memory he returned to when fearful or discouraged, and on government stationery bearing the logo "Canadian Army Active" he began to write.

> Darling Buck,
>
> Here it is again the ninth of May, and just a few hours before this letter was written I believe around 3 p.m. we were well in the swing of things, eh hon? Gee it seems longer than two years when you sit down and write and think back of how are knees were knocking and our throats felt like it could do with a good drink of _____ to take that feeling out of it.
>
> Well, even if I can't be with you I'll still be thinking of them hours we had. They were happy hours for me.

He ended with a poem. During the worst of the war, the night Dee Byrom died and much of the regiment was slaughtered, he had to wonder just why he was there, away from where he wanted to be. With that theme in mind he continued scribbling:

Though we are now far apart Sweetheart
the memory of you will forever Be within my heart
Each and every moment
Through the day

It was Spring and the year 1942,
God gave us freedom and you, brave and true
Knew what we had to do. We lived and planned,
But someone else Was planning too
And we know that His plans will not Come true
No matter what he Tries to do
We know the struggle
Though hard to endure But through God's Grace
We will Come Through

And when we do Darling, We will come
Straight back to Ones like you
Well now before I part You know you are
The one who holds my heart
God bless Mom, Pop, and you,
Chins up until the day we are back with you

Yours ever loving
For Evermore
—Art

Dora would be touched by the poem that in Art's small way tried to articulate the plight of their generation.

Arsennek's introspection was understandable. The grinding beachhead stalemate had gone on too long. But by the time of Dora and Art's anniversary clear signs were emerging that it was coming to an end. Headquarters had already begun ordering daylight reconnaissance patrols. A massive breakout offensive was in the works, and General Truscott wanted VI Corps trained, poised, and ready. At first, officers railed against this, arguing that incursions other than at night would bring needless casualties. In his book, Adna Underhill expressed the general feeling: "Shit, we all know, and Headquarters must, too, that those places are occupied and fortified. Why do we need to go out in broad daylight and be shot at to prove it?" But the FSSF were the only soldiers on the line conducting operations exclusively at night, so any concerted VI Corps operation would necessarily begin after sunup.

Joe's Glass's first daytime raid had taken place more than a month earlier, on April 15. Most of 2nd Regiment was involved, and the mission was to attack German forces that seemed to be congregating on the right side of the line, east of Gusville, near a village called Cerreto Alto. On that raid Joe went into battle a newly promoted acting sergeant. His promotion was a testament to the valuable scouting work he and Waling, who was also promoted to sergeant that day, had been doing.

For Joe, the Cerreto Alto raid had been memorable for two reasons. The first was the tanks. Joe and the others attacked alongside the M4 Sherman medium tanks and M5A1 Stuart light tanks and Grayhound armored cars of the First Armored Regiment and the Eighty-first Reconnaissance Battalion. And once again Lieutenant Colonel Bob Moore would personally lead the attack, whose violently simple strategy was, according to Captain Adna Underhill, "to inflict maximum damage on their troops, kill or capture all if possible, and then pull back." Moore's raiders identified two strategic targets on which to inflict their damage: the enemy concentration at a plantation near Cerreto Alto, and a cluster of buildings roughly to the south along the coastal road, Strada Litoranea. As far as Joe could figure it, headquarters wanted to give him and the others experience fighting alongside tanks in preparation for a possible push from the beach. Underhill's raiders in 5th Company moved out before dawn. They circumvented a minefield without being detected, and slunk into an irrigation ditch a mere 150 meters away from their objective when two light tanks arrived in the clear light of morning, and opened fire on the farm houses where the Germans were garrisoned. The tanks were lucky enough to catch the enemy by surprise. Underhill watched Germans soldiers, seven by one count, barrel from the entrance of a building only to be "mowed down" by tank and small-arms fire. But still the enemy managed to man a machine-gun nest set behind the houses that began pouring fire on the Force men taking cover behind the tanks.

Unwisely, the gun pit was nestled beneath a haystack. One of Underhill's men silenced it by shooting Johnny gun tracers into the hay, which quickly kindled the dry grass into an inferno, and sent the enemy gunners scrambling. The armor, which now included two additional Shermans, turned their cannons on the buildings as the Force men closed in. The result was an eruption of white surrender flags as the Germans and Italians burst from windows and doors "waving towels, shirts, or any thing white they could find." After a single machine-gun placement, just off the east, was silenced by one of Underhill's men, the raiders hung around and savored their victory until the 88 shells started falling in from a battery located beside Borgo Isonzo.

Joe Glass fought on the raid at the coastal road alongside the Shermans. Assigned to clear four farm buildings, identified as Houses 9 through 12, which the Germans used as barracks, Joe and the others, who hailed mainly from 4th Company, advanced on the roadside and in the ditches while the tanks rolled along the road. But right away Joe could see that the tanks were not right for this particular raid. Because the fields were marshy, the armor had to remain on the roads, and this made them easy targets for the tank mines and the Germans' fearsome 88s. The 4th

Company raiders found the first three barracks, Houses 9 to 11, empty, and their advance was halted on the way to House 12 while sappers cleared the road of tank mines. The mines were a clear a sign that House 12 would not be empty, and sure enough, the enemy, from the building and from gun nests and entrenched spots located around it, opened up on them as they approached.

From the cover of a drainage ditch, Joe watched the 88s rake the vehicles, and he couldn't help but think, "Those poor bastards in the tanks." Still, the tankers fought hard. One Stuart traversed its turret gun and fired on a house the Germans were shooting from. The blast from the cannon's muzzle blew Joe's helmet clear off his head and the shell opened an aperture in the building the vehicle could easily have rolled through.

At one point a German ambulance appeared near the intersection that led to Fogliano, and Herby Forester, standing not far from Joe, mumbled, "What the hell is this, now?" and took off for a closer look. The ambulance flew no white flags, but Joe and Lorin, his chief mortar man on raids like this, held their fire nonetheless because you never wanted to shoot at an ambulance. They watched the medical vehicle pull up to a point along the road. The back doors flew open, and a squad of soldiers carrying an antitank gun piled out and disappeared into the drainage ditch alongside.

"Jesus Christ," Joe thought. Just then Herby Forester ran back. He had found a vantage point where he could see the Germans lying in wait in the ditch. He and Joe quickly figured the distance, and then Lorin went into action with his mortar: he pulled pins and dropped live grenades into the tube so fast that they burst from the barrel like automatic fire and fell almost directly on the antitank crew. The Germans tried running down the ditch and climbing onto the road to escape the shrapnel, but the razor-sharp hail cut them down to a man. Amazingly, within seconds of the ambulance's arrival, every German who had ridden in it was dead.

Joe heard clapping, and when he turned he realized it was none other than the Old Man: Frederick. The commander was right there, clean-shaven as always, dressed in his combat green and a helmet that boasted a single star radiating from its center.

"Good job," Frederick said, referring to the mortar work. "That was a good job."

Frederick had every reason to be pleased. Although the Force's intelligence chief would describe it as only a "workmanlike" effort, the raid, which ended around 9 a.m., had been a success. Forty-four Germans and seventeen Italian marines had been captured, and nineteen enemy soldiers had been killed. On the Allied side, the armor took the worst beating, with two tanks and two tank destroyers lost.

There were subsequent raids on the same area, but they were less charmed, mainly because the enemy bolstered its line and improved its response with each attack. However, the Germans knew as well as the Allies on the beachhead that a breakout was as inevitable as the end of winter. Momentum was building, and not all of it at Anzio. By the spring of 1944 the Allied command in the Italian theater, and particularly Mark Clark, were feeling the pull of history. What had once been the spear-point of the free world's assault on Europe had begun to look like an embarrassing sideshow, as the German rearguard action bottled up the vastly superior Allied force at the mouth of the Liri. But the tide began to turn with the offensive of May 11. In addition to their three-to-one superiority in infantry strength, the Allies enjoyed an overwhelming preponderance in artillery, limitless ammunition, and control of the skies. German prisoners led to the Allied rear were astonished by the Allies' stores of materiel waiting to be moved to the front.

All this might was brought to bear on the Germans who controlled the heights at Cassino and had thwarted the Allies with their ability to cover one summit with fire from the adjoining peak.

The key to Operation Diadem, as the breakout was called, was the Free French assault on Monte Maio, one of the gateposts at the mouth of the Liri. In a risky gambit not unlike the FSSF assault on Difensa, the French scaled the cliffs of the south-western German flank on May 13 and drove in the thin edge of the wedge that cracked the German defense at Cassino. On May 18 another army of expatriates looking for vengeance, the 12th Podolski Lancers, finally laid claim to the monastery after suffering appalling losses, and raised a makeshift Polish flag over the ruins. Estimates of the casualties at Cassino ran as high as 350,000.

This brought to an end what many German troops considered the bitterest fighting of the war. But it was not a collapse. The Wehrmacht had simply made a tactical withdrawal to prepared defensive positions, as the 1 Canadian Corps was to find when they set off in pursuit. But the deadlock had been broken, and the pressure was off the men at Anzio. General Alexander told Mark Clark that it was time to break out of the beachhead.

———

The beachhead was ready. In March alone 14,000 replacement troops had joined the besieged Anzio force. The British Fifth Division relieved the Fifty-sixth Division, and the U.S. Thirty-fourth Division took the place of the 504 Parachute Infantry Regiment of the 82nd Airborne Division between the U.S. 45th Infantry and the FSSF. The Force itself might have been relieved if they had not been so effective and essential. By May 1, the First Armored Division, Combat Command B was in place, and the Thirty-sixth Division was on its way.

The Force had received replacements from the Canadian army in late February. In the months after their trial by fire on Difensa, the Force men had become legendary in the Italian the-ater, particulary among Canadian units, of which there were many: the Princess Patricia's Canadian Light Infantry, the Hastings and Prince Edward Regiment (the famous Hasty Ps), the Kent Regiment (Joe Glass's former unit), the Royal Canadian Regiment, the 48th Highlanders of Canada, the Loyal Edmonton Regiment, the Royal 22nd Regiment, the Carleton & York Regiment, the West Nova Scotia Regiment, and the Seaforth Highlanders of Canada. A call for volunteers for the Force had met with an enthusiastic response. An untold number signed up. Fifteen Canadian officers and 240 enlisted men eventually passed muster. After enduring three weeks of specialized training in Santa Maria under the guidance of the martial artist, Pat O'Neill, and the senior Canadian officer, Jack Akehurst (who was recovering from serious wounds suffered in the mountain campaign), these soldiers became Force men in uniform and name.

The lives of many of these young men would be the toll exacted by the Germans for the decisions made by the Allied strategists. General Frederick knew this better than anyone. This was perhaps one reason why he continually put himself in harm's way. In March he was awarded the Silver Star, and the Oak Leaf Cluster to the Silver Star. These citations were just the beginning. Frederick would also earn two Distinguished Service Crosses, second only to the Congressional Medal of Honor in distinction in the U.S. Army, and two Distinguished Service Medals. On at least one occasion, General Clark came to the beachhead and decorated Frederick personally. Nevertheless, Clark still thought Frederick eccentric and "crazy" for the conduct and strategy that was winning him these awards.

Ironically, despite Frederick's continued presence on the front lines, his closest scrape came that winter on the beachhead when an aide brought a charcoal stove to his bunker at Anzio and fired it up. The hot furnace offered relief from the biting cold but, unbeknownst to him, was filling the room with carbon monoxide gas. Writing a letter home at the time, Frederick faded mid-sentence, scribbling "Suddenly I feel so ti—" as he passed out.

He was found a short time later, unconscious but alive, and with no obvious impairment save that his heart became enlarged as it laboriously attempted to pump oxygenated blood through his suffocating body.

Frederick's damaged heart may have been a fitting metaphor for the conflict inside him. The pressure was mounting. Almost without relief, Frederick had been engaged in intense front line combat for six months. Nearly every combat officer in Europe, from lieutenants leading platoons to company commanders such as Mark Radcliffe, suffered the burden of command. This was not the same burden endured by most generals, who were largely spared the firsthand images of carnage and death that their battle captains saw daily. General Frederick's rare determination to be on the line during an operation made him an exception. His men's suffering would have been easier to accept had he not been haunted by the thought that many of the deaths were unnecessary.

Frederick always worried that most of the top brass had no idea how to utilize the Force. He had selected the best soldiers from two national armies and created a unit unique in U.S. Army history, only to be given missions of frontal attack. The decision from the top to send the Force men out on daylight raids put them at great risk at best, and at worst made them little more than cannon fodder. Now, as the momentum for the breakout began to build, Frederick could only hope that the push to Rome would see his men used to their best advantage. In fact, the battle for the Eternal City would prove to be the Force's crowning achievement, the culmination of a journey begun on the frigid slopes of Monte la Difensa a half year before.

PART III

THE CITY

CHAPTER 15

THE QUARRY

On the morning of May 21, 1944, Joe Glass climbed onto a truck for what would be the last daylight raid before the breakout from Anzio beachhead. As he and the others from I-2 bounced toward the line, he had a look around at the other worn, scarred, gaunt faces staring across at each other from opposite sides of the transport, lingered on Herby Forester's mug, and said "Either you or me are gonna get hit today."

Forester asked him what he meant.

"Just look at it, Herb," Joe said. "We're the only two guys in the platoon who haven't got hit yet." Joe had never considered his battered thumb or temporary blindness suffered on Monte la Difensa as real wounds.

The two men had only to look around them. There was Percy Crichlow, now a lieutenant. "Crich" had been given a commission in April, and no sooner had he been promoted than Joe and

Lorin Waling had evicted him from their foxhole. But while still a sergeant, Crich had been hit in the leg during a raid.

Joe eyed the chain-smoking Jimmy Flack, whom he and Lorin had once kicked out of their foxhole to make room for Crich. Flack was a good combat man. He was small as a rooster, but always went on patrol lugging a heavy .30-caliber machine gun. Flack had also been hit, and survived. Joe spotted Kenny Folsom, who had been grievously wounded on Monte la Difensa. After months in the hospital he returned to the company at Anzio, but Joe realized he shouldn't have. He was constantly in pain, and Joe always wondered why the hell he had been made to return. On it went down the line. There was Kenny's friend Lew Weldon, whose bottom-heavy face and sad eyes always reminded Joe of Buster Keaton.

Rusty Kroll also glared from the lineup, conspicuous because his face was the profile of a private, while nearly everyone else from the old 3rd Platoon were sergeants or higher. Other visages were conspicuous by their absence, the most obvious being Lorin Waling, who was alive, but would be attacking elsewhere on the line with another group of 2nd Regiment raiders. With the war about to leave the static battleground of Anzio, the two friends were again being separated. Lieutenant Piette was missing as well; he had been transferred to 6-2 about the time Crichlow received his commission. Most of the other absent men were wounded or KIA. Sergeant Schumm, whom the boys used to tease for his German ancestry, had died in late February. In truth, he didn't die so much as disappear. He went missing on patrol and was eventually declared Presumed Dead. For Joe, it was as if he had vanished from his foxhole in his sleep: there one night, gone the next morning.

Joe recognized familiar faces from the company: Van Ausdale and Joe Dauphinais and the Montana cowboy Johnny Walter were still around. There was Captain Gordon, who would be leading that day's raid. And there were new faces: several brooding Rangers, including Roy Houseman, who was still cold toward Joe after he taught his brother Dick to scout.

There were more new faces than old ones. "This is probably our last raid before the breakout," he said. "Something's gotta happen today to one of us."

Forester couldn't quarrel with Joe's logic. Only a handful of the originals from 3rd Platoon were still around; Glass and Forester were lucky to be alive. For the veteran Force men, there was no average life expectancy. Inexperienced replacements usually died or were wounded quickly, but the longevity of the originals varied. Many 1-2 men, such as Syd Gath, died within minutes of entering their first battle, on Difensa. Others, like Don MacKinnon, who lost a leg on Monte Majo, survived unscathed until January. Some men, including Joe Dauphinais, had been wounded, hospitalized, and then returned to the line after their recuperation. But there were almost no combat Force men like Joe and Herby. That neither had suffered a substantial wound in almost six months of fighting was astounding. Joe believed it couldn't last.

———

On the morning of May 21, Joe Glass, Herby Forester, and elements of what was left of 2nd Regiment arrived at the canal and jumped from transport trucks to the ground.

Joe and everyone else knew that the breakout was imminent. They also knew this raid was a foray into the Quarry area just north of Borgo Piave, meant to gauge the strength of the German forces there. As they set out, Joe couldn't fathom marching in broad daylight onto a battlefield he had known only in the dark. So he was expecting the worst as Captain Gordon led the men over the canal and then across a treacherously open field on the way to the German line. Admittedly, the Force had pushed the Germans back several kilometers at this point, but Joe couldn't figure out how a company could march across exposed ground in daylight without a single shot fired against them. But march they did, led by their scouts across the German minefield.

Finally the men, still edging forward in silence, cut their way through a wire fence, squeezed through the jagged opening, and filed into what Joe recognized as the German position. The operation had turned surreal. Not only had they crossed Anzio's no man's land without detection, they had penetrated the enemy outpost, and found no one at home.

A ditch that served as a convenient trench for the Germans ran parallel to the boundary of the outpost, and the men filed into it, wondering what to do next. Captain Gordon was seemingly as baffled as anyone that they had made it this far without incident. Perhaps lulled by the quiet, Gordon stood up and mounted the bank of the ditch to get his bearings and see if he could spot the enemy.

The others may have been relieved they hadn't needed to fight their way in, but they were keeping cautiously low all the same, and Joe, just off to the side, hissed: "Gordon, what the hell you doing up there?"

Just then a shot rang out, and a bullet ripped open the throat of a soldier near Joe. A German sniper, shooting from some vantage point above them, had hit a former Ranger named Carter who was crouching beneath Gordon. Baffled no longer, Gordon leaped down as the Ranger died.

Perhaps not understanding what they were facing, the Germans focused their defense on a small hill that lay just ahead of the ditch. The Force men, using the trench as cover, opened fire with their M1s and Thompsons as the Germans came down and around the hill only fourteen meters away.

Almost immediately, the thunder of a firefight sounded from down the line, which meant that Lorin Waling's group from 2nd Regiment had also engaged the enemy.

In Joe's trench, Jimmy Flack quickly noticed that their ditch opened up on the right into another trench, more like a path, which seemed to intersect it. Within moments German soldiers were racing down this path and by the opening. Seeing that the enemy were trying to outflank them, Flack set up his Browning, leveled the barrel down the length of trench at the intersection, and opened fire, cutting the Germans down as they tried to pass.

Joe, for his part, had little time to worry about Flack's problems on the flank. As the head of a mortar team, he immediately prepared to fire. His chief mortar man was the Ranger Roy Houseman, who seemed to forget how much he disliked Joe and immediately set to work. Houseman was at hand with the mortar tube and ammunition, but somehow the base-plate man had become separated from them, and was somewhere behind with the rest of the company, which hadn't caught up with Gordon's advance force yet. So Houseman grabbed a helmet, tipped it over, and, sticking the tube inside it, began unleashing rounds. The helmet worked fine as a base plate, and Joe began directing fire against the hill as the Germans swarmed around it.

Joe and Roy Houseman beat the exposed Germans on the hill like a sledgehammer with that 60 mm mortar. The Germans were taking heavy losses. But Force men were also falling. Looking to his side, Joe saw poor Kenny Folsom lying on the bottom of the ditch, and beside him Folsom's friend, the Buster Keaton look-alike, Weldon. The sniper who had killed the Ranger had now killed Kenny and Lew as well, but with the Germans attacking from the hill ahead of them, Joe was too busy to figure out where the sniper could be.

Men were also falling on the far left side of the ditch, where a squad including Dauphinais and old Van Ausdale had positioned themselves to guard the flank. Although they were holed up as much as 270 meters from where Gordon and the main body of men were firing on the hill, these men were taking fire, and Dauphinais realized it had to be a sniper. With virtually everyone else dead, he knew he needed to get out of this trench and behind better cover. So he scrambled to the bank and impulsively began implementing a technique that—as he told oral historian Joe Springer—he had learned from a German during a battle in the mountains. "This German was a great big bugger, and when I was shooting at him with my Tommy gun, he began walking . . . sideways to my fire," Dauphinais recalled. "These bloody Germans were damn good soldiers . . . We learned a lot of things by watching how they survived. And this one bugger meant to survive." Dauphinais stood up and, resisting the urge to run (because, as he told Springer, "I always thought that if you were running, you would run into [the bullets]"), edged sideways toward a trench he had spotted to the left. An incredulous Van Ausdale followed, moving with him to the edge of the ditch. Van Ausdale, after shooting a German face-to-face, leaped into the new position barely a moment after Dauphinais. "You almost died there, did you know that?" Van Ausdale told Dauphinais as they collected themselves.

While Dauphinais and Van Ausdale were finding cover, Joe Glass finally spotted the sniper. The man was in a tree, firing down into the ditch. Bullets might have knocked the sniper from his perch, but Joe decided to use the best weapon he had at his disposal. Eyeballing the distance and making a quick calculation, Joe pointed his bayonet into the air and told Houseman to lob a shell just over the gun dagger's tip; that was the trajectory he needed. Houseman measured it up, fired, and an instant later the tree exploded and the sniping stopped.

But the Germans kept coming. According to Dauphinais, they stormed the trench in "human waves," and at one point it appeared as if the company was surrounded. A German officer called out for them to surrender, and when Captain Gordon didn't, heavy fire from an 88 began peppering their position. At that stage it was all over. Crichlow told Joe to grab his mortar man and retreat back through the line the same way they had come. Joe gave the word to Houseman, turned, and jumped over the dead men Folsom and Weldon.

———

The attack that 2nd Regiment launched farther down the line had been as fierce and violent as Gordon's raid. Beating a retreat across the minefields and the open meadow, Lorin Waling was near the canal and about to climb onto a transport truck when he heard Herby Forester's voice shout out his name. He turned just as a jeep pulled up carrying Forester, Crichlow, and Johnny Walter. Stretched out across the back of the vehicle, Waling noticed, was a bloodied body, the almost lifeless form of a wounded Force man coming in from the raid. Forester, sitting in the back with the wounded man, said, "Lorin, it's Joe."

Waling approached the jeep and saw that the almost unrecognizable wounded man on the hood was indeed Joe Glass. Looking down on him, Lorin knew that Joe's wounds were severe. Blood flowed from his mouth, and his chest was awash in red. He was semiconscious. For the first time in the war, Lorin Waling wept.

Shards of the 88 mm shells bombarding their position had hit Joe Glass squarely in the back just as he was leaping over his two dead friends, throwing him to the ground. Glass knew that he was hit, but he felt no pain, just a spreading numbness. At first he tried to rise, but he no longer had the use of his legs. The numbness turned to warmth, and Glass almost didn't notice that he was coughing blood. A wonderful drowsiness started to envelop him. In spite of it, Joe suddenly experienced clarity. He understood that he was gravely wounded and would not be going back with the others. He knew that he couldn't walk, and if he couldn't walk, how was he going to make it through the mine-field and across the clearing to the canal? And he also knew that there would be no chance of becoming a POW. Who would want a soldier with a sucking chest wound as a prisoner?

Jimmy Flack's face appeared above him. "How you doing, Joe?" Flack said.

"Say good-bye to my wife and son," he said. Flack, the most sea-soned soldier in the platoon, inspected Joe's wounds, considered the distance they would have to travel to get back, and realized that Joe was right to think he would never see his family again.

Jimmy's face disappeared from view. Joe didn't mind. The drowsiness and warmth began to feel welcoming. Pleasure, calm, and extreme comfort covered Glass like a quilt and slowly lulled him to sleep. Right then Joe had the sense that even if his legs worked, he wouldn't want to go anywhere; it simply felt too good where he lay. Joe was prepared to sink fully into this feel-ing, never looking back, when he felt himself waking up. He almost tried to fight it, but the fog cleared around him, his eyes opened, and there was the face of Percy Crichlow.

Crichlow was speaking, but not to Glass, whose head he was holding up by the hair. He was speaking about him. From a long way off, Joe heard Crichlow say: "He's still alive."

Suddenly Joe was on his feet, supported by Crichlow and Johnny Walter, who trailed the last of the raiders as they retreated completely from the compound. In the first instant Joe was annoyed, angry even, wanting to go back to that peaceful place he had just been wallowing in. But the experience of being dragged by Crich and Johnny, flopping between them like a man-sized doll, perhaps triggered enough pain to pull Glass closer to the living. He was still numb in some places, though. He didn't feel it when another hunk of shrapnel tore open his arm and clipped Walter's neck. The metal did more damage to Glass than to Walter, and the three soldiers made it out of the minefield.

Farther on, Crichlow and Walter caught up with some of the others and lay Joe down. The Force men were near a road, and a jeep rolled up, probably dispatched from the canal either to pick up stragglers or to inspect the aftermath of the raid. Crichlow commandeered it and the men stretched Joe out in the back. Mercifully, someone gave him a shot of morphine, and Joe, still conscious, asked Forester for a smoke. Herby lit him a cigarette, put it in his mouth, and then took it away when he noticed smoke wafting out of a hole in Glass's back.

Moments later they were off, speeding toward the canal. Crichlow stopped the jeep when he spotted an ambulance in the assembly area. With the help of Lorin Waling, Glass was transferred to the ambulance and was rushed to an aid station.

As Waling climbed into the swaying transport and rode it toward the bivouac area, this bloody, dying mess was his last image of Joe Glass on the beachhead at Anzio. Lorin would not have time to grieve. Barely two days later, after languishing on the Italian coast for close to four months, the Allied Forces, with the First Special Service Force in the lead, would storm across the line and clash head-on with the German defenders.

The Force's long night on the Anzio beachhead would soon be over.

CHAPTER 16

BREAKOUT

Before dawn on May 23, men of the First Special Service Force crouched in trenches and waited under a shower of light rain as 500 artillery pieces and sixty bombers pounded Cisterna to cut a path for the VI Corps breakout.

The Allies' ultimate destination was Highway 6 at the village of Valmontone, a mere thirty-two kilometers away. The strategy called for VI Corps to cut off the German Tenth Army as they attempted to retreat from the Winter Line under the weight of the exploitation of Operation Diadem. The U.S. Fifth Army would swing north from the coast to meet and bolster VI Corps. Caught by the Americans on one side, the British and Canadians on the other, the German Tenth Army would face checkmate. Highway 6 was the only escape route from the Liri Valley for the Germans.

The Force men were poised along three thousand meters of

the Cisterna Canal, where Cooky Marshall's 1st Regiment (backed up by the 1st Battalion of 2nd Regiment) were positioned, and the Mussolini Canal, where Ed Walker's 3rd Regiment (supported by the other half of 2nd) nervously waited. The men crouched in the rain, but there was no wind. The poplars were still and "blood-red" poppies, as one soldier described them, poked from the grass, a gorgeously grim foreboding for every soldier who remembered the poem "In Flanders Fields."

The Force men knew that once the order was given to attack, 1st Regiment would lead the assault, acting as the spearhead of the spearhead. Third Regiment (with tanks and tank destroyers in tow) would attack from across the Mussolini Canal, farther down the line.

Despite the grinding rigors of the last ninety-eight days, the FSSF was up to the task of leading the advance, at least in terms of bodies. The 384 Force men who had died, disappeared, or been wounded on the Anzio line had been replaced by fresh recruits (American as well as Canadian) and mended Force men back from the hospital, some of whom had gone AWOL from their sick beds. By the beginning of May, with 104 officers and 1,966 enlisted men, the FSSF was above full strength, but not the same. Replacements had been carefully selected and trained, but even the Force's intelligence chief, Robert Burhans, admitted that "the old bite" was gone. "The acid," he mused, "had become slightly diluted."

Even the fighting would be different. The breakout would not be another daring Difensa operation. The night before the attack, the men journeyed to the front and, like their fathers a generation earlier, slipped into trenches in advance of the morning's battle. For Major Ed Thomas, the breakout as conceived was alarmingly conventional. "Just like WWI," he would later say, "out of the trenches at daybreak."

Despite their unique education as commandos, the Force

men, now cogs in the U.S. Fifth Army machine, were fighting an infantryman's war that, as Thomas later said, "didn't make a lot of sense." General Frederick probably didn't like the strategy any better than Thomas, but he viewed the coming battle as another test for a unit that had never failed a mission, no matter how arduous. In a message given his men before the battle, Frederick said:

> You have overcome the obstacles of nature and of the enemy. No hardship, however great, has stopped you, and you have endured conditions that only real men and real soldiers could stand. The Force has never moved backward. Every day of its existence has been one of progress. In battle, we have never lost an inch to the enemy . . . The eyes of Canada and the United States are upon us. Let them see that, as in the past, we move only forward.

In this case they were moving toward Rome. But at 5 a.m., when the beachhead artillery began its shelling, followed by mortar fire at about 6:30 a.m., the Eternal City seemed much farther than forty-eight kilometers, and the Force men's route would be even more circuitous than the rest of VI Corps's, taking them into the Lepini Mountains in order to guard the high ground on General Truscott's right flank as he moved north. Once again the outfit would be fighting on crags, draws, and narrow trails etched over the centuries by donkey hooves.

As morning began to break on the 3rd Regiment line, Sergeant Herb "Muscles" Morris waited in his trench, poised for the "go" order. The battalion scout, Tommy Prince, was also raring to go, scheduled to advance with battalion headquarters.

The 2nd Regiment men slated to fight in the first phase of the attack included Sergeant Lorin Waling, Howard Van Ausdale, Joe Dauphinais, Tom Gordon, Herby Forester, Sam Eros, and Jimmy Flack, to name a few of the Force veterans still alive and on the line.

First Regiment was equally ready to go, although 1st Company didn't include Herb Peppard, the Truro, Nova Scotia, native, or Spud Wright, Waling's childhood friend from Grande Prairie, Alberta. Both men were alive, but away from the beachhead on a mission as forward observers. Sergeant Sam Finn, the former Ranger who had survived the debacle at Cisterna and joined the Force's 1st Company (1-1), waited for the attack to begin, along with Lieutenant Bill Airth from Montreal, who was one of the best-liked platoon leaders in 1st Regiment. Airth had won the lifelong loyalty of one of his privates, a Toronto boy named MacIver, when the officer saved him from drowning in the frigid Bering Sea during the Kiska operation. In early May, after elements of 1-1 had moved to the rear for rest and relaxation, MacIver's foxhole had received a direct hit. MacIver died instantly, as did his best friend, Ray Briddon, moments later when shrapnel cut him down as he left his hole to go to MacIver's aid. Airth wept as he told Peppard the news. And despite the unspoken ethic of toughness that permeated the Force, Peppard admired Airth for his heart. "MacIver had been like a son to him," Peppard wrote in his memoirs. "And we understood his reaction."

Not far from Sam Finn in the trenches and foxholes of 1-1 Company crouched Sergeant Art Arsennek, with his best friend, Lieutenant Ed Kelly.

That the breakout would be one of their toughest fights yet dawned on Arsennek, Kelly, and the men of 1-1 when Germans returned fire with fire and lobbed mortars into their heavily concentrated positions. No one was underestimating the Wehrmacht, the army that had conquered western Europe with seeming ease and penetrated Russia as far as the Volga. Even a year after the destruction of the Sixth Army at Stalingrad, the Germans could maul the Allies in Italy even as they slugged it out with the Red Army—the largest fighting force the world had ever seen—on the other side of the continent. Though the Allies controlled the skies and enjoyed enormous advantages in manpower and equipment, Germany was far from beaten in May 1944, and the soldiers arrayed against Arsennek and Kelly could not be taken lightly.

Around Ranger Finn, men were getting hit even before the attack had begun. The situation worsened the moment the order was given to advance, sometime around 7 a.m. On some parts of the line the Germans, despite the artillery barrage that should have been a clear broadcast of Allied intentions, were caught by surprise and in their underwear—literally—in their foxholes.

Along the Cisterna Canal, the enemy was deadly vigilant when 1-1 went over the top of the trench. Machine guns swept the front like searchlights in impenetrable lines of fire. However, when the friends Art Arsennek and Ed Kelly crossed an open field with the bulk of their platoon, it was not gunfire but artillery that irrevocably changed their war. In a sudden barrage, a shell exploded so near to Kelly that only the shield of another man's body prevented him from being shredded by shrapnel. The force of the blast threw Kelly to the ground, and when he arose and shook himself back to the present, he realized the body that had shielded him had been Art Arsennek's.

After scrambling out of his trench, Sam Finn ran forward with a squad of about eight men, and in the excitement he and the others had covered about a kilometer of territory and had approached an empty German trench before Finn realized he was standing in the middle of a minefield. The man right behind took a step that triggered a deafening explosion, which threw him into air, dead and dismembered. As Finn would later recall, he picked a path out of the mines, and as he gingerly stepped to safety he could not quite believe he hadn't detonated one himself.

Finn and 1st Company (1-1) had made great progress. Within an hour of the breakout they had covered almost two kilometers and were halfway to the first strategic prize of the advance: Highway 7, the lifeline of the German defenders. Two hours later, the soldiers had run through a storm of artillery fire (racing forward to get ahead of the metal as much as to get at the enemy) and made it as far as the highway. They had now effectively cut off Cisterna, which had to be a great feeling for the Ranger Finn, but the situation began to unravel by the minute as nine Tiger tanks, by Finn's count, appeared to the left of 1-1. In the face of this devastating fire, mainly from the 88s, the company hunkered down along the railway line and did their best to hold their ground. But the tanks kept advancing, and the battle degenerated into a chaotic mess remarkable even for wartime: "It was so screwed up and no one seemed to know what the hell was going on." Finn and some others started to make for cover, and in the melee Lieutenant Airth was killed. As Finn and the others tried to regroup, an officer came up, stood beside a disabled Allied tank, and told them to keep advancing. Then a shell howled in and killed him.

The Allied armor fared almost as badly as the infantry. In the prewar years the U.S. Army had determined that in future wars tanks would support infantry and not engage other tanks. As a result, the U.S. mainly stocked its armored battalions with medium and light vehicles such as the Stuart, which weighed only fourteen tons, making it, as one historian described, "a fast, agile deathtrap with a 37 mm gun known to American tankers as the 'squirrel rifle.'" British armor was no better when represented by tanks like the Valentine, which "fired two-pound shells comparable to heaving loaves of hard bread at the enemy."

The enemy tanks, by comparison, were beasts from the Book of Revelation. German armor strategists had been visionaries. Conceiving a battlefield where steel monsters fought steel monsters, they concentrated on size, power, and lethality, creating weapons such as the MK VI Tiger: sixty tons in weight, protected by frontal armor ten centimeters thick, and armed with the dreaded 88 mm cannon. Even the American Sherman, with its 75 mm gun, was no match for the Tiger. The German armor at Anzio lived up to its brutal potential. One tank supporting 1st Regiment rolled up behind a farmhouse in the path of the advancing German armor. "One Tiger on the highway," wrote the Force's intelligence chief, Burhans, "fired a round that penetrated the house, went through the tank, and traveled another thousand yards."

The German tanks also managed to savage 3-1, which suffered as much as Finn's unit. Those 3-1 men who weren't "badly cut up," as one officer put it, were captured. Behind them, 2nd Regiment's 1st Battalion endured a numbing loss only minutes into the breakout when its commander, Lieutenant Colonel Walter Gray, was cut down by machine-gun fire after advancing barely forty-five meters into no man's land. Not long before he died, he told his bodyguard, Peter Cottingham, a young sergeant from Swan River, Manitoba, that he wanted to be at the head of the leading company of his regiment.

The German panzer column lost four tanks in the onslaught, and withdrew as their infantrymen dug in. Finn and the survivors of 1st Company backed up over the tarmac of the hard-won Highway 7 and also dug in. Their day's battle, for the most part, was over.

———

Herb Morris's departure from the beachhead featured the same mad forward rush into mayhem. Racing toward the German line, Morris and 3rd Company–3rd Regiment dodged the same intensity of machine-gun fire and mortars that had cut into 1st Regiment farther down the line. "We were being badly chewed up," Morris would later say. Men from 3-3 including Corporal Wall and Private Storey fell as their bodies caught shrapnel and bullets that somehow missed others such as Herb Morris, who did the only thing they could do in such a hailstorm: they continued forward and hoped for the best.

Morris's unit reached the highway, encountered more fire, and then crossed the tarmac, stopping only when they finally reached their objective for the day: a clearing on the edge of some woods, which was to be a rendezvous point for a friendly force occupying the treed area.

The only thing for it was to dig in and wait. So Morris moved forward and began setting up a machine-gun post. In order to better work a shovel, he put down his rifle and removed his jacket and suspenders. He was digging furiously when a squad of Germans emerged from the trees a short distance away.

Sergeant Bray, part of his machine-gun team, saw them too, and he looked at Morris, made a decision, and said: "Herb, get out of here, I'll cover ya." Morris obeyed him, able to grab only his rifle as he sprinted back a dozen meters or so to the strong point where the others were. Gunfire ruptured the air, and Morris planned to turn and lay down enough fire for Bray to join him. But when he turned, he saw Germans where their machine-gun pit was supposed to be, and Bray lying dead. Morris was alone: the rest of the men had already abandoned the position.

Morris realized what Bray had done. The sergeant hadn't decided to cover Morris's advance. In a cruel calculation of odds, he had realized that only one of them could get away alive, and Bray had selected Morris to do the living; Bray would do the dying. As far as Morris knew, this act of sacrifice would earn Bray no medals or honors. The only thing he would win was Morris's life. As he had in the wake of those few lucid moments on the beachhead, Morris left the scene of Sergeant Bray's death a different man than he had been an instant before.

By the time night fell, one element of 2nd Regiment (3rd Company) stood vigil on a bridge on Highway 7 and guarded the new front line. The 133rd Infantry replaced Sam Finn and 1st Regiment, and the 100th Battalion replaced Herb Morris and 3rd Regiment. The Force had lost thirty-nine men that day. As Herb Peppard would realize when he rejoined the outfit the next day, most of the casualties came from his company. Nine 1-1 men were dead and eight were missing. If not dead, those eight were beginning long ordeals as POWs.

The Force's fortunes on May 23 mirrored VI Corps's, which was somehow unable to translate their breakout into a striking advance. Dead and wounded for the Third Division alone numbered 950. German defenses to the south were just as formidable but, like the beachhead line, were also beginning to buckle. Kesselring's forces were standing the line in the Liri Valley, but just barely. While the Force and VI Corps rolled north from the beachhead, in the Liri the Canadians and Brits battered the wire, bunkers, and stubborn fire of the Hitler Line from the front while the French attacked from the south, where they had emerged from the mountains. The Canadians of the Second Brigade (the Princess Patricia's Canadian Light Infantry and the Seaforth Highlanders) who led the attack against the line took devastating losses in the first hours. Mines prevented tanks from supporting the infantry, and the men were cut to pieces by machine-gun fire. The Princess Pats were reduced to a mere seventy-seven men. As one historian observed: "An unreal orgy of killing was spiralling across the Liri Valley." The Hasty Ps were thrown into the fight, and launched "virtual suicide missions" across open ground covered with daisies and poppies. Nevertheless, these advances were applying irresistible pressure, which finally breached the Hitler Line (hastily renamed the Senger Line for symbolic reasons) like water through a collapsing dam—first as a trickle, then a flow.

The Canadians had broken through at the center. Kesselring was still laboring mightily, with some success, to finesse the rout into a controlled withdrawal. When Mark Clark's II Corps, fighting along the coast, breached German defenses at Terracina, Kesselring—faced with an uneven front—decided to retreat to yet another defensive front called the Caesar Line, a chain of fortifications boasting razor wire, trenches, and obstacles twelve meters deep in places, which he had erected south of Rome. As the Allies expended blood and tears, Kesselring was retreating to a position that he—ever the optimist—believed he could hold long enough to allow Wehrmact engineers enough time to complete the fortification of the Gothic line to the north. The Allies advanced to find not an open road to Rome littered with the detritus of German retreat, but the prospect of another bloody set-piece battle.

By the afternoon of the second day, the Force embarked on its return to the mountains. The U.S. 133rd Regiment was earmarked to push past Highway 7, and once there, the Force would launch itself from this line and seize Mount Arrestino, the beginning of the high ground on the right of VI Corps's path to Valmontone. The 133rd did its job in the early morning of May 25, and Colonel Walker's 3rd Regiment moved out. Second Regiment followed, and on that march a shard of shrapnel penetrated the tough skin of Bob Moore, who had been given command of 2nd Battalion when the highest-ranking Canadian in the Force, Lieutenant Colonel Jack Akehurst, took over command of 2nd Regiment after returning from the hospital. Still alive, Moore was rushed off the line, becoming the second battalion commander to fall since the breakout. Major Stan Waters, who had joined the Force as a second lieutenant out of Brockville, Ontario, replaced Moore, and the advance continued.

Private Herb Morris, his coat and suspenders still littering the ground near Sergeant Bray's body, climbed Arrestino in a "drab olive shirt." His soldierly belongings had been reduced to an ammunition belt, a rifle, and a pistol. He used none of these to any extent on Arrestino, which the Force seized easily. For the most part, trees populated the mountaintop, not Germans. Morris and the others could now stare south, slack-jawed with fascination, at the vulnerable lowlands they had occupied for almost one hundred days. When Herb Peppard saw the view from Arrestino, he wondered: "How in hell did we hold that beachhead?"

The Force then turned northwest and marched into the village of Cori. Again, they received no resistance. The Germans had already abandoned the high-mountain village in such desperate haste they left torched panzers on the roads as obstacles to the Allies. The townsfolk were nowhere to be seen, having taken refuge in nearby caves. A patrol from 1-1 flushed two German medics out of a farmhouse and found a wine cellar intact in the basement. When word spread about the booze, the warriors attacked the casks in full force and held an impromptu party, some of them spending the night exactly where they had passed out.

Lorin Waling's journey from the Anzio line to Cori had not been his worst experience. He and the rest of the battalion followed 1st Regiment, which took the brunt of the violence of the breakout. As Waling moved forward, he watched the flotsam of the fighting, wounded men and prisoners, stream by him on their way to the rear. Like everyone, he was awed by the destruction the German panzers had wrought but ebullient at the amount of ground seized when he dug in along Highway 7 that night. Casualties in the march to the mountains had been reduced only because Waling and the others were advancing so far ahead of the line that enemy shelling was landing behind them. From time to time Waling thought of Joe Glass. His wartime partnership with Glass had been so enduring that some of the men had confused them. The next time Waling encountered 2nd Regiment surgeon Evashwick, the heavyset doctor recoiled as if he were looking at a ghost. "Damn it, kid," he said. "I thought you were gone."

"You mean Joe," Lorin replied.

Like Herb Peppard and his company, Lorin would find Cori to be a harmless place. Second Battalion's commander Stan Waters would find it positively friendly. In the mountains Waters came across a guerrilla band, what seemed to be a sextet of haggard peasants but turned out to be five escaped British and American POWs and one Italian. The Italian stole up to Waters and in English introduced himself as Tito Gozzer, an army lieutenant searching for a lost brother. Waters sent the stranded flyers to the rear but kept Gozzer, who spoke good English and knew the lay of the land.

Despite Cori's seeming calm, other Force men fell into a momentary frenzy when word spread that General Frederick had been captured by an enemy patrol just outside the village. The rumor proved false; Frederick was still at large and—as always—keeping pace with the advance. He already had his eyes set on the next objective: Artena, the last village before Valmontone, and Highway 6. Artena would be a deadly, fiery ordeal, and not because of anything Frederick had or hadn't done.

On May 25, Fifth Army commander Mark Clark shocked Truscott, and surprised even those aides well acquainted with his ambitiousness, by abandoning the original plan to continue north, cross Highway 6, and encircle the German Tenth Army with the help of the Brits and Canadians pushing from the other end. Instead, Clark had decided to turn the bulk of VI Corps north and drive straight for Rome to take his place among the illustrious generals who have conquered the Eternal City. Clark's superior, General Alexander, was philosophical about the change in the Fifth Army's course, and made no protest. Alexander seemed simply relieved that the endless stalemate of the past seven months was history and the Allies were advancing on the enemy on all fronts. But Clark's decision not to cut off Highway 6 would allow the German Tenth Army to escape encirclement and destruction in the Liri Valley, reorganize itself at the Gothic Line, and fight again.

Truscott protested Clark's order. He worried that the forces between VI Corps and Rome—the 65th, 4th Parachute, and 3rd Panzer Grenadier Divisions—were too tough to take on alone. But "the boss" thought only of the capital. Wrote the historian Blumenson: "Clark saw Rome as belonging rightly to his own Fifth Army." He and his men, Clark believed, deserved the glory, and the headlines, of liberating Europe's first capital.

So Truscott turned his corps toward the Alban Hills, and Clark ordered the Third Division, elements of the First Armored Division, and Frederick's FSSF to continue north through the village of Rocca Massima in the direction of Valmontone. They— a single division, some tanks, and a commando force of two thousand men—were to do what VI Corps was originally supposed to accomplish: sever the long-contested Highway 6 and block the escape route of the German Tenth Army. If Frederick saw vanity in Clark's decision, he didn't protest. As always, he accepted the tough assignment and set about fulfilling it.

The village of Artena stood on the northern tip of the Lepinis. Quaint and as ancient as any village on the peninsula, Artena was a queer-looking place. To Herb Morris it was as if a giant had thrown a fistful of stone houses against an almost sheer mountainside, where both the dwellings and their inhabitants clung for their lives. With upper and lower sections of the town connected by impossibly steep switchbacks, Artena did not look like any village Morris had seen in New Jersey. Sadly, it was about to endure a level of violence remarkable even for wartime Italy. When the Force men arrived on the outskirts of the village on May 27, Third Division had already conquered it, and like firemen after a forest fire they were stamping out the last of the flames. But the Germans controlled the ground just outside the village, and it was ground they wanted to keep. To the north, visible from some of the hills, lay Highway 6, and for those Force men who found a proper vantage point, this vista was every bit as fascinating as the beachhead seen from Arrestino. The route was the scene of a historic flight, as transport after transport carried men and weapons of the retreating German Tenth Army out of the Liri Valley and into the relative safety of the far side of the Caesar Line. These were the troops Mark Clark had allowed to escape.

The next day, May 28, the Force men took their first tentative step toward that highway when they attacked on either side of the road linking Artena and Valmontone. But the Germans had dug in a line of tanks along a railway line just outside the town, and responded furiously, opening up on the Force men with both 88 mm cannon fire from the armor and 20 mm shells from anti-aircraft guns mounted on *Flakwagens*. The fire was devastating. "To walk the narrow, climbing streets of Artena was quick death," Burhans observed. The Force men made ground anyway, but they paid for every step of the three hundred meters gained.

During the fighting Colonel Walker was in a foxhole dug into a hillside when a particularly lethal barrage fell in. Just outside the hole, the shrapnel caught and cut down Walker's XO, Major Jack Secter, the Winnipegger who had been famous for wandering the Anzio line armed only with a swagger stick. Despite the metal raining down, Walker lunged out and dragged his second-in-command back to safety. But there would be no safe haven for "Black" Jack Secter, who died in Walker's arms. According to some accounts, the normally stoic Texan cradled his XO like a baby and wept. Such acts of selflessness and open emotion were becoming more common among men who had been in combat too long and had watched too many comrades disappear. Herb

Morris experienced this sentiment during a hail of fire that had trapped his platoon on a narrow trail. With no place to take cover, Morris simply crouched as low as he could against a boulder, when he realized that his sergeant, another Texan by the name of Virgil Farmer, was leaning over him, actually shielding him with his body.

Morris and Farmer survived the firefight unscathed, but many others didn't. Major Evashwick, 2nd Regiment's quarterback-sized surgeon credited with saving so many lives, was struck from behind with shrapnel as he tended a wounded soldier. Still living, he was evacuated from the line. In words that were almost poetic in their sparseness, intelligence chief, Burhans, described the attrition: "Lieutenant Coleman, a new Canadian officer just joined, had died from a tree-burst that morning. Private Ball, a Service Company litter bearer plainly marked with the Geneva Red Cross, had been killed by a sniper. Sergeants Bivins and Guerin, Privates Gable, Hicks, and Hoffard, Sergeant Lawrence, and many more, were lost . . ."

The problem was that the FSSF and Third Division stuck into the German lines "like an exposed thumb." With the rest of VI Corps attempting to crawl over the Alban Hills to Rome, the Allied troops at Artena were facing the panicked might of the Tenth Army, including their old foes, the Hermann Göring Division. The savage give-and-take continued: patrols were met with counterattacks, and shells were lobbed back and forth. On May 30, having had quite enough, Frederick was able to enlist the help of big guns from Fifth Army's Field Artillery Group and II Corps (which had slugged its way from Terracina to Anzio to Artena), and they unleashed a barrage on the line of German armor near the railway station, destroying both the station and a formation of enemy infantry who had been assembling to attack.

Two divisions of II Corps joined the line, and by June 2 Kesselring had given the order for a full retreat through Rome.

On that day the Fifteenth Infantry mounted Artena's steep, pock-marked streets and officially relieved the Force men, who were weary and bloodied but on their way to being reenergized. Their war was about to take a northeastern turn. The day before, the Force had been transferred from the jurisdiction of Truscott's VI Corps to II Corps, commanded by Major General Geoffrey Keyes. A plump former cavalryman, Keyes was the officer who had promised the Force men on the eve of their attack against Monte la Difensa: "If you fellows can take this mountain, we'll be in Rome in two or three weeks." Keyes had been dead wrong, but now he was making good.

Mark Clark wasn't the only general who wanted to get to Rome first. Keyes summoned Frederick to his HQ and informed him that II Corps would now be pursuing the enemy and marching on Rome along the newly secured Highway 6. Keyes wanted the Force to lead the corps in, and wanted to ensure that a II Corps unit would be the very first to enter and officially liberate the city. This would be no easy task given that Truscott's VI Corps, after a tough slog over the Alban Hills and through ferocious stretches of the Caesar Line, was bearing down on the capital along Highway 7.

Keyes had a plan, and Frederick had a man in mind to carry it out.

CHAPTER 17

THE FLYING COLUMN

As his comrades planned and prepared on the Anzio beachhead, Captain Mark Radcliffe had languished in a hospital in Naples, as miserable as a bedridden boy on the first day of snow. His misery had little to do with his throat wound, the legacy of the clubbing he'd received from his interrogator in Littoria, an act that stole his voice for weeks; or his bum leg, which was virtually mended, although it still ached when he exercised it in physical therapy. What bothered Radcliffe was the prospect of missing the upcoming action. Military secrets are the worst-kept, and rumors spread through the hospital like a virus that a breakout was imminent. When that happened, the Force would barrel off into the war, and Radcliffe, when he was ready for action, would have to report to a "repple depple," a replacement depot where he would be randomly assigned to almost any sorry outfit in the army.

As he lay in bed and contemplated his military career, he decided there was one solution: he had to go AWOL. Conning an orderly into fetching his uniform, he slipped from the hospital, a former TB sanatorium perched high on the hill overlooking the city, and began to activate the plan he had been hatching. The war zone was truly a small world, and a friend of Radcliffe's from his days at the University of Utah regularly flew mail into the beachhead aboard a sparrow-sized Piper Cub. Once free among Naples's narrow streets, Radcliffe made his way to the airfield, found his friend Chuck, and asked if he was scheduled to make a run to Anzio. When Chuck said yes, Radcliffe countered: "How about taking me?"

"I can't take you. It's against regulations."

Radcliffe worked on him, and finally Chuck agreed to fly him in so long as Radcliffe jumped out of the airplane the moment they touched down, so that there would be no witnesses. Radcliffe agreed, and later that day he was huddled in the cramped seat of the bouncing Piper, airborne for Anzio.

It was dark when they touched down. True to his word, Radcliffe ducked out the door while the plane was still taxiing, and made his way to 3rd Regiment headquarters. Within a short time Radcliffe would realize that he had made the right decision in hurrying back. Early the next morning, on May 23, 1944, a crushing artillery barrage from the Allied side of the line preceded attacks along the length of the beachhead front. Captain Mark Radcliffe had returned just hours before the Anzio breakout. Still healing from his wounds and back too soon to assume his old job, Radcliffe witnessed the breakout as another officer led 3-3.

By June 2, Radcliffe was decidedly fitter and ready for an assignment when Frederick sent word through 3rd Regiment HQ that he wanted to see him. Radcliffe hurried to Force headquarters, to be briefed by his commander. Radcliffe would be commanding a special mission on behalf of II Corps. He then marched to II Corps HQ, where General Keyes, also a son of New Mexico, told him why an FSSF officer had been chosen for the job: "Because of the Force's ability to get the job done," he said. Within minutes Radcliffe was clear on his mission and ready to move.

As Radcliffe and every soldier in the theater were aware, the Fifth Army was closing in on Rome. Less well known was the fact that the Fifth Army's top commanders, Truscott of VI Corps and Keyes of II Corps, were jockeying to be the first ones in. Radcliffe's mission was to ensure that Keyes and II Corps won the race.

Radcliffe was to form and lead a combat patrol capable of moving in a flying column down Highway 6 toward the Eternal City. On the final approach, Radcliffe's patrol would rendezvous with an armored group, the steel tip of II Corps's advance on the city, called Task Force Howze. The task force's leader and namesake was Hamilton H. Howze, a no-nonsense soldier who had served as operations officer of Old Ironsides, the troubled First Armored Division, in North Africa. Howze was both capable and given to rhetoric in the George Patton style. (Howze described fear in a battle as "a monkey's paw that squeezes your liver in a heavy grip.")

After meeting up with Howze's tanks, Radcliffe's patrol would lead them into the city, lay claim to Rome, and get a measure of enemy strength and the Germans' inclination to fight before pulling out. Kesselring's intentions in Rome were still a question mark. The German command had declared Rome "open" and stated they would not endanger the ancient city by contesting it. But few in the Fifth Army were willing to stake their lives on this promise, and Radcliffe's greeting at Rome's gates would be a solid indication of what they could expect. (The Germans had made a similar offer to spare the ancient monastery of Cassino, and the Allies had sparked a storm of condemnation when they flattened it. But the Germans had stored its most precious artifacts and shipped them to the Vatican in a propaganda coup the Allies no doubt wanted to avoid permitting them to repeat.)

Radcliffe's assignment had a strong PR element as well. At Keyes's insistence, a journalist, two photographers, and "one movie camera man" would go along to capture the mission for posterity. Lastly, and importantly, Radcliffe's men were to post blue-colored signs along all prominent streets and squares in the city that stated: "Follow the Blue to Speedy Two." These would serve as calling cards to Truscott, reminding him who had entered the capital first.

As for the unit itself, Radcliffe was to select a top man from each of the three regiments in the FSSF and top soldiers from every unit in II Corps. Radcliffe left II Corps HQ with passes endorsed by General Keyes himself that would allow him and his men to travel any road in Italy under Allied control.

With only hours to get on the road, he assembled the Force men first, tapping K. R. "Mike" Meiklejohn, a tough first sergeant from Edmonton, Alberta, to represent 2nd Regiment; Sergeant Thomas Philips, a Texan, from 1st Regiment; and a New Jersey native by the name of Sergeant John Brannon from 3rd Regiment. Radcliffe then combed II Corps for their best. Based on Keyes's instructions, he made sure every unit was represented, from infantry to artillery to MPs. Even men from engineering units found a spot in the patrol, which had become a representation of II Corps itself, distilled to absolute excellence.

The squad pulled out from the II Corps line at 2 p.m. on June 3: sixty men riding in eight jeeps, and two M-8 armored cars. As he led the convoy forward, Radcliffe was worried. He had a high-octane unit, the very best of II Corps, but none of the men had ever worked together. He had tried to remedy that by devising elaborate plans and going over them before their departure, but Radcliffe knew as well as anyone how a plan could become utterly forgotten once bullets started flying.

The convoy raced forward, headed for the village of Frascotti, where the 398th Infantry were bivouacked. Radcliffe's squad would arrive at their lines and at that point connect with an element of the Howze armor, specifically a unit from the 92nd Reconnaissance Squad, commanded by an officer named Ellis. The 92nd was already assigned to move on Rome in that sector, and had been told to expect Radcliffe. But when Radcliffe's jeep rolled up to the 398th line, the commanding officer of their Second Battalion told him Ellis had passed through about an hour ago.

Radcliffe's elaborate plans were unraveling. He had no choice but to try to catch Ellis's men. But with an hour's head start, they could well be in Rome already. The convoy pulled out and sped along as fast as possible, Radcliffe praying that something hadn't gone wrong.

The going was smooth, the only interruption being a handful of tanks and infantry that were bottlenecked on the road about fifteen minutes from the line. Radcliffe yelled out to a soldier: "Who the hell are you with?" The Eighty-eight Division, he was told. "What's the holdup?" Snipers.

German sharpshooters had pinned down the convoy, but Radcliffe couldn't be bothered with either. He had his men drive around the traffic jam, and sensed the frustration of the convoy's officer when he passed him at the head of the column and was shot a bewildered stare as Radcliffe and his men sped by, determined to keep on going until they reached either Ellis or Rome.

They advanced quickly but not recklessly, keeping their speed at twenty-four kilometers per hour and the vehicles well spaced. Radcliffe wasn't too worried about heavy resistance at this point, figuring the most likely obstacle would be snipers; and sure enough, five minutes after passing the stranded Eighty-eighth Division column, bullets started raining down on them from farmhouses off to the side. Radcliffe dispatched a squad to clear them out, and seconds later a volley of fire erupted and then died down. His men returned with two German prisoners in tow. There were two other snipers in the houses, Radcliffe was told. Both were dead.

The soldiers climbed back in their jeeps and the patrol pushed on. But Radcliffe's hope that snipers would be their only concern before reaching Rome died only a few kilometers down the bare tarmac. Radcliffe's convoy collided with a serious enemy outpost, consisting of two German Self-Propelled (SP) guns supported by machine guns. More and more, as the German army retreated, these SPs were being left behind to fight from the rear.

Radcliffe ordered his patrol to fan out, and he was planning to use an antitank weapon against the SPs when the Eighty-eighth Division armor he had passed chugged up, having heard the shooting from down the road. The tanks knocked out one of the German guns and sent the other one fleeing in retreat. The armor had brought along some troops, and Radcliffe's men teamed up with a platoon of infantrymen and pushed ahead, finding yet another German position a short distance away.

The Germans had set up a roadblock at the head of a destroyed bridge, and fortified it with infantrymen and machine guns. Given the might of Kesselring's Tenth Army, Radcliffe could see that this was a suicide detail, a handful of men ordered to hold off the Allied onslaught for as long as possible. In this case, the delay would not be long.

The skill of his men, particularly Meiklejohn, shone as a group of them converged on the gun pit. Their tactics were standard— the laying down of covering fire as men swooped into the position from the flanks—and utterly irresistible. Within minutes the position was overrun. Two Germans were killed, two wounded, and four taken prisoner. As a bulldozer appeared to cut a detour around the collapsed bridge, Radcliffe walked down the column of tanks to have a chat. He found a captain, who greeted him with the words: "What the hell are you doing here? Are you crazy or lost?"

He might have answered: neither and both. But Radcliffe told the captain that he was under orders to find a tank unit commanded by Ellis.

"Hell, man!" the captain said. "That's us."

Radcliffe could only shake his head. As he would later write: "We had been leading the main Task Force for the last seven miles without knowing it." Once the bulldozer had finished its work, the patrol, now a bona fide task force, pressed on. The resistance from the enemy increased the closer the convoy moved toward the city, which was long visible, albeit shallow and small on the horizon.

At first the task force encountered small-arms fire from snipers that fell on the convoy in two separate incidents from the front and the side of the road. Then they were ambushed by a modest contingent of tanks and infantry in what turned into a vicious brawl. The task force beat the attack off, but not before Ellis's column lost a tank and a tank destroyer. When darkness fell, Radcliffe and the others were on the southern cusp of the city. Radio towers loomed off to the side, a clear broadcast to the task force that they were close to their objective. But a line of enemy tanks—again, enough armor to slow their advance but not enough to contest it—stood in their way. So they deployed and shot their way into an open area near *via Tuscolana* and what looked like a moviemaking complex—studio buildings the size of airplane hangars. They fought within sight of this studio until dawn broke and the enemy's battered rearguard began to pull back into the city.

The retreating tanks, this close to the municipal limits, were like a door opening. Radcliffe marshaled his men and prepared to sweep ahead of Ellis's tanks, and plow on through this door in order to fulfill the mission given him by Keyes and Frederick. Just then, Radcliffe received word that another element of Howze's armor was approaching the city on the right. The armored contingent had a regiment of the FSSF in tow. Truly, every road was leading the Force men to the capital.

CHAPTER 18

SIX BRIDGES

On June 4, Herb "Muscles" Morris and the 3rd Regiment of the FSSF had arrived on the outskirts of the ancient city.

The men had traveled in six-by-six trucks down Highway 6 during the night. The trucks stopped on the approach and the men got out, moving the rest of the way gingerly on foot. After night turned to morning, Morris and 3-3 reached their objective, the Ponte Margherita that stretched over the Tiber. The Force's assignment that day had been to penetrate the city and secure all six of Rome's main bridges, an act designed to win Rome for the Fifth Army and, in no small measure, the Force.

There had been virtually no fighting for this bridge. The night before, their trucks had taken some fire from a German SP that lobbed shells as it sped away. Otherwise the morning had simply been tense. The tension, of course, dissipated in the air once the Margherita bridge fell into their hands. And Morris and Sergeant

Jim Kurtzhal, a friend who hailed from Oregon, stared in wonder at the marvelous stone crossing, something that had no equivalent in North America.

Morris was pleased to be with Jim. Boisterous, bold, mischievous, and tough, Kurtzhal was a type proudly represented in the Force. Like Captain Gus Heilman of 2-1, he was not a spit-and-polish soldier, and in another unit he might have been designated a troublemaker. But in the Force's unique culture, where strength, resilience, and audacity were prized and harmless rebelliousness and quirks were ignored, he excelled. Morris would have bad memories of the war; but at the end of the day, Kurtzhal would represent the happier and more innocent ones, such as the time they crossed enemy lines on patrol and Kurtzhal spotted a cherry tree, and convinced Morris to fill his pockets and bring the fruit back for the rest of the guys. When they emerged at the Force outpost, the soldiers who greeted them stared as if they were seeing walking corpses, and immediately wanted to call for medics. Morris peered down, and understood the problem: the crushed cherries in their pockets had stained their lower bodies blood-red, turning both into the goriest casualties imaginable. This was one of the few occasions Morris could laugh about a mortal wound.

Now here they were together in Rome on a morning of relative quiet. Suddenly, the war interrupted their chat. A car started speeding toward the bridge. Morris could see that there was a German officer inside, trying to barrel his way north across the Tiber in a desperate attempt to escape. Somebody opened up with a Thompson, bullets bore into the windows and doors, and the car came to a stop with the German dead inside.

Kurtzhal looked at the car and then said to Morris: "Would you like to ride into Rome?" They had reached the river, but they hadn't really reached the center of the city. "Why not!" Morris said. They climbed in, and with wild Jim Kurtzhal at the wheel, they drove into the silent, empty streets of Rome in style.

———

Not every entrance into the city of Rome would be so charmed. After the conclusion of the Artena operation, General Frederick rode with the advance armor of the Howze Task Force. Frederick got so bold in his pursuit of the city, 2nd Regiment's commander Jack Akehurst was forced to politely ask the general not to get ahead of advance units.

According to some, the act of securing Rome's bridges was more symbolic than strategic, an order that gave Frederick and the Force a stake in winning the capital. But he took the order seriously, as did his 1st Regiment commander, Cooky Marshall. On the morning of June 4, Marshall's men penetrated the city to spearhead the seizure of the bridges. Some of his units, such as Gus Heilman's 2-1, rammed up against solid resistance: stubborn German SPs and *Flakwagens* that were again ordered to slow but not stop the Allied march into the city. Worried about how his units were faring as they made their way to the Tiber, Marshall and his young radio operator, Norm Smith, ranged ahead as Marshall desperately tried to keep tabs on the operation.

Frederick was in the same situation. At a critical point in the morning, he had received no word on the fate of several crucial bridges. As the main column ploughed into Rome, to be met by crowds of jubilant citizens who had swarmed out to meet their liberators, Frederick ordered his driver to take a side street in order to reach the river. Arriving at Ponte Margherita, the same bridge Muscles Morris would liberate later in the morning, Frederick ordered the men with him to scan the structure for any demolition charges. In addition to his driver and a "hitchhiker," a young soldier AWOL from the hospital trying to get back to his unit, Frederick had his aide and bodyguard, Captain George McCall, with him.

As they reconnoitered the bridge, the realization came to all of them that they had ranged too far ahead when a German squad appeared and began advancing on them from the far bank of the Tiber. The enemy was too close to run from. So Frederick shouted, "Halt!" ("[I] could think of nothing else to do," he would say later.) Both sides opened fire on each other on the bridge, and within seconds his driver was slumped over the wheel dead and Frederick too had been hit. Still able to move, he and the others climbed behind the vehicle for cover as McCall frantically returned fire, and the Germans gave up the fight and withdrew. Checking himself, Frederick realized he had been hit twice, in the shoulder and the leg. It was time to go back to their lines.

Frederick was ushered to a field hospital at Anzio, where he spent the night surrounded by wounded German prisoners moaning in pain. He stayed awake listening to the enemy groans and could only wonder what was happening in the city.

That same day, Cooky Marshall, who had also ventured deep into the city, worried that he hadn't heard from his 1st Battalion in hours. He had continually asked his radio man to raise the battalion commander, but Smith simply couldn't reach him. So he ordered Smith and their small entourage to move ahead through the city streets on foot in the hope of rendezvousing with the unit.

As they crossed a street, Smith noticed a German tank up ahead, pointing its cannon in their direction. The muzzle spat fire and Smith dove for cover. When he turned back from the safety of a doorway, he could see Colonel Marshall sprawled out on the street, motionless. Smith and the others ran out and pulled Marshall to the sidewalk. But they needn't have. Marshall's wounds were severe. As far as Smith could tell, 1st Regiment's commander had died instantly.

In his own way, former Ranger and 1-1 Force man Sam Finn would get revenge for Marshall's death. He and the rest of his company rolled across the city limits at 6:30 a.m., riding atop their armored escorts, and officially entered the capital. It was early enough that the Germans were still putting up a fight. An antitank gun appeared mysteriously from an aperture in a stone wall, opened up, and suddenly two tanks exploded. Finn and his companions weren't on the savaged tanks, but they jumped to the ground anyway and continued on foot.

Trying to swing behind enemy positions still operating in the city, Finn was among a squad of six men advancing down a narrow Italian street when they found themselves approaching the unsuspecting rear of a German machine-gun nest. One of the gunners eventually saw the Force men, and in a panic they began struggling to swing the big barrel of their gun around behind them. Before they could get it in place, Finn bolted, running at them and blazing away with his Thompson as the others in the squad laid down covering fire.

The German gunners threw their arms skyward and surrendered before Finn and the others managed to shoot them. The Force men took away their guns and told them to march to the rear and turn themselves in. As a band of Italian partisans appeared from nowhere to lay claim to the machine gun, the Force men continued on their way into the heart of the city.

When they entered the Piazza Venezia, they realized their war was over for the day. This main square had already erupted into a joyous party as Italians danced, sang, and frolicked in celebration of the departure of the Germans and the end of the war in their streets. As the men in his squad received handshakes and swigs of wine, Finn focused on the monolith off to the side and pondered it: the Palazzo Venezia, one of the city's first palaces of the Renaissance. Although Finn didn't know it at the time, the

Venetian Pope Paul II erected the structure in the late fifteenth century. What Finn did know was that Mussolini had used it as his headquarters, and greeted followers from a perch on the high grand balcony that overlooked the square.

With the help of a local, Finn was able to get inside the palace and identify the upper room that Mussolini had used as an office. When he entered it, Finn realized immediately that he was in the right place. The room was magnificent—spacious and large, with a desk situated at the far end. Finn crossed the room in his leather jump boots, eased behind the elaborate writing table, and did what any man would do in his situation: sat in the chair and plopped those heavy boots on Mussolini's desk. It was not bloody revenge, but Sam Finn relaxed in Benito Mussolini's ornate chair as if he owned it, and rested his tired feet on the same table from which Mussolini had waged his war. Afterward he walked out onto the balcony, and the crowd below went wild. The people cheered as if he were Italy's new leader, and Sam shouted the first thing that came to mind: "Viva Italiano."

Lorin Waling's entrance into the city was every bit as charmed as Sam Finn's. Like Finn, he had to cross a threshold of fire on the outskirts. Waling's company, which made its final approach about 3:30 p.m., was immediately met by resistance. The fight was sudden and ugly, and a few of the men got wounded, including Captain Tom Gordon.

Despite these casualties, Waling and the others in 1st Battalion pressed the Germans back and eased into a city that suddenly became eerily quiet. It was as if everyone, not just the Germans, was in retreat. Advancing down these streets, Waling and the others—Van Ausdale, Herby Forester, Jimmy Flack, and all the rest—moved toward their objective: a five-street junction beside the San Lorenzo railway station. As they made their final approach, the men realized they didn't have to hurry. Stan Waters's 2nd Battalion was already in place. They had somehow beaten them to the objective, and Waters had just received a special welcome.

Waters had advanced to the station, as he had from the mountains, with Tito Gozzer, the Italian partisan he had happened upon near Cori, in tow. As a translator and local guide, Gozzer was useful for Waters. But Gozzer had his own reasons for following the 2nd Battalion into the city. This was evident a few moments before 1st Battalion's arrival, when Waters, Gozzer, and a Force patrol continued past the station and edged toward the Porta Maggiore. As they drew up beneath the arch of this famous and ancient gate into Rome, Gozzer leaped through the passage ahead of Waters, turned, and said: "Welcome to Rome, Major." Years later Gozzer would write: "I do not know if [Waters] understood how much it meant to me to take those two or three steps ahead of him. I only know that he smiled and cordially shook my hand."

After their arrival at the station, firing in the area died off, and Lorin Waling and the others noticed people tentatively appearing at doorways and moving into the streets. Confident that it was safe, this trickle turned into a flow, and before long the area was awash with people. For happy-go-lucky Lorin Waling, the joy was intoxicating. Women kissed him. Men pumped his arm. And sometimes, women shook the soldiers' hands and men kissed them. This quarter of the city, like almost every other, made up for years of deprivation. Everyone found what he wanted most. Lorin Waling marched to a hotel and fell asleep in a bed—the first bed he had spent the night in for almost a year.

Herby Forester would later state: "We shall always insist we were the first troops in the City, and received a grand and glorious welcome—wine, women, and song." Forester may have been right about the wine, women, and song, but he was wrong about who entered Rome first.

———

That prize fell to the one Force man who fought his way into Rome without the Force. Early on June 4, after fighting on the outskirts for most of the night, Mark Radcliffe seized the moment and led his II Corps patrol through the narrow doorway that was swinging open. Radcliffe's vehicle rolled under a highway overpass that had been rigged with explosives but not yet detonated. The men cut the lines and pressed on.

At 6 a.m., Radcliffe passed through the gate at *via Tuscolana*, becoming the first Allied soldier to enter Rome, and his cameraman took the shots to document it.

When the II Corps patrol eventually left the city, Radcliffe had his entire complement with him. Not a single man had been killed, although Ellis's armored group had received casualties, and partisans who had joined the column inside the city had died. Every man in Radcliffe's outfit won the Bronze Star. Radcliffe himself received the Silver Star. And Radcliffe knew that every other Allied soldier who passed into the city that day was "following the Blue to Speedy Two."

General Clark got his wish: the Fifth Army had liberated Rome. But liberation wasn't the only thing on his mind. On June 4, Clark and Keyes descended from the Alban Hills in a jeep and found Frederick on the outskirts of Rome, directing the Force's early hazardous forays into the capital. Clark was impatient. "What's the holdup?" he asked.

Minutes later, after Clark, Keyes, and Frederick had their photo taken under a nearby reflector-studded road sign that read *Roma*, a German sniper opened fire on the group and everyone threw themselves onto the ground for cover. "That is what's holding up the First Special Service Force," Frederick told Clark as they crawled to safety.

When Clark left, Frederick asked Keyes why their boss was so impatient to get into Rome. "France is going to be invaded from England the day after tomorrow," he said, "and we've got to get this in the paper before then." Clark later had the sign sent home as a personal trophy.

———

Early the next morning, a convoy of jeeps cruised through the narrow streets of the city. They carried General Clark and his entourage, and their destination was the Capitoline Hill, where Clark planned to meet with his top generals in what one general had called Rome's "town hall"—the Campidoglio, where the Roman senate had once sat. Clark's convoy got lost and ended up in St. Peter's Square, where a helpful English-speaking priest gave the Fifth Army's commander directions.

Clark's jeeps finally wound their way to their objective, the entourage led by an Italian kid on a bicycle, Clark recounted, "pedaling along . . . and shouting to everybody on the street to get out of the way because General Clark was trying to get to Capitoline Hill."

In a strange metaphor for his campaign, Clark's attempt to heroically enter the hall where generals such as Julius Caesar had been lauded was thwarted by a locked door. Clark knocked. There was no answer. Even he later admitted he was "not feeling much like the conqueror of Rome."

Shortly after Clark and his entourage gained entrance to the building, a horde of foreign correspondents arrived. Clark and his generals, Truscott, Keyes, and the French General Alphonse Juin, were in the process of congratulating each other. Even though the journalists had been tipped off by Clark's PR officer,

Clark expressed surprise at seeing them. "Well, gentlemen," he said. "I didn't really expect to have a press conference here—I just called a little meeting with my corps commanders to discuss the situation. However, I'll be glad to answer your questions." Clark then gave a short victory speech that stated what a great day this was "for the Fifth Army and for the French, British, and American troops of the Fifth."

Clark's startling failure to mention the true benefactors of this victory (including the British, Canadians, and South Africans of the Eighth Army who broke the Gustav Line, and the Poles, Indians, and New Zealanders at Cassino) shocked famed broadcast correspondent Eric Sevareid, who stood among the press. "It was not, apparently, a great day for the world, for the Allies, for all the suffering people who had desperately looked toward a time of peace," Sevareid later wrote. "On this historic occasion, I feel like vomiting."

Journalists had the leisure of outrage. After the jubilation of their welcome by the Romans, the Force men felt simple relief and exhaustion. "The long campaign had left the regiment very tired and needing rest," wrote Major Ed Thomas of 2nd Regiment. "Before dozing off that night I doubt many of us reflected on what a memorable [day] we'd just been through."

CHAPTER 19

SOLDIER'S FAREWELL

After the grand party subsided, a semblance of normalcy appeared in Rome as citizens and soldiers attempted to resume lives as if the war hadn't happened. When Lorin Waling rose the next day after his first restful night's sleep in Italy, he looked out his window and saw trams on the streets and Italians rushing off to work. But reminders of the war were inescapable, because soldiers were everywhere. Rome was utterly unlike the freebooters' paradise of Naples. The southern city had been poor and shabby even before it was contested between armies. But Rome remained a beacon of civilization in a dark world, and Allied troops, many of them from small North American towns, had never seen anything like its magnificence. They were in awe.

Rome was transforming by the minute. As hours passed, more troops entered the city, and immediately a black market economy flourished. Waling found a barbershop where goods could be had—alcohol, food, cigarettes, and so on—and it was at this shop that he ran into a fellow Force man. Lorin and the kid didn't know each other—they were from different regiments—but they recognized each other's uniforms, and the kid gave Lorin the news: the Force was being moved to a rest area outside the city.

The new Force bivouac area was Lago di Albano, an alpine lake about thirty-two kilometers southeast of Rome. Quiet, secluded, and pristine, the lakeshore served as a sanitorium for the more war-weary men, a place where mail could be read, letters written, and home missed. It was a party for those determined to burn off energy. But for some, Rome's allure was too great. Lorin Waling got a pass and returned to the capital. Sam Finn, after his personal victory over fascism, decided to become as close as he could to a tourist. He descended into the catacombs and explored the Coliseum, an ancient ruin that suddenly looked contemporary beside the millions of modern ruins across Italy and Europe. He went to a show: Irving Berlin's *This Is the Army*. And Finn spotted Humphrey Bogart in the city.

At Albano, men commandeered jeeps and raided adjoining units, villages, and storehouses for alcohol, food, or whatever they lacked. They wanted for little, actually. The water and clean air and baseball games were enough to satisfy most of the men. Living soldiers were paid; dead soldiers were remembered in memorial services. But the rest and the victory that had preceded it would be fleeting. On June 6, men huddled around their radios and cheered as they listened to news reports of the largest amphibious attack in history then taking place on the beaches of Normandy, France. The war in Europe had shifted from the Italian campaign in the south to France in the north, where Allied armies under Dwight Eisenhower prepared for the long march to Berlin.

Mark Clark had, as he later wrote, "got to Rome before Ike got across the English Channel to Normandy." But this Italian victory would be forgotten faster than Clark could have imagined. The Italian war—with the troubled Salerno landings, the grinding attrition of the advance north, the long stalemate at the Gustav Line, the carnage at Cassino, and the disappointment of the Anzio landing—had always been difficult for the public to comprehend. Where the Italian campaign had been a long, anticlimactic slog on Europe's periphery, the invasion of Normandy, the beginning of the battle to liberate France, was exhilaratingly clear. The Allies were now marching on Paris and Berlin. And with each step taken by Eisenhower's armies, the Italian war seemed more distant and superfluous.

This sentiment received a voice when a story spread that British Conservative MP Lady Nancy Astor had criticized the soldiers of the British Eighth Army for "dodging" the real war in France. In response, British soldiers composed a song called "The Ballad of the D-Day Dodgers," which soon became the anthem of the warriors of the Italian campaign. Although some argue the story of Lady Astor's criticism is apocryphal, the lyrics underscore the irony and bitterness that the soldiers in Italy felt after June 6, the disenchantment of the men who had gone toe-to-toe with the Wehrmacht when it was still lethal, when the outcome of the war still seemed to hang in the balance, only to be shrugged off as history turned its gaze to the northwest.

> We're the D-Day Dodgers, here in Italy
> Drinking all the vino, always on a spree
> We didn't land with Eisenhower
> And so they think we're just a shower
> For we're the D-Day Dodgers
> Out here in Italy

We landed in Salerno, a holiday with pay
Jerry brought the band out to cheer us on our way
Showed us the sights and gave us tea
We all sang songs, the beer was free
To welcome D-Day Dodgers
To sunny Italy

If you look around the mountains in the mud and rain
You'll find scattered crosses, some which bear no name
Heartbreak and toil and suffering gone
The boys beneath them slumber on
For they're the D-Day Dodgers
Who stayed in Italy

═══

Just as Normandy changed the dynamic of the war, for the Force men nothing would be the same after the liberation of Rome. General Frederick arrived at Albano, taking advantage of the tranquility to recover from his wounds. He had spent only one night in the Anzio field hospital among the groaning enemy. On June 5 he returned to Rome and rested in a hotel room before moving on to Albano, where he shared a villa with his fellow officer and friend, Ken Wickham, who was recovering from wounds to his leg.

Frederick had ordered Wickham's return from a hospital in Naples where surgeons were contemplating whether or not to amputate two of his fingers. A Force physician had fetched him, telling the Neapolitan surgeons that if the patient's fingers worsened, he could remove them at his station; but Wickham had to go: General Frederick needed him. "Our commander has lost the use of his leg," the surgeons were told. "Wickham has the use of his, so the commander wants him back."

The two officers rested in a grand villa that was decorated with furniture from Castel Gondolfo, the summer residence of the Pope. The Vatican authorities weren't bitter about the borrowed items. In fact, they invited Frederick and Wickham to dinner, where they feasted on turkey served by a surprisingly tempting waitress. Back at Albano, Frederick spoke often with Wickham. The general's mood must have been soulful, because Wickham would later say that he "found him hungry for company."

If Frederick was rueful and introspective, he had obvious reasons to be. Albano was a recess after almost seven months of relentless combat and death, much of which Frederick had witnessed firsthand. His nine wounds attested to his constant proximity to slaughter. But Frederick had other concerns as well, notably an order that had just come down promoting him to major general. Just thirty-seven years of age, Frederick's new rank was as unprecedented as his wounds. He was the youngest major general in the U.S. Army ground forces.

The rank had implications. These became clear on June 23, when the men were called and asked to meet in the courtyard of the villa that served as the Force headquarters. Frederick, dressed in crisp fatigues, his cuffs tucked into his jump boots paratrooper-style, and a simple overseas cap on his head, stepped up and told the men that he had an announcement. He was leaving the Force. In receiving another star, General Frederick was being promoted out of the outfit, and would soon be given another command: an airborne unit slated to spearhead the upcoming invasion of southern France ahead of the Seventh Army.

The men were stunned. "A discernible, protesting gasp broke the hush in the ranks of men who normally withheld such sentiments," wrote intelligence chief Burhans years later. And each man, Burhans said, seemed to dwell on his individual memories of Frederick, or "Fredericks" as the few pioneering Force men from Fort Harrison still called him. Men sorted through memories of Frederick in terrible places they had never expected to encounter a general, of his generosity with cigarettes when touring those places, and of his fearlessness.

"We respected him because he was always with us, and he was one of us," Herb Peppard of 1-1 would later say. When he absorbed the news, Lorin Waling fought back a tear, but he noticed that many others couldn't. Years later he admitted, "There wasn't a dry eye anywhere."

Then, in order to tell everyone good-bye individually, Frederick received and shook hands with each man in the Force. The procession was funereal: somber, silent, and slow. Frederick was the only one who smiled good-naturedly at the men as they approached.

As for a new leader, Frederick had selected 3rd Regiment commander Edwin Walker to replace him. Respected, hard-driving, and, as Frederick had stated, "an outstanding soldier," Walker was the obvious choice. Everyone knew that. But no one was happy.

CHAPTER 20

RIVIERA WARS

For Lorin Waling and the others, Lago di Albano had changed from a resort to a barracks overnight. On June 12, eleven days before Frederick announced he was leaving, combat training began in earnest. The men resumed long marches, honed rested bodies with exercise and calisthenics, and ranged out on mock patrols. Captain O'Neill tutored replacements in hand-to-hand combat, his classroom the surface of the nearby tennis court. The holiday had ended.

And the war resumed. In early July the Force men ventured south to prepare to pick up where they had left off. Bouncing in the rear of trucks, they drove to Anzio and experienced a strange war homecoming. For front-line scouts like Waling, the former beachhead was eerily quiet. It was hard to believe this lazy port had been the target of so much condensed fear, violence, and aggression. They boarded Liberty ships at Anzio and sailed south to Salerno, the scene of the Allied invasion of Italy in September 1943. *Was it really less than a year ago?*

From Salerno, they rode train cars about sixty-five kilometers, then hiked the rest of the way into an ageless Italian fishing village: Santa Maria di Castelabate. Their first base in Italy had been Santa Maria Capua Vetere; this was the second tribute to Holy Mary they would call home.

The Force that arrived at this Santa Maria was considerably different than it had been when it took up residence in the shattered barracks of Capua Vetere. The outfit had new leaders to replace Frederick and Ken Wickham, who had accompanied his friend to the airborne division. When Walker assumed command of the Force, a polished Canadian lieutenant colonel named Bill Becket took over 3rd Regiment, becoming Mark Radcliffe and Herb Morris's regimental boss. Bob Moore resumed command of 2nd Regiment, and Jack Akehurst took command of 1st Regiment, still mourning the death of Cooky Marshall.

And the war itself had changed in the interim. The Force had come to the southern coast of Italy to prepare for the invasion of southern France, an Allied stab into the French Riviera that was scheduled to take place in six weeks' time. Along the way, the Force had left Mark Clark's Fifth Army and been transferred into the Seventh Army.

Clark had expressed sadness at losing the men. He sent a farewell letter that seemed to indicate he recognized just how arduous their campaigns had been. "The grueling fighting which you went through on the main front in the dead of winter, the way in which your relatively small Force maintained an aggressive offensive on a front equal to that held by any full division," Clark wrote, "have entered history and forged a bright new link in our military tradition." Some of the men were wistful when they read the letter and assessed their war so far. Wrote Force man Adna Underhill: "It was a good letter and generally appreciated, but there were some who hoped that their new commander might be more able to use the Force for the type of missions for which they had been formed and trained." No matter how they would be used, the shift to this theater meant that the commandos would be joining the war's endgame as Eisenhower's armies slugged their way across Europe toward a German frontier that still seemed a long way off.

The biggest difference between 1942 and 1944 was felt within the men themselves. How could they have emerged unchanged from the hell of the last eight months? They had watched too many friends disappear, dead or wounded. In this pause between battles, the men began to feel how combat had changed them.

Some of the lost Force men did come back. During the summer, 663 Force men returned to camp from hospitals, recovered and ready for duty. One sunny day in July, during training to assault rocky beaches in rubber boats, a bone-thin, dark-haired jackknife of a soldier, cradling a bad arm, limped into an area where 2nd Regiment was bivouacked. Lorin Waling was the first to recognize him.

"You sonofabitch," Waling said to Joe Glass, "how'd you get down here?"

The two friends hooted and embraced. Other original 1-2 men ran up to greet Joe, whose appearance answered a question Waling had been pondering right up to that day: Did Joe Glass die on the beachhead? In truth, he almost did. His wounds had been severe. He had so much blood in his lung that the doctor gave him a pack of Lucky Strikes and told him to smoke it out. The cigarettes hurt like hell, but Joe smoked every one and gradually coughed the dried blood out of his system. From Anzio, Glass had been shipped to the hospital in Naples. He was out of immediate danger of dying, and his badly mangled arm had been saved, but he was weak, and his chest wound was far from healed. By July he was able to get around well enough, and he missed the boys, so he found out where the Force base was and hitched a ride in with a group of replacements. Joe was reporting for duty. He wanted back into combat.

Of course everyone, including Waling, laughed. Joe was almost an invalid. But he was part of the Force, so he was told by one of the doctors to swim in the sea as much as he could; it would strengthen his arm.

While Glass recuperated, the men trained. Wearing shorts and lifebelts, they scrambled from landing craft into rubber rafts and paddled themselves ashore through crashing waves. They trained to assault cliffs as well as beaches, scaling rock faces with full equipment. The Mediterranean sun and beech trees didn't distract them for a moment. The soldiers tackled their training with as much intensity as ever. Two men would die in training; over six hundred would be injured in some way.

Herb Morris thrived in Santa Maria di Castelabate. He was delighted that Radcliffe was back with the Force after his absence during the assault on Rome. But Radcliffe was no longer his company commander. Battalion commander Canadian Tom Gilday had just been promoted to headquarters, and the big Louisianan Ray Hufft had taken his place. Major Hufft was a newcomer to the Force and his "Boudreaux" Radcliffe was his new XO. Morris got a strong sense of Hufft in the training. It was no coincidence he had found his way into the Force; he was a gungho soldier cut from exactly the same cloth as Frederick and Walker.

On August 7, the Force men packed up and left Castelabate, bound for their new mission directly linked to Operation Dragoon, the Seventh Army's invasion of southern France. (Originally named "Anvil," the operation's name was reportedly changed by Churchill, who opposed the plan and complained that he had been "dragooned" into it by the Americans.) The Îles d'Hyères, a three-island chain eleven kilometers from the French coast, were located to the immediate left of the landing zone. The Force was ordered to occupy two of these islands—Île de Port-Cros and Île du Levant—and destroy the enemy there, and a collection of artillery on Levant powerful enough to threaten the invasion force.

Waling and 2nd Regiment waved good-bye to Joe Glass. He still wanted to go along, and they still wouldn't have him in combat. Glass was allowed to report to the other Santa Maria to help train and brief replacements. When the new boys took a look at his battered physique, they asked him what it was like to get hit. "Don't worry about getting hit," Glass said. "Because if you get hit, you ain't gonna know it anyway. And if you get hit like I did, you ain't gonna feel it." Joe, as he would later say, "had given them the biggest line of shit I could." But the boys were kids, and he didn't want to scare them.

When Joe had a chance, he returned to Naples to visit friends in the hospital on the hill. One day he was negotiating a wide ward full of beds when a voice from behind said, "Joe." The voice was weak, and unrecognizable. He turned and his eyes fell on a sliver of a soldier lying flat as a sheet on a bed. The face was gaunt and pale, but Joe could still recognize it.

"Art?" Joe said.

"How you doin', Joe?" the voice said, confirming what Joe had figured. The wounded man was Art Arsennek. And God, what a surprise. Joe remembered Poison. He was the husband of Dorothy's friend Bucky, who had worked with Dorothy at Eddy's Bakery in East Helena. Joe and Dorothy had sometimes chummed with Art and Bucky because the girls were friends. But Art was in 1st Regiment, and once they arrived in Italy, Joe had lost track of him. Joe couldn't remember seeing Art once on the beachhead, and he certainly hadn't heard that he'd been hit. In fact, he could not have heard that Arsennek had been wounded for the simple reason that it occurred two days after Joe himself fell in battle.

Living with her parents in the town of St. Catharines, Dora Arsennek knew about the wounding of her husband almost immediately. She had received a telegram notifying her of it, even before a prognosis had been declared on his condition. The telegram was mercilessly direct. It described the loss of his two fingers, and the shrapnel in his buttocks and stomach. The cable was so matter-of-fact and undramatic, she couldn't help but feel as if everything would be okay. Joe Glass didn't know the details of Art's wounds, but he had the feeling he wouldn't be all right. Art looked very bad.

————

On the night of August 14, U.S. Navy destroyers slipped into waters just off the Îles d'Hyères. On board, the three regiments of the First Special Service Force made ready to mount the nets and climb down into the landing craft and rubber boats jostling in the sea below. Mark Radcliffe and many of the men of 3rd Regiment would be embarking on full stomachs. Radcliffe had never forgiven the navy for feeding him sauerkraut before the invasion of Kiska Island. A soldier about to hit the beach was supposed to have beef. So Radcliffe approached the cook in the ship's mess and asked him, "What about our steaks?"

The cook had stared impassively. But Radcliffe made it clear that he and his men had a right to steaks, and they wanted their steaks. The cook listened, grumbled, and stalked off.

When chow time came, sure enough, the Force men were treated to a feast of fine beef, as much as they could eat. Radcliffe ate with satisfaction, and when he saw the navy cook next, he wanted to thank him. But the cook didn't seem to want gratitude.

"I hope you liked your steak, you sonofabitch," he said.

————

Radcliffe, Morris, Tommy Prince, and the others from 3rd Regiment climbed into rafts that were bound for the same island that Waling, Van Ausdale, Dauphinais, and the others would be attacking: Levant. Port-Cros was 1st Regiment's target, and they were at that moment scrambling off another destroyer.

The sea was still as a lake when the men of 2nd and 3rd Regiments made their way to Levant in rafts towed by landing craft. They chugged along as slowly as possible, keeping engine noise to a murmur in the utter silence. This attack was to be a surprise. The shrewd Colonel Walker had fought hard to make it so. He had chosen some of the most inaccessible reaches of the island as landing zones (LZs), guessing that these would also be the least defended. The Seventh Army had balked at the cliffs he had chosen as his LZs. But Walker knew his men could surmount them. The important thing was that they land where the enemy wasn't.

The landing craft released the rafts about nine hundred meters from shore, and the men—1,200 in all—gripped paddles and dipped them into the sea. In a stillness where even small splashes were audible, the men paddled as cautiously as possible to their respective LZs. At 2 a.m. both Waling and his comrades in 2nd Regiment and Radcliffe and 3rd Regiment had left their rafts and were standing on the shore.

The granite face that Waling and the men of 2nd Regiment climbed was steep but not high. Third Regiment reached its assembly area with similar efficiency, and by approximately 3 a.m. both regiments were moving out in the direction of their targets. Of the objectives, Colonel Walker was most concerned about where Hufft's men were headed. First Battalion was assigned to take out a battery of 164 mm guns that menaced the beaches on the mainland. Sources in the French forces claimed they had scuttled the guns when they abandoned the fort, but the army had taken aerial shots and the cannons were clearly there, aimed at the coast where troops would be landing in only a few hours. The mainland LZs spanned over fifty-six kilometers of shoreline, and the cannons had the range to attack every bit of it. So menacing were these weapons that one infantry division had made their removal a prerequisite for hitting the beaches.

After assembling at the top of the cliffs, Hufft and his battalion quietly began to move east. The battery was in a fort almost directly beside the Phare de Titan lighthouse. Both Hufft and Radcliffe expected the worst. They had come ashore without incident, but the guns would be heavily guarded, of that there could be no doubt. Suddenly they realized that the guns weren't their only concern. The ground was covered with a thick brush that the locals called *maquis,* and fighting through it in the dark was a battle in its own right. The three hundred men in Hufft's battalion cursed it silently as they plodded up the island to the northeast end, where the battery was entrenched.

As dawn approached, the men were within sight of the lighthouse and the cannons. Even with the morning, the island where they stood remained bizarrely quiet. They were a battalion of men and should have been spotted, but as of yet there was no firing. The assault company got into place, and within minutes Captain Mark Radcliffe was inside the silent fort. There had been no guards to resist them. As far as he could tell, there were no Germans there, just straw mannequins posing as guards near the battery. And when he walked close to the guns, he and everyone else could clearly see that they were a ruse as well, painted tubes covered with camouflage. Hufft immediately phoned Walker's HQ to relay the good news.

Then mortar fire began to fall in.

As Hufft's men overtook the empty gun emplacement, 3rd Regiment's other battalion had managed to swing in behind their target: a contingent dug in and guarding a stretch of beach near Point du Liserot that looked like a prime LZ.

Second Battalion hit this position from the rear, and the defenders became so disoriented that as many as sixteen gave themselves up. But the shooting had awakened the Germans in the center of the island just as Lorin Waling and the rest of the men in Major Ed Thomas's 1st Battalion approached Port du Grand Avis.

The enemy's fire came in on fixed lines designed to protect the approach. Machine-gun fire swept in, and mortars began to erupt around the battalion. Section leader Sergeant Lorin Waling was shepherding his men forward when 88 mm rounds began to rupture the earth around them. Waling felt himself rise in the air, and when he hit the ground, he noticed a bloody arm in front of him. It was his own right arm, and from the way it was twisted he wondered if it was still attached. He flipped it up with his other arm, and felt a surge of relief when it remained attached to his body. Scanning around him, Waling could see as many as seven men, most from his section, lying on the ground in approximately the same state of mutilation as himself. The rest of the company was advancing toward the bunkers that were responsible for the fire.

Then Waling's eyes focused and he saw a figure approaching. The man was Doug Edgelow, a sergeant like himself. Edgelow had seen Waling fall and was coming back to see how his friend was. Edgelow's expression told Waling everything. "Oh my God," Edgelow said, "your face." Waling could feel the blood on his face, and he knew he had a large hole in his chest—blood spurted from the wound between his ribs. Edgelow leaned Waling up against a rock; Waling felt himself sitting. Edgelow said he had to go on. "Take care of yourself," he said, and then was gone.

With nothing else to do, Waling decided there was one thing he needed more than anything: a smoke. With his left arm, which was chewed up as well but still working, he fished out a cigarette and put it between his lips. He tried his awkward best with his bloody left hand to light it, but he could only fumble with the matches and curse. Off to the side lay a Ranger who had also been hit by the mortars. As Lorin struggled to light a match, the Ranger began crawling toward him. In contrast to Waling, the Ranger's arms were all right. It was his legs that were injured: both broken, with bones sticking from the skin like little spears. The Ranger pulled himself the distance of three meters right up to Lorin, fished a lighter out of his pocket, and lit the cigarette Waling still had hanging from his lips.

When the medics arrived, Lorin shouted for them to take the others back first. He was section leader, after all; he should be the last. The medics complied, and within minutes Waling was the only man there—the only living man. He was waiting for the medics to get back when suddenly the environment around him changed as if a cloud was passing overhead and blocking the sun. It became quiet: no shooting, no explosions. The air went still, and a feeling of warmth began spilling over him like water. Waling felt relaxed. More than that, he was happy. If he could have described what he was feeling, he would have said "freedom."

―――

By about 8:30 p.m., the Force's 2nd and 3rd Regiments had pacified Île du Levant, with ten Force men dead and many more injured. While the battle raged, medics carried wounded Force men to the beaches, where landing craft ferried them to the hospital ship lying offshore. Three surgeons had worked around the clock to keep sixty-one wounded commandos alive. First Regiment's battle for Port-Cros offered up casualties as well.

One of the saddest casualties of the entire campaign was the medic Sergeant Jake Walkmeister, from Suttercreek, California.

Attached to 1st Regiment HQ, Walkmeister had been a lion throughout the war, risking life and limb to aid wounded Force men. According to one history, shrapnel tore into Walkmeister early in the invasion of Port-Cros when he left the cover of a hastily erected aid station to help a wounded man to safety. Walkmeister died on the hospital ship, and was buried at sea.

—

Once on the mainland the Force was reunited with General Frederick when assigned to Frederick's 1st Airborne Task Force, whose British and American paratroopers had spearheaded the landings. Frederick's operation dropped ten thousand men by parachute and glider behind enemy lines just ahead of the main invasion force and landed almost unopposed. Frederick had jumped along with his men. His leg still wounded, Frederick parachuted "into southern France with the first wave, a blue flashlight in hand, .45 on hip, his shattered leg strapped to a board."

Frederick's division, along with the FSSF, was assigned to attack along the Franco-Italian border: a lackluster conflict some of the Force men would call the "Champagne Campaign." The Force men's introduction to Dragoon was almost solemn, given the missionary retreat at Sylvabelle that served as their first barracks after their arrival on August 17, 1944. Set on the coast near Cavalaire, the survivors of the Îles d'Hyères invasion enjoyed a brief respite on the beaches and watched the supplies and troops, mainly soldiers from France's colonies, stream ashore. After their three-day rest ended and the Black Devils officially joined Frederick's Airborne Task Force, they replaced the British Red Devils of the Second Parachute Battalion, who were bivouacked inland from Cannes. (The Allies had devils of many colors: the "Blue Devils" of the 88th Infantry Division, the "Blue and White

Devils" of the 3rd Infantry Division, the "Red Devils" of 1/504 Battalion of the 82nd Airborne Division, and the "White Devils" of 2/504th. On the German side, the "Green Devils" of the 1st Parachute Division were formidable opponents—the uncompromising defenders of Cassino.) Even from their first engagement, pushing north toward the village of Le Veyans, Burhans admitted that "enemy resistance was sparse and scattered."

The Force men's first major engagement was the liberation of Tanneron, conducted by Akehurst's 1st Regiment, which the Germans of the 148th Reserve Division contested with surprising vigor. At the same time, Becket's 3rd Regiment, on Akehurst's left, seized the south bank of the Siagne River, and 2nd Regiment, in reserve but also protecting the right flank, was dispatched to seize the fragrant little town of Grasse, which they managed by enlisting the help of a "Cannon Platoon" to remove a pair of 88s menacing them in the area, and then by circling the objective, a center of the region's perfume industry, while 1st Regiment hit the town from the highway. Grasse fell on August 24, and the Force netted eighty-three prisoners.

And on it went. Declared Burhans: "With the enemy on the run there was no time for play. The long march continued." The countryside was picturesque, but the men slogged through it on foot, and Underhill lamented: "We can't walk as fast as Jerry can run away in his vehicles."

The battles continued to be uneventful. Mougins offered only enemy invalids, a hospital abandoned in the haste of retreat. Valbonne was utterly empty.

But the setting was perfect for a "Seventh Army side-show, an improvised sealing of the flank." Ordered to advance east along the Riviera coast, the Force men were conquering past paradise, securing or simply brushing past peasant villages and resort towns that until then were the domain of the European elite. The FSSF marched past Cannes, Antibes, and eventually Nice, with their ultimate destination being the mountains that stood along the French-Italian border.

———

Sergeant Joe Glass returned to France and tried again to join the Force, now missing his friend Waling. Still a walking invalid, Glass was assigned guard duty and spent a lot of time in bars in Nice. He could have returned home to North America, but he couldn't stand to leave his "family," or at least those original men from 1-2 who remained. And incredibly, a few remained. Van Ausdale, one of the oldest in the outfit, had survived into France without a scratch, even though he had manned the front lines of some of the Force's most dangerous operations. Tommy Fenton, Percy Crichlow, and Jimmy Flack were all still alive. And so was Herby Forester. After Lorin, Joe was probably closest with Herby, and they shared a few good times. Once, on the prowl together in Nice, they walked by a bar tucked into a basement that was brimming with music and laughter. Herby insisted on going in, even though the party was a private one. Joe followed, and watched Herby while the night away dancing with kind women who towered over him.

Only casualties reminded the Force men that war in southern France, no matter how surreally charmed, was not a holiday. Soldiers continued to fall. And because the casualties in southern France were fewer than in the Italian war, each death brought an especially poignant sadness. Moreover, it was clear the war would soon be over, and no one wanted to die now that the outcome had been decided.

On the evening of August 25, 6th Company–2nd Regiment, now under Captain Larry Piette, Joe Glass's platoon commander on Monte la Difensa, stormed a charming château in the high village of Villeneuve by way of the cellars and flushed out a squad of Germans taking a stand there. By the next morning 2nd

Regiment controlled both the château and the town itself. They spent a day driving off counterattacks, and then on August 27 advanced again and took the small village of Cagnes-sur-Mer near the coast.

After being relieved at Cagnes, company commander Piette had one casualty report to file. In street fighting in the previous days, one of his sergeants had been clipped by a spurt of fire coming from the machine pistol of a German trapped in the basement of a house. The bullets had torn into the sergeant's thigh, severing his femoral artery. The soldier was Floyd Schmidt from Elmira, Ontario—the childhood friend of and best man to Captain Herb Goodwin, the 1st Regiment officer who had lost "damn near" all his men when he was ordered up Remetanea. Lieutenant Bill Story of Winnipeg was with "Smitty" when he died, the life leaking out of him in powerful artery-red spurts no one could stop.

A friend broke the news of Schmidt's death to Goodwin, and it was difficult for him to accept. Firstborn in a family of ten, Goodwin had grown up poor in Elmira, right next door to Smitty. During the worst days of the Depression, Goodwin found himself admiring Floyd, an only child who didn't seem to have the worries that Goodwin did. Sometimes, on his way to work, Herb would spot Floyd playing tennis. Goodwin had been surprised to run across him at Fort Harrison. The two childhood friends, quite independently of each other, had volunteered for the same unit. As a fixture of his past, Schmidt merged into Goodwin's future when he stood up for Herb at his wedding. Smitty had asked to be placed in Goodwin's platoon, but Herb refused. Although he never told Schmidt this, he didn't want a friend from home to die under his command. But Schmidt's death in 2nd Regiment was still a heavy blow. It was so close to the end, Goodwin thought, and he knew that there would soon be great terrible grief in his neighborhood.

In mid-October, the Force parted with General Frederick again when his division was transferred to the Sixth Army Group. A shift in resources prompted Colonel Walker to reduce the contingent and send some support personnel home. One of these was Joe Glass, who had been doing his bit as a camp guard. Walker shook hands with every man who left. When he got to Joe, he said, "I'm sorry to see you go."

The one man who couldn't tear himself away from the Force was General Frederick. Joe Glass was limping down a street in Nice one day when General Frederick's jeep sped by, flags waving. Frederick spotted Joe's uniform, immediately ordered his jeep to stop, and came over to shake his hand and ask him how he was.

====

In November 1944, the Second World War entered its fifth winter, and every sign suggested it would not see another. Germany's greatest general, Erwin Rommel, was dead, forced to commit suicide after supporting a coup attempt against Hitler. Advancing Soviet armies several times larger than the forces under Eisenhower's command had already liberated the Baltics and were advancing on Germany with the inevitability of a tidal wave across a front that spanned the continent. On October 21, the historic German city of Aachen, birthplace of Charlemagne, fell to the American Thirtieth and First Divisions.

Only those Germans utterly detached from reality (and there were many) believed anything but total defeat was their future. In late 1944 Hitler still entertained the hope that some turn of fate would save Germany from annihilation in the same way providence had preserved Prussia and Frederick the Great during the Seven Years War. (The providential death of the Czarina Elizabeth in 1762 caused Russia to leave the alliance of enemies that had virtually destroyed Prussia on the battlefield.)

Soon, German officers would be fighting not so much to stave off defeat as to influence who would defeat them. Between the Red Army, grinding its way toward Berlin from the east, and the Americans, British, French, and Canadians pressing from the west, many Germans prayed their western enemies would conquer them first, although the Wehrmacht doggedly continued to resist in the west. "I hoped the Americans would hurry up and get it over because we expected nothing good from the Russians," said one major in the German army. The German military, aware of the savagery of its invasion of the Soviet Union, expected the Red Army to exact horrific revenge. They would be correct. The Red Army would drive the Wehrmacht from eastern Europe and liberate Auschwitz on their way to Berlin. And according to historian Antony Beevor, they would vent an almost diabolical hatred for the enemy by raping 1.4 million women in East Prussia, Silesia, and Pomerania, and as many as 130,000 women when they got to the German capital. In a matter of months Germany would cease to wage a world war and begin a struggle for survival.

In late November 1944, General Frederick visited Force headquarters in the coastal town of Menton looking wistful. He was saying goodbye yet again. The First Airborne Task Force had been disbanded and Frederick was leaving the theater to be reassigned. His Task Force had been scrapped by the Allies because its light infantry mandate did not fit with the strategy that was currently winning the war: sweeping the Germans before them with massed artillery and air power. The invasion of Normandy and the collapse of German forces in the Soviet Union had created a conflict where massive armies of historic proportions were bearing down on Germany. There was no place for the First Airborne Task Force in this colossally scaled new war, which few in the Allied command expected to last into 1945. And there was something in Frederick's good-bye that hinted that the FSSF faced the same fate.

=====

The inevitable came for the Force in early December 1944. The Force was bivouacked at Villeneuve-Loubet, and on December 5 the order went out for a parade. The Force men fell in as they had so many other times in the past, to witness the awarding of medals, to receive news. Rumors had been spreading that something was up, but the men knew it could be anything. The Force might be leaving the theater. Colonel Walker could be leaving the Force. Some men seemed to know as well as General Frederick what the future held; others would claim to be utterly surprised. But the news became clear as the men stood at attention on open ground outside Villeneuve-Loubet called Loup River flats, and looked on at Walker standing at the fore beneath the outfit's three flags: Old Glory, the Union Jack, and the Force colors.

Chaplains led the Force men in prayer for those who had been lost during the campaign in France. And then Walker, who had guarded his charges as obsessively as any officer in the U.S. Army, announced the Force's death. The First Special Service Force was being disbanded. As proof the Force's flag, a black dagger framed in a white shield, was rolled up on its pole and placed in a sleeve while the Force men saluted.

There was silence on the parade ground, and disbelief when the next order came: "Americans stand fast. Canadians step forward in a column of threes." The Canadians were being asked to step from the ranks. There was hesitation and bewilderment. The soldiers had long ago stopped identifying themselves by nationality—that had ended when they first shed blood for each other, so long ago that no one could quite recall when nationhood, or anything, took precedence over the outfit. The bond had begun in Fort Harrison, but it was sealed in every bloodletting along the way. "It was never Canucks and Yanks," wrote Burhans; "the

pervading thought that tied the men together under their leadership was the esprit of the Force itself."

The scouts Tommy Fenton and Howard Van Ausdale stood in
the same platoon rank, and Van Ausdale saw Fenton step forward. Jimmy Flack looked on as Herby Forester left the rank.
Herb Morris saw Tommy Prince step away. Rusty Kroll watched
Joe Dauphinais march forward. Bill Story stepped forward. Tom
O'Brien stepped forward. Stan Waters stepped forward. And on
and on down the line.

Then the order came: "Canadians! Form up." When the
Canadian soldiers obeyed, they turned and found themselves
staring across a narrow and yet unbridgeable chasm at soldiers
who moments before had been comrades. The Force had just
been dismembered. The Americans honored their friends by
refusing to fall in and fill the spaces where the Canadians had
been. This gesture was not lost on Herb Peppard, who was overwhelmed by a surge of emotion. "It seemed fitting that the
Americans left gaps in their line, out of respect for their departing comrades," Peppard wrote. "I had a great lump in my throat
and I fought back tears."

The 442nd Regimental band was on hand, requisitioned by
Force HQ for the ceremony, and they struck up a march while
the Canadians, with the Union Jack flapping above their formation, paraded by the Americans, who still had not closed ranks.
What a strange sight, some of the Americans thought; it's as if
they are a different army. Suddenly, these 40 officers and 585
enlisted men had been transformed into a separate battalion.
A single order to "step forward" had in a matter of seconds
accomplished what the Panzergrenadiers of central Italy and
the Hermann Göring Division of the Anzio beachhead and the
defenders of the Îles d'Hyères had been unable to bring about
during a year of almost constant combat: the liquidation of the
First Special Service Force.

That night in camp, the men drank, wandered from tent to tent, and said their good-byes. The next day the Canadians would board trucks and be redeployed. Most would be shipped back to Britain.

In the morning the Americans gathered as the Canadians scrambled into the backs of transports and rumbled away while their erstwhile comrades looked on. Some, such as Mark Radcliffe, had witnessed a few of these same men stepping off the train at the Fort Harrison siding two years before, and now they were watching them leave. Men wept, and as the trucks pulled out, a few of the American boys ran along behind, not quite able to let go.

Joseph Springer's oral history of the Force preserves Joe Dauphinais's last image: as his truck pulls from the Loup River bivouac, he sees the soldier Jimmy Flack, arguably one of the toughest man-killers the Force ever produced, running after the Canadians at full speed. He refuses to slow down or give up, running on after the others have stopped, and his face is wet with tears as he weeps like a child.

CHAPTER 21

HOMECOMING

After being discharged from the FSSF in October 1944, Joe Glass was shipped to Great Britain. Separated from the Force and from his friends, unable to fight or go home, Joe was in limbo. In England, he was assigned to a rest camp for convalescing soldiers at Fleet, just down the road from Aldershot, the location of a major Canadian military camp. The rest camp was as quiet as a sanatorium, and as boring. There were some brighter moments. Joe's brother Charles, serving with the Victoria Rifles of Canada, managed to swing leave and came to Fleet to see him. They spent a day together, mainly drinking, before Charles had to return to London to make his way back to his unit. Then in January 1945 the nearby Aldershot base filled with old Canadian friends from the Force, including Herb Goodwin and Tommy Fenton. When the Canadians had climbed on the trucks at Villeneuve-Loubet, Aldershot was the final destination for most. Joe had a few raucous reunions with them, but for the most part they were as miserable as he was. Herb Goodwin called the boredom and inactivity of Aldershot the worst episode of the war. "I was in purgatory," he said.

The rest camp was working to redeploy some of the soldiers as drivers and motor pool sergeants. Joe was asked if he was willing to do this and he said: "Sure, send me to Germany." On the Continent, Germany was reeling from the failure of their attack in the Ardennes, a desperate offensive to seize the Allies' supply base and drive a wedge between the Americans on one side and the British and Canadians on the other that would become known as the Battle of the Bulge. Despite catching the Americans off their guard and making dramatic initial gains, the exhausted Germans quickly ran out of momentum and fuel for their panzers. When the chastened Americans regrouped, they were able to retake lost ground quickly, leaving the Germans weaker than ever. They flattened out the "Bulge" by mid-January. By February the Canadian First Army reached the Rur River on the German frontier. Nazi Germany itself was about to be invaded. But the authorities scoffed at Glass's desire to go to the front even as a driver; he was too disabled. So Joe said: "If you're not going to send me to Germany, you better send me home."

The rest camp commanders were reluctant even to do that until an event one night in the sergeants' mess, where Joe and friends were staging a big party. One of the camp's officers hated airborne men, and on that night he got drunk, stumbled into the mess, and started abusing Joe and a few other convalescing paratroopers. Joe and the others understood the officer. Paratroopers' swaggering confidence and accomplishments on the battlefield often generated resentment among regular infantrymen. What the officer probably disliked most in elite soldiers such as Joe was their disdain for meaningless decorum. Another soldier might have stomached the tirade, but Sergeant Joe Glass threw the man out the door. Technically an assault on a superior, Joe might have been court-martialed had the officer not been drunk and abusive. Unable to press charges against Joe without having charges brought against himself, the officer sent Joe and another recuperating Force man named Davie Woon packing to Glasgow, where they climbed aboard a cruise liner being used as a troopship.

The ship was packed to the gunwales with convalescent soldiers bound for home. Most, like Joe, were healthy enough to gamble, and Joe, an accomplished poker player, joined a game and parlayed his last army pay into a $6,000 jackpot. In 1945 this was a small fortune. Joe decided to turn it into an even larger fortune, and elbowed his way onto the edge of a crowded dice table, where "the biggest crap game" he had ever seen was taking place. By the time the troopship docked at Halifax, Joe had lost every penny. A fellow soldier lent him money to buy a bottle of Coke.

From Halifax, Joe boarded a train destined for Sarnia. The train, like the ship, was chock full of homebound soldiers. A lot of booze flowed, and by the time Joe arrived at the Sarnia station, he was good and drunk. When he stepped onto the platform, Dorothy, his young son, Charles, now a toddler, his mother and father, and a marching band organized by Joe's Uncle Willy, mayor of Sarnia, were there to greet him. Dorothy, almost two years older and, as a young mother, infinitely wiser, was not the same woman he had known in Helena. Joe had changed even more. He had survived a year of murderous combat and had witnessed all of the horrors and grand gestures mankind is capable of—the deaths of friends and enemies, displays of heroism, sacrifice, fear, and cowardice by comrade and foe alike. He had seen men's bodies mutilated and dismembered, he had seen them implode spiritually and psychologically to become little more than shells. He had killed, and escaped those utter strangers who had tried to kill him. He had survived these attacks, but his body had been ruptured in ways he could never have imagined—

muscle torn from bone, ribs smashed, a lung transformed by shrapnel into a blood-filled sack. Joe had healed well enough to make this return, but he too stood on that train platform a very different man from the husband to whom Dorothy Glass had bid good-bye in 1943.

The eradication of the FSSF was immediately clear to Dorothy too. Gone was Joe's smart Force uniform with the billed cap that made him look like an officer. In its place Joe wore standard Canadian army issue, which Dorothy didn't like nearly as much.

Joe embraced everyone, and was introduced to the son he had never met. Meeting a son who was both familiar and unknown generated deep emotions that hundreds of thousands of returning soldiers across North America would soon be confronting: to have traveled so far away in every sense and then, against great odds, to return to loved ones whom time and circumstance have reduced to strangers.

The Glass family immediately retreated to Joe's aunt's house, where Dorothy and his parents now lived. Dorothy had smelled alcohol on Joe the moment she kissed him, and she was furious. In anticipating their romantic reunion, an alcohol-sodden husband had never figured into the fantasy. Not long after they got to the house, Joe went off to his room and passed out. He slept for hours and hours. Dorothy knew he was sleeping off the revelry. Joe's mother was distraught. "The poor boy's weak from his war wounds," she said.

Joe was indeed weak from his wounds. Right away he visited a military doctor, who gave him a thorough examination. Based on his reduced pulmonary capacity Joe was declared 50 percent disabled, and was immediately sent to another military rest camp for treatment. But he did not linger there long. He left the camp after a brief sojourn, and after the war officially ended on September 2, 1945, he was "de-mobbed" from the Canadian army. There was no time for reflection on the horrors of the past and on friends lost; Joe had a family to provide for, and opportunities came his way. His childhood Sunday school teacher was a supervisor at the Dow Chemical plant in the city. He gave Joe a great job in the electrical room, and said he wanted to send him to McGill University to study electrical engineering so that he could return to the plant as an engineer. Joe's family was growing as well. In late 1945 his son Bob was born, and Joe moved Dorothy and the kids into a big two-story house on Collingwood Street, with an ample yard, a master bedroom, and a full basement. Joe rented the house and filled it with eight hundred dollars' worth of furniture he got on credit, and then the owner offered to sell him the house for a relative song: $6,500. With a family, a job, and a future, Joe was perfectly set up—and unhappy.

A man couldn't call a place home where he was not able to breathe, and because of his lung condition Joe continually wheezed and coughed from the pollution that Sarnia's industries created. His breathing was at its worst at the plant where he worked, and where Mr. Phelps wanted him to work out his years. In August 1946, Joe took his holidays and promptly quit his job. He and Dorothy and the kids climbed aboard a train, rode it south and west, and stepped off it at the only other place they could imagine living: Helena.

Joe had once thought that Sarnia was home. But his adult life had begun when he had stepped onto the dust of Fort Harrison, and from that time Helena became his hometown, and the other Force men were his adopted family. Going there meant filling a void, which is what hundreds of thousands of Canadian and American veterans returning from Europe and the Pacific had within them.

Soon after arriving at the station, Joe, Dorothy, and the boys appeared on Ma and Pa's porch in East Helena. The elder Strainers had not seen their son-in-law or their grandson Charles since

1943, and they had never met the newest addition, Bob. As Joe and Dorothy settled in and caught up with news, Ma said to Dorothy: "Did you know that Steffie's back?"

Given that Dorothy had been in faraway Sarnia, the phones were so bad, and Steffie was on the move, Dorothy hadn't heard much from her old friend since Steffie had heard about Lorin.

———

In August 1944, Sergeant Lorin Waling, his body peppered with shrapnel, his shoulder pumping blood, and one arm mangled, had waited on a battlefield of Île du Levant for the medics to return for him. While he waited, Lorin heard footsteps behind him. The sound of footfalls interrupted a wonderful slumber. Moments before, he had been numbed, and alarmed by the obscenity of his wounds: the way his arm hung twisted and life-less, the blood flowing from his shoulder, the numerous leaking shrapnel holes. But now he felt comfortable and warm. In fact the sensation was more than physical comfort; it was an emo-tion—happiness. Lorin felt as if he could fall into a deep sleep. Only the loud approaching footsteps snapped him awake, shak-ing him from his slumber. The steps were heavy and crisp, and Lorin knew they had to be the footfalls of a German stealing up from behind and closing in for the kill.

The steps came closer and closer, and finally stopped directly behind him. Lorin tried to look but could not turn himself, and then, suddenly understanding what was happening to him, he visualized Steffie and spoke out loud to her.

"It's not over yet."

Summoning all the strength he had left, Waling pulled him-self to his feet, staggered up to the road, and began making his way to his line. He didn't get far. But he no sooner collapsed than a soldier he would never identify found him and helped him to the beach, where medics loaded him onto a landing craft. The craft delivered Waling to a hospital ship named the *Prince Henry,* and once aboard Lorin wasn't too delirious to forget where he had seen this ship before. Temporarily patched and infused with blood, Lorin was placed on the floor of a passageway to wait while doctors treated the more serious cases. While there, a sailor bent over him and asked if there was anything he could do.

"Yeah," said Lorin. "Can you get Billy Lindsey?"

They summoned Billy, the Great Lakes seaman who had sailed with Joe Glass before the war, had stumbled into Joe at Anzio. Billy was shocked to see Lorin in that state, but he sat with him all night, and Lorin did his part by remaining alive.

Lorin was taken to Britain, where he went from hospital to hospital. Along the way he caught up with one or two fellow Force men, who passed on news. One item was particularly bad. Lorin was told the fate of his friend Don Edgelow, who had rushed back during the firefight on Île du Levant to see if Waling was all right. Don was cut down storming a German position shortly after leaving Lorin. When Edgelow went down, he refused to stop, clawing forward on the ground with his hands until he died.

At one point Lorin found himself in the same hospital as Spud Wright, his childhood friend from Grande Prairie who had been in 1-1 with Herb Peppard. Spud had been shot on Port-Cros the day after Lorin had been hit. But Spud was so badly mangled he couldn't talk. Finally, one day an American colonel came to the hospital and presented Spud with a Distinguished Service Medal (DSM), one of the highest citations that can be given to a foreign soldier. Spud gasped, strained, and with much effort was able to mumble his first complete sentence to the colonel: "I just want to be back with the boys."

When he returned to Canada, Lorin went to Edmonton to try to find his family and get word to Steffie. He didn't know where anyone was. He knew his mother and siblings had moved to the Alberta capital from Grande Prairie, but he had no idea where in the city they were living. Waling had been in so many different hospitals that mail from home never reached him, and he was no longer sure if Steffie was still in Spokane. Lorin's older sister, Maxine, was worried by his silences and serious wounds. She had known he would be coming home sometime but had no idea when, and so she had gone daily to the train station to meet troop transports in the hope that Lorin would be on one of them. One day, finally, he was. Maxine could only look at her brother in awe. He had left home a smooth-skinned boy; now he was a scarred man.

As soon as they returned to Maxine's place, Lorin phoned Steffie's sister, Ann, in Helena to find out Steffie's whereabouts, and was surprised to learn that Steffie was there with her. She had come home from Spokane thinking that Lorin would return to Helena. Lorin might have gone to her immediately had he not still been in the army. He needed to report for duty, and as a convalescing soldier he also needed to see army doctors. In addition to everything else, Lorin was scheduled to have his appendix removed. So Steffie came north to be with him.

After his discharge, Lorin, like Joe, quickly got on with life. He had gone to trade school during his last stretch in the army, studying to become an electrician, and after the war he opened a repair shop, Electric Motor Repair and Rewinding. But like Joe, Lorin found he wasn't satisfied with his job or his life in Edmonton. He and Steffie talked about it, and they decided to go home. The Walings returned to East Helena in August 1946. This small collection of houses in the shadow of a smelter's dome, which stood on the Montana plain almost like an afterthought, was really where Lorin's life had begun—his life as a man, anyway. East Helena was where he had first met Steffie, and it was also where he had met Joe Glass. In the confusion, excitement, and mass movements of people that marked the war's end, Lorin had had no better idea of Joe's whereabouts than Joe had had of Lorin's. Waling had assumed that his best friend was alive, but he hadn't heard any more. So he was astonished and delighted when Joe appeared at their door in East Helena barely a week after he and Steffie had returned.

Lorin recognized his friend despite the changes. Heavier now, after almost a year of Dorothy's cooking, Joe no longer had the physique of a ration-fed front-line soldier or of an invalid. But he acted exactly the same. The two friends threw their arms around each other, laughed, and caught up with each other's lives. When the conversation eventually swung in the direction of other Force men, there was a lot to talk about. Some were making their way back to Helena; many more wouldn't be returning at all; and others they just didn't know about.

———

Sergeant Art Arsennek, "Poison" to his friends in 1st Regiment, whom Joe had met during a visit to the hospital in Naples, couldn't go home in the weeks after he was wounded in the breakout from the Anzio beachhead; his condition was too serious. Art's wife, Dora, whom Dorothy Glass had worked with at Eddy's Bakery in East Helena, was at home in St. Catharines when word of Art's wounding reached her by way of a telegram. Simply knowing he was alive had been comforting. Despite the tally of the wounds to his fingers, stomach, and buttocks, there was nothing in the description to suggest his condition was grave. But when Dora received a letter from Art that had been written for him by Doc Kessinger, a friend and Force medic from Nebraska, Dora became worried. Art was not able to write for himself. Again addressed to "Darling Buck" and dated June 15, 1944, the missive began:

Just a few lines to let you know how well and still kicking I am. I'm having Doc write this letter for me as I am not able to write with my one arm in a cast.

Don't take the government notice too hard as I am not that bad off.

How are things going with you folks at home. This is a nice hospital and the people here do all they can for a person. I expect to be coming home but am not sure. I sure hope so.

Oli Pederson is in here and comes down to see me. I see several of the fellars.

I think it's awful good of Doc to write for me, don't you?

Hope you ever received those souvenirs I sent . . .

The souvenirs were the five cameos that Art had purchased in an Italian market, and mailed to her with instructions that they be made into a bracelet to mark their second wedding anniversary. Dora had dutifully taken the cameos to a jeweler. He inspected them, and she was upset when he told her that the cameos were poor quality, that if he tried to work on them they would surely crack and disintegrate. As for the letter, it had been cheerful, but she read the implications: her husband was seriously ill.

Her worries were confirmed when she received another package from Art, who had instructed a nurse from the Naples hospital who was planning leave in Rome to mail Dora a gift. The woman included a letter she had written independently of Art, and in it she had been mercifully honest with Dora. The nurse had probably witnessed too much death in the Naples hospital to do otherwise. Art was getting progressively worse, she informed Dora. She didn't think he was going to make it.

The nurse wasn't alone. Joe hadn't thought Art was going to make it when he saw him that summer. Art had looked alarmingly gaunt and weak. Lieutenant Ed Kelly, Art's best friend at the beachhead, who had been with Art when he was wounded, noted that Art himself seemed to know he was dying.

The letters, of course, made Dora Arsennek frantic. She sensed her husband slipping away and was carefully informed of his slow decline, but she could neither be with him nor help him, and for all communication she was at the mercy of others. There was no one she could contact. Maddeningly, infuriatingly, she could only wait for letters and cables. But she waited nevertheless.

The summer ended, and sometime after September 13, 1944, Dora Arsennek received a telegram. Sergeant Art Arsennek had died of his wounds. The cable expressed the government's sympathy, and in future correspondence Dora Arsennek was invited to write an epitaph for her husband's grave in the Commonwealth military cemetery at Caserta. Dora ultimately chose a phrase she had come across on a sympathy card:

I cannot say
And I will not say
That he is dead
He is just away

The words seemed to express the strange quality of Art's departure from her life. He had been grievously wounded, but she never saw him mutilated. He died, but she never saw a body. Nor did she attend a funeral. Like every other wife, mother, sister, and daughter of a dead soldier, Dora had only a handful of cables and letters as tangible proof. She had no doubt Art was dead, but the reality was: Art had left to go to war and simply stayed away.

Dora settled her young, dead husband's affairs, and began a new chapter of her life as a twenty-two-year-old widow.

Those Force men who did not find a grave in Italy or southern France streamed home. Not long after Art Arsennek had been mortally wounded during the beachhead breakout, fellow 1st Regiment Force man Herb Peppard had been wounded on a hill above the town of Velletri. He had been shot high in the inner thigh. In his pocket he carried a letter from his girlfriend, Greta, that he had read many times. Because his wound was so high and his flesh so numb, he feared he had been ruined as a man and would never be able to marry or have children. He summoned the courage to look down when a medic sliced off his pant leg, and felt awash with relief when he could see that he was still intact. Peppard's wound sent him to the Naples hospital, but it wasn't serious enough to send him home. Peppard convalesced, recovered, went AWOL for a spell, and returned to the Force in France, where he received a reprimand and a Silver Star. The reprimand was for going AWOL; the Silver Star was for bravery he had exhibited during a patrol at Anzio.

Peppard returned to the outfit just in time for the parade on the Loup River flats near Villeneuve-Loubet that marked the FSSF's breakup. Afterward he went with the rest of the Canadians, first to England and then, when it was time to go home, across the Atlantic on a troopship, the *Isle de France*, which streamed into Halifax harbor amid the welcoming spray of fire boats and the cries of people crowded on the pier. Peppard and the others were so excited by the scene that they swarmed along the rail nearest the shore and almost capsized the ship.

When Peppard returned home to Truro, Nova Scotia, and entered the front gate for the first time, he was quaking, and he marveled that amid the convulsions of war, his home had remained unchanged. "The ten maples that ringed the house I'd grown up in were in full foliage, green and fresh," he wrote. "The garden that Dad planted was laid out in perfectly straight rows, as only Dad could do it. The house, which was Mum's domain, was spotless. The shiny wood stove, with its attached reservoir, reminded me of many a succulent family meal . . . I knew every nook and cranny in this house, as though it were part of myself." Peppard closed his eyes and said: "Thank God, I'm home."

———
———

After the interminable wait at Aldershot, with the war's end Captain Herb Goodwin also boarded a troopship, landed at Halifax, and returned to his family in Elmira. His parents were relieved, and not only because Herb had survived the war. Mr. and Mrs. Goodwin had ten children, and four of them were in uniform. When the war ended in September 1945, all were alive and well, and now Herb was home. The only sadness in Herb's Elmira homecoming was the specter of the Schmidt house, which loomed in the neighborhood like a crypt. Floyd Schmidt, Goodwin's childhood friend and best man, had died over a year before, but his family still grieved. During his stay Goodwin dutifully paid them a visit to offer his sympathies. Mrs. Schmidt was tearful, and she asked Goodwin repeatedly about the exact circumstances of the death of her only child. Goodwin could only answer that he didn't know. Floyd was in a different regiment, he explained. When informed that Floyd had died on August 27, 1944, Goodwin had been told only (and incorrectly) that a mortar had struck him down. Goodwin didn't know any more.

"I can't understand it," Mrs. Schmidt said. "Your mother had all those boys, and she didn't lose one of you. And all I had was Floyd."

Herb spent more awkward moments with Mrs. Schmidt, and left her as inconsolable as he had found her. Due to the intense pain of the visit, he never went back. Eventually, Goodwin's mother also stopped visiting, unable to bear Mrs. Schmidt's laments.

After his discharge and visit to Elmira, Herb returned to Helena, but not immediately. Goodwin got off the train at Bozeman, about 160 kilometers short of his destination, where his wife, Doris, had suggested they meet and spend a night alone together before returning to her family. In Bozeman they mended a two-year absence and resumed a six-week-old marriage. Then they returned to Helena, ready to make it their home.

———

After the breakup, Mark Radcliffe was sent east to fight in the final battles against Germany and to guard the peace after the war's conclusion. At one point he found himself in a tank battalion attached to General George Patton's Third Army. During parade, a gunner in one of Radcliffe's tanks lifted the hatch of the vehicle and raised an unhelmeted head covered by a scruffy wool hat. Radcliffe, close to both the tank and the notoriously irascible general, saw Patton's arm go up and point at the man as he motored by. Sure enough, after the parade Radcliffe was hauled in to see the general.

"One of your men was out of uniform," Patton ranted. "He was without his helmet. That man is to be severely reprimanded."

Radcliffe gave the only answer he could. "Yes, sir. I'll take care of it, sir."

Naturally, Patton never realized the irony of the exchange. He was chewing out the first Allied combat soldier to enter Rome, and a man who had escaped from a German headquarters behind the lines at the Anzio beachhead, all for the high crime of having a tanker in his unit who failed to wear a helmet during parade.

Radcliffe went to Norway after the war and served with the 474th Infantry. When it was time to come home, he got the opportunity to fly. There was no room for his gear, so he stowed his two duffle bags on a ship. When the bags finally reached him stateside, they had been pilfered. He lost a prized possession: his Force jump boots. Bootless, Radcliffe, like Joe Glass and Lorin Waling, ended up in Helena, Montana, where he was reunited with Edith and his young daughter, Caroline, by all accounts the first child of the FSSF.

———

Ostensibly, the war had been good to General Robert T. Frederick. He had commanded two impressive units—the FSSF and the First Airborne Task Force. In both assignments Frederick had displayed unique leadership that was not lost on his superiors. Given command of the Forty-fifth Division, Frederick fought at the Battle of the Bulge. Under his command the Forty-fifth advanced into the ruins of Germany; it crossed the Rhine, and won the city of Nuremberg, arguably the symbolic heart of the Nazi party. Finally, it liberated the death camp of Dachau, surely another symbol of all the Allies were fighting against. "The Forty-fifth left one of the greatest division records of the war," wrote Frederick's daughter and biographer, "and Gen. Frederick was acclaimed as knowing how to beat the enemy's best."

In the four years between Pearl Harbor and Japan's surrender, Frederick had risen from lieutenant colonel to major general, an ascendancy equaled by few soldiers, the most notable exception being General Dwight Eisenhower, who also began the war as a temporary colonel. The possessor of eight Purple Hearts, Frederick remained the war's premier fighting general. By 1945 he had become a bona fide army star.

Along the way Frederick had traded fortunes with his rough counterpart, Colonel William O. Darby, who—in contrast to Frederick—had experienced a charmed early career but endured only tragedy and missed opportunity later on. The two leaders' fates overlapped briefly, at Anzio. There, Frederick was able to make his brigade-sized force do the work of a division. Darby's Rangers, on the other hand, met with extinction. Immediately after the debacle at Cisterna, Darby was given command of the 179th Infantry Regiment of the 45th Division at Anzio, which he led for two months. In April 1944 he was transferred to the War Department in Washington and given a desk in the Operations Division, where Frederick's ascendancy had begun two years before. He had been sent home out of Mark Clark's desire to spare a few of the war's combat heroes "for inspirational purposes." Darby excelled in the military bureaucracy but soon grew restless, and in March 1945 he arranged a return to Europe. As assistant divisional commander of the Tenth Mountain Division, Darby was leading a task force in northern Italy on April 30 when a single fragment, smaller than a fingernail, of an 88 mm shell pierced his heart and killed him. William O. Darby died the same day Hitler committed suicide. He was thirty-four years old.

While Frederick lacked Darby's personal flair as a battle captain, he may have surpassed him in vision. But ultimately, Frederick had escaped Darby's fate simply by being luckier. All the same, Frederick's stature at the war's end could not compensate for the fact that his greatest contribution to the U.S. Army, the First Special Service Force, had been disbanded and largely forgotten.

Former Force men such as Joe Glass and Lorin Waling wasted no time worrying about the Force's legacy. With families to feed, Joe and Lorin got down to the immediate concerns of life. They each landed jobs driving cab for rival taxi companies. The war was over. Real life, whether they wanted to face it or not, had begun.

EPILOGUE

Like the Force men, who limped home, shed their uniforms, and continued their lives, the unique special-warfare concept that General Marshall and Lord Mountbatten had jointly fathered seemed to retire with the advent of peace. The FSSF was not the only special unit to disappear from the postwar landscape. The OSS was disbanded in September 1945. Although it did not grow from that fateful London meeting in April 1942 that gave birth to both the FSSF and the Rangers, an arm of the OSS mandated to infiltrate and operate behind the lines in occupied France trained in Scotland with Mountbatten's commandos and its agents named themselves the Jedburghs after the castle in Scotland where they received their special schooling. Ultimately, the deactivation of the Rangers in 1951 seemed to suggest that the modern American military had no room for the branch of warfare Frederick and Darby had pioneered.

This was only partly true. In the early 1950s, the strategy of the postwar U.S. Army—mass attack by great armies bolstered by heavy armor and overwhelming airpower—paid little heed to commando warfare. But in select corners of the army establishment a few innovators had not forgotten the potential of small, versatile, exquisitely trained units like the FSSF, Rangers, and Jedburghs, and were determined to keep the experiment alive.

In June 1952, the 10th Special Forces Group was inaugurated, and although a strategic backwater in the U.S. military, the army leadership rooted it in the establishment by creating the Psychological Warfare Center and School at Fort Bragg, which was later renamed the Special Warfare Center. Eight years after Mark Radcliffe, Bill Story, and Herb Morris witnessed the death of the FSSF on the Loup River Flats, the army had resurrected special operations. According to Tom Clancy and General Carl Stiner in their book *Shadow Warriors*, the watershed year for the concept as it is known today was 1961 when President Kennedy visited Fort Bragg and inspected a group of Special Forces wearing their trademark rebellious green beret. He immediately recognized their potential for the era then unfolding. Immediately after WWII, the army establishment quite rightly foresaw a conflict with the Soviet Union as a clash of titanic armies in Europe. By the 1960s, Kennedy presciently foresaw the Cold War being fought on dozens of small, innocuous fronts around the globe (Asia, Africa, and even South America) where the world's two superpowers would battle for influence, primarily through the locals whom Special Forces commandos would nurture, train, and often lead.

This new mandate represented the merger of the two branches of special warfare that emerged from WWII: the light-infantry commando school (represented by the FSSF and the Rangers), and the OSS, which emphasized psychological warfare and the organization of indigenous resistance fighters. For the most part, this amalgamation characterizes the Special Forces of today. After 1952, special warfare, of course, was championed by visionary offi-cers like Robert McClure, a pioneer of psychological warfare; Aaron Bank, a former Jedburgh who commanded the 10th Special Forces Group in the 1950s; and Bill Yarborough, the politically savvy commander who led the Special Forces through their coming-of-age in the early 1960s. Conspicuously absent from this roster were the names Robert T. Frederick and Edwin Walker.

Frederick and Walker may have survived the war, but they ultimately became casualties of the grand experiment they obses-sively pursued. General Frederick ended the war a bona fide star destined for great things, but his wartime successes proved to be almost an impediment in peacetime.

Frederick became the subject of envy when he returned to the U.S. to command the Coast Artillery School at Fort Monroe, Virginia. Long accustomed to the pure pragmatism of the battle-field, Frederick, wrote his daughter, was "deeply affected" by army politics. Perhaps believing he might excel in an overseas assign-ment, Frederick accepted an offer in 1948 to lead the European Command in Austria. As the ranking American officer in Vienna at the inception of the Cold War, Frederick stood up to Soviet gen-erals and recognized the coming confrontation with the East. But only five months into this posting Frederick asked to be reassigned.

In 1951 he received an equally crucial job: command of the U.S. Military Aid Group to Greece. In this role Frederick dis-played characteristic insight and mettle, which is why many in Greece and the Pentagon were shocked when he tendered his resignation from the mission and the army only a year later. He was forty-five years old. At first the army refused to let him go, arguing that his "value to country" was too great. But he had come to the end of his endurance. According to his daughter, Frederick's "mental, physical, and spiritual expenditures in war were catching up with him."

Clearly, Frederick had given too much on the battlefield. "[W]ar nerves kept him pacing at night," wrote Anne Frederick-Hicks, "[and there were] tears at mention of his men killed in action." He was still a young man, but he was as hollow as a spent cartridge. He drifted into retirement, purchasing land in California and becoming, in his daughter's description, "a gentleman farmer."

Frederick's successor, Edwin Walker, also revealed the strains of command, but in a different way. In 1959, the tall Texan, by then a major general, was dispatched to Germany to assume command of the Twenty-fourth Infantry Division. Walker's war record as a soldier, commander, and strategist made him perfectly qualified for this responsibility. But when his superiors learned that Walker was lecturing his troops on extreme right-wing politics supported by texts from the John Birch Society, he was relieved of duty by the Kennedy administration. Walker temporarily lost his command, pending an investigation, but resigned from the army anyway. In 1961 he revealed his zeal for reactionary politics by journeying to the University of Oxford in Mississippi to object to the admission of African American student James Meredith. For his agitations in Mississippi, Walker was arrested by order of Attorney General Robert Kennedy under charges of seditious conspiracy and rebellion. Walker declared himself a "political prisoner" of the Kennedy presidency.

Walker passionately opposed the president, but, ironically, he and Kennedy shared a common enemy, a fact that would titillate conspiracy theorists for a generation. In April 1963, Walker was in his study in his Dallas home when a bullet passed just inches from his head and slammed into the wall. A gunman had tried to kill him, and after Kennedy's murder seven months later forensic tests proved that his would-be assassin was the president's murderer, Lee Harvey Oswald.

Oswald had targeted Walker after the former general became a spokesman for the ultraright. In 1962, Walker went to Stanford

University to give a speech, and Frederick, who lived in retirement in nearby Palo Alto, attended. Frederick had heard Walker
speak two years earlier, and was as shocked the second time as
he had been the first. Walker railed against the United Nations,
spouted extremism, and, as Frederick later said, "just rambled on
and on and on."

The "irrational" figure Frederick saw and heard on the lecture
tour in 1962 was not the same "outstanding soldier" he had commanded in battle. He had to wonder: Had the war created a
vacuum in Walker that was now filled with rage?

If so, Frederick could commiserate. Although he retired at
forty-five, Frederick never regained his strength. In a car accident
he would suffer a head injury that he attributed to memory loss
later in life. According to some, he struggled with alcoholism. He
was a commander who had not merely given too much of himself
during the war; he had given everything. He had lovingly created
the First Special Service Force, a new paradigm in warfare, and
filled it with the best soldiers of two nations and a single generation. Then, in the course of two years, he had watched the lion's
share of his boys, and the experiment itself, die. He continued to
serve the men he had once commanded by devoting much of his
retirement to corresponding with Force veterans and with the
families of fallen men, and helping when he could.

Frederick would live to see his visions for special warfare vin-
dicated. In 1960 he and a group of Force veterans were invited to
ceremonies at Fort Bragg, North Carolina, during which the FSSF
campaign history and battle standard were officially attached to
the U.S. Special Forces. Ironically for Edwin Walker, President
Kennedy would be the Special Forces' most valuable patron. He
promoted the outfit against the wishes of many in the military
establishment, and it was he who permitted its members to wear
as an official part of their uniform the green beret. In Canada, the
airborne legacy lived on in the Canadian Airborne Regiment,

which would stand as the country's elite airborne unit until it was disbanded by the federal government in 1995 after a series of scandals, the most serious being charges that soldiers from the regiment had been involved in the torture and death of a sixteen-year-old local during a humanitarian mission in Somalia. Today in Canada, the special forces paradigm is best represented by Joint Task Force 2, Canada's premier special operations and counterterrorism unit which, like the U.S. Special Forces, fought in Afghanistan after the attacks of September 11, 2001.

The U.S. Special Forces' success in toppling the Taliban in late 2001 has been called their greatest achievement. Sadly, Robert T. Frederick did not live to see this day. He died in 1970 at the age of sixty three, just as quietly as he had lived during the previous two decades. According to his daughter, Frederick had never fully recovered after being poisoned by the fumes of a gas stove in his quarters on the Anzio beachhead, an accident that caused significant enlargement of his heart. That heart finally gave way, and Frederick was interred at the cemetery of the Presidio in San Francisco, the military base where young Bob Frederick a half-century before had first spotted soldiers on parade and dreamed of glory. Today Frederick's career remains both an ideal and a cautionary tale: a style of leadership that was unique, inspired, brilliant, and tragically costly.

Other key players in the Force's history met equally tragic ends. The British defense scientist, Geoffrey Pyke, who first conceived of Project Plough, went to Washington, and assisted then Colonel Frederick in the early stages of the plan. But Canadian and U.S. military leaders tired of his odd behavior and Pyke was ultimately sent home. He pursued other controversial and exotic ideas to win the war, including a scheme to build glacier-sized battleships from a special type of highly dense ice he called Pykrete. Churchill, Mountbatten, and even President Roosevelt were supposedly fascinated by Pykrete's potential, and Canadian researchers built a small prototype ice ship on an alpine lake in Alberta in 1943. But like Pyke's vision for Mastery of the Snows, this plan was eventually scrapped. After the war Pyke became a recluse, devoting nearly all of his time and energy to a search for an all-encompassing theory that would make sense of international economics. The theory proved elusive and Pyke grew despondent. Still, when Pyke killed himself with sleeping pills on February 21, 1948, even his enemies were shocked. There seemed to be no real reason for his suicide, other than an eccentric intelligence that had driven and haunted him throughout his life.

Britain's premier commando leader, Lord Mountbatten, excelled both during the war and after it. Different from Frederick, he was far enough removed from the human losses under his command to escape permanent scars. Only slightly older than Frederick but equally as gifted, Mountbatten was given the post of Supreme Allied Commander South East Asia Theater in 1943. Like Eisenhower, Mountbatten's greatest talent as supreme commander may have been an ability to work with his temperamental Allied counterparts, such as U.S. General Joe Stilwell. Nevertheless, Mountbatten supervised the liberation of Burma during the war, and after, took on the delicate and explosive task of overseeing the dismantling of British colonial rule in India. Later, he returned to the Royal Navy, became First Sea Lord, then chief of the Defense Staff, and finally in August 1979, perished along with his fourteen-year-old grandson and two others after a bomb planted on his yacht exploded while he vacationed in the Republic of Ireland. The IRA later claimed responsibility for Mountbatten's "execution."

As for the fighting men of the FSSF, forty Force men eventually made their way back to Helena to settle. Many had local wives, but most—like Glass and Waling—seemed to view the birthplace of the FSSF their true homes. There was Eugene "Peltchie" Pelletier who fought in Mark Radcliffe's company.

During training at Fort Harrison Pelletier met Loraine Lager on a blind date and married her. He returned to her after the war, taking a job at the Northern Pacific Railroad and beginning a marriage that would produce nine children. There was John Marshall who also met and married a local girl, and after the war ran a heating and refrigeration business. There was Dave Woon, who sailed home on the same troopship as Joe Glass. Woon married a local woman, moved from Helena to Cut Bank, Montana, and opened a lumberyard. Force man Roy Hudson and his wife Eileen ran a furniture store. James "Stoney" Wines became a deputy sheriff.

Even though he was a professional soldier, the 1-2's Jimmy Flack returned to Helena in 1946 to be with his wife, the former Marguerite MacDonald, another Helena girl who had worked with Dorothy Glass at Eddy's Bakery. Flack had gone AWOL, and compounded his crime by cruising around Helena in taxis and charging the fares to Joe and Lorin, who, ironically, were were working as cab drivers themselves at the time. For reasons still not clear, Jimmy turned himself in at the sheriff's office for violating his leave, and Joe and Lorin, despite the crushing taxi bill Flack had run up, bailed him out. Jimmy and Marguerite eventually moved on to Oregon, but not before attending the first Force reunion, organized by Mark Radcliffe.

In August 1947, nearly every Force man who could walk descended on Helena for what would become an annual get-together. Some veterans, such as Don MacKinnon, who had lost a leg on Monte Majo, limped into town, but they did so proudly. Joe, Lorin, MacKinnon, a former 1-2 warrior named Dennis George, and a few others descended on a bar on Last Chance Gulch and drank a few for old times' sake. Some local cowboys recognized the group as former Force men and called them outside. Don MacKinnon and Dennis George took up the challenge, and fought the men on the street. Dennis George received an awful beating. But even on one leg, young Don MacKinnon gave better than he got, exhibiting the pluck he would display throughout his life. MacKinnon was already on his way to completing a bachelor's degree and launching a career in advertising. He would be one of the early users of state-of-the-art technology for the physically challenged that would allow him to ski. As for Dennis George, the next day, bruised and swollen, he decided to skip town early. Lorin Waling took him to the airport, bought his flat-broke former comrade-in-arms a ticket, and saw him off. When Lorin returned to town, the grand reception was in full swing, and Helena was glad to have the Force men back.

Bill Story stayed with his Helena family, the local Methodist preacher whose wife made those wonderful apple pies. Herb Morris was reunited with friends from 3-3 including Radcliffe, Gene Pelletier, and Roy Hudson. From 1-2, diminutive Herby Forester returned with a gift for his friends: a history he had written of the company, summarizing their war. "Throughout all campaigns, [1st] Company has maintained a brilliant combat record and has taken a heavy toll of the enemy." He listed their casualties as thirty-one killed and ninety-four wounded. "Score of Jerries," he wrote. "Killed—well over fifty. Wounded—beaucoup."

There is no record of the native warrior Tommy Prince going to Helena in 1947, but he had a reunion of another sort. After the war, Prince was summoned to London, invited to Buckingham Palace, and decorated with the Military Medal and Silver Star by King George VI. He returned to the Brokenhead Reserve, one of only three Canadians to possess both the Silver Star and Military Medal. His other citations included the Italy Star, the 1939–1945 Star, the France & Germany Star, the Defense Medal, and the Canadian Volunteer Service Medal with Clasp, making him one of the most decorated native soldiers to emerge from the Second World War. He too picked up where he had left off. He grabbed a saw, headed into the bush, and resumed his life as a logger. But

Prince was never able to adjust to civilian life. He died destitute in a veterans' hospital in 1977.

In 1948, Joe Glass started working for Helena Sand and Gravel in the summer while driving a taxi in the winter. He had two more daughters, and as he later wrote in a memoir to his children, "our little family was complete." A man had to be flexible to make a living in the West, and in 1949 Joe left both jobs to manage the Moose Club, a local social hall. After that, he sold insurance, built and ran a stock car racing track, worked for a dairy, sold cars at the Dodge City dealership, and finally won permission from the sheriff (later bolstered by a bona fide gaming license) to run poker and bingo games. Joe held the poker games just outside the city limits and kept them going twenty-four hours a day. Poker players shut out at 2 a.m. when the games closed in the city would stream to Joe's tables to continue throughout the night. Joe built a fish-and-chip restaurant beside his casino to feed the customers, and he did well.

Lorin and Steffie Waling were living in a veterans' housing unit in Helena when their firstborn, Jerry, arrived. More and more work came as an electrician, and by the time their second son, Dave, was born in 1950, Lorin was building his first home.

Mark Radcliffe returned to school to study engineering while providing for and raising a family of two children. After becoming qualified to practice engineering, Radcliffe set up shop in Helena, joined the army reserves, and eventually learned to fly. Herman "Chet" Ross, the Force man who had lent Radcliffe a car for his honeymoon, married a Montana girl, settled just outside Kalispell, became a veterinarian, and also earned a flying license. He used a small plane to visit ranchers and tend to sickly cattle in far-off areas, but sometimes he would fly to Helena just to meet Radcliffe for lunch at the airport. Herb and Doris Goodwin eventually opened a convenience store across from the junior high school called Herb's Quick Service. Students flooded into their shop throughout the day, and Herb and Doris became fixtures of the childhoods of a generation or more of young Helenans.

If Glass, Waling, Radcliffe, Marshall, Woon, Pelletier, and the other prominent Force men wrestled with ghosts from the war, terrible memories, and inner scars, they fought their battles silently. And some Force men did fight battles. Young Herb Morris was one. Returning to Denville didn't mean that he had come home. On patrol, in slit trenches, and wielding and pondering the beauty of a V-42 dagger, Morris knew that he had strayed so far from his former self he wondered if he could ever return. After the breakup of the Force, he was eventually posted to Norway. Even after the war had ended, he slept with a pistol under his pillow.

Back in the United States, he no longer needed a gun, but he wasn't able to slip back into his old life. As if the war was still on, he kept in close touch with Force men: Mark Radcliffe, of course, Ray Hufft, who was in the regular army, and Jim Kurtzhal, who moved between Oregon and California. Many of the men were as pensive as he was about postwar life. In early 1946, Hufft wrote a letter confessing that he pined for his old friends. "I will never find words to express my feeling when I tell you how much I missed the grand bunch we had in the Force," he wrote.

Yearning for the wilderness, Morris went to Alaska, scratched around for work, and was in a cafeteria when a bigger man sized up Morris, who was still slight, and began to provoke him. They couldn't go outside because of the cold, so they fought in the boot-and-jacket room just inside the door. Morris still lived by the credo: don't give a guy an even break. The bully was twice his size, a head taller, and still the fight was hopelessly unfair. Returning to the mode of fighting Pat O'Neill had taught him, the only type of fighting he knew, Morris was mauling his opponent in a full rage when someone screamed: "You're going to kill him!" Morris stopped. Long ago, when deadly violence became part of his life, the boundary between fist fighting and killing had disappeared. Now he knew what he really yearned for: "I wanted to be a person again." Morris left Alaska and tried his hand at several things, including a job with a private detective agency in Yakima, Washington, and, over time, began to think more and more about the spirituality he had encountered on the battlefield.

He pondered the reasons why he had been spared so many times, and the feeling he'd had then that he was placed there for a purpose. For men who knew Morris, his decision ten years after the war to enter a seminary should have been no surprise. Still, some of his old friends were nonplussed. "Dear Rev. Muscles," Hufft wrote in January 1955. "It is hard for me to picture you in a black robe as I can well remember you full of mud with a Tommy gun in the right hand and being master of the descriptive adjective. Muscles, I am proud of you as I have always been."

In the seminary, Morris reflected on the self-sacrifice he had witnessed: Sergeant Bray, on the day of the Anzio breakout, dying to ensure Morris's escape; Sergeant Farmer using his own body to shield Morris from mortar fire at Artena. Morris recognized these acts as a spiritual phenomenon, and called them "vicarious suffering." It was this deep compulsion to sacrifice for another that lay behind many soldiers' decisions to risk their lives for their comrades and the society they hailed from. Morris was ordained a Methodist minister, and regularly gave the invocation at Force reunions.

For every Force man who got on with his life, there was a loved one of a fallen soldier who grieved, struggled, and tried to cope, often in vain. In the years after the war, FSSF reunions were occasionally visited by parents of dead soldiers looking for information. There had been a bookish kid in Joe's platoon named Ray Holbrook. Slight, studious-looking, and bespectacled, Ray came from a town in Washington State, and besides a slightly pedantic manner, Ray's most memorable attribute was that he worried constantly about his mother. On March 30, after two months on the beachhead, Ray was picked to go out on patrol, and as he was leaving he took Joe Glass aside and said: "I've got an awful feeling today."

"I'll pray for you while you're gone," Joe said.

When the patrol came back, it brought news: Ray had been killed in a minefield. According to Joe Dauphinais, Holbrook had thrown himself onto a "Jumping Jesus"—a German antipersonnel mine designed to leap into the air before discharging shrapnel—to save the rest of the patrol. It was as if Holbrook had stepped through a door into another place. Dauphinais would later say there was nothing left of Holbrook after the blast, or at least no remains that anyone ever found. During one of the first reunions Holbrook's bereaved mother appeared, spent the day with the veterans, and asked the men in Ray's company how her son had died. She wanted to know if he had suffered. "I feel bad, but we never told her what really happened to Ray," Joe Glass said. "How could we?"

Later, FSSF reunions were visited by other young people searching for information about dead soldiers who were not their fathers but who had never been forgotten by their mothers. Of course, over the years, countless sons of Force men wrestled with the outfit's legacy and came to terms with their fathers, both living and dead. Tom MacWilliam, Jr. was born after his father died after leading the assault on Monte la Difensa. Force men such as Stu Hunt, Lieutenant Colonel MacWilliam's young bodyguard, and Major Ed Thomas, MacWilliam's good friend and XO, would become surrogate fathers to Tom Junior. Forty years after the battle, MacWilliam visited Italy and climbed to Difensa's peak to personally stand on the spot where his father's legendary but brief military career began and ended.

Implausibly, for some Force men the war was simply a recess in their lives, giving them neither wounds nor wives. When peace arrived they carried on as though the Second World War had never happened. No one really knows what bloody memories the scouts Howard Van Ausdale and Tommy Fenton wrestled with, but by all accounts both men emerged from the war unscathed, and immediately returned to the bush and mountains they had left behind.

Van Ausdale continued to winter in Arizona and summer in Oregon, prospecting and trapping. He attended the first reunion in 1947, but none thereafter until Joe Glass and Tommy Fenton persuaded him to appear at a big gathering in Helena in 1980. He seemed to enjoy meeting with old friends, but never attended another reunion. Sometime around 1982, Lorin Waling was visiting his daughter in Idaho and on impulse drove across the border, made for the town of Baker City, and arrived on the front steps of the modest house where Van Ausdale lived. The old scout took one look at Waling and said, "Hi, kid." The two men visited for an hour or so. Van Ausdale proudly showed Lorin some skins he had trapped and kept in the freezer. He also showed Lorin a few nuggets he had panhandled from a creek. He talked enthusiastically, and was clearly the same person he had always been: a solitary man who relished friendship. Lorin left that day and never saw Van Ausdale again. The old scout died in Baker City in February of 1983.

Tommy Fenton also returned to the bush, spending years in British Columbia and the Yukon. He kept in touch with Van Ausdale and Joe Glass, returning to Helena for reunions now and then. As with Van Ausdale, the years did not change Fenton. He stayed, as one woman remembered, "a wild man." He loved to drink and smoke and carouse. He regularly wintered in Costa Rica, and simply wandered. He died in 1995.

It didn't take long after coming home for the Force men to realize that peacetime could hold as much irony and tragedy as war. Herby Forester survived every engagement of the FSSF without receiving a blemish. On the day Joe and Herby embarked on their last battle before the Anzio breakout, they feared that one of them would be hit that day. It was Joe. Forester had a charmed war. After its conclusion Forester found work as a traveling salesman, and in early December 1958, one day after the fifteenth anniversary of the battle of Monte la Difensa, he was driving through Snohomish County in Washington State when his car left the road and crashed into a pillar supporting an overpass. Severely injured, Forester was rushed to a hospital in nearby Everett, Washington. Shortly afterward, a county deputy sheriff was glancing at a car accident report when he recognized Forester's name. Don Fisher, the 1-2 veteran whose blindness after the battle of Difensa proved temporary and who had joined the Snohomish sheriff's office after the war, went to the hospital, where Forester's wife, Rose, was standing vigil at his bedside. The vigil lasted six days, ending with Herby Forester's death on December 10 at the age of thirty-seven. For Fisher, who was seeing Forester for the first time since the war, the vigil had been a sad and strange reunion.

Grant Erickson, the soldier who found Mark Radcliffe in no man's land after Radcliffe had escaped from the German HQ at Littoria, married a Helena girl and settled in town. He died in a parachuting accident.

Those Helena Force men who didn't die young in cars or planes began to disappear in the 1980s and 1990s as time caught up with them. The inexhaustible Jimmy Flack faded away in a veterans home in 1984 after a long illness. Joe and Lorin visited regularly, and brought him whiskey that the orderlies gave him in small, regulated doses. Don MacKinnon, the youngest in 1-2, lived a vigorous life with his wife, Heather, until dying in Kingston, Ontario, in 2002, at the age of seventy-seven.

Joe and Dorothy, and Lorin and Steffie, remained healthy and active well into the 1990s, and continued to meet regularly. On

November 1, 1996, they sat together at a big dinner at the Montana Club and had a particularly festive night. Afterward, while standing in the parking lot before heading home, Steffie turned to Lorin and said: "Something is wrong with me." Then she died.

When the 1990s ended, Helena had lost most of its Force men. Even such fixtures of the community as Johnny Marshall, Gene Pelletier, and Davie Woon had disappeared. By the winter of 2003, only seven FSSF veterans remained, including Joe Glass, Lorin Waling, and Herb Goodwin, who had lost Doris some years before. But the reunions continued yearly, and the Helena veterans continued a tradition that had been going on for years: a monthly dinner together in Jorgenson's restaurant on the east end of Helena. To ensure a turnout, Joe Glass would phone every vet and urge him to attend. Sickness and age often kept half of them away, but the monthly dinners were often well attended by widows and sons and daughters of dead Force men who were determined to continue the legacy, and members of the regional Special Forces group, who found the Force's legacy irresistible.

For the veterans scattered across Helena and North America, meetings and reunions were more than get-togethers; and the friendships forged during the war more enduring than any made before or after. This fact became clear to the author of this book while chatting with Mark Radcliffe over a morning coffee at the airport diner in Helena in October 2004.

"You know, we're shutting down the outfit," Radcliffe said.

At first, Radcliffe's statement seemed perplexing in light of the fact the "outfit," as veterans referred to the FSSF, had been shut down sixty years before. Radcliffe was referring to the FSSF Veterans' Association, which had voted to disband after one final valedictory reunion in Helena in 2006. But Radcliffe's grim expression revealed a simple truth: for he and many of the Force men, the FSSF association and the FSSF had been one and the same. More precisely, the Force still existed whenever two or more former Force men congregated, so strong was the bond between them, and the memories of accomplishments and terrors.

This bond had withstood the passage of more than sixty years. In some cases, it extended over thousands of miles, and resisted sickness and the infirmities of old age. One day in January 2004, Joe Glass's phone rang, and when he answered, it took him a while to identify the caller. Joe knew he was a Force man from 1-2 because the weak, aged voice spoke of their first battle on Monte la Difensa. So Joe talked a bit, listened more, and then realized: it was Piette—Larry Piette, his lieutenant from 3rd Platoon, the officer who had arrested him for bringing in the New Year in 1943 while AWOL, and the leader who had given him the order to fix bayonets the moment he set foot on Difensa's cold, still plateau on December 3 that same year. He hadn't recognized Piette's voice because he hadn't spoken to Larry for years. Piette, who had returned to his home in Wisconsin after the war, rarely came to reunions. He had attended one of the last big gatherings in Helena but no others that Joe had attended, and Joe had heard that Larry was very ill.

For a while Joe didn't quite know why Piette had called. But he began to understand as their conversation drew to a close. Dying and virtually bedridden, Larry Piette had trouble walking, dressing, and bathing himself, but damn it he could still remember, and he phoned Joe to revel in the accomplishment that nearly every man wants, but few have had.

"Joe," Piette said finally, "we really took that mountain, didn't we?"

Joe, another old soldier who in his youth had had the rare good fortune to conquer a peak and survive, agreed.

"Yeah, Larry. We sure did."

NOTES

PROLOGUE

2   The 25:1 killing ratio and 235:1 POW ratio found in *Daring to Die: The Story of the Black Devils*, produced by Northern Sky Entertainment for Canada's History Television, 2003. Directors Greg Hancock, Wayne Abbott.

CHAPTER 1

15   "At approximately 4:30 p.m. . . . . Company History, 1st Company–2nd Regiment, 1st Special Service Force," by FSSF veteran H.G. Forester, undated, but probably written in 1946.

CHAPTER 2

17   "A meeting took place . . ." April 11, 1942 minutes of meeting "to consider the Snow Plough scheme," records found in UK National Archives, Kew, UK.

18   "Your visits always have a tonic effect . . ." Roy Jenkins, *Churchill* (London: Pan Books, 2002), p. 686. Jenkins cites Robert Sherwood (ed.), *White House Papers of Harry L. Hopkins*, Vol. II (New York: Harper and Brothers, 1948) as original source.

18   No lover ever studied . . . Roy Jenkins, *Churchill* (London: Pan Books, 2002), p. 784.

19   "Even to the end . . ." ibid.

19   "We've got to go to Europe and fight . . ." Stephen Ambrose, *Eisenhower* (New York: Pocket Books, 2003), p. 57.

20   "Dear Winston" letter from Roosevelt to Churchill . . . Martin Gilbert,

Winston Churchill: Road to Victory, 1941–1945 (London: Houghton Mifflin Co., 1986), p. 83.

21   "The enemy in the West must be pinned down," Marshall quote . . . Robert Sherwood, *Roosevelt and Hopkins: An Intimate History* (New York: Grosset & Dunlap, 1950), p. 519.

21   "He had them under consideration for many weeks . . ." ibid, p. 523.

22   "I'm favourably disposed to it . . ." Martin Gilbert, *Winston Churchill: Road to Victory, 1941–1945* (London: Houghton Mifflin Co., 1986), p. 86.

22   "A river of blood . . ." Sherwood, p. 8.

23   "Churchill went a long way," Hopkins's paraphrase of Marshall's words after the first meeting with Churchill on April 8 between 4 and 6 p.m. at 10 Downing Street. Sherwood, p. 523.

25   "Lord Mountbatten, you need me on your staff . . ." David Lampe, *Pyke: The Unknown Genius* (London: Evans Brothers, 1959), p. 88.

26   Pyke's undiagnosed epilepsy . . . Clifford Pickover, *Strange Brains and Genius: The Secret Lives of Eccentric Scientists and Madmen* (New York: Plenum Trade, 1998), p. 142.

27   "We must obtain mastery of the snows . . ." Memorandum "Mastery of the Snows," by Geoffrey Pyke, British National Archives at Kew, UK.

28   "Never in the history of human conflicts . . ." Churchill quote recounted by Mountbatten in a letter to Harry Hopkins, dated 24 Sept. 1942, British National Archives, Kew, UK.

CHAPTER 3

29   "We are definitely committed to one concept of fighting . . ." Stephen Ambrose, *Eisenhower: Soldier and President* (London: Pocket Books, 2003), pp. 57 and 58.

29   Roosevelt cable . . . Sherwood, p. 542.

30   Marshall memo on "Plough," Frederick Papers, Hoover Institution.

30   "Curiousity . . ." Robert Burhans, *The First Special Service Force* (Nashville: Battery Press, 1996 reprint), p. 8.

31   "Plough was a beautiful paper concept but . . ." ibid, p. 9.

32   "General Eisenhower was very much . . ." "Plough Project Diary," p. 1, report by Robert T. Frederick, undated, Frederick Papers, Hoover Institution.

32   "would be to keep 8,000,000 Russians in the war," Eisenhower memo, July 19, 1942. Eisenhower Library.

33   "If the project was really going . . ." "Plough Project Diary," p. 13, report by Robert T. Frederick, undated, Frederick Papers, Hoover Institution.

33   "Every man will be sacrificed" . . . "The War Made Him, Peacetime Broke Him," by Anne Frederick-Hicks, *Army* magazine, Sept. 1982, p. 50.

35   "Maj. Frederick, we are not much impressed . . ." ibid, pp. 48–55.

36   "He wasn't looking for anything unusual . . ." Anne Frederick-Hicks interview with the author, Aug. 2004.

36   "I've got to go to Canada . . ." Anne Frederick-Hicks interview with the author, Aug. 2004.

38   Frederick orders for Plough Project, Frederick Collection, Hoover Institution.

43   "Single men . . ." Burhans, p. 14.

44   Mark Radcliffe interview with the author, Oct. 5, 2004.

CHAPTER 4

46	"Pleased with the progress that had been made . . ." Robert T. Frederick, "Plough Project Diary," Robert T. Frederick papers, Hoover Institution, pp. 113 and 114.
47	"There are excellent sites . . ." Robert T. Frederick, "Plough Project Diary," Robert T. Frederick papers, Hoover Institution, pp. 113 and 114.
47	"Was four times as large . . ." Ken Wickham, *An Adjutant General Remembers,* (Fort Harrison, Indiana: Adjutant General's Corps Reg. Assoc., 1991), pp. 18–20.
47	"Blunt, go-getter . . ." Robert T. Frederick, "Plough Project Diary," Robert T. Frederick papers, Hoover Institution, pp. 113–114.
48	The naming of the FSSF . . . Burhans, pp. 15–16.
49	Radcliffe account of Fort Harrison . . . Interview with Mark Radcliffe, Helena, Montana, Oct. 5, 2004.
50	"Yard training instructions . . ." Colonel Adna H. Underhill, *The Force* (Tuscon: Arizona Monographs, 1994), p. 7.
51	"Sixty-two years . . ." Interview with Mark Radcliffe, Oct. 5, 2004.
52	"You men will be making your first jump . . ." Underhill, p. 11.
52	"Keep your feet together . . ." Video documentary, *First Special Service Force, July 1942–December 1944,* FSSF Association.
56	"Plaid trousers, better known as trews . . ." William Story, "The Early Days of the Force," article available through the First Special Service Force Association.
57	"I watched with some apprehension . . ." "Address by Major General Frederick to Atlanta Chapter, Reserve Officers Assn., 14 January 1948," p. 7 of transcript, Robert T. Frederick Papers, Hoover Institution.
57–58	Waling's arrival . . . Lorin Waling interview with the author, January 2004.
60	"Forget it . . ." Transcript, "Interview with Ken Wickham, Falls Church, Virginia, 16 December 1963," p. 5, Adleman Collection, Hoover Institution.
61	Marriage between a Force man and Ida's girl . . . Robert Adleman, George Walton, *The Devil's Brigade* (London: Corgi, 1968), p. 68. Veteran Adna Underhill mentions unnamed comrades who corresponded with Ida.
62	"This bunch of ivory-peckered bastards . . ." Fred W. Naegele interview with the author, Oct. 6, 2004.
62	"A Yank's . . ." Adleman and Walton, p. 68.
64	"I really felt . . ." Memoir entitled "From Joe Glass to his children," Oct. 14, 1991. Courtesy of Joe Glass.
65–66	Demolition training . . . Transcript, "Interview with Ken Wickham, Falls Church, Virginia, 16 December 1963," p. 7, Adleman Collection, Hoover Institution.
66	"In several instances . . ." Address by Major General Frederick to Atlanta Chapter, Reserve Officers Assn., 14 January 1948," p. 11 of transcript, Frederick Papers, Hoover Institution.
66–67	Hand-to-hand training . . . "Dermot M. O'Neill: One of the 20th Century's Most Overlooked Combatives Pioneers," by Steven C. Brown, *Journal of Asian Martial Arts,* p. 22, Vol. 12, No. 3, 2003.
67	Blood was spilled . . . ibid, p. 24.
68	Shinberger and snakes . . . Mark Radcliffe interview with the author, Oct. 5, 2004.

72   Bill Story, "The Early Days of the Force," FSSF Living History Group.

73   Correspondence between Robert T. Frederick and Irving Berlin . . . Frederick Papers, Hoover Institution, Frederick letter dated Dec. 12, 1942; Berlin letter, Dec. 31, 1942.

74   "There were very few of these cases . . ." Wickham, p. 32.

74–75   Transcript of "Talk Delivered over Radio Station KPFA, August 31, 1942 (8:45 pm)," pp. 5 & 6, Frederick Collection, Hoover Institution.

CHAPTER 5

77   "Toy land" from the air . . . Untitled typewritten diary for Robert T. Frederick, dated Tues. Sept. 8–Nov. 1, 1942, p. 11, Frederick Papers, Hoover Institution.

78   "Possibly the blackest in history . . ." Ambrose, p. 66.

78   "Although he was interested . . ." Untitled typewritten diary for Frederick, Tues. Sept. 8–Nov. 1, 1942, p. 13, Frederick Papers, Hoover Institution.

78   "Progress and planning . . ." Untitled Frederick diary, p. 11, Frederick Papers, Hoover Institution.

78   Six hundred Lancaster bombers . . . Wickham, p. 33.

78–79   "When the project . . ." Untitled Frederick diary, p. 13, Frederick Papers, Hoover Institution.

79   Brooke quotes on Mountbatten . . . Alan Brooke, *War Diaries 1939–1945 Field Marshal Lord Alan Brooke* (London: Phoenix Press, 2002), p. 236.

80   "To demonstrate how difficult was a landing on a fortified coast . . ." Jenkins, p. 692.

81   Jupiter quotes . . . Brooke, pp. 321 & 322.

82   They even believed an invasion of Europe might not be necessary . . . Ambrose, p. 115. According to Ambrose, General Carl Spaatz of the US Eighth Air Force shared this view.

83   "Suspend effort . . ." Incoming Message, War Department Classified Message Center, No. 2742 (declassified July 7, 1976), dated September 26, 1942. Frederick Papers. Hoover Institution.

83–84   Truscott's thinking on speed of mobilization . . . Lucien K. Truscott, Jr., *Command Missions: A Personal Story* (New York: EP Dutton & Co., 1954), p. 533.

84   "To do all in our power . . ." April 27, 1942 diary of Mackenzie King, National Library and Archives of Canada, pp. 4 & 5.

85   Brian Nolan, *King's War: Mackenzie King and the Politics of War, 1939–1945* (Toronto: Random House, 1988), p. 134.

85   "The US should turn to the Pacific for decisive action . . ." Rick Atkinson, *An Army at Dawn* (London: Abacus, 2003), p. 14.

85   Marshall appealed to Ottawa. Stanley Dziuban, *Military Relations Between the United States and Canada, 1939–1945.* (Washington, DC: Department of the Army, Office of the Chief of Military History; 1959), p. 261.

86   Someone had plans for them . . . Underhill in *The Force* wrote that the Johnson's replacement of the BAR gave "officers . . . an inkling as to the special treatment the Force was getting . . ." Underhill, p. 43.

86   Shinberger "irrational" . . . Transcript of Robert Adleman interview with Robert T. Frederick, Sept. 20–21, 1963, Adleman Collection, Hoover Institution.

94   "Which in total number 30,000 Americans and Canadians . . ."
         Designated Amphibious Training Force 9, the contingent had 34,426
         men, of which 5,300 were Canadian.

95   "There was nobody home . . ." *Daring to Die: The Story of the Black
         Devils*, produced by Northern Sky Entertainment for Canada's History
         Television, 2003. Directors Greg Hancock, Wayne Abbott.

CHAPTER 6

102   "Whenever they reached a peak, they would be counterattacked off of
         it," "much to the fury of Clark . . ." Matthew Parker, *Monte Cassino:
         The Hardest-Fought Battle of World War II* (New York: Doubleday, 2004),
         pp. 58–59.

103   "I had my doubts about Monte la Difensa . . ." Emil Eschenburg inter-
         view with the author, September 17, 2004.

104   "Rothlin was quiet but 'very dedicated' . . ." Ed Thomas interview with
         author, December 14, 2004.

106   "We'll be in Rome in two or three weeks . . ." Tom O'Brien interview
         with the author, January 2004.

106   Herby Forester threatened to tear off Sergeant's stripes . . . "Memories
         of the Battle of Monte la Difensa, December 2–8, 1943," by Donald
         MacKinnon, undated.

107   "Glamour boys . . ." Joseph A. Springer, *Black Devil Brigade: An Oral
         History* (New York: ibooks, 2003), p. 74.

107   Frederick and Williamson speeches . . . recalled by Joe Glass (Feb. 2,
         2004) and Stuart Hunt (Jan. 4, 2005) in interviews with the author.

108   20,000 rounds over a single hour of firing . . . Martin Blumenson,
         Salerno to Cassino, (Washington, U.S. Army Office of Military History,
         1969), p. 265.

108   "Shells roared . . ." "Memories of the Battle of Monte la Difensa,
         December 2–8, 1943," by Donald MacKinnon, undated.

110   The column stopped at 10 p.m. . . . History of 1st Company–2nd
         Regiment entitled "Company History," p. 6, by H.G. Forester.

110   "Every little noise seemed amplified . . ." Ibid. p. 6.

111   Van Ausdale spots the sentry on the summit of Difensa . . . , p. 75.

113   Kicked Callowhill in the head . . . Jack Callowhill interview with the
         author, June 2, 2004.

113   "like jelly . . ." Chet Ross interview with the author, Oct. 8, 2004.

115   Joe Dauphinais account . . . "My Memories of Monte Difensa," by J.J.
         Dauphinais, undated unpublished memoir.

116   1st Platoon's Pvt R.E. Daigle from Lynn, Massachusetts died on Difensa
         on Dec. 3, 1943. Crichlow account of the death of Daigle and Deyette
         taken from Adleman and Walton, p. 119.

119   Rothlin and Gath's death . . . Joe Glass interview with the author, Oct.
         2, 2004.

119   MacKinnon's recollection of the death of Syd Gath . . . "Memories of the
         Battle of Monte la Difensa, December 2–8, 1943," by Donald MacKinnon,
         undated.

120   "MacWilliam's death . . ." Stu Hunt interview with author, Jan. 5,
         2005; Ed Thomas interview with the author, Dec. 20, 2004.

120   Sgt. Carl Siebels . . . The death of Staff Sergeant Siebels was described
         by Ed Thomas in correspondence to the author dated Dec. 22, 2004.

From Monticello, Iowa, Siebels is incorrectly identified in Burhans's *First Special Service Force* as Sgt. Seiber, and is not listed in Burhans's casualty roster.

121   Death of Kotenko . . . "Memories of the Battle of Monte la Difensa, December 2–8, 1943," by Donald MacKinnon, undated.

122   "So these are supposed to be German supermen" . . . Joe Glass interview with the author, Oct. 3, 2004.

123   This portrait of the aftermath of the Difensa battle compiled from interviews with Chet Ross (Oct. 9, 2004), William Magee (June 1, 2004), and Tom O'Brian (Jan. 10, 2004).

123   Cuff's recollections . . . Adleman and Walton, p. 124.

124   When Colonel Frederick met them at the aid station . . . William "Sam" Magee interview with the author, June 1, 2004.

124   "fought like they didn't have any intention . . ." Springer, p. 110.

124   "Oh my boys, oh my boys" . . . Lorin Waling interview with the author, March 2004.

CHAPTER 7

127   Harriet MacWilliam . . . Tom MacWilliam, son of subject, interview with the author, Dec. 21, 2004.

128   Hibbard and Montana Club . . . Bill Story interview with the author, December 21, 2004.

129   "to let R.O. keep his arms and legs . . ." Georgina Morgan letter to author Dec. 1, 2004.

129   "The banker is the closest" . . . Alfred T. Hibbard interview with Helena *Independent Record*, June 3, 1962, p. 10.

134   You have to promise us . . . Herb Peppard interview with author, Jan. 14, 2005.

134–135   "I was born to be a lover not a soldier . . ." Herb Peppard phone interview with the author, Jan. 14, 2005. "Mama, mama, mama . . ." Herb Peppard, *The Lighthearted Soldier*, (Halifax: Nimbus, 1994), p. 82. The Dee Byrom episode is also related in Peppard's memoirs.

136   First Lt. A.J. Ariott was from London, Ont. Sgt. A.O. Gunderson was listed as a citizen of Helena, Montana. Hibbard mentions both men in a letter dated Jan. 4, 1944, addressed to Col. Robert T. Frederick. Letter courtesy of the Frederick Papers, Hoover Institution.

137   "Be used for the erection of a memorial fund . . ." Letter from Robert T. Frederick to A.T. Hibbard, dated 13 Dec. 1943, Frederick Papers, Hoover Institution.

137   A.T. Hibbard letter to Col. Robert T. Frederick, Jan. 4, 1944, Frederick Papers, Hoover Institution.

138   "The most difficult . . ." Ed Thomas interview with the author, June 2004.

CHAPTER 8

140   Despite the losses they sustained . . . "War Diary of the 2nd Canadian Parachute Battalion," Dec. 12, 1943 entry. Canadian National Archives, Ottawa.

141   "I'm going to give you all . . ." Peppard, p. 93.

143   "cold, cold rain . . ." Peppard, p. 93.

143   "mortar and artillery . . ." Burhans, p. 134.

143   "Marshall assumed command . . ." Burhans, p. 136.

144   "His death was a terrible blow to me . . ." Peppard, p. 96.

145   Radicosa patrol . . . Burhans, p. 143.

145–146 "Bypass Radicosa on the north and east," "As is rarely the case, . . ." p. 167.

146–147 "Strong winds," "Light fire fight," "We were standing alertly . . ." Burhans, p. 145.

147   "These German soldiers were cold, tired, disorganized," "These Krauts who are manning . . ." pp. 169 & 170.

148   "Established a rest camp . . ." FSSF "BATTLE REPORT 3rd Co. 3 Jan to 17 Jan 1944," courtesy of Mark Radcliffe.

150   Saulteux . . . Bruce Sealey and Peter Van De Vyvere, *Thomas George Prince* (Winnipeg: Peguis Publishers Ltd., 1981), pp. 8 & 9.

151   "like a shadow," "Prince had done a beautiful job . . ." Mark Radcliffe interview with the author, Oct. 5, 2004.

152   "prevent ambush, take enemy snipers under fire" . . . FSSF 3rd Company, 3rd Regiment battle report on the Monte Majo assault, dated Dec. 21, 1943– Jan. 6, 1944.

152   "Austrians and Poles out of the 132d Regiment" Burhans, p. 152.

153–154 The Force had barely taken Monte Majo . . . Copy of affidavit by Lieutenant Mark Radcliffe describing the battle for Monte Majo on January 6, 1944 to support bravery citations forwarded to Sergeants Rich and Swisher. Undated. Courtesy of Mark Radcliffe.

154   "outstanding NCOs . . ." FSSF Battle Report, Jan. 3–17, 1944, courtesy of Mark Radcliffe.

155   "Scissored back and forth along its length," "moon was full," "Casualties were heavy on this flank," 2nd Battalion operations . . . Burhans, pp. 152, 150.

157   "wore himself out," An outstanding soldier . . . Robert T. Frederick interview with Robert Adleman, Sept. 20–21, 1963, Adleman Collection, Hoover Institution.

159   "Fuzzy and inaccurate . . ." Burhans, p. 153. Burhans suggests that "the Germans had taken up positions behind heights not even mapped."

161   Perry's death described in letter from Tom Gilday to Daniel P. Gallagher, undated but probably written in the early 1990s. Gilday wrote: "Captain Perry was killed a bullet through the head in a kneeling position and continued to kneel there with rifle armed . . ." Letter courtesy of Mark Radcliffe.

161–162 "Radcliffe also set up dummy . . ." FSSF "BATTLE REPORT 3rd Co. 3 Jan. to 17 Jan. 1944."

163   "Lay in piles on the hill . . ." Burhans, p. 154.

166   Joe Glass, on Majo with MacKinnon, stated the ordnance that debilitated him was a dud shell. In MacKinnon's interview with Joseph Springer he stated: "To this day, nobody knows for certain what caused it [the explosion]. Some think it must have been a land mine, given the wounds to my feet."

CHAPTER 9

172   "old men in the outfit . . ." Peppard, pp. 93 & 94.

172   "boy wants a smoke . . ." "Devils in Baggy Pants," *YANK: The Army Weekly,* Dec. 29, 1944. New York. Quote of Sgt. Carl Ward of Fort Worth, Texas.

173   "crazy S.O.B. . . ." p. 49.

173   "Hearty congratulations . . ." US cipher message, no. R-230-23, courtesy of Frederick Papers, Hoover Institution.

173   "very proud of you . . ." Letter from War Department General Staff, Operations Division, dated April 19, 1944.

174   "Last night we labored . . ." Poem courtesy of the Frederick Papers, Hoover Institution. Signed by Fay Sager, Jean McKnight, Ellen Keegan, Marguerite Draeger, Lois Olson, Madelaine Cagle, Catherine Petterson, and Derie Henderson.

175   Churchill quotes "dazzling vision" and "passionately" taken from Martin Blumenson, *Anzio: The Gamble That Failed* (New York: Cooper Square Press, 1991 reprint), p. 9. Letter to Mark Clark, William Darby, William Baumer, *Darby's Rangers: We Led the Way* (New York: Ballantine Books, 2003 reprint), p. 173.

176   "In effect, the first attack on the Gustav Line . . ." Ken Ford, *Cassino 1944: Breaking the Gustav Line* (Oxford: Osprey, 2004), p. 28.

CHAPTER 10

178   "like a big business . . ." Martin Blumenson, *Anzio* (New York: Cooper Square Press, 2001 reprint), p. 78.

180   "opportunities for observation . . ." Battle Report, Chapter XVI, "Anzio Beachhead Operations—February 1944," Frederick Papers, Hoover Institution.

181   "Darby was born to command . . ." Rick Atkinson, p. 436.

183   "every year of it . . ." Blumenson, p. 58.

184   "There were Germans . . ." Military History of Samuel W. Finn, 1992 unpublished account, by Sam Finn.

184   "Shooting from the hip . . ." Mir Bahmanyar, *Darby's Rangers, 1942–1944* (Oxford: Osprey, 2003), p. 52.

185   "They had lost too many . . ." Springer, *Black Devil Brigade,* p. 171.

185   "Wildcat . . ." Jenkins, *Churchill,* p. 729.

186   According to Herby Forester's 1st Company history, Gordon was promoted on May 9.

188   "a kind of no man's land . . ." Battle Report, Chapter XVI, "Anzio Beachhead Operations—February 1944," Frederick Collection, Hoover Institution.

188–189 "the only good German . . ." Underhill, p. 195.

190   "For 7 days, 2 to 9 February, the Force was busy . . ." Underhill, p. 200.

190   "knifed into," "pushed the line back . . ." Battle Report, Chapter XVI, "Anzio Beachhead Operations—February 1944," Frederick Papers, Hoover Institution.

CHAPTER 11

200   "captured 145 of the enemy . . ." Battle Report, Chapter XVI, "Anzio Beachhead Operations—February 1944," Frederick Collection, Hoover Institution.

200   "Getting diminished . . ." Springer, p. 144.

201   "That murdering FSSF . . ." ibid, p. 161.

202   "Were falling like leaves . . ." Underhill, p. 209.

203   "Reports from Sessuno . . ." Burhans, pp. 177 & 178.

203   The documentary film *Daring to Die: The Story of the Black Devils* (Canada's History Television, 2003) reported that the authenticity of these diaries has been called into question.

203   "Slicing his throat . . ." Springer, p. 166.

204   "Hunting moose . . ." *Forgotten Warriors*, documentary film of National Film Board of Canada, 1996.

204   "Reward enough . . ." Springer, p. 177.

204   "strict disciplinarian . . ." Donald Ballantyne correspondence with the author, Jan. 5, 2005.

205   "slit their throats . . ." Blake Heathcote, *Testaments of Honor: Personal Histories of Canada's War Veterans* (Toronto: Doubleday, 2002).

205   "Chief William Prince . . ." "Voyageurs on the Nile," by John Boileau, *Legion* magazine, Ottawa, January/February 2004 edition.

205   24 percent death rate . . . "Canada's First Nations: A Legacy of Institutional Racism," by Claire Hutchings, <www.tolerance.cz/courses/papers/hutchin.htm>. Hutchings states the investigation found a 24 percent death rate among "fifteen prairie schools."

205   "five bullets . . ." Sealey & Van De Vyvere, *Manitobans in Profile: Thomas George Prince* (Winnipeg: Peguin, 1981), p. 14.

206   "A better man . . ." "Prince of the Brigade," article posted by Veterans Affairs Canada, <www.vac-acc.gc.ca/general/sub.cfm?source=history/other/native/prince>

206   "Prince kept quiet . . ." Bill Story interview with the author, Jan. 4, 2004.

206   "smoke signal," "chicken Indian . . ." Sealey & Van De Vyvere, *Manitobans in Profile: Thomas George Prince* (Winnipeg: Peguin, 1981), pp. 19, 21, 24.

207   Mark Radcliffe testifies the *das dicke* cards were in use as early as Monte Majo.

207   "All my life . . ." Hansard, Legislative Assembly of Manitoba, Thurs., May 13, 2004.

209   "Prove he is brave . . ." Sealey & Van De Vyvere, p. 5.

210   "Is this real?" Herb Morris interview with the author, Oct. 15, 2004.

212–213   "profound anxiety to the allied command," "refused to break," "Kesselring thought it was probably already too late . . ." Blumenson, pp. 124, 133, 134.

CHAPTER 12

215   "kill as many Krauts . . ." Underhill, p. 194.

217   "my guts . . ." Nielson's wounding during the raid on the Quarry is also included in Sgt. John Dawson's testimony in Springer, p. 154.

217–218   "Nearly one in ten . . ." Max Hastings, *Armageddon: The Battle for Germany 1944–1945* (New York: Knopf, 2004). The figure Hastings cites is 8.9 percent. The soldier referred to here as Lester Granville would recover, return to combat, and later earn the US Silver Star for valor.

220 "Was slowly realizing . . ." Burhans, p. 181.

222 "As we lay . . ." unpublished poem courtesy of Herbert Morris.

224 "Others lost all restraint, and killed easily." Note this testimony by 5-2's Walford Michaelson: "There was nothing left after we got through with a raid. We were trained to destroy, and we destroyed everything. We were a bunch of crazy men. Nuts! No fear at all." Springer, p. 167.

224 "Silent Death . . ." Stanzas 1 and 3 of this unpublished four-stanza poem have been included here. Courtesy of Herbert Morris.

CHAPTER 13

227 As many as 89,000 Polish soldiers deserted the Wehrmacht in WWII. The Free Polish Brigade in Britain, made up of Polish soldiers who had escaped the Continent after the German occupation of Poland, was made up of 100,000 men. Twelve percent of the RAF during the Battle of Britain was Polish nationals, and the Polish Armored Division fought with the First Canadian Army throughout much of WWII.

229 "Tins of beef . . ." Andrew Clark, *A Keen Soldier* (Toronto: Alfred A. Knopf Canada, 2002), p. 198.

234 "Fanatical suicide troops . . ." Appendix "A" to S-2 Periodic Report NO./93 "INTERROGATION REPORT OF ESCAPED AMERICAN OFFICER," undated photo copy, Source: Adleman Collection, Hoover Institution.

235 Also spelled Urlig in one report. The official reports state that Erlich/Urlig was a Captain in the Hermann Göring Division. In interviews Radcliffe has suggested he may have been a member of the SS.

235 "Don't you know . . ." Appendix "A" to S-2 Periodic Report NO./93 "INTERROGATION REPORT OF ESCAPED AMERICAN OFFICER," undated photocopy, Source: Adleman Collection, Hoover Institution.

CHAPTER 14

240 "Happy Birthday . . ." Frederick Papers, Hoover Institution.

241 "Something of a victory," "worn out," Blumenson, pp. 139, 186.

242 "The whole thing" and "Map room . . ." Transcript of Dec. 16, 1963 interview with Kenneth Wickham, p. 16, Adleman Collection, Hoover Institution. Frederick stated in his interview with Adleman, Sept. 21, 1963, (Frederick Col., Hoover Inst.): "They stole the wine, and VI raised hell . . . but they were too embarrassed to take any action."

242 "Darby's Rangers . . ." Communiqué from H.S. Alcorn, Asst. Adjutant General to Frederick, marked SECRET, dated Feb. 20, 1944, with subject heading Disposition Ranger Units. ". . . YOU WILL GROUP ALL REMAINING RANGERS IN THE FOURTH RANGER BATTALION AND ATTATCH SAME TO SSF. . . ." Frederick Papers, Hoover Institution.

242 Ernie Pyle dispatch. David Nichols, ed. *Ernie's War: The Best of Ernie Pyle's World War II Dispatches* (New York: Random House, 1986), pp. 236–238.

243 "Suspiciously cheerful . . ." Appendix "A" to S-2 Periodic Report NO./93 "INTERROGATION REPORT OF ESCAPED AMERICAN

OFFICER," undated photocopy. Source: Adleman Collection, Hoover Institution. "According to the French PW the 7th Lufftwaffe Jaeger Bn. was being relieved the night of Mar. 14, by the 735 I.R. It seemed that every body was very happy about something."

244   "If you can't do this . . ." Text of Aug. 19, 1992 interview with Gerald McFadden. Montana Historical Society. '20th Century Montana Military Veterans' oral history project.

244–245 "witty, polished," "post officers seized the opportunity," transcript of Sept. 21, 1963 interview, Adleman Collection, Hoover Institution.

244   "One of the best officers . . ." Norm Smith interview with the author, Jan. 16, 2005.

245   "Big, tough, mean, and resentful . . ." Adleman, p. 77. Marshall "cross the canal . . ." Robert Burhans, *The First Special Service Force* (Nashville: Battery Press, 1996 reprint), p. 171.

245–246 *Gusville Herald Tribune*, undated original copy bearing the name "General Frederick," Frederick Papers, Hoover Institution.

246   "Each morning would show . . ." Burhans, p. 187.

247   "a herd of cattle . . ." "Devils in Baggy Pants," by Sgt. James O'Neill, *Yank: The Army Weekly*, Vol. 1, No. 39, Dec. 29, 1944. "Henhouses . . ." Burhans, p. 188. "The Germans were besieged in the hen house for several hours until they surrendered at daylight."

248–249 Transcript of Art Arsennek letter courtesy of Dora Stephens.

250   "to inflict maximum . . ." Underhill, p. 228.

251   "mowed down," " waving towels," ibid., p. 229.

256   "Crazy," "Suddenly I feel so ti— . . .," p. 51.

256   "most of the top brass . . ." Anne Frederick-Hicks interview with the author, July 2004.

256   Schumm is officially listed MIA, PD. Sam Eros of 1st Company (1-2) stated that Schumm was somehow separated from a patrol with Eros in no man's land on or about Feb. 24, 1944, and was likely discovered by the enemy and killed.

CHAPTER 15

263   Weldon is officially listed MIA-PD, a classification Joe Glass doesn't understand given that his death seemingly had numerous witnesses. Glass theorizes that his dog tag wasn't taken before the company withdrew.

264   "Sideways to my fire . . ." Springer, p. 196. "You almost died," ibid., p. 197.

CHAPTER 16

269   "Old bite . . ." Burhans, p. 212.

269   "Just like WWI . . ." "didn't make sense" . . . Springer, p. 207.

270   "You have overcome . . ." Burhans, pp. 215–216.

271   "MacIver had been like a son . . ." Peppard, p. 133. Peppard also recounts Airth saving MacIver at Kiska.

271–272 Finn . . . Military History of Samuel W. Finn, 1992 unpublished account, by Sam Finn.

273   U.S. M5 General Stuart, British Valentine tank, and German MK VI Tiger . . . Atkinson, pp. 187, 176, 223.

274   "one Tiger," "badly cut up . . ." Burhans, p. 217.

275   Burhans writes that Gray died from a mortar wound (*FSSF*, p. 216), but eyewitness Cottingham, in a memoir retained by the FSSF Association (compiled in the booklet "Rome Stories," 1994), stated that he died from a "burst of machine gun bullets."

275   "Death of Sgt. Bray . . ." Herb Morris interview with author, Oct. 15, 2004, and "Badly chewed up," taken from Herb Morris account collected in "Rome Stories," FSSF Assoc., 1994.

276   "An unreal orgy of killing," "virtual suicide missions . . ." Clark, pp. 85, 86.

278   "How in hell had we held . . ." Peppard, p. 137. Cori wine cellar . . . ibid., pp. 139–141.

279   "Damn it, kid . . ." Lorin Waling inteview with author, Oct. 1, 2004.

280   "Clark saw Rome as belonging to his own 5th Army . . ." Blumenson, p. 190. "The boss," ibid., p. 191.

281   "Artena was a quick death . . ." Burhans, p. 229.

281   Jack Secter's death . . . Interview with Herb Morris, Oct. 15, 2004. See Adleman, p. 194.

282   "Lieutenant Coleman . . ." ibid, p. 232.

282   "Like an exposed thumb . . ." Underhill, p. 252.

283   Keyes statement "If you fellows can take this mountain" recounted by FSSF veteran Tom O'Brien (5-2) in interview with the author, Jan. 2004.

CHAPTER 17

286   "The Force's ability to get the job done . . ." Battle report by Mark Radcliffe for General Frederick, entitled "Patrol to Rome," undated, Adleman Collection, Hoover Institution.

286   Howze quote, "A monkey's paw . . ." Atkinson, p. 511.

278–291 Patrol into Rome . . . Battle report by Mark Radcliffe for General Frederick, entitled "Patrol to Rome," undated, Adleman Collection, Hoover Institution.

CHAPTER 18

295   "I could think of nothing else . . ." Transcript of interview with Robert T. Frederick, Sept. 20–21, 1963, Adleman Collection, Hoover Institution.

295   Marshall's death . . . Norm Smith interview with the author, Jan. 16, 2005.

296-297 Sam Finn in Rome. Interview with the author, June 2004. Also described in Finn's unpublished memoir.

298   Tito Gozzer quote . . . Rome Stories, oral history collection, FSSF Association.

298   "We shall always . . ." "Company History, 1–2, FSSF," Herby Forester, undated personal account.

299   "Our camera man took documenting pictures" . . . Battle report by Mark Radcliffe for General Frederick, entitled "Patrol to Rome," undated, Adleman Collection, Hoover Institution.

299–301 "reflector-studded," the story of Clark, Keyes, and Frederick at the *Roma* sign was later recounted by both Frederick (to the writers Adleman and Walton, *The Devil's Brigade*) and Clark in his memoirs. This account taken from Robert Katz, *The Battle for Rome: The Germans, The Allies,*

The Partisans, and the Pope, September 1943–June 1944 (New York: Simon & Shuster, 2003), pp. 316, 317. The convoy to Capitoline Hill and the press conference recounted in Katz, *The Battle for Rome*, pp. 321, 322. Sevareid's account comes from Eric Sevareid, *Not So Wild a Dream.* (New York: Atheneum, 1978). Clark's account, Mark Clark, *Calculated Risk.* (New York: Harper, 1950).

300   "got to Rome before Ike got across the English Channel to Normandy" . . . Robert Katz, *The Battle for Rome* (New York: Simon & Schuster, 2003), p. 321.

301   "The long campaign had left the regiment very tired and needing rest" . . . Ed Thomas memoir, "Rome Stories," privately published, FSSF Association, June 4, 1944.

CHAPTER 19

305   "Our commander has lost" . . . Wickham, p. 46.

306   Gondolfo dinners, "found him hungry for company . . ." Transcript of Interview with Kenneth Wickham, Dec. 16, 1963, Adleman Collection, Hoover Institution.

306   "A discernible, protesting gasp . . ." Burhans, p. 249.

307   "We respected him because . . ." Herb Peppard interview with the author, Jan. 2005.

307   "There wasn't a dry eye . . ." Lorin Waling interview with the author, Oct. 1, 2004.

CHAPTER 20

309   Mark Clark farewell letter . . . Burhans, p. 250.

310   "It was a good letter . . ." Underhill, p. 275.

311   Non-battle casualty numbers at Castelabate . . . Robert Todd Ross, *Supercommandos* (Atglen: Schiffer, 2000), p. 240. Ross reports total training casualties to be 688.

312   Art Arsennek in Naples . . . A description of Arsennek's condition gathered from interviews with Joe Glass (Oct. 2, 2004) and Dora Stephens (Dec. 10, 2004).

313   "I hope you liked your steak . . ." Mark Radcliffe interview with author, Oct. 8, 2004.

316   "Oh my God, your face . . ." Lorin Waling interview with author, Oct. 10, 2004.

317–318   "Walkmeister's death . . ." Adleman and Walton

318   1st Airborne Task Force routs a "confused" enemy, "into southern France with the first wave . . ." p. 54.

319   "enemy resistance was sparse . . .," "cannon platoons," "With the enemy," "Seventh-army sideshow" . . . Burhans, pp. 272, 273.

319   "We can walk . . ." Underhill, p. 275.

321   Death of Floyd Schmidt . . . Bill Story interview with the author. Jan. 2004. Also Herb Goodwin interview, Oct. 2004.

323   "I hoped the Americans . . ." Quote by Major Hannibal von Luttichau taken from Stephen Ambrose, *Citizen Soldiers* (New York: Touchstone, 1998), p. 452.

323   1.4 million women in East Prussia, Silesia, Pomerania . . . Antony Beevor, *The Fall of Berlin 1945.* (New York: Viking Press, 2002).

324   "Americans stand fast . . ." Springer, p. 253.
324–325   "It was never Canucks and Yanks," Burhans, p. 298.
325   "Canadians!" "it seemed fitting . . ." Peppard, p. 175.

CHAPTER 21

335   Frank E. Kessinger from Bancroft, Nebraska. Letter courtesy of Dora
          Stephens.
336   Ed Kelly's assessment of Art's condition based on a letter written to
          Arsennek's sister. "I visited him in the hospital before my return to the
          Force," wrote Kelly. "He was cheerful but knew he was not going to win
          the battle." Letter courtesy of Dora Stephens.
338–339   "The ten maples that ringed the house . . ." Peppard, p. 188.
341   "The 45th left one of the greatest division records . . ." Anne
          Frederick-Hicks, p. 54.
342   "For inspirational purposes . . ." Baumer, p. 213.

EPILOGUE

345   "Throughout all campaigns . . ." "Company History, 1st Company–
          2nd Regiment, 1st Special Service Force," by Herby Forester, undated.
348   "I will never find words . . ." Letter from Ray Hufft to Herb Morris,
          Jan. 30, 1946, courtesy of Herbert Morris.
348   "Dear Rev. Muscles . . ." Letter from Ray Hufft to Herb Morris, Jan. 3,
          1955, courtesy of Herbert Morris.
349   "an eloquent and emotional introduction . . ." Sealey and Van De
          Vyvere, p. 29. That his boldness was endangering the lives of his men
          . . . ibid p. 35.
350   "There is little doubt . . ." Sealey, Van De Vyvere, p. 45.
351   For further information on the history of Pykrete see Lampe, David. *Pyke:
          The Unknown Genius.* London: Evans Brothers Limited, 1959; Fergusson,
          Bernard, *The Watery Maze: The Story of Combined Operations.* London:
          Collins, 1961.
352–353   Fredericks-Hicks, p. 54.
354   "Just rambled on and on and on," "obviously irrational," "outstanding
          soldier" turned "right" . . . Transcript of Robert Frederick interview
          with Robert Adleman, George Walton, Sept. 20–21, 1963. Adleman
          Collection, Hoover Institution.
357   Copy of the Charlie Kelly letter to *The Toronto Sun*, dated Dec. 23, 2001,
          courtesy of Dora Stephens.
358   Dauphinais account of Ray Holbrook's death . . . Springer, p. 177.
361   The Don MacKinnon memorial, written by friends Bill Harris and Bill
          Halewood, appeared in the Lives Lived section, *The Globe and Mail*,
          Feb. 11, 2003.

SOURCES

NOTE ON SOURCES

Historians of the First Special Service Force have paid tribute to Robert Burhans and his landmark book *The First Special Service Force: A War History of the North Americans, 1942–1944*, and I am no exception. Burhans' role as the Force's intelligence chief gave him access to reports, data, intelligence, and accounts, which makes his work more than definitive, and I—like my colleagues—consulted it like a road map. Burhans, though, was never on the front lines, and he is not right about everything, his account of the death of Bill Rothlin on Difensa being one example. Apart from the best sources of battle scenes, the accounts of surviving eyewitness, I found Adna Underhill's *The Force* a fascinating contribution. Underhill, a 2nd Regiment officer, wrote *The Force* as a historical novel. Still, in operations, such as the Sessuno raid at Anzio, in which Underhill was a primary participant, I selectively quoted the book's general description of certain events, assuming that the author would draw on his memory, diaries, and battle reports when describing the background of these actions. Some readers may disagree with this decision, but I found *The Force* too rich a resource to ignore. Herb Peppard's *The Lighthearted Soldier*, the memoir of one of the Force's more colorful members, was equally rich, and I used it to extrapolate on information garnered from conversations and interviews with Peppard both in Rome in June 2004, and afterward. Joe Springer's *The Black Devil Brigade* also served to confirm much information I gained from interviews since some of my sources, namely Glass and Waling, were also interviewed for Springer's book. In certain instances I quoted from Springer, particularly the words of Force men who have since died. Robert Adleman's *The Devil's Brigade* is also cited, but I found his papers (the interviews, notes, and such that he used to write his book) available at the Hoover Institution infinitely more useful, and I have quoted his interviews of Wickham and Frederick repeatedly. Wickham's memoir *An Adjutant-General Remembers* also proved an invaluable source on the origins of this historic unit.

BOOKS

FSSF and Fort Harrison

Adleman, Robert; Walton, Col. George. *The Devil's Brigade.* London: Corgi, 1968.

Burhans, Robert. *The First Special Service Force: A War History of the North Americans, 1942–1944.* Nashville: Battery Press, 1996 reprint.

Dzuiban, Stanley. *Military Relations Between the United States and Canada.* Washington: Government Printing Office, 1959.

Paladin, Vivian; Baucus, Jean. *Helena: An Illustrated History.* Montana Historical Society Press, 1996 reprint.

Peppard, Herb. *The Lighthearted Soldier: A Canadian's Exploits with the Black Devils in WWII.* Halifax: Nimbus, 1994.

Ross, Robert Todd. *Supercommandos.* Atglen: PA, Schiffer Books, 2000.

Sealey, D. Bruce and Van de Vyvere, Peter. *Manitobans in Profile: Thomas George Prince.* Winnipeg: Penguin Publishers Ltd., 1981.

Springer, Joseph. *The Black Devil Brigade: The True Story of the First Special Service Force.* New York: ibooks, 2001.

Underhill, Adna. *The Force.* Tuscon: Arizona Monographs, 1994.

Wickham, Kenneth, Maj. Gen. *An Adjutant-General Remembers.* Fort Harrison: The Adjutant-General's Corps Regimental Assoc., 1991.

Special Forces, Rangers, Airborne

Ambrose, Stephen. Band of Brothers: E Company, 506th Regiment, 101st Airborne from Normandy to Hitler's Eagle Nest. New York: Simon & Schuster, 2001.

Bahmanyar, Mir. *Darby's Rangers: 1942–45.* Oxford: Osprey Publishing, 2003.

Clancy, Tom; Stiner, Gen. Carl. *Shadow Warriors: Inside the Special Forces.* London: Pan Books, 2002.

Darby, William O.; Baumer, William. *Darby's Rangers: We Led the Way.* New York: Presidio, 1993.

Horn, Bernd; Wyczynski, Michel. *Paras Versus the Reich: Canada's Paratroopers at War, 1942–45.* Toronto: The Dundurn Group, 2003.

King, Michael J. *William Orlando Darby: A Military Biography.* Hamden, Conn.: Archon Books, 1981.

Ladd, James. *Commandos and Rangers of WWII.* New York: St. Martin's Press, 1978.

Nolan, Brian. *Airborne: The Heroic Story of the 1st Canadian Parachute Battalion in the Second World War.* Toronto: Pearson, 1995.

Paddock, Alfred H., Jr. *U.S. Army Special Warfare: Its Origins. Psychological and Unconventional Warfare, 1941–1952.* Washington, D.C.: National Defense University Press, 1982.

Combined Operations

Fergusson, Bernard. *The Watery Maze: The Story of Combined Operations.* London: Collins, 1961.

Lampe, David. *Pyke: The Unknown Genius.* London: Evans Brothers Limited, 1959.

Loewenheim, Francis; Langley, Harold; Jones, Manfred. *Roosevelt and Churchill: Their Secret Wartime Correspondence.* New York: Dutton, 1975.

Ziegler, Philip. *Mountbatten: The Official Biography.* London: Collins, 1985.

Plough Project and Background to 1942/43

Alanbrooke, Field Marshal Lord. *War Diaries: 1939–1945.* London: Phoenix Press, 2001.

Ambrose, Stephen. *Eisenhower: Soldier and President.* London: Pocket Books, 2003.

Chandler, Alfred D., ed. *The Papers of Dwight David Eisenhower, The War Years: I.* Baltimore, Johns Hopkins, 1970.

Chandler, Alfred D., ed. *The Papers of Dwight David Eisenhower, The War Years: III.* Baltimore, Johns Hopkins, 1970.

Churchill, Winston. *Memoirs of the Second World War.* London: Mariner, 1991.

Churchill, Winston. *The Second World War, Volume III: The Grand Alliance.* Boston: Houghton Mifflin Company, 1950.

Gilbert, Martin. *Winston Churchill: Finest Hour 1939–1941.* London: Heinemann, 1983.

Gilbert, Martin. *Winston Churchill: Road to Victory, 1941–1945.* London: Houghton Mifflin Co., 1986.

Jenkins, Roy. *Churchill.* London: Pan Books, 2002.

Nolan, Brian. *King's War: Mackenzie King and the Politics of War, 1939–1945.* Toronto: Random House, 1988.

Pogue, Forrest C. *George C. Marshall: Ordeal and Hope.* New York, Viking Press, 1966.

Pogue, Forrest C. *George C. Marshall: Organizer of Victory.* New York, Viking Press, 1973.

Sherwood, Robert. *Roosevelt and Hopkins: An Intimate History.* New York: Grosset & Dunlap, 1950.

Cassino, Rome, and the Italian War

Blumenson, Martin. *Mark Clark.* New York: Congdon and Weed, 1984.

Blumenson, Martin. *Anzio: The Gamble That Failed.* New York: Cooper Square Press, 2001.

Blumenson, Martin. *Salerno to Cassino.* Washington: U.S. Army Office of the Chief of Military History, 1969.

Clark, Andrew. *A Keen Soldier: The Execution of Second World War Private Harold Pringle.* Toronto: Alfred A. Knopf, 2002.

Clark, Mark. *Calculated Risk.* New York: Harper, 1950.

Ellis, John. *Cassino: The Hollow Victory.* London: Aurum Press, 2003.

Ford, Ken. *Cassino: Breaking the Gustav Line.* Oxford: Osprey, 2004.

Heathcote, Blake. *Testaments of Honour: Personal Histories of Canada's War Veterans.* Toronto: Doubleday, 2002.

Katz, Robert. *The Battle for Rome: The Germans, the Allies, the Partisans, and the Pope, September 1943–June 1944.* New York: Simon & Schuster, 2003.

Jackson, W.G.F. *The Battle for Italy.* London: Harper & Row, 1967.

Parker, Matthew. *Monte Cassino: The Hardest-Fought Battle of World War II.* New York: Doubleday, 2004.

Pyle, Ernie; Nichols, David, ed. *Ernie's War: The Best of Ernie Pyle's World War II Dispatches.* New York: Random House, 1986.

Sevareid, Eric. *Not So Wild a Dream*. New York: Atheneum, 1978.

Truscott, Lucien K. Jr. *Command Missions: A Personal Story*. New York: EP Dutton & Co., 1954.

Science and Warfare

Eggleston, Wilfred. *Scientists at War*. Toronto, Canada Oxford University Press, 1950.

Pickover, Clifford. *Strange Brains and Genius: The Secret Lives Of Eccentric Scientists And Madmen*. New York : Plenum Trade, 1998.

Thistle, Mel, ed. *The Mackenzie-McNaughton: Wartime Letters*. Toronto: University of Toronto Press, 1975.

WWII

Ambrose, Stephen. *Citizen Soldiers: The U.S. Army from the Normandy Beaches to the Bulge to the Surrender of Germany June 7, 1944–May 7, 1945*. New York: Touchstone, 1998.

Atkinson, Rick. *An Army at Dawn: The War in North Africa, 1942–1943*. London: Abacus, 2003.

Beevor, Anthony. *The Fall of Berlin, 1945*. New York: Viking Press, 2002.

Beevor, Anthony. *Stalingrad*. London: Penguin Books, 1999.

Eisenhower, Dwight D. *The Great Crusade*. Baltimore: Johns Hopkins, 1997 reprint.

Fussels, Paul. *Wartime: Understanding and Behavior in the Second World War*. New York: Oxford Univ. Press, 1989.

Hastings, Max. *Armageddon: The Battle for Germany*. New York: Knopf, 2004.

Keegan, John. *The Second World War*. New York: Viking, 1989.

Keegan, John. *A History of Warfare*. London: Pimlico, 1994.

Keegan, John. *The Mast of Command: A Study of Generalship*. London: Pimlico, 1987.

ARTICLES

"The Fearless Innovator," *The Times* (London), 26 Feb. 1948. (On Pyke.)

"Devils in Baggy Pants," *YANK: The Army Weekly*, Dec. 29, 1944.

Brown, Steven C. "Dermot M. O'Neill: One of the 20th Century's Most Overlooked Combatives Pioneers," Journal of Asian Martial Arts, Vol. 12, No. 3, 2003.

Frederick-Hicks, Anne. "The War Made Him, Peacetime Broke Him." Army 32, Sept. 1982.

Frederick-Hicks, Anne. "'Rugby Force': Fist in War's Uppercut." Army 36, April 1986.

Harris, Bill: Halewood, Bill. "Lives Lived: Don MacKinnon." *Globe and Mail.* Feb. 11, 2003.

Perutz, Martin. "Enemy Alien." *The New Yorker,* 12 Aug. 1985. (British scientists at Combined Ops.)

Mackenzie, Porter. "Warrior: Tommy Prince." *Maclean's,* Sept. 1952.

Synness, Curt. "Meet the Devil's Brigade." *Helena Independent Record.* C-1, Aug. 11, 2002.

Story, William. "The Early Days of the Force." First Special Service Force Association.

Veterans Affairs Canada. "Prince of the Brigade." Available online at www.vac-acc.gc.ca>

VIDEOS

Daring to Die: The Story of the Black Devils. Directors Greg Hancock & Wayne Abbott. Northern Sky Entertainment for Canada's History Television, 2003.

First Special Service Force. Narrated by Bill Story. FSSF Association.

Forgotten Warriors. National Film Board of Canada. 1996. (Transcript of interview obtained.)

UNPUBLISHED ACCOUNTS, MEMOIRS, REPORTS, SPEECHES

Dauphinais, J.J. *My Memories of Montel Difensa*. Undated.

Finn, Samuel. *Military History of Samuel W. Finn*. 1992.

Thomas, Gen. Ed, ed. *Rome Stories: June 4, 1944*. FSSF Association. 1994.

Forester, H.G. *Company History: 1st Company – 2nd Regiment*. Undated.

Frederick, Robert T. *Plough Project Diary*. Frederick Collection, Hoover Institution.

Frederick, Robert T. *Talk Delivered Over Radio Station KPFA, Helena, Montana. Montana Radio Forum*. (Transcript.) Aug. 31, 1942, 8:45 p.m.

Frederick, Robert T. *Battle Report, Chapter XVI*, "Anzio Beachhead Operations—February 1944." Frederick Collection, Hoover Institution.

Glass, Dorothy. *Dorothy (Strainer) Glass*. Undated.

Glass, Joe. *From Joe Glass to his children*. Oct. 1991.

MacKinnon, Donald. *Memories of the Battle of Monte la Difensa, December 2–8, 1943*. Undated.

Radcliffe, Mark. *Patrol to Rome*. Battle report on June 3–4 incursion into Rome for Brig. Gen. Robert T. Frederick. Courtesy of Mark Radcliffe.

Radcliffe, Mark. Affidavit (copy) on actions of Sgts. Rich and Swisher during Majo attack, Jan. 6, 1944. Written for Ken Wickham. Courtesy of Mark Radcliffe.

Radcliffe, Mark. *FSSF Battle Report 3rd Co. 3 Jan to 17 Jan 1944*. Courtesy of Mark Radcliffe.

Waling, Lorin. *As I Remember*. Undated.

INTERVIEWS—SELECT LIST OF PRIMARY SOURCES

Ballantyne, Donald. Email: Jan. 5,6, 20, 2005. **Callowhill, Jack.** Notes from interviews June 2004 (Rome). **Eros, Sam.** Phone: Nov 30, 2004. **Eschenburg, Emil.** Taped Oct. 3, 2004. Phone:

Sept. 17, 2004. **Finn, Samuel.** Notes taken from two interviews June 2004 (Rome). **Frederick-Hicks, Anne.** Phone: July 2004. **Glass, Joe.** Taped interviews Oct. 2, 3, 2004. Notes taken interviews Oct. 2–9, 2005. Phone: Feb. 2, Mar. 9, Dec. 8, 2004, Jan. 2005. E-mail correspondence: Feb. 18, 26, 27; Mar. 9, 22; April 25, 27, 28, 2005. **Goodwin, Herb.** Taped Oct. 5, 8, 2004. **Hunt, Stuart.** Phone: Jan. 8, 2005. **Jones, Ken.** Notes from interview June 2004 (Rome). **Magee, William 'Sam.'** Notes from interviews June 2004 (Rome). Email: July, August, November 2004. **Mann, Charlie.** Notes from interviews June 2004 (Rome). **Morris, Rev. Herb.** Taped interviews Oct. 15, 2004. Phone: Mar. 9, 2004. Email: Jan. 27, 2005. **O'Brien, Tom.** Phone: Jan. 10, 2004. **Peppard, Herb.** Notes in meetings: June 1–4, 2004. Phone: Dec. 2004. **Poirier, Roland.** Phone interview Feb. 2004. **Radcliffe, Mark.** Tape recorded interviews Oct. 5, 7, 8, 2004. Phone interviews: Feb. 2004, Jan. 2005. **Ross, Herman 'Chet.'** Taped interview Oct. 9, 2004. Notes from interview June 2004 (Rome). **Stephens, Dora.** Phone: Dec. 2004. **Story, William 'Bill.'** Phone interviews: Jan. 4, Jan. 6, July 5, Mar. 18, Dec. 21, 2004. **Thomas, Gen. Ed.** Transcripts of interview (Rome) June 1, 2004. Phone: Mar. 9, Dec. 15, 2004. **Turner, John Cliff.** Phone: Nov. 2004. **Waling, Lorin.** Taped interviews Oct. 1, 7, 2004. Phone: Feb., Mar. 2004.

ARCHIVAL

British National Archives, Kew, Surrey. (Telegram to Field Marshall Dill on Mastery of Snows, April 3, 1943; Combined Operations HQ Master of Snows proposal, Geoffrey Pyke; Churchill Telegram to Harry Hopkins, July 7, 1943; Mountbatten correspondence on Plough; Minutes April 11, 1943 meeting at Chequers with Marshall, Churchill, Mountbatten, and Hopkins.)

Canadian National Archives, Ottawa. ("War Diary of the 2nd Canadian Parachute Battalion," PM Mackenzie King diary entries for 1942.)

FSSF Museum Fort William Henry Harrison, Helena, Montana (maps, photos obtained).

Hoover Institution, Stanford University, Stanford, Calif.

*Papers of Robert T. Frederick (correspondence, battle reports, diaries, speeches)

*Papers of Robert Burhans (FSSF battle reports, declassified intelligence data, information used in the writing of *The First Special Service Force: A War History of the North Americans*).

*Papers of Robert Adleman (transcripts of interviews of Robert T. Frederick, Ken Wickham; battle reports, correspondence generated in the research and writing of *The Devil's Brigade*).

JFK Special Warfare Museum, Fort Bragg, North Carolina (Lew Merrim photos obtained).

Montana Historical Society (transcript of interview with Gerry McFadden, Aug. 19, 1992. Helena Independent Record obituaries on Jack Haytin, A.T. Hibbard, George S. Morrell).

ACKNOWLEDGMENTS

Many thanks to Ron Doering, Al Zuckerman, Nick Garrison, Susan Ginsburg, Maya Rock, and Adi Haspel for shepherding this book from idea to proposal to publication. A special thank you to friend and novelist Olen Steinhauer for reading this manuscript, and offering invaluable suggestions. Erika Papp, Rick Bruner, Mirco Tonin, Pam Clarke, Michael Nadler, Chris Condon, Robin Hunt, Adam LeBor, Randall Crow, and Doug Jones (son of Force man Ken Jones) offered much appreciated personal support.

John Dallimore of the FSSF Living History Group shared his knowledge, contacts, and trove of photos, some of which appear in this book. Thanks as well to FSSF aficionados Bruno Aklil of France and Paul Dray of Britain. Greg Hancock, filmmaker and grandson of Force man Gord Hancock, also provided photos, insights, and sources. His definitive film on the FSSF, *Daring to Die,* (co-directed with Wayne Abbott of Northern Sky Entertainment) was an essential resource. Jodie Foley of the Montana Historical Society opened wide his files on the FSSF. In Europe, historian Gianni Blasi of Alatri, Italy, generously guided me through the area around Monte la Difensa and the Liri Valley, and shared his definitive knowledge. Historian Alessandro Campagna of Frosinone, Italy, shared personal research and unique insights on the battle for Cassino and the Mignano Gap.

Special thanks to Brian Nolan, Klaus Pohl, Carly Stagg, and Brett Popplewell for Canadian archival research, and to my good friend, the British filmmaker Jonathan Schutz, who combed the British national archives for documents on Plough Project. Geoff Slee of Combined Ops.com offered insight into the Combined Operations HQ, and put me in touch with Rob Silcocks, the possessor of the most comprehensive collection of Geoffrey Pyke memorabilia, who provided the Pyke portrait, which appears in this book. Thanks as well to the JFK Special Warfare Museum, the Eisenhower Library, and ARMY Magazine for documents and photos.

My greatest resource has been the veterans. Bill Story, the longtime executive director and the heart of the FSSF veterans' association, gave generously of his time and knowledge, and for this I am grateful. Story and General Ed Thomas graciously allowed me to join a FSSF veterans' tour in Rome in June 2004, and visit former battlefields with the old soldiers. Anne Frederick-Hicks offered insight into the character and past of her father, Robert T. Frederick. And a special thank you to Andre and Kaija Kucharek who billeted me in Stanford while I conducted research at the Hoover Institution.

Joe and Dorothy Glass, and Rev. and Mrs. Herb Morris welcomed me into their homes and exhibited a trust that was inspiring. Lorin and Irene Waling, Sam Magee, Mark Radcliffe, Herb Goodwin, Herb Peppard, Emil Eschenburg, and Chet Ross were equally as generous. Sam and Rhea Finn kindly provided photos, and a copy of Finn's unpublished wartime memoir. Tom MacWilliam, Jr., Dora Stephens, and Robin Bowman allowed me to pry into intimate recesses of their pasts. Force man Donald Ballantyne offered sober insight into the characters of Tommy Prince and Tom Gilday. Heather MacKinnon provided photos and information on her late husband, Don; and FSSF children Pam Davidson and Bill Woon shared information on their fathers, John Marshall and Dave Woon.

In telling the stories of the men of the FSSF, my only conundrum was which ones to tell. I desperately wanted to tell all the stories related to me, but decided to center this narrative on the Force men who settled in Helena because they represented the spirit and experiences of all. John Dallimore expressed it best when I once pressed him to name a veteran whose exploits were particularly special. "They're all special," he said, and after thousands of miles and hours of research I now realize how right he was.

John Nadler
August 2005

INDEX

JOHN NADLER is a war correspondent and feature writer who has covered conflicts in Kosovo, Macedonia, and Serbia. He lives with his wife in Budapest, Hungary.

Printed in the United States
by Baker & Taylor Publisher Services